Dreamweaver®
MX 2004:
Comprehensive
Course

BILL LEWALLEN
President and Founder of VisionMagic

LABYRINTH
PUBLICATIONS®

El Sobrante, CA

Dreamweaver MX 2004: Comprehensive Course
by Bill Lewallen

LABYRINTH
PUBLICATIONS®

Labyrinth Publications
3314 Morningside Drive
El Sobrante, California 94803
800.522.9746
On the Web at labpub.com

President and Publisher:
Brian Favro

Editorial Director:
Ted Ricks

Series Editor:
Russel Stolins

Developmental Editor:
Carol Pritchard-Martinez

Managing Editor:
Laura A. Lionello

Production Manager:
Rad Proctor

Editorial/Production Team:
Kelly Burch, Cici Kinsman, Interactive
Composition Corporation (ICCorp),
and Carolyn Stratton

Indexing: Joanne Sprott

Cover Design:
Seventeenth Street Studios

ISBN 1-59136-063-3

Manufactured in the United States of America.

05 06 07 08 09 10 9 8 7 6 5

Dreamweaver MX 2004: Comprehensive Course

Contents in Brief

UNIT 3 ADVANCED SKILLS

Contents

UNIT 2 BEYOND THE BASICS

List of Quick Reference Tables

List of Keyboard Shortcuts

Automation Tasks

To insert an editable region
WIN ONLY `Ctrl` + `Alt` + `V`
MAC ONLY `Option` + `⌥⌘` + `V`

To open the Snippets panel
WIN AND MAC `Shift` + `F9`

Document Tasks

To create a new document
WIN ONLY `Ctrl` + `N`
MAC ONLY `⌥⌘` + `N`

To insert an image
WIN ONLY `Ctrl` + `Alt` + `I`
MAC ONLY `⌥⌘` + `Option` + `I`

To open the CSS Styles panel
WIN AND MAC `Shift` + `F11`

To open a page in the primary browser
WIN AND MAC `F12`

To open a page in the secondary browser
WIN ONLY `Ctrl` + `F12`
MAC ONLY `⌥⌘` + `F12`

To open an existing document
WIN ONLY `Ctrl` + `O`
MAC ONLY `⌥⌘` + `O`

To open the Page Properties dialog box
WIN ONLY `Ctrl` + `J`
MAC ONLY `⌥⌘` + `J`

Dreamweaver Configuration Tasks

To display preferences
WIN ONLY `Ctrl` + `U`
MAC ONLY `⌥⌘` + `U`

To open the Preferences dialog box
WIN ONLY `Ctrl` + `U`
MAC ONLY `⌥⌘` + `U`

To show/hide panels
WIN AND MAC `F4`

To show/hide the Insert bar
WIN ONLY `Ctrl` + `F2`
MAC ONLY `⌥⌘` + `F2`

To show/hide the Properties panel
WIN ONLY `Ctrl` + `F3`
MAC ONLY `⌥⌘` + `F3`

To toggle between Design and Code views
WIN AND MAC `Ctrl` + `~`

Frame and Frameset Tasks

To open the Frames panel
WIN AND MAC `Shift` + `F2`

To select a frame in the Document window
WIN ONLY `Alt` + Click
MAC ONLY `Shift` + `Option` + Click

HTML Tasks

To cycle through the three quick tag modes
WIN ONLY `Ctrl` + `T`
MAC ONLY `⌥⌘` + `T`

To open the Quick Tag Editor
WIN ONLY `Ctrl` + `T`
MAC ONLY `⌥⌘` + `T`

To run Validate Markup
WIN AND MAC `Shift` + `F6`

To set new HTML document preferences
WIN ONLY `Ctrl` + `U`
MAC ONLY `⌥⌘` + `U`

Layers Tasks

To open the Behaviors panel
WIN AND MAC `Shift` + `F4`

To open the Layers panel
WIN AND MAC `F2`

To open the Timelines panel
WIN ONLY `Alt` + `F9`
MAC ONLY `Option` + `F9`

To toggle the display of visual elements
WIN ONLY `Ctrl`+`Shift`+`I`
MAC ONLY `⌘`+`Shift`+`I`

Link Tasks

To insert a named anchor
WIN ONLY `Ctrl`+`Alt`+`A`
MAC ONLY `⌘`+`Option`+`A`

To open the Page Properties dialog box
WIN ONLY `Ctrl`+`J`
MAC ONLY `⌘`+`J`

To open the Styles panel
WIN AND MAC `Shift`+`F11`

To remove a link
WIN ONLY `Ctrl`+`Shift`+`L`
MAC ONLY `⌘`+`Shift`+`L`

To Show/Hide all invisible elements
WIN ONLY `Ctrl`+`Shift`+`I`
MAC ONLY `⌘`+`Shift`+`I`

Site Management Tasks

To open the Link Checker tab on the Results panel group
WIN AND MAC `Shift`+`F8`

To open the Results panel group
WIN AND MAC `F7`

Table Tasks

To add a column to the left of the current table column
WIN ONLY `Ctrl`+`Shift`+`A`
MAC ONLY `⌘`+`Shift`+`A`

To add a single row above the current table row
WIN ONLY `Ctrl`+`M`
MAC ONLY `⌘`+`M`

To delete a table column
WIN ONLY `Ctrl`+`Shift`+`-`
MAC ONLY `⌘`+`Shift`+`-`

To delete a table row
WIN ONLY `Ctrl`+`Shift`+`M`
MAC ONLY `⌘`+`Shift`+`M`

To display the Insert bar
WIN ONLY `Ctrl`+`F2`
MAC ONLY `⌘`+`F2`

To insert a table
WIN ONLY `Ctrl`+`Alt`+`T`
MAC ONLY `⌘`+`Option`+`T`

To merge cells
WIN ONLY `Ctrl`+`Alt`+`M`
MAC ONLY `⌘`+`Option`+`M`

To select a single cell
WIN ONLY `Ctrl`+`A`
MAC ONLY `⌘`+`A`

To select a table
WIN ONLY `Ctrl`+`A`, `A`
MAC ONLY `⌘`+`A`, `A`

To split cells
WIN ONLY `Ctrl`+`Alt`+`S`
MAC ONLY `⌘`+`Option`+`S`

To switch in and out of Expanded Tables mode
WIN AND MAC `F6`

Text Tasks

To apply bold or italic
WIN ONLY
`Ctrl` + `B`
`Ctrl` + `I`
MAC ONLY
`⌘`+`B`
`⌘`+`I`

To display the Page Properties dialog box
WIN ONLY `Ctrl`+`J`
MAC ONLY `⌘`+`J`

To insert a line break
WIN ONLY `Shift`+`Enter`
MAC ONLY `Shift`+`Return`

Preface

Dreamweaver MX 2004: Comprehensive Course provides complete coverage of Dreamweaver MX 2004 software. The book supports both Windows® and Macintosh™ platforms.

The lessons are divided into three units. Unit 1: Basic Skills provides an introduction to Dreamweaver. Students learn about building Web sites with text and images and applying anchors and links. They are also introduced to site management techniques. In Unit 2: Beyond the Basics students build on the knowledge they gained in Unit 1 as they make their Web sites more robust with tables, cascading style sheets (CSS), frames, snippets, library items, and templates. Finally, in Unit 3: Advanced Skills, students tackle the more complex topics of working with forms, behaviors, layers, and hand coding HTML. This book assumes that students understand how to use a mouse and drop-down menus, how to save files to some type of storage media, and how to perform other basic skills required to run Windows and Macintosh programs, but there are no specifics prerequisite skills needed for either platform.

Labyrinth has been writing and publishing Microsoft® Office courses for more than 10 years. We are now expanding our book list to include other application programs including Macromedia® Dreamweaver®, Intuit® QuickBooks®, digital photography, and more. Labyrinth has developed a unique instructional design that makes learning faster and easier for students at all skill levels. Teachers have found that the Labyrinth model provides effective learning for students in both self-paced and instructor-led environments. The material is carefully crafted and built around compelling case studies that demonstrate the relevance of the subject matter. Mastery of this subject matter is ensured through the use of multiple levels of carefully crafted exercises. This book includes Concepts Review quizzes, and Hands-On, Skill Builders, Assessment, and Critical Thinking exercises.

Dreamweaver MX 2004: Comprehensive Course has a companion online testing package based on the Blackboard Learning System™ so students can study effectively at home or in the office and with minimal need to contact an instructor for assistance. This book is also supported on the Labyrinth Web site with a comprehensive instructor support package that includes a printable solutions guide, detailed lecture notes, PowerPoint® presentations, a course syllabus, extensive test banks, and more.

We are grateful to the many instructors who have used Labyrinth titles and suggested improvements to us during the 10 years we have been writing and publishing various best-selling series of textbooks. *Dreamweaver MX 2004: Comprehensive Course* has benefited from the review and suggestions of Shirley Dayton, dGroup Learning Center (Cortland, NY); David Karlins, San Francisco State University (San Francisco, CA); Kathy Lavieri, Great Oaks Institute of Technology and Career Development (Cincinnati, OH); Darin Murphy, South Puget Sound Community College (Puget Sound, WA); Monika Olson, Diablo Valley Community College (Concord, CA); and Gordon Pike, Haywood Community College (Haywood, CA).

About the Author

Bill Lewallen is an independent technical trainer, writer, and Web design consultant with more than 20 years of experience using communication and technical writing skills with Fortune 50/500 companies in the United States, Germany, and Mexico. Bill wrote and developed the first Web publishing courses for Oracle University, Charles Schwab University, Hewlett-Packard's Enterprise Workforce Development, and others. He has designed numerous Web sites for business professionals and non-profit organizations. He has trained thousands to create Web pages, and has authored courses on HTML for end-users and developers. It is Bill's fondest hope that your skillful mastery of the tools presented here will help you become leaders in the competitive world of information exchange.

Introduction

Welcome to Labyrinth Publications, where you'll find your course to success. Our real world, project-based approach to education helps students grasp concepts, not just read about them, and prepares them for success in the workplace. Our straightforward, easy-to-follow language is ideal for both instructor-led classes and self-paced labs. At Labyrinth, we're dedicated to one purpose: delivering quality courseware that is comprehensive yet concise, effective, and affordable. It's no wonder that Labyrinth is a recognized leader in Microsoft Office and operating system courseware.

More than a million users have learned Office our way. At Labyrinth, we believe that successful teaching begins with exceptional courseware. That's why we've made it our goal to develop innovative texts that empower both teachers and students. We give educators the necessary resources to deliver clear, relevant instruction and students the power to take their new skills far beyond the classroom.

Labyrinth Series Give You More Choices

Labyrinth offers seven exceptionally priced series to meet your needs:

- ProStart™ Series—This new series of full-length, full-featured texts teach professional-level skills in popular application programs for media arts, small business management, and more using Labyrinth's accessible and efficient methods. As they complete work projects and critical thinking tasks, students learn how to create deliverables that are ready for primetime.

- Briefcase™ Series—The popular and inexpensive choice for short classes, self-paced courses, and accelerated workshops (or mix and match for longer classes), these concise texts provide quick access to key concepts. Many are Microsoft Office Specialist approved.

- Microsoft Office 2003 Series—These full-length, full-featured texts explore applications in the Office 2003 system. All application specific books in this series are Microsoft Office Specialist approved for the Microsoft Office 2003 certification exams and the Word and Excel books are also approved for the Microsoft Office 2003 Expert certification exams.

- Silver™ Series—Designed especially for adult learners, seniors, and non-native speakers, this series includes larger fonts and screens, our unmistakable straightforward design, and fun hands-on projects.

- ProStart Foundations™ Series—These full-length, full-featured texts for operating systems and applications include the new Microsoft Windows titles and are designed to lay a solid foundation for students.

- ProStart Series for Office XP—These full-length, full-featured texts walk students through the basic and advanced skills of the primary Office XP applications. Most are Microsoft Office Specialist approved. The Office XP Essentials and Comprehensive courses offer surveys of all the primary Office XP applications.

ProStart Series Teaching Resources

Instructor Support Material

To help you be more successful, Labyrinth provides a comprehensive instructor support package that includes the following:

Teaching Tools

- Detailed lecture plans, including a topic sequence and suggested classroom demonstrations

- PowerPoint presentations that give an overview of key concepts for each lesson (also available online for students)

- Answer keys for the Concepts Review questions in each lesson

- Comprehensive classroom setup instructions

- A customizable sample syllabus

- A teacher-customizable background knowledge survey to gather information on student needs and experience at the beginning of the course

Testing Tools

- Printer-friendly exercise solution guides and solution files for Hands-On, Skill Builder, Assessment, and Critical Thinking exercises

- Teacher-customizable, project-based Assessment exercises

- Teacher-customizable test banks of objective questions for each lesson and unit

- TestComposer™ test generator for editing test banks with Microsoft Word (and for creating new question banks and online tests)

These resources are available on our Web site at labpub.com and on our instructor support CD, which you can obtain by calling our customer service staff at 800.522.9746.

Web site

The Web site labpub.com/learn/dw04/ features content designed to support the lessons and provide additional learning resources for this book. This main page contains links to individual lesson pages. Some of the items you will find at this site are described below.

PowerPoint Presentations The same presentations available to instructors are accessible online. They make excellent tools for review, particularly for students who miss a class session.

Downloads Required course files can be downloaded on the lesson pages.

Student Exercise Files The student files needed to complete certain Hands-On, Skill Builder, Assessment, and Critical Thinking exercises are available for download at labpub.com/students/fdpro05.asp.

Distance Learning Courses

Labyrinth offers distance learning courses for the Blackboard Learning System platform that leverage the strengths of both online and print-based content to deliver a rich learning experience. To find out about implementing a Blackboard distance learning program at your campus, contact your Labyrinth sales representative.

Labyrinth's Successful Instructional Design

In conjunction with our straightforward writing style, Labyrinth books feature a proven instructional design. The following pages point out the carefully crafted design elements that build student confidence and ensure success.

Lesson introductions present clear learning objectives.

Case studies introduce a practical application that integrate topics presented in each lesson.

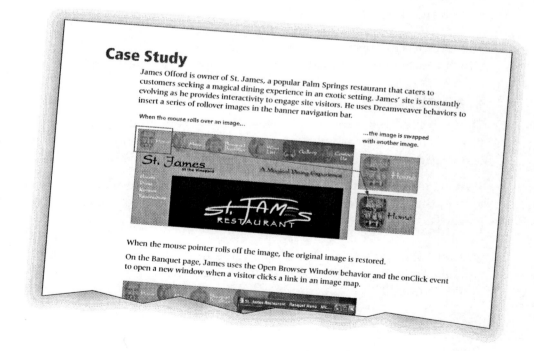

Concepts discussions are kept concise and use illustrations for added clarity and to help students understand the material introduced.

Quick Reference tables provide generic procedures for key tasks that work outside the context of the lesson.

Hands-On exercises are detailed tutorials that help students master the skills introduced in the concepts discussions. The illustrations provide clear instruction and allow unparalleled ease of use.

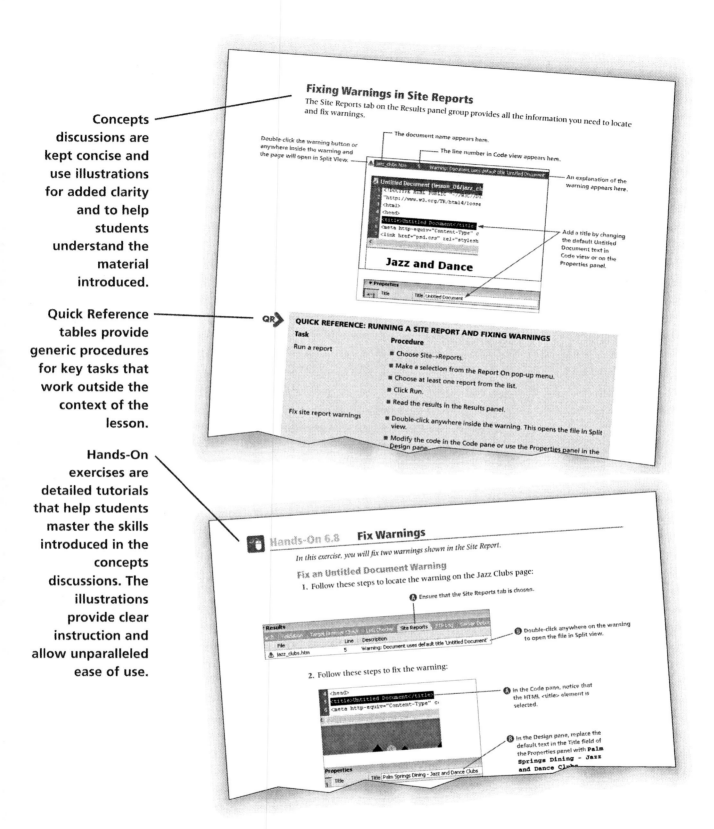

Fixing Warnings in Site Reports

The Site Reports tab on the Results panel group provides all the information you need to locate and fix warnings.

Double-click the warning button or anywhere inside the warning and the page will open in Split View.

The document name appears here.

The line number in Code view appears here.

An explanation of the warning appears here.

Add a title by changing the default Untitled Document text in Code view or on the Properties panel.

Jazz and Dance

QR **QUICK REFERENCE: RUNNING A SITE REPORT AND FIXING WARNINGS**

Task	Procedure
Run a report	■ Choose Site→Reports.
	■ Make a selection from the Report On pop-up menu.
	■ Choose at least one report from the list.
	■ Click Run.
	■ Read the results in the Results panel.
Fix site report warnings	■ Double-click anywhere inside the warning. This opens the file in Split view.
	■ Modify the code in the Code pane or use the Properties panel in the Design pane.

Hands-On 6.8   Fix Warnings

In this exercise, you will fix two warnings shown in the Site Report.

Fix an Untitled Document Warning

1. Follow these steps to locate the warning on the Jazz Clubs page:

Ⓐ Ensure that the Site Reports tab is chosen.

Ⓑ Double-click anywhere on the warning to open the file in Split view.

2. Follow these steps to fix the warning:

Ⓐ In the Code pane, notice that the HTML <title> element is selected.

Ⓑ In the Design pane, replace the default text in the Title field of the Properties panel with **Palm Springs Dining - Jazz and Dance Clubs**.

The Concepts
Review section
at the end of
each lesson
includes both
true/false and
multiple choice
questions.

Concepts Review

True/False Questions

1. Cascading style sheets can control the appearance of a single page, or multiple pages.   TRUE   FALSE
2. Before adding CSS styles to an existing Web page, remove any preexisting formatting.   TRUE   FALSE
3. External styles override internal styles.   TRUE   FALSE
4. Internal styles are embedded within HTML tags, such as headings and paragraphs.   TRUE   FALSE
5. A CSS selector style is always an HTML tag.   TRUE   FALSE
6. A style sheet is a group of CSS styles.   TRUE   FALSE
7. A declaration consists of a style property and its value.   TRUE   FALSE
8. Class selector styles are automatically applied to HTML elements.   TRUE   FALSE
9. If you want to modify the format of any paragraph text that appears inside a table cell, you can use the contextual selector "p td."   TRUE   FALSE
10. The Page Properties dialog box offers the most options for creating and modifying CSS styles.   TRUE   FALSE

Multiple Choice Questions

1. Which of the following are pseudo-class

3. Which of the following CSS categories is

Skill Builders,
Assessments,
and Critical
Thinking
exercises
provide fun,
hands-on
projects with
reduced levels
of detailed
instruction so
students can
develop and
test their
mastery of the
material.

Skill Builders

Skill Builder 8.1   **Align and Populate Table Cells**

In this exercise, you will design a basic page layout and use Expanded Tables mode, insert images, set cell alignment, add spacers, and set page and table background color.

1. Open entertainment.htm from the review_08 f...

Assessments

Assessment 8.1   **Design a Basic Page Layout**

In this exercise, you will design a page with a nested table.

...new HTML document and save it as **tango.htm**. Store the file in the review_08

Critical Thinking

Critical Thinking 8.1   **On Your Own**

Just in Time Design is recruiting new employees to help them with their demanding Web design schedule. Justin distributes a picture of a Web page to your Dreamweaver class and asks anyone interested to recreate the liquid page layout design. The winner will receive a $500 hiring bonus and an extra week of paid vacation.

...ising the d...   ...the following il...   ...in this Web...

How This Book Is Organized

The information in this book is presented so that you master the fundamental skills first, and then build on those skills as you work with the more comprehensive topics.

Visual Conventions

This book uses many visual and typographic cues to guide you through the lessons. This page provides examples and describes the function of each cue.

Type this text — Anything you should type at the keyboard is printed in this typeface.

 — Tips, Notes, and Warnings are used throughout the text to draw attention to certain topics.

Command→Command — This convention indicates multiple selections to be made from a menu bar. For example, File→Save means to select File, and then to select Save.

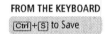
FROM THE KEYBOARD
[Ctrl]+[S] to Save — These margin notes indicate shortcut keys for executing a task described in the text.

 — Quick Reference tables provide generic instructions for key tasks. Only perform these tasks if you are instructed to in an exercise.

 — Hands-On exercises are introduced immediately after concept discussions. They provide detailed, step-by-step tutorials so you can master the skills presented.

(Win) (Mac) — Content and instructions specific to the Windows platform or the Macintosh platform will include this notation.

 — The Concepts Review section includes both true/false and multiple choice questions designed to gauge your understanding of concepts.

 — Skill Builder exercises provide additional hands-on practice with moderate assistance.

 — Assessment exercises test your skills by describing the correct results without providing specific instructions on how to achieve them.

 — Critical Thinking exercises are the most challenging. They provide general instructions, allowing you to use your skills and creativity to achieve the result you envision.

Dreamweaver MX 2004: Comprehensive Course

Unit 1

Basic Skills

Dreamweaver MX 2004 is Macromedia's professional Web design and Web site management program. In this unit, you will be introduced to the visual Designer workspace and many of the toolbars, panels, and inspectors that can be shown or hidden as needed. You will learn how to format HTML documents and set basic Cascading Style Sheet (CSS) page properties. You will also learn how to insert and modify images, and how to create text and graphic links within your site, to email, and to resources on the Internet. The last lesson in this unit teaches you how to set up and transfer files on your local file storage location to a remote location, find and fix broken links, run site reports, and synchronize local and remote files.

Lesson 1: Getting Started

Lesson 2: Working with HTML Documents

Lesson 3: Working with Text

Lesson 4: Working with Images

Lesson 5: Working with Anchors and Links

Lesson 6: Working with Site Management

LESSON 1

Getting Started

Welcome to Dreamweaver! Dreamweaver MX 2004 is a professional, visual, Web design program for the creation, organization, and maintenance of Web sites and private company intranets. In this lesson, you will learn how to create new files and folders that will house your new Web site. You will also learn how to navigate the Dreamweaver workspace. Dreamweaver's integrated workspace is occupied by flexible panels and toolbars that you can hide or show to accomplish certain tasks. Dreamweaver preferences can be tailored to your settings and help is available in many forms.

Case Study

Janet Saxon is publisher of Palm Springs Dining, a monthly magazine. Many of her subscribers have encouraged her to create a Web site to enable them to get up-to-the-minute information on dining in Palm Springs. It seems new restaurants are opening daily in the desert.

An absolute novice, Janet researched all of the WYSIWYG (What You See Is What You Get) Web design programs and chose Dreamweaver MX 2004 because of its powerful, easy-to-use visual layout tools. She's relieved that she doesn't have to know anything upfront about HTML, CSS, or any other Web language to get started.

Janet begins her Web design journey by using Dreamweaver to create a site on her local computer that she can use to store all of the files and folders for her Palm Springs Dining site. Although tempted to start with the glamorous page design process, Janet says, "I will take the time now to master the mechanics so I won't waste time looking for tools and then figuring out how they work when I need them."

Janet browses the visual interface and discovers an array of features that will dramatically speed up the design process.

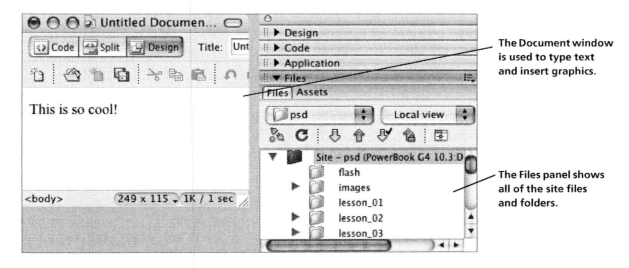

The Document window is used to type text and insert graphics.

The Files panel shows all of the site files and folders.

After taking another sip of double espresso, Janet rolls up her sleeves and jumps into the beginning of the Web design process—learning the Dreamweaver interface.

Understanding the Project Files

The project files for the lessons in this book are based on a series of fictional Web sites, including Palm Springs Dining, and a real Web site named St. James Restaurant. The skills you develop while working on the project files will enable you to build and manage your own Web site.

 NOTE! *In this book, when variations occur between the Windows and Macintosh versions, you will see special notations such as (Win), (Mac).*

Storing Your Exercise Files

Throughout this book you will be referred to files in your "file storage location." You can store your exercise files on various media, such as a USB flash drive, the My Documents folder (Win), Documents folder (Mac), or to a network drive at a school or company. See the appendix for additional information on alternative file storage media.

 NOTE! *If you have not copied the student exercise files to your local file storage location, please see the appendix for instructions on how to do this. The student exercise files will need to be in place before you begin the first Hands-On exercise.*

The Save In box as it appears in the book

The Save In box as it might appear if you are saving your files to a USB flash drive

Introducing Web Design

Dreamweaver provides users of all levels the visual tools needed to create, modify, and publish Web pages. Beginners are not forced to learn HTML or CSS to put Dreamweaver to work right away. Advanced users are provided the option of working directly with HTML (HyperText Markup Language) and other coding languages, if they so choose. The powerful support of CSS (cascading style sheets) layers, tables, behaviors, templates, advanced error checking, and find and replace make Dreamweaver a tremendous tool for Web designers at any skill level.

HTML and CSS in a Nutshell

HTML and CSS are text-based languages that any computer can read. HTML is used to define the structure of an HTML document (Web page). Structure refers to the organization of content including headings, subheadings, paragraphs, lists, and tables. CSS is used to define the presentation (formatting) of an HTML document. Presentation elements include the page font and font size, foreground and background color, margins, word and letter spacing, alignment, and much more. You will be gradually exposed to both of these languages throughout many lessons in this book, beginning with Lesson 2, Working with HTML Documents. By the time you complete this book, you will be well versed in both languages without having to spend any time outside of Dreamweaver.

Creating a Web Site

The term Web site, or site, refers to a collection of related Web pages along with their supporting files and folders. A site does not have to be hosted on a Web server and made available to the public. For example, a site might be stored on a private intranet and made available only to a company's employees. A site may also reside on a network drive to be shared by a team of users. Regardless of where your site resides, visitors typically enter through the front door, called the homepage. A homepage serves as an index or table of contents to other documents stored on the site.

Defining Homepage Filenames

Your homepage filename is determined by your Web server's operating system or your Web server administrator. The most common homepage filenames are:

- index
- default
- welcome

All homepage filenames in this book use index.htm. (You'll learn about the .htm filename extension in Lesson 2, Working with HTML Documents.)

 TIP! *You don't have to know your homepage filename in order to begin building your site. When in doubt, use index.htm. If you have to rename it later, Dreamweaver takes care of updating your entire site to reflect the new filename.*

Launching Dreamweaver

The first time, and only the first time, you start Dreamweaver, a Workspace Setup dialog box opens (Win) and you must choose either the Designer or Coder workspace.

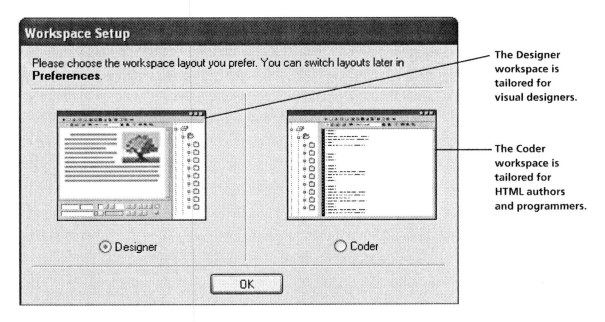

The Designer workspace is tailored for visual designers.

The Coder workspace is tailored for HTML authors and programmers.

The following exercise assumes that this is the first time Dreamweaver is being launched on your computer. For Windows users, if Dreamweaver was previously opened, you will not see the Workspace Setup dialog box but will be taken directly to the workspace that was chosen by the last user. If you need to change the workspace, please see the following Quick Reference table.

QUICK REFERENCE: CHANGING THE WORKSPACE (WIN)

Task	Procedure
Change the workspace	■ Choose Edit→Preferences.
	■ Select the General category, and then click the Change Workspace button.
	■ Restart Dreamweaver.

 Hands-On 1.1   **Launch Dreamweaver for the First Time**

In this exercise, you will launch Dreamweaver. Because of program differences, the steps for Macintosh users and Windows users are not identical.

Before you begin: *If you have not done so already, please turn to the Downloading the Student Exercise Files section of the appendix (page 492), for instructions on how to retrieve the student exercise files for this book from the Labyrinth Web site, and to copy the files to your file storage location for use in this and future lessons.*

1. Launch the Dreamweaver application using the Start button (Win) or the Finder (Mac).
    The Workspace Setup dialog box opens (Win). The Designer workspace opens for (Mac) users; skip to step 3.

2. (Win) Choose the Designer workspace, and then click OK.
    Dreamweaver opens in the Designer workspace.

3. Leave the workspace as it is and continue with the next topic.

NOTE! *All of the lessons in this book use the Designer workspace.*

Exploring the Workspace

The Dreamweaver workspace contains the Insert bar, Start page, Panel groups, and Properties panel (also known as the Property Inspector). The Insert bar and the Properties panel are dimmed when the Start page is active. When you begin working with Web pages, these and many other panels are available.

The Workspace Layout (Mac)

The Macintosh workspace features a floating workspace layout. Each workspace element is in its own individual window. Panel groups are initially docked together, but can be undocked and moved to another location.

The Insert bar has buttons for inserting objects, such as images and tables, into a document.

Panel groups are sets of related panels grouped together under one heading.

The Start page enables you to open existing or create new documents. Learn more by taking a product tour or a tutorial.

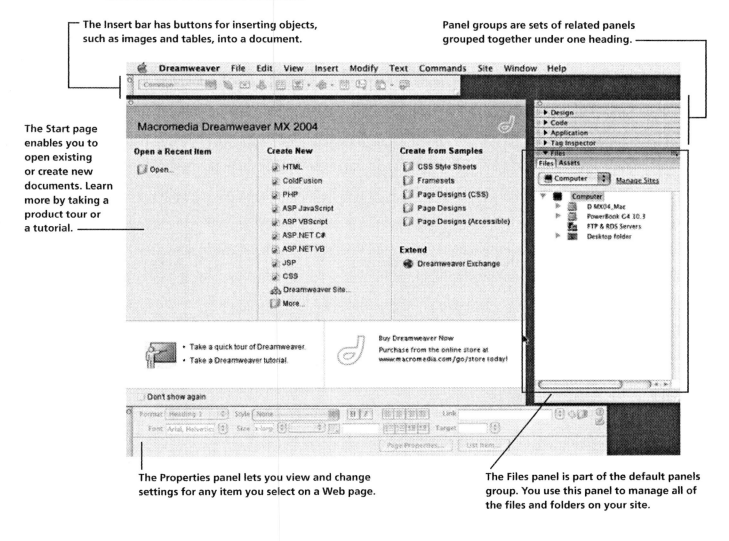

The Properties panel lets you view and change settings for any item you select on a Web page.

The Files panel is part of the default panels group. You use this panel to manage all of the files and folders on your site.

The Workspace Layout (Win)

The Windows workspace provides an all-in-one-window integrated layout. All windows and panels are merged into a single application window. Panel groups are initially docked together, but can be undocked and moved to another location.

The Insert bar has buttons for inserting objects, such as images and tables, into a document.

Panel groups are sets of related panels grouped together under one heading.

The Start page enables you to open existing or create new documents. Learn more by taking a product tour or a tutorial.

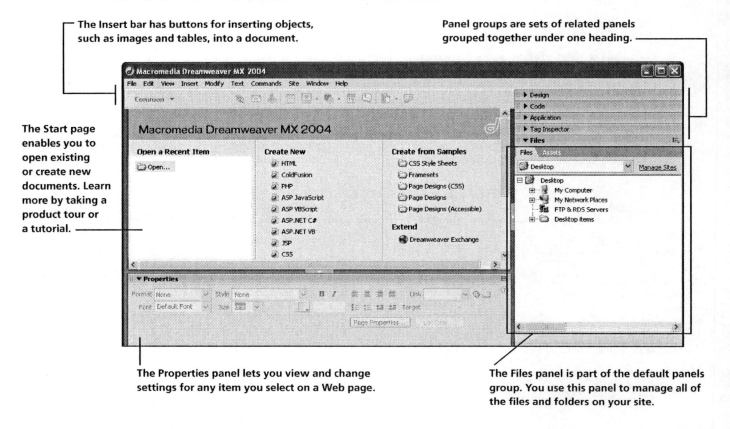

The Properties panel lets you view and change settings for any item you select on a Web page.

The Files panel is part of the default panels group. You use this panel to manage all of the files and folders on your site.

WARNING! *You can customize the workspace elements, dock them to the right or left, or move them into a floating position in the workspace. You should NOT attempt to close or hide any of the panels until you understand how to open them again.*

The Start Page

The Start page appears in the left window of the workspace the first time you open Dreamweaver MX 2004. The Start page provides a visual interface for frequently used tasks including:

- Opening recent documents

- Creating new documents

- Creating new documents from samples

- Taking a product tour or a tutorial

- Creating a new Dreamweaver site

The Start page temporarily closes each time you create a new document or open an existing document. When all documents are closed, the Start page reappears and will continue to appear each time you open Dreamweaver unless you disable it by placing a checkmark in the Don't Show Again checkbox located in the lower-left corner of the page. You must then restart Dreamweaver for the change to take effect. If you do not see the Start page, follow the steps in the following Quick Reference table to enable it.

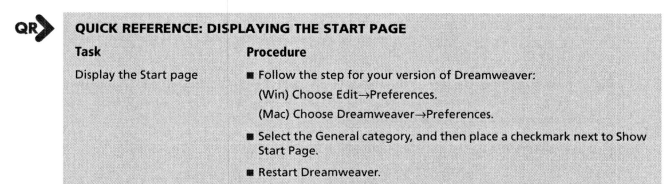

QUICK REFERENCE: DISPLAYING THE START PAGE

Task	Procedure
Display the Start page	■ Follow the step for your version of Dreamweaver: (Win) Choose Edit→Preferences. (Mac) Choose Dreamweaver→Preferences. ■ Select the General category, and then place a checkmark next to Show Start Page. ■ Restart Dreamweaver.

Defining a Local Site

The Web site creation process in Dreamweaver begins by defining a local site. You do this by creating a folder on your file storage location to store all the content for your site. Then, you use Dreamweaver to designate that folder as the local root folder. The local root folder and its contents form your local site. You create and manage all of the site contents on your local site. When you're ready, you publish the contents to your server, which is called the remote site. The creation of a local root folder prevents you from storing any files there that are not associated with your site. This restriction is a safeguard to ensure that you won't inadvertently link to files that aren't available when the local site is published to your remote server.

When defining a name for the local root folder, choose a brief descriptive name so you can easily identify it when you have more than one site to manage. The name of the local root folder can be the name of your site, an abbreviation of the name, or any name you choose. The name of the root folder is for internal file management purposes only; it doesn't appear anywhere when you publish your site.

The following illustration is an example of what a local root folder and its contents might look like for a very small site.

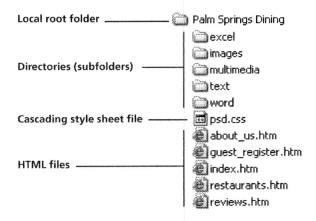

WARNING! *Never create a local root folder, or save any of your site files, inside the Dreamweaver program folder. If you ever have to reinstall Dreamweaver, all of your files may be deleted. It is always a good practice to separate the files you create from the program files of the creating application.*

TIP! *Use folders as necessary to keep the files of your Web site well organized.*

Local Sites Compared to Remote Sites

When you are ready to make your site available to others, you use Dreamweaver site management tools to publish the contents of your local site to the remote site (a location not connected to your own computer). The remote files may be stored on a Web server anywhere in the world or on a local network drive.

In this lesson, you will define a local site and use it for all of the lessons in this book. In Lesson 6, Working with Site Management, you will learn how to transfer a copy of any folder or the contents of the entire local site, to another location on your file storage device, a network drive, or to a remote server.

 TIP! *While you are developing your site, it is a good idea to frequently backup all of your files to a location other than your hard drive.*

 QR

QUICK REFERENCE: DEFINING A LOCAL SITE	
Task	**Procedure**
Define a local site	■ Click the Dreamweaver Site button on the Start page.
	■ Ensure that the Basic tab is chosen.
	■ Follow the instructions in the Site Definition dialog box.
	Or,
	■ Choose Site→Manage Sites.
	■ In the Manage Sites dialog box, click the New button, and then choose Site.
	■ Ensure that the Basic tab is chosen.
	■ Follow the instructions in the Site Definition dialog box.

 Hands-On 1.2   Define a Local Site

In this exercise, you will set up the new Palm Springs Dining's Web site. You will use the student exercise files you previously copied to your file storage location.

1. Click the ⊞ Dreamweaver Site... icon located in the Create New column of the Start page. *The Site Definition dialog box opens.*

2. Make sure the Basic tab is chosen.

3. Type **unit1** in the What Would You Like to Name Your Site field.
   The name you choose is not seen by visitors to your site.

4. Click Next.
   Part 2 of the dialog box opens. The site name appears in the title bar of the dialog box.

5. Click No, I Do Not Want to Use a Server Technology.
   You are creating a site that does not use databases or other server technologies.

6. Click Next.
   Part 3 of the Site Definition dialog box opens.

7. Click the Edit Local Copies on My Machine option. Do NOT click next.

8. Click the folder ⬚ button to the right of the text field and browse to and select the unit1
   folder you copied to your file storage location.

9. Click Next.
   Part 4 of the Site Definition dialog box opens.

10. Choose None from the pop-up menu below the text, "How do you connect to your remote
    server?"

11. Click Next.
    The Summary section of the Site Definition dialog box opens.

12. Review the Summary section. If the information is correct, click Done. (Or, click the Back
    button and correct any errors.)
    *The local root folder unit1 appears in the Files panel. The path to your file storage location will likely
    differ from the following illustrations.*

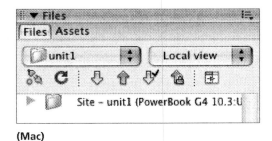

(Mac)

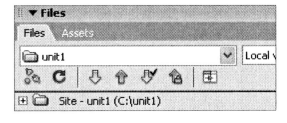

(Win)

Time Well Spent

You are probably anxious to take a leap of faith and begin working on your site. However, there are a few things that you need to know up front. If you are accustomed to working exclusively in Microsoft Office applications that use an all-in-one window approach and have never used a Macromedia integrated program, you might find managing multiple panels and toolbars challenging in the beginning. That's OK. You will soon learn that you can display only the panels and toolbars you need for a specific task.

 TIP! *Mastering the interface now will help you later when you want to focus on the design of your site, not the mechanics.*

Working with Panels

Most Dreamweaver controls are available from panels that are grouped under one heading. There are five default panel groups:

- Design
- Code
- Application
- Tag Inspector
- Files

Each panel group can be expanded or collapsed by clicking the Expand/Collapse arrow located to the left of the panel group name.

Expand/Collapse arrrows ———

When you expand a panel group, you will see two or more panels. In the following illustration, the active panel is Files. You can switch to another panel within the group by clicking the panel name.

Files panel group ———
Files tab (the active panel) ———
Assets tab (the inactive panel) ———
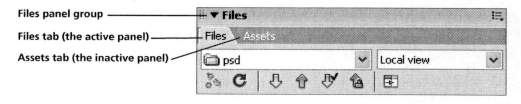

Docking and Undocking a Panel Group

You can undock a panel from its docking station and move it into a floating position in the workspace, or you can dock the panel in another location. You can also rename panels and move them around in the panel groups. However, until you are comfortable using panels, it is recommended that you not move them, rearrange, or rename them.

⚠ NOTE! *All of the lessons in this book assume that you are using the default panel configuration.*

The majority of Dreamweaver panels can be docked in the panels group. Two exceptions are the Properties panel and the Results panel. These two panels can appear as floating panels in the workspace, or they can be docked at the top or bottom of the workspace.

Showing and Hiding Panels

FROM THE KEYBOARD
To show/hide panels:
WIN AND MAC
[F4]

This lesson provides an overview of how to manage the panels that appear in the workspace. Until you are familiar with the workspace, you should work with a limited number of choices. Dreamweaver's interface allows you to display only the panels you need to accomplish the current task.

You can toggle panel display by choosing Window→Hide Panels or Window→Show Panels. (Win) When all panels are hidden, only the Start page is shown in the workspace (assuming it has not been disabled). (Mac) When all panels are hidden, the Start page is also hidden.

Hiding Individual Panels (Win)

When you are designing Web pages, the Panels group and the Properties panel can be distracting, as they both take up quite a bit of room in the workspace. You can selectively hide or show each panel by clicking the tiny arrow next to the panel.

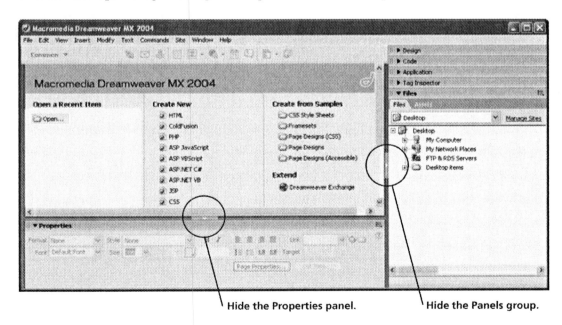

Hide the Properties panel.   Hide the Panels group.

When you hide a panel in this manner, the panel collapses and only the arrow remains. To open the panel again, you must click the arrow.

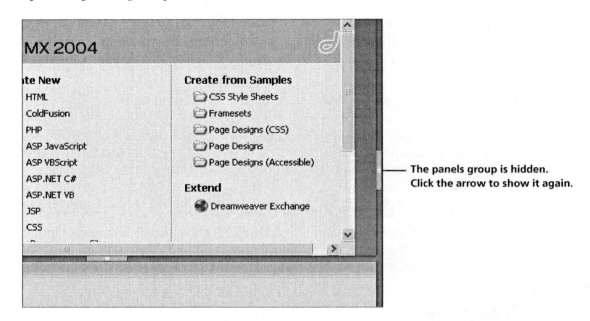

— The panels group is hidden.
Click the arrow to show it again.

TIP! *Individual panels can also be shown or hidden by choosing the panel's name from the Window menu.*

SHOWING AND HIDING PANELS

Panel	Windows Shortcut (Win)	Macintosh Shortcut (Mac)
Properties panel	Ctrl + F3	⌘ + F3
Files panel	F8	F8
All panels	F4	F4

 ## Hands-On 1.3   Show and Hide Panels

In this exercise, you will hide all panels, show all panels, and show and hide individual panels.

1. Choose Window→Hide Panels.
   This hides all open panels.

2. Choose Window→Show Panels.
   This opens the hidden panels.

3. Choose Window→Properties from the menu bar.
   This closes the Properties panel.

4. Choose Window→Files.
   This closes the Files panel.

5. Choose Window→Properties.

This opens the Properties panel.

6. Choose Window→Files.

This opens the Files panel. Keep the Files panel open for the next exercise.

Using the Files Panel

The Files panel serves as a file management control center. All site management tasks, such as adding or moving Web site files and folders, should be done inside the Files panel. This way, Dreamweaver can keep track of where your files are and how they're organized. This is especially critical when you begin modifying pages that are linked to images or other pages.

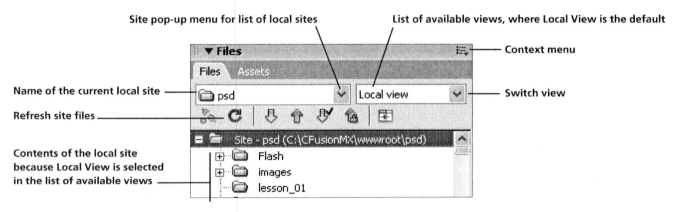

Many file management tasks are accessible through the context menu. The following illustration displays the expanded context menu.

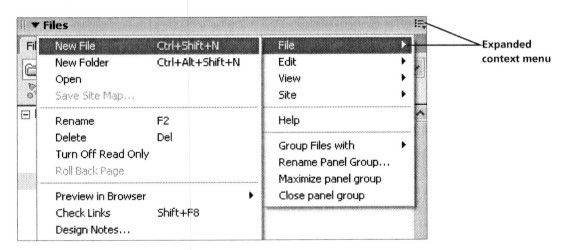

Adding New Files and Folders

When you are creating a site from scratch, you can use the Files panel to quickly add new, blank files that serve as placeholders and blank folders to store the files.

Renaming Files and Folders

New folders and HTML files initially appear selected, as shown in the following illustration.

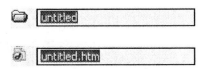

While a file or folder name is selected, you can change the default name "untitled" to something meaningful. When renaming files, be sure to include the .htm extension, which identifies the file type as HTML. Also, use lowercase names with no spaces for both folder names and filenames. You will learn more about file extensions and file naming conventions in Lesson 2, Working with HTML Documents.

Moving Files and Folders

Always use the Files panel to move files and folders, not Windows Explorer or Macintosh Finder. The main purpose of the Files panel is to keep track of your site's content. If you move a file or folder using Windows Explorer or Macintosh Finder, Dreamweaver has no way of changing the path to linked documents and those pages will result in a "File not found" error when you try to preview them in a Web browser.

Deleting Files and Folders

When you use the Files panel to delete a file or folder that is linked to other files, Dreamweaver displays an alert box that identifies the linked documents and you are given a chance to change your mind. If you proceed, the file or folder is deleted and the action cannot be undone.

 TIP! *Windows users can locate the deleted file in the Recycle Bin and use the Restore feature to send the file back to the Files panel. When you do this, you may need to click the Refresh button on the Files panel toolbar. Macintosh users can move the file out of the Trash, and then move it back to the Files panel.*

Refreshing the Files Panel

When you're organizing files and folders, you should occasionally tap [F5] or click the Refresh button on the Files panel menu bar to refresh the Files panel.

QUICK REFERENCE: WORKING WITH THE FILES PANEL

Task	Procedure
Refresh the Files panel	■ Click the Refresh [C] button on the Files panel toolbar or tap F5.
Add new files and folders	■ Right-click (Win) or Ctrl+click (Mac) the area inside the Files panel where you want to add a new file or folder. ■ Choose New File or New Folder from the context menu.
Rename files and folders	■ In the Files panel, click one time on the file or folder you want to rename. ■ Tap F2. ■ Type the new name over the existing name. ■ Tap Enter or Return.
Move files and folders	■ Click on the file or folder and drag and drop it in a new location in the Files panel.
Delete files and folders	■ Click one time on the file or folder, and then press Delete.

 Hands-On 1.4   Organize Files in the Files Panel

In this exercise, you will use the Files panel to add, rename, move, and delete two new files and a folder.

Before you begin: The Files panel must be open. If you do not see the Files panel, tap F8.

1. Right-click (Win) or Ctrl+click (Mac) the lesson_01 folder.

2. Choose New Folder from the context menu.
   An untitled folder appears inside the lesson_01 folder.

3. While the folder is highlighted, type **new_restaurants**, and then press Enter or Return.

4. Right-click (Win) or Ctrl+click (Mac) on the lesson_01 folder.

5. Choose New Folder from the context menu.
   Another untitled folder appears inside the lesson_01 folder.

6. While the folder is highlighted, type **restaurant_reviews**, and then press Enter or Return.

7. Right-click (Win) or Ctrl+click (Mac) on the new_restaurants folder, and then choose New File from the context menu.
   An untitled HTML file is added to the new_restaurants folder.

8. While the file name is highlighted, type **st_james.htm**, and then press Enter or Return.

9. Right-click (Win) or Ctrl+click (Mac) on the restaurant_reviews folder, and then choose New File from the context menu.
   A new untitled HTML file is added to the restaurant_reviews folder.

10. While the filename is highlighted, type **the_falls.htm**, and then press Enter or Return.

11. Drag and drop the_falls.htm into the new_restaurants folder.
This opens the Update Files dialog box.

12. Tap Update.
The File manager updates the new file location.

13. Right-click (Win) or Ctrl+click (Mac) on the_falls.htm.

14. From the context menu, choose Edit→Rename.

15. Type **the_falls_steakhouse.htm** and press Enter or Return.

16. Select the restaurant_reviews folder.

17. Tap Delete.

18. Tap Yes when prompted, "Do you really want to delete the selected file(s)?"

19. Click the Refresh C button on the Files panel.

Accessing Files on Your Computer

The Files panel is a gateway to all of the files and folders located on your computer or local storage device. To access files on your Desktop or local or network drive, click the arrow located to the right of the root folder name and make a selection from the pop-up menu.

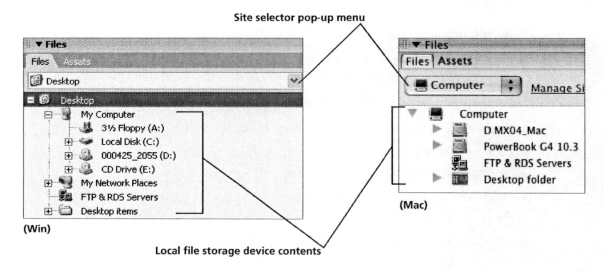

Site selector pop-up menu

(Win)

(Mac)

Local file storage device contents

When you use the Files panel to browse the contents of your computer, folders that you have designated as local root folders are colored light green; all other folders are colored yellow (Win) or blue (Mac). You can drag and drop (or copy and paste) any file located on your computer to the desired local root folder in the Files panel. The file is copied to the new location and the original file remains intact.

Setting General Preferences

FROM THE KEYBOARD

To display preferences:

WIN ONLY
[Ctrl]+[U]

MAC ONLY
[⌘]+[U]

Because all of us work differently, Dreamweaver provides many preferences that you can set so Dreamweaver works with you, not against you. You access the Preferences dialog box by choosing Edit→Preferences (Win) or Dreamweaver→Preferences (Mac).

This is a list of preference categories.

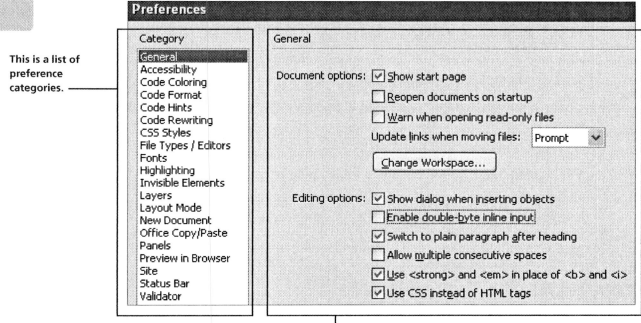

Settings for the selected category are displayed here.

> **⚠ NOTE!** *The Change Workspace button shown in the preceding illustration is not available on the Mac.*

You will use the Preferences dialog box throughout this course to set preferences in various categories. In this lesson, you will set general preferences. General preferences are divided into two subcategories: document options and editing options. Some of the editing options refer to HTML and CSS. It is not important that you understand the HTML tags and the use of CSS at this time; however, later lessons that cover these topics assume that you have set these general preferences.

RECOMMENDED GENERAL PREFERENCE SETTINGS

Recommended Setting	Description
Show Start page	This displays the Dreamweaver Start page every time you launch Dreamweaver.
Update links when moving files	This determines what Dreamweaver does when you move, rename, or delete a linked document within your site. The recommended setting is Prompt, which is the default.

RECOMMENDED GENERAL PREFERENCE SETTINGS (CONTINUED)

Recommended Setting	Description
Show dialog when inserting objects	This is a time saver that enables you to set properties for various objects when you insert them.
Switch to plain paragraph after heading	This specifies that when you create a heading and then press Enter or Return, Dreamweaver changes the format to a new paragraph, not another heading.
Use <strong> and <em> in place of <b> and <i>	The <b> and <i> tags are obsolete. The <strong> and <em> tags should be used instead.
Use CSS instead of HTML tags	This specifies that Dreamweaver uses CSS styles instead of HTML to format Web pages.

 QUICK REFERENCE: SETTING GENERAL PREFERENCES

Task	Procedure

Set general preferences	■ Follow the step for your version of Dreamweaver:
	    (Win) Choose Edit→Preferences.
	    (Mac) Choose Dreamweaver→Preferences.
	■ Choose the General category.
	■ Make the desired settings, and then click OK.

 ## Hands-On 1.5   Set General Preferences

In this exercise, you will set general preferences. For the remainder of this course, it will be assumed that all these settings are in place.

1. Choose Edit→Preferences (Win) or Dreamweaver→Preferences (Mac).
   The Preferences dialog box opens.

2. Choose the General category.

Set Document Options

3. Follow these steps to set document options:

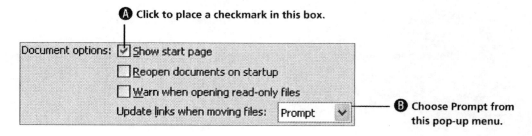

Ⓐ Click to place a checkmark in this box.

Ⓑ Choose Prompt from this pop-up menu.

Set Editing Options

4. Check the Editing Options shown in the following illustration:

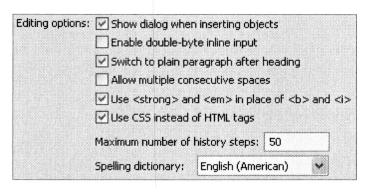

5. Click OK.

6. Leave the workspace as it is.

 **Concepts Review**

True/False Questions

1. The term Web site refers to a collection of related Web pages along with their supporting files and folders. TRUE FALSE

2. A local root folder should be stored in the Dreamweaver program folder. TRUE FALSE

3. Remote files are typically stored on a Web server or on a local network drive. TRUE FALSE

4. Panels can be shown or hidden by tapping the F4 key. TRUE FALSE

5. You should occasionally use Windows Explorer or Macintosh Finder to move or rename linked files. TRUE FALSE

6. Dreamweaver preferences can be set by choosing Edit→Preferences (Win) or Dreamweaver→Preferences (Mac). TRUE FALSE

7. When setting Editing options in Preferences, you should not choose the option to use CSS instead of HTML tags. TRUE FALSE

8. CSS is used to define the document structure; HTML is used to format the page font, font size, color, margins, and other page properties. TRUE FALSE

9. The Properties panel and the Results panel cannot be docked in the panels group. TRUE FALSE

10. You should refresh the Files panel after moving, deleting, or renaming files and folders. TRUE FALSE

Multiple Choice Questions

1. Which of the following statements best describes HTML and CSS?
   a. They are programming languages.
   b. They are scripting languages.
   c. They are text-based languages that any computer can read.
   d. None of the above

2. Which of the following names are commonly used for homepages?
   a. index.htm
   b. default.htm
   c. myplace.htm
   d. Both a and b

3. Which of the following elements appears in the default Dreamweaver workspace?
   a. Insert bar, Standard toolbar, and Properties panel
   b. Start page, Help window, and Insert bar
   c. Insert bar, Start page, Panels group, and Properties panel
   d. Designer bar, Insert bar, and Piano bar

4. The Dreamweaver site design process begins with creating a(n) _____ folder.
   a. HTML
   b. Images
   c. Local Root
   d. All of the above

Skill Builders

Skill Builder 1.1   Define a New Local Site

In this exercise, you will define a new local site, add new files and folders, and then remove the new site using the Manage Sites dialog box.

1. Use Windows Explorer or Macintosh Finder to create a new folder anywhere in your file storage location.

2. Name the folder **Project**, and then return to Dreamweaver.

Define a New Local Site

3. Use the [⬚⬚ Dreamweaver Site...] button on the Start page to open the Site Definition dialog box.
   If you don't see the Start page, close all open files.

4. Type **project** in the What Would You Like to Name Your Site field.

5. Click Next.

6. Choose the option No, I Do Not Want to Use a Server Technology.

7. Click Next.

8. Choose the option Edit Local Copies on My Machine, Then Upload to Server. Do NOT click Next.

9. Click the folder icon to the right of the text field and browse to the location you used to store the practice folder in your file storage location.

10. Click Next.

11. Below the question, How Do You Connect to Your Remote Server, choose None from the pop-up menu.

12. Click Next.

13. If the information in the Summary section is correct, click Done.

Add Files and Folders

14. Right-click (Win) or [Ctrl]+click (Mac) the project folder in the Files panel and choose New File from the context menu.

15. Type **index.htm**, and then tap [Enter] or [Return] to name the file.

16. Use the technique outlined in steps 14 and 15 to create two more files: **chess.htm** and **checkers.htm**.

17. Right-click (Win) or [Ctrl]+click (Mac) the project folder in the Files panel, and then choose New Folder from the context menu.

18. Type **games** and tap [Enter] or [Return] to name the folder.

19. Drag and drop the chess.htm and checkers.htm files into the games folder.
The Update Files dialog box opens.

20. Press Update.

Remove the New Project Site

Unless you want to continue practicing, you should remove the project Web site.

21. Choose Site_Manage Sites.

22. Choose project from the site list, and then click Remove.
This removes the project site. The project folder remains in your file storage location.

23. Choose unit1 from the site list, and then press Done.

Skill Builder 1.2   Show and Hide Panels

In this exercise, you will practice showing and hiding the panel groups and the Properties panel.

1. Click on the Window menu and verify that checkmarks appear next to Properties and Files.
This guarantees that the panels are displayed.

2. Click the Window menu to close it.

3. Tap [F4] to hide the open panels.

4. Tap [F4] again to display the hidden panels.

5. Choose Window→Properties.
This hides the Properties panel.

6. Choose Window→Properties.
This opens the Properties panel.

 # Assessments

Assessment 1.1   Create a New Local Site

In this exercise, you will create a new local site.

1. Use Windows Explorer or Macintosh Finder to create a new folder named **Blog** in your file storage location.

Define a Local Site

2. Use Dreamweaver to define a local site named **MyBlog** using the Blog folder as the local root folder.

Add New Folders and Files to the New Site.

3. Add two new folders and five new files to the MyBlog site.

4. Rename the untitled folders and files and organize them as shown in the following illustration:

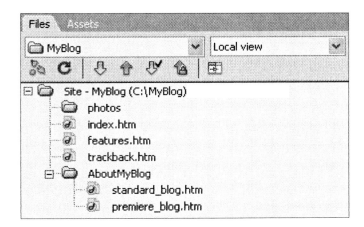

Remove the MyBlog Site

Unless you want to keep the MyBlog site for additional practice, you should remove it from the Manage Sites dialog box.

5. Choose Site→Manage Sites.

6. Choose MyBlog from the site list, and then click Remove.
   The site is removed from the Manage Sites dialog box. The folder remains in your file storage location.

7. Delete the folder from your file storage location.

Assessment 1.2   **Hide and Show Panels**

In this exercise, you will hide and show panels.

1. (Win) Arrange the panels so that only the Start page is visible.

2. (Mac) Hide all of the panels and the Start page.

3. (Win) Arrange the panels so that only the Start page and the Properties panel are visible.

4. Arrange the panels so that only the Start page and the panels group are visible.

5. Arrange the panels so that the Start page, Properties panel, and all default panel groups are visible.

Critical Thinking

Critical Thinking 1.1 On Your Own

Heather Madden recently graduated from high school and is off to San Francisco State University to begin work on a broadcast journalism major. This is the first time Heather has been away from home and she knows she will miss her family and friends, but she has a plan.

Heather researched San Francisco State's Web site and found that the university offers free Web services to SFSU departments, faculty, staff, and students. Armed with graduation gifts that include a new notebook computer, Dreamweaver, a digital camera, and now a free Web hosting service at SFSU, Heather has all the tools she needs to create a Web site that brings her friends and family together on the Web.

Since you already know how to set up a local site in Dreamweaver, Heather has asked you to help get her started. How can you say no to your best friend?

To get started, you need to create a local root folder on your file storage location. Name the folder **Freshman Scrapbook**. Next, use Dreamweaver to define a local site based on the local root folder.

Select topics that might be of interest and create files on them for Heather's Web site. (There is no need to put content in the files right now.) Topics might include dining hall hours, dining hall menus, dorm rooms and prices, Biology 1, English 1a, Social Studies 10, Modern Dance, Precalculus, Journalism 52, Technology offerings, family newsletter, etc. You can add any other topics that you think could be in her freshman scrapbook site.

For the purpose of this exercise, restrict filenames to one word or two words using the underscore (_) character. For example, dorm_room.htm, dining_menus.htm or dorm_prices.htm.

Critical Thinking 1.2 On Your Own

This exercise requires that you have completed Critical Thinking 1.1. Now that you have a list of possible files, create folders with the appropriate names, such as dining hall, courses, dorm, newsletters, and classmates.

For the purpose of this exercise, restrict folder names to one word or use the underscore (_) character; for example, dining_hall, dorms.

Critical Thinking 1.3 With a Group

Each individual in a group of two to six classmates chooses a college or university to compare with San Francisco State, creating pages that correspond to those Heather Madden has included in her freshman scrapbook site.

The group may want to create a new amazing Dreamweaver site based on a composite of the best features reviewed by each member of the group.

Working with HTML Documents

In this lesson, you will learn about the most fundamental type of Web page—the HTML document. You will learn how to create and modify HTML documents and to become even more proficient using the Dreamweaver workspace. Because HTML is a universal language, any computer can read it. You do not have to know anything about HTML to use Dreamweaver. However, there are a variety of things you need to understand about working with HTML documents because they are quite different from documents created by word processing and page layout programs.

IN THIS LESSON

Case Study

Justin Timberland is a recently unemployed computer technical support engineer. Having more time on his hands than usual, Justin has agreed to help his fiancée, Janet, get the Palm Springs Dining site online. Justin and Janet have mastered the process of creating a local site and organizing files and folders. Now they're ready to explore tools they can use to create and manage HTML (Web page format) documents. Neither Justin nor Janet knows anything about HTML and Janet would rather read the back of her Nordstrom's credit card than read HTML code. Curious Justin, however, has discovered several powerful tools they can use to explore HTML without leaving the visual design workspace. Justin can't wait to show Janet the Tag Selector, which identifies the HTML tag (descriptive marker) of any element on the page.

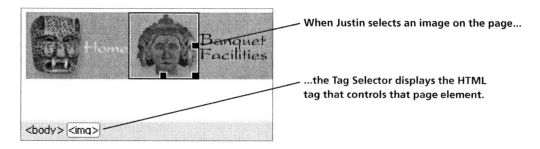

When Justin selects an image on the page...

...the Tag Selector displays the HTML tag that controls that page element.

The Properties panel, shown in the following illustration, changes to reflect the settings of each selected element. Justin and Janet soon learn that this panel is probably the one they will use more than any other.

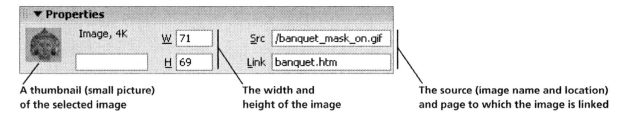

A thumbnail (small picture) of the selected image

The width and height of the image

The source (image name and location) and page to which the image is linked

Justin is confident that the new skills he's learning will help him start a new, exciting career in Web design and he can stop fretting over the great job that he lost.

Setting New HTML Document Preferences

FROM THE KEYBOARD

To set new HTML document preferences:

WIN ONLY
Ctrl + U

MAC ONLY
⌘ + U

The default new document type is HTML; however, Dreamweaver provides settings to create other types of documents, such as ColdFusion, ASP, JSP, and PHP. If most pages in your site use a language other than HTML, you can set document preferences that automatically create new documents of the specified file type.

All of the exercises in this book use HTML as the new default document type. To ensure that this setting has not been changed on your computer, please refer to the following table.

RECOMMENDED NEW DOCUMENT PREFERENCE SETTINGS

New Documents Preferences	Recommended Settings
Default document type	HTML
Default encoding	(Win) Western European (default setting)
	(Mac) Western (Latin1) (default setting)
Unicode Normalization Form	None (default setting)
Include Unicode Signature (BOM)	Leave this box unchecked
Show New Document dialog box on Ctrl+N (Win) or ⌘+N (Mac)	Leave this box unchecked
Make document XHTML compliant	Leave this box unchecked

QUICK REFERENCE: SETTING NEW DOCUMENT PREFERENCES

Task	Procedure
Set preferences for new Dreamweaver documents	■ Follow the step for your version of Dreamweaver: (Win) Choose Edit→Preferences from the menu bar. (Mac) Choose Dreamweaver→Preferences from the menu bar. ■ Choose New Document in the Category list on the left side of the dialog box. ■ Make the desired settings and click OK.

Hands-On 2.1   Set New Document Preferences

In this exercise, you will display new document preferences and make sure the recommended settings are in place for the rest of this lesson.

1. Choose Edit→Preferences (Win) or Dreamweaver→Preferences (Mac) from the menu bar. *This opens the Preferences dialog box.*

2. Follow these steps to set recommended new document preferences:

Ⓐ From the Category column, choose New Document.   Ⓑ For the default document type, choose HTML.

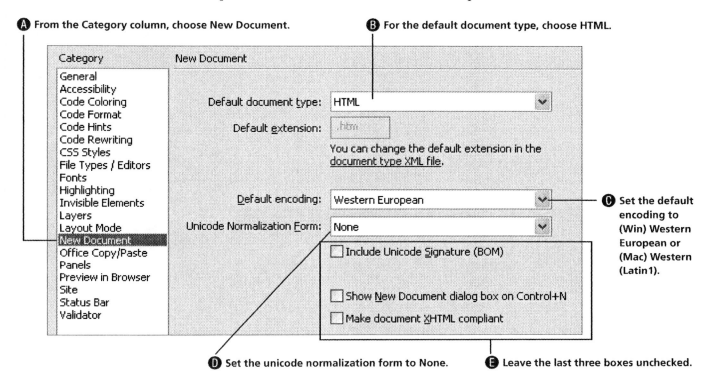

Ⓒ Set the default encoding to (Win) Western European or (Mac) Western (Latin1).

Ⓓ Set the unicode normalization form to None.   Ⓔ Leave the last three boxes unchecked.

3. Click OK.

Creating New, and Opening Existing, HTML Documents

Dreamweaver provides many options for creating new, and opening existing, HTML documents. Here we explore the most commonly used methods.

Creating a New HTML Document

FROM THE KEYBOARD

To create a new document:

WIN ONLY
[Ctrl]+[N]

MAC ONLY
[⌘]+[N]

By default, when you choose File→New from the menu bar, a comprehensive dialog box provides options for creating many new document types. Since our goal in this lesson is to create only new HTML documents, we will use a shortcut in the next exercise to bypass the dialog box.

Saving an HTML Document

When you create a new HTML document you should save it immediately. Do this before inserting objects (such as graphics) or creating links to other pages. (Links, also called hyperlinks, provide navigation through your site.) If you try to insert an object without first saving the document, Dreamweaver promptly warns you to first save the file.

If you see this dialog box, you should:

- Click OK to close the dialog box.
- Save the file.
- Insert the object or create the link.

 WARNING! *If you ignore this prompt, Dreamweaver will not be able to write the correct code to link the object to the page you're saving. This results in links that do not work when the page is published to your remote site. (You will learn how to create links in Lesson 5, Working with Anchors and Links. You will learn how to find and fix broken links in Lesson 6, Working with Site Management.)*

 TIP! *Save your HTML documents **immediately** after creating them and frequently as you revise them.*

Naming HTML Documents

Naming a file for use on a Web server is somewhat different from naming files stored on your computer. When you're ready to upload files from your local site to a Web server, you'll need to identify the Web server's operating system. The most common operating systems are Windows, Macintosh, Unix, and Linux.

The naming convention used on each of these operating systems is different. For example, Unix servers are case-sensitive. This means the following three filenames are unrelated on Unix servers.

- index.htm
- INDEX.HTM
- Index.htm

Use lowercase letters for all filenames to simplify the naming process and to eliminate the guessing game regarding which case to use.

Specifying a Filename Extension

When you save a file, Dreamweaver automatically adds the .htm extension to the filename unless you override this by typing the .html extension in the Save As dialog box. You can use either extension, but they are not interchangeable. Any server will recognize either extension but a file named resources.htm is not the same as a file named resources.html. In most cases, it is best to use the Dreamweaver default .htm filename extension.

 TIP! *Make sure **all** of the pages on your Web site use a consistent filename extension.*

To ensure that your Web pages will work on any Web server where they may be hosted, review the rules in the following table. These rules apply to naming both files and folders.

RULES FOR NAMING WEB PAGES

- Use only alpha characters (A–Z) and numbers (0–9).
- Use only lowercase letters.
- Don't use spaces. Instead, use hyphen or underscore characters (customer_information.htm).
- Don't use special characters (%, *, >, or /), periods, or commas.
- Keep folder names and filenames short and descriptive. The folder name becomes part of the Web address or URL.
- Use the filename extension .htm.

 NOTE! *Uniform Resource Locator (URL) identifies a unique file on the Internet. It is referred to as the Web address. Every Web site has a unique URL. For example, http://www.labpub.com is the URL of Labyrinth Publications.*

Hands-On 2.2   Create, Save, and Modify an HTML Document

In this exercise, you will create a new HTML document and save it to a folder in your file storage location.

1. Press ⌈Ctrl⌉+⌈N⌉ (Win) or ⌈⌘⌉+⌈N⌉ (Mac) to create a new document.
   A new, untitled document opens in the workspace.

2. Choose File→Save from the menu bar.
   The Save As dialog box opens and lists all of the files and folders in the local site.

3. Locate and open the lesson_02 folder.

4. Replace the default filename with **getting_started.htm.**

5. Press the Save button.

6. Choose File→Close from the menu bar.

FROM THE KEYBOARD

To open an existing document :

WIN ONLY
⌈Ctrl⌉+⌈O⌉

MAC ONLY
⌈⌘⌉+⌈O⌉

Opening Existing Documents

In Dreamweaver, you can open an existing HTML document or text document, (any document with a .txt extension) even if it wasn't created in Dreamweaver. When you choose File→Open from the menu bar, the Open dialog box looks in the last folder that you opened within the current local site, your computer, or a network drive location.

 QR

QUICK REFERENCE: CREATING, SAVING, AND OPENING HTML DOCUMENTS	
Task	**Procedure**
Create a new document	Choose File→New from the menu bar.
Save a new document	Choose File→Save from the menu bar.
Save a document with a different name	Choose File→Save As from the menu bar.
Open an existing document	Choose File→Open from the menu bar.
Reopen a recently opened document	Choose File→Open Recent from the menu bar.

TIP! *You can also open a document by double-clicking on the filename in the Files panel.*

 Hands-On 2.3   Open an Existing HTML Document

In this exercise, you will open an HTML document from the lesson_02 folder.

1. Choose File→Open from the menu bar.
   The Open dialog box opens.

2. Navigate to the lesson_02 folder.

3. Double-click to open bubbas.htm in the file list.
   The document opens in the Document window.

4. If any panels are open, press the `F4` key to hide them.
   This hides all panels and allows you to focus on the Document window.

5. Leave the document open.

Exploring the Document Window

The Document window is where you are likely to spend most of your time building Web pages. This window shows the body of the page. This is where you can insert, modify, and delete the wide variety of elements (graphics, words, objects) that make up a Web page. The Document window approximates how your page will appear in a Web browser.

Several important items appear in the Document window, as identified in the following illustration.

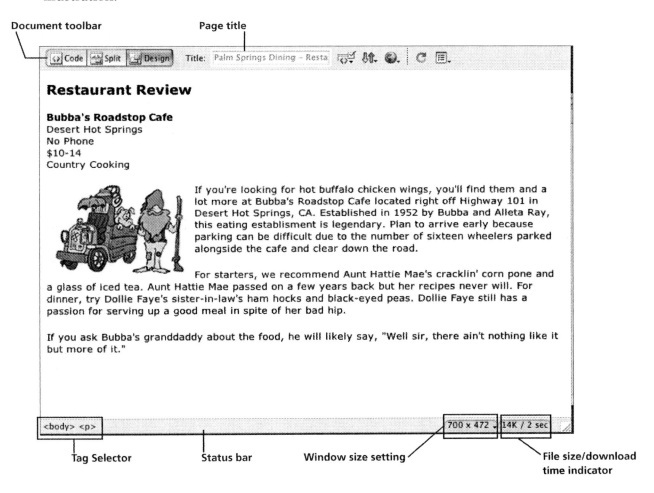

The Window Size Menu

The Window Size menu enables you to preview how your pages will appear at various screen resolutions. The menu contains a list of popular window sizes followed by the corresponding screen resolution in parentheses. You can customize the list by choosing Edit Sizes at the bottom of the list.

 NOTE! *(Win) To access settings in the Window Size menu, you must first click the Restore/Maximize button on the Document window—not the Restore/Maximize button for the entire application. The Document window will reduce to a floating window in the workspace. You can only adjust the window size in this view. If you cannot see the Window Size menu, choose Window→Cascade from the menu bar. This is a sure way to restore the Document window.*

First, click this Window Size setting.

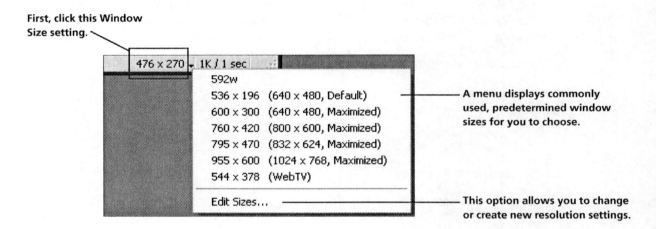

A menu displays commonly used, predetermined window sizes for you to choose.

This option allows you to change or create new resolution settings.

What Is Resolution?

Resolution refers to the sharpness and clarity of an image. The term is most often used to describe monitors, printers, and graphic images. For monitors, the screen resolution signifies the number of pixels (colored dots) on the entire screen. For example, a 640×480 pixel screen is capable of displaying 640 pixels on each of 480 lines, or about 300,000 pixels. As the number of pixels increases, so does the screen resolution. The greater number of pixels, the clearer the image and, sometimes, the slower the download time.

What Is a Pixel?

Short for picture element, a pixel is a collection of three dots that form the colors red, blue, and green. Graphics monitors display pictures by dividing the display screen into thousands (or millions) of pixels, arranged in rows and columns. The pixels are so close together that they appear connected. The following illustration shows a small portion of an image scaled to 800%. At this increased size, you can see the individual pixels that make up the image.

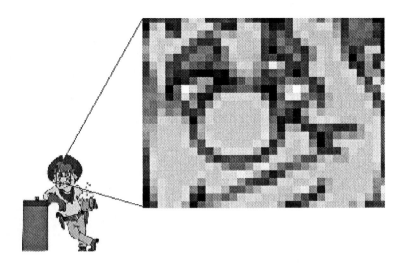

Choosing a Window Size for Testing

Currently, the most commonly used screen resolutions are 800 × 600 pixels and higher. You won't always know the screen resolution your visitors use so you should test your pages at a window size of 760 × 420 (800 × 600, maximized) to make sure that a horizontal scroll bar does not appear when the browser window is maximized. (It is bad practice to force your site visitors to scroll horizontally to see all of the content on a Web page.) You will learn more about this feature in Lesson 8, Working with Page Layout Tables.

Download Time

Download time refers to the number of seconds it takes to completely display a Web page. When the Web was new, people were willing to wait several minutes for a page to download; not anymore. Today, Web usability studies rate the following download times:

- Excellent—2 seconds or less

- Good—3 to 5 seconds

- Average—From 6 to 10 seconds

- Poor—More than 10 seconds

Throughout this course, you will learn ways to optimize your pages to achieve an acceptable download time. The estimated download time shown on the Status bar is based on the default setting of 28.8 kilobytes (K) per second. You can modify the default speed in Dreamweaver's Preferences dialog box to more closely match your target audience. Set the download speed setting to 56 kilobytes per second to view the speed of most users who rely on a dialup modem for their Internet connection.

QUICK REFERENCE: SETTING THE DOWNLOAD TIME PREFERENCE

Task	Procedure
Set the download time preference	■ Follow the step for your version of Dreamweaver: 　(Win) Choose Edit→Preferences from the menu bar. 　(Mac) Choose Dreamweaver→Preferences from the menu bar. ■ Display the Status bar category. ■ Make the desired Connection Speed setting.

 Hands-On 2.4　Choose Window Size and Check Download Time

In this exercise, you will choose a different window size and check the download time.

Before you begin: The bubbas.htm file should be active.

1. If the Document window is maximized (Win), then click the Restore Down document (not program) window sizing button.

The Document window becomes a floating window and the Document toolbar is no longer attached.

2. Click anywhere on the Window Size setting at the lower-right corner of the document window.

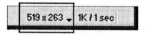

This opens the Window Size pop-up menu.

3. Choose 600 × 300 (640 × 480, Maximized.)
The window resizes to 600 pixels wide by 300 pixels high. Notice the horizontal scroll bar that appears below the document. (A vertical scroll bar is acceptable; a horizontal scroll bar is not.)

4. Display the Window Size menu again, and this time choose 760 × 420 (800 × 600, Maximized).
The window resizes to 760 pixels wide by 420 pixels high and the horizontal scroll bar disappears.

5. Observe the file size and estimated download time on the Status bar.
The file size is 14K and the estimated download time is 4 seconds using a dialup modem speed of 28.8K per second.

6. Press F4 to show the hidden panels.

7. Leave the file open.

Using the Standard Toolbar

The Standard toolbar contains buttons used to perform common tasks. These buttons are available in most Windows and Macintosh applications. If you do not see the toolbar you need, make sure a document is open, choose View→Toolbars, and then make a selection from the list. A checkmark indicates which toolbars are currently visible. You can dismiss a toolbar by simply choosing it again from the View→Toolbars menu.

 TIP! *You can also display a list of toolbars by right-clicking (Win) or* `Ctrl`*+clicking (Mac) anywhere on the Document toolbar.*

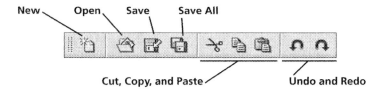

 Hands-On 2.5   Use the Standard Toolbar

In this exercise, you will display the Standard toolbar and use a few of its most common features.

1. If the Standard toolbar is not visible, choose View→Toolbars→Standard from the menu bar. Otherwise, skip to step 2.

2. Click once (don't double-click) on this image to select it.

Sizing handles indicate that the image is selected.

3. Click the Cut ✂ button on the Standard toolbar.
   Dreamweaver cuts the image to the Clipboard.

4. Click the Undo ↶ button on the Standard toolbar.
   Dreamweaver restores the image.

5. Leave the file open.

Using the Insert Bar

FROM THE KEYBOARD

To show/hide the Insert bar:

WIN ONLY
[Ctrl]+[F2]

MAC ONLY
[⌘]+[F2]

The Insert bar contains buttons for inserting various types of objects to dress up your document, such as images, hyperlinks, tables, layers, special characters, and HTML elements. Insertable objects are grouped into eight categories in the menu at the far left of the bar:

■ The Common category includes frequently inserted objects such as images, tables, and email links.

■ The Layout category contains tools to assist you while working with page layout tables, layers, and more.

■ The Forms category helps you create forms that visitors to your site may fill out.

Check out these and other insert options at your leisure.

Here, the Common category is chosen. To change categories, click the arrow next to Common and then make a new selection from the menu.

When you make a selection, it becomes the default action for the button. To change the default action for the current button, make another selection from the menu.

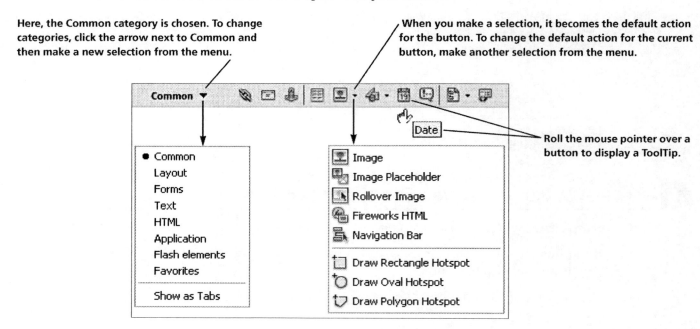

Roll the mouse pointer over a button to display a ToolTip.

 Hands-On 2.6   Use the Insert Bar

In this exercise, you will use the Date button on the Insert Bar to insert the current date into a document.

Before you begin: The bubbas.htm file should still be selected and the Insert bar should show the Common category.

1. Position the insertion point after the text Restaurant Review, and then press [Enter] or [Return].
   The insertion point moves directly below the heading Restaurant Review.

2. Click the Date 🗓 button on the Insert bar.
   The Insert Date dialog box opens.

3. Choose the settings shown in the following illustration:

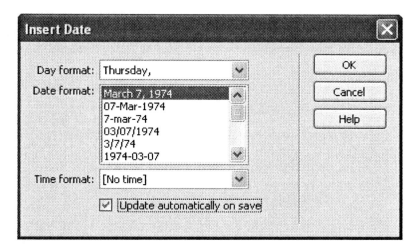

4. Click OK.

The current date appears below the heading at the top of the page.

5. Save the document.

6. Choose File→Close All from the menu bar.

All open documents are closed and the Start page reappears.

⚠**NOTE!** *The simple exercises in this lesson are designed to familiarize you with frequently used tools and how to use them. You will perform much more advanced exercises using these tools as you progress in this course.* ▪

Exploring the Tag Selector

As your documents become more complex, you will use the Tag Selector often to quickly identify the HTML tag of any element on the page. When you select an element, its corresponding HTML tag appears on the Tag Selector.

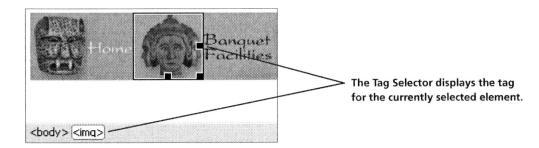

The Tag Selector displays the tag
for the currently selected element.

About HTML Tags

HTML tags instruct Web browsers how to display information on a Web page. Each tag is associated with formatting instructions. Headings, subheadings, paragraphs, lists, images, etc., each have unique predefined tags.

The <h1> tag is used to instruct browsers to display a level one heading.

A Web browser displays level one headings in large, bold text.

The Tag Selector displays the tag for the currently selected element.

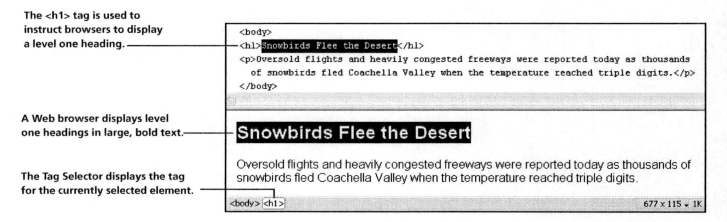

```
<body>
<h1>Snowbirds Flee the Desert</h1>
<p>Oversold flights and heavily congested freeways were reported today as thousands
   of snowbirds fled Coachella Valley when the temperature reached triple digits.</p>
</body>
```

Snowbirds Flee the Desert

Oversold flights and heavily congested freeways were reported today as thousands of snowbirds fled Coachella Valley when the temperature reached triple digits.

<body> <h1>   677 x 115 ▾ 1K

 Hands-On 2.7   Explore the Tag Selector

In this exercise, you will use the Tag Selector to explore the HTML tags of various Web page elements.

1. Open index.htm from the lesson_02 folder.
   The document contains an image, followed by a heading, then a paragraph, and finally a bulleted list.

2. Click to the right of the graphic at the top of the page. Do NOT click on the graphic.
   This ensures that the insertion point is at the top of the page.

3. Observe the Tag Selector.

The Tag Selector shows the <body> tag. All of the visual content in an HTML document follows this tag.

4. Click once to select the image on this page.

The Tag Selector shows the <body> tag, followed by the image <img> tag. The image tag is highlighted to identify it as the currently selected element on the page.

5. Click anywhere inside the word Formal, which is the first item in the bulleted list.

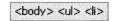

The Tag Selector shows the <ul> and <li> tags. A bulleted list is called an unordered list in HTML. Items in the list are called list items. You will learn how to create lists in Lesson 3, Working with Text.

6. Click the <ul> tag on the Tag Selector.

All of the list item elements are selected on the page. The <ul> tag is highlighted.

7. Leave the file open.

Using the Document Toolbar

The Document toolbar contains a series of menus and buttons you can use to perform routine tasks such as switching the document view, setting the document title, previewing the page in a browser, and setting view options. If you do not see the Document toolbar, choose View→Toolbars→Document from the menu bar.

(Mac) The Document toolbar is part of the Document window, as shown in the following illustration. All of the menus and buttons work identically on Windows computers.

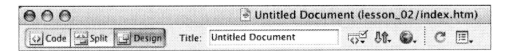

(Win) The Document toolbar, shown in the following illustration, is a standalone toolbar that can be moved to different locations in the Document window.

Use the Code, Split, and Design view buttons to switch views.

Use the Preview in Browser button to see how your page will look in a Web browser.

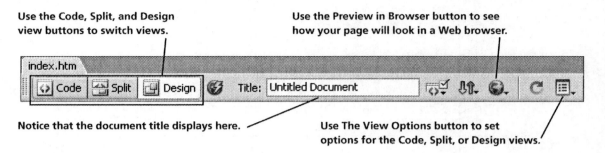

Notice that the document title displays here.

Use The View Options button to set options for the Code, Split, or Design views.

Previewing Your Pages in a Browser

The Document window approximates what you'll see when you preview the page in a Web browser. Not all Web browsers display pages exactly the same. If you're designing a complex site and plan to have a wide variety of visitors, it's a good idea to preview your pages in Internet Explorer, Netscape Navigator, and (Mac) Safari. To make your pages accessible to users with visual impairments, you may want to test your pages using a text-only browser such as Lynx.

The Preview in Browser 🌐 button located on the Document toolbar will display a menu that lists the currently installed browsers on your computer.

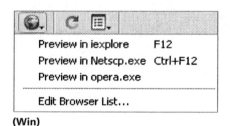

(Win)

(Mac)

FROM THE KEYBOARD

To open a page in the primary browser:

WIN AND MAC
[F12]

To open a page in the secondary browser:

WIN ONLY
[Ctrl]+[F12]

MAC ONLY
[⌘]+[F12]

The browser listing shown in the preceding illustration may not match the browsers in your list. That's OK, as you can easily add and remove browsers from the list by setting Preview in Browser preferences.

Setting the Primary Browser

The primary browser is the browser Dreamweaver displays first in the Preview in Browser menu on the Document toolbar. You can use a function key to quickly open a Web page in either the primary or secondary browser.

QUICK REFERENCE: SETTING PREVIEW IN BROWSER PREFERENCES

Task	Procedure
Add a new browser to the Preview in Browser list	■ Follow the step for your version of Dreamweaver: (Win) Choose Edit→Preferences from the menu bar. (Mac) Choose Dreamweaver→Preferences from the menu bar. ■ Ensure that the Preview in Browser category is chosen. ■ Click the Add Browser ⊞ button. ■ Click the Browse button, navigate to the program folder for the desired browser, choose the program file, and then click Open. ■ If desired, indicate whether this browser is to be the primary or a secondary browser for previews.
Edit settings for a browser	■ Follow the step for your version of Dreamweaver: (Win) Choose Edit→Preferences from the menu bar. (Mac) Choose Dreamweaver→Preferences from the menu bar. ■ Display the Preview in Browser category. ■ Choose the browser you wish to edit in the Browsers window, and then click Edit.
Preview using temporary file	■ Remove the checkmark for this option and Dreamweaver will automatically update the document without creating a temporary copy. ■ Click OK to confirm your preferences and close the box.

Defining a Page Title

Every HTML document should have a descriptive title that identifies the contents of the page. The title text is displayed in a browser's Title bar and appears as the bookmark name (Netscape, Mozilla, Opera, Safari) or in Favorites lists (Internet Explorer). Some search engines display the page title in search results lists. If you don't specifically give your page a title, the default text Untitled Document is used.

The page title appears in the browser's title bar when it displays your Web page. ——————

When there is no page title, this is the result. ——————

Page Title Recommendations

Always use a phrase that describes the document's content. Each page in your site should have a unique title. Here are a few examples of well-defined page titles.

■ Charles Schwab—Financial Goals

■ Macromedia—Dreamweaver Support Forums

■ St. James Restaurant—Entrees and Appetizers

You'll learn much more about optimizing your Web page titles in Lesson 15, Working with HTML.

Hands-On 2.8   Define and Preview a Page Title

In this exercise, you will use the Document toolbar to enter a descriptive page title, and then you will preview the file in your browser.

Before you begin: The index.htm file should still be active.

1. Type **Palm Springs Dining** in the Title text field on the Document toolbar.

2. Press [Enter] or [Return].
   The default title is replaced by the new title.

3. Click the Preview in Browser 🌐 button on the Document toolbar.

4. Select a browser from the list.

5. If you are prompted to save changes, choose Yes.
   The page opens in the browser. Notice that the page title appears in the Title bar of your browser.

6. Close the browser and return to Dreamweaver.

7. Save the file. Leave it open for the next exercise.

Switching the View

FROM THE KEYBOARD

To toggle between Design and Code views:

WIN AND MAC
[Ctrl]+[̄]

The Document toolbar contains buttons you can use to switch from one view to another. Dreamweaver allows you to view a document three ways:

- Code view—Displays a text environment for writing and editing HTML or other code

- Design view—Displays a design environment for visual page layout

- Split view—Displays both Code view and Design view for the same document in a divided window

Hands-On 2.9   Switch Views

In this exercise, you will use the Tag Selector to select an element on a Web page. While the element is selected, you will switch views to see the HTML code.

Before you begin: The index.htm file should be selected.

1. If any panels are open, press F4 to hide them.
   This allows you to focus on the task at hand without distractions.

2. Click the <body> tag on the Tag Selector. (The <body> tag is a container for all of the elements that appear on a Web page.)
   The entire page contents are highlighted. Do NOT click anywhere on the page.

3. Click the ⟨⟩ Code button.
   The entire page contents are highlighted in Code view.

```
<body>
<img src="../images/psd_mountains.gif" width="398" height="140" alt="">
<h1>Welcome to Palm Springs Dining</h1>
<p>We provide  dining resources in the following categories:</p>
<ul>
   <li>Formal</li>
   <li>Casual</li>
   <li>Ethnic</li>
   <li>Take-Out</li>
</ul>
</body>
```

4. Click the ⊟ Split button.
   This splits the view into two panes, which are separated by a movable horizontal border. You can click and drag the horizontal border up or down as needed.

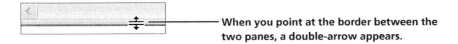
When you point at the border between the two panes, a double-arrow appears.

5. Click on the horizontal border and drag it up or down to create approximately a 50/50 split in each pane.

6. In the design pane, click once on the image of the mountain to select it.
The code for the selected element is highlighted in the code pane.

7. Practice selecting elements in the design pane and observe the code in the code pane.

8. Practice selecting code in the code pane and observe the element in the design pane.
Be sure to select only code that appears below the <body> tag.

9. Click the [Design] button.
This switches you back to Design view.

10. Press [F4] again to display the hidden panels.

11. Leave the file open.

Exploring the Properties Panel

FROM THE KEYBOARD

To show/hide the Properties panel:

WIN ONLY
[Ctrl]+[F3]

MAC ONLY
[⌘]+[F3]

Each element on a Web page has a unique set of properties that you can view and modify with the Properties panel (also called the Property inspector). Each time you select an element on the page, the content of the Properties panel switches to display the property settings for that element. For example, when you select text, the Properties panel changes to display text properties (such as headings, font types, and font sizes). When you select an image, the Properties panel changes to display width, height, border, and other image properties.

If the Properties panel is collapsed, additional properties may not be visible until you expand the panel by clicking on the tiny down triangle at the bottom-right corner of the panel. (If the triangle is up, the panel is expanded.)

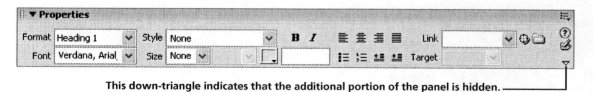

This down-triangle indicates that the additional portion of the panel is hidden.

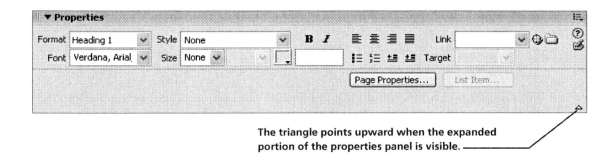

The triangle points upward when the expanded
portion of the properties panel is visible. —

 Hands-On 2.10   **Explore the Properties Panel**

In this exercise, you will use the Properties panel to explore common properties of various HTML elements.

Before you begin: The index.htm file should be active in Design view.

1. Click once on this image to select it.
   Sizing handles appear around the image, and the Properties panel changes to display image properties.

2. Observe these settings on the Properties panel:

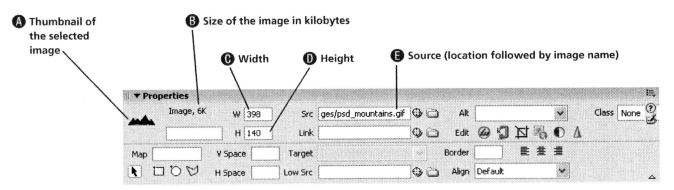

3. Click anywhere inside the heading Welcome to Palm Springs Dining.
   The Properties panel changes to display text properties.

4. Observe these setting on the Properties panel:

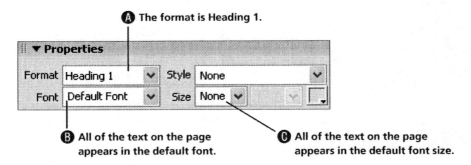

A The format is Heading 1.

B All of the text on the page appears in the default font.

C All of the text on the page appears in the default font size.

5. Leave the file open.

Setting Basic Page Properties

FROM THE KEYBOARD

To open the Page Properties dialog box:

WIN ONLY
Ctrl + J

MAC ONLY
⌘ + J

When you want to change properties that apply to an entire page rather than a single element such as a heading or paragraph, you can use the Appearance category of the Page Properties dialog box. Using this approach, Dreamweaver insert the <style> tag in the head (top) of your document (in Code view) that contains the CSS style rules a browser uses to format your page. (You may recall that CSS is used to style your pages, HTML is used to define the document structure.)

⚠WARNING! *If your Page Properties dialog box doesn't contain the categories and features you see in the following illustration, review the Setting General Preferences section of Lesson 1, Getting Started, before you begin. If you review the settings, make sure there is a checkmark next to Use CSS instead of HTML tags.*

This list shows the page property categories.

Properties of the selected category are displayed here. ──

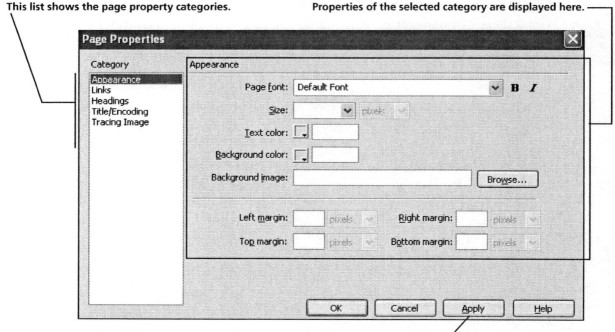

The Apply button provides instant visual feedback on any property settings you modify.

Setting Background Color Properties

The color box is located on the Properties panel and the Page Properties dialog box. The color box opens the color picker, which you can use to set color properties for an entire page background or for a variety of other elements on the page.

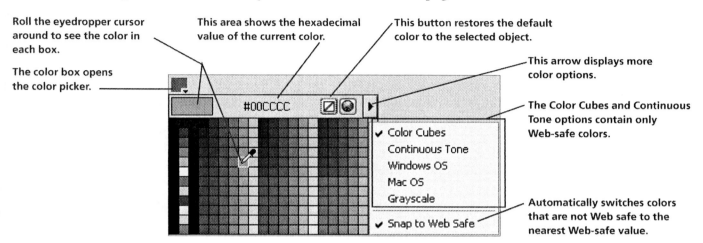

Roll the eyedropper cursor around to see the color in each box.

The color box opens the color picker.

This area shows the hexadecimal value of the current color.

This button restores the default color to the selected object.

This arrow displays more color options.

The Color Cubes and Continuous Tone options contain only Web-safe colors.

Automatically switches colors that are not Web safe to the nearest Web-safe value.

TIP! *You should always specify a background color (even if it's white) to ensure that older browsers won't display your pages with a default dark gray background.*

Web-Safe Colors

Web-safe colors are the 216 colors that display exactly the same on all computers, regardless of the operating system. If you use Web-safe colors, you reduce the risk that your colors will shift when visitors view your pages using an operating system or browser that is different from yours.

TIP! *Creating a color scheme for your site can be a daunting task unless you are a graphic designer, or really have an eye for color. If you find yourself stressing over a color scheme for your Web site, a number of online design studios provide free color schemes and other design advice. Links are provided at, labpubcom/learn/dw04/.*

Using a Background Image

When a Web browser opens a page that contains a background image, the image is repeated horizontally and then vertically, filling the entire background of the page. This repetitive process is called tiling.

In the following illustration this single spiral image is tiled against the page background.

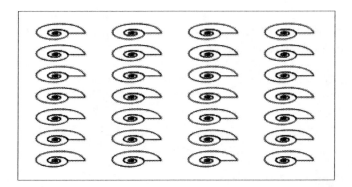

!TIP! *When using a background image, always specify a background color in case the image cannot display.*

Setting Page Margins

The Page Properties dialog box can also be used to specify left, right, top, and bottom margin properties to control how close to the edge of the browser window the design appears. You can also set each of these to zero if you do not want a margin; otherwise, try different combinations until you find the spacing you want.

Changing the Page Font

The default font for Web pages is either Times or Times New Roman. While these fonts work well for print media, they are not the ideal choices for HTML documents. You can choose from a group of related fonts such as Verdana, Arial, and Helvetica or you can edit the font list to include your favorite fonts. However, be aware that site visitors must have the fonts you specify installed on their computer or the page will appear in the default font.

!NOTE! *You will learn much more about page properties, including font choices and sizes, in Lesson 3, Working with Text.*

QR▶ **QUICK REFERENCE: SETTING THE APPEARANCE PROPERTIES OPTIONS**

Task	Procedure
Make appearance settings for the current page	■ Display the page for which you wish to set appearance properties. ■ Click the Page Properties... button on the Properties panel or choose Modify→Page Properties from the menu bar. ■ Choose the Appearance category. ■ Make the desired appearance settings.

Hands-On 2.11   Set Page Properties

In this exercise, you will use the Appearance category of the Page Properties dialog box to set the page font, background color, background image, and left margin. You will leave the font size at its default setting.

Before you begin: The index.htm file should be selected.

1. Choose Modify→Page Properties from the menu bar.
   The Page Properties dialog box opens.

2. Follow these steps to change the page font, add a background color, a background image, and a left margin to the page:
   Be sure to take advantage of the Apply button's instant visual feedback each time you modify a property setting.

A Verify that the Appearance category is chosen.

B Choose Verdana, Arial, Helvetica, sans-serif from the Page Font pop-up menu.

C Click the Background Color box and choose a color from the palette or type **#FFFFCC** in the text field.

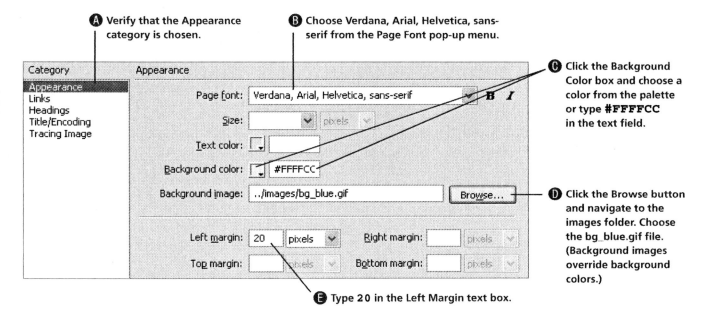

D Click the Browse button and navigate to the images folder. Choose the bg_blue.gif file. (Background images override background colors.)

E Type 20 in the Left Margin text box.

3. Click OK.

The image tiles to fill the page background and the left margin is offset by 20 pixels.

4. Save and close the file.

 **Concepts Review**

True/False Questions

1. When you create a new HTML document you should save it immediately before inserting objects or creating links to other pages.   TRUE   FALSE

2. The naming conventions for HTML documents are identical to those used on Windows, Macintosh, Unix, and Linux.   TRUE   FALSE

3. The .htm and .html filename extensions are interchangeable so you can use both on your site to refer to the same document.   TRUE   FALSE

4. Web-safe colors display exactly the same on all computers, regardless of the operating system.   TRUE   FALSE

5. The Tag Selector is a useful tool for quickly identifying the currently selected element on a Web page.   TRUE   FALSE

6. HTML tags instruct Web browsers how to display information on Web pages.   TRUE   FALSE

7. The filenames index.htm, Index.htm, and INDEX.HTM can be used interchangeably on UNIX servers.   TRUE   FALSE

8. The Document window displays your pages exactly as they will appear in a Web browser.   TRUE   FALSE

9. Every HTML document should have a descriptive title that identifies the contents of the page.   TRUE   FALSE

10. Each time you select an element on a Web page, the contents of the Properties panel switches to display property settings for that element.   TRUE   FALSE

Multiple Choice Questions

1. The most fundamental type of Web page uses _____.
   a. PHP
   b. JavaScript
   c. HTML
   d. XML

2. Which window size setting should you use to test your pages for the average Internet user?
   a. 760 × 420 (800 × 600, maximized)
   b. 600 × 300 (640 × 480, maximized)
   c. 544 × 378 (WebTV)
   d. 955 × 600 (1024 × 768, maximized)

3. The Standard toolbar can be used to perform which of the following tasks?
   a. Creating a new document
   b. Saving the current or all open documents
   c. Cutting, copying, and pasting
   d. All of the above

4. How many colors appear in the Web-safe color palette?
   a. 256
   b. 1,248
   c. 216
   d. 1,650,000

# Skill Builders

Skill Builder 2.1   Work with HTML Documents

In this exercise, you will create, modify, and save a new HTML document.

Create a New HTML Document

1. Press (Win) Ctrl+N or (Mac) ⌘+N.

2. Choose File→Save from the menu bar.

3. Save the file as **street_fair.htm** in the review_02 folder.

4. Select the default text in the Title text field on the Document toolbar and type **Palm Springs Dining – Street Fair.**

Open an Existing Document

5. Open street_fair.txt from the review_02 folder.

6. Tap F4 to hide the panels.
   This provides a much larger work area.

7. Choose Window→Tile Vertically (Win) or physically arrange the two documents side-by-side.
   This enables you to work more easily with two documents.

Copy and Paste Text

8. Click anywhere in street_fair.txt and choose Edit→Select All.

9. Use the Copy button on the Standard toolbar or choose Edit→Copy from the menu bar.
   This copies the contents to the Clipboard.

10. Click inside street_fair.htm and choose Edit→Paste.

11. Close the text file.

12. Tap F4 to show the panels.

13. Save and close the file.

Skill Builder 2.2   Set Page Properties and Window Size

In this exercise, you will set the page font, background image, and margin properties. You will also set the window size to WebTV and observe what happens when the horizontal content on a page is too wide for the chosen window size.

1. Open st_james.htm from the review_02 folder.

2. Set the properties shown in the following illustration or use your creative expression to spruce up the page:

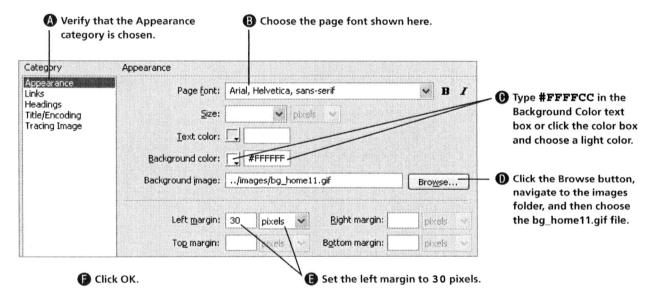

A Verify that the Appearance category is chosen.

B Choose the page font shown here.

C Type **#FFFFCC** in the Background Color text box or click the color box and choose a light color.

D Click the Browse button, navigate to the images folder, and then choose the bg_home11.gif file.

E Set the left margin to 30 pixels.

F Click OK.

3. Save the file.

Set the Window Size

4. Click the Window Size pop-up menu and choose 544 × 378 (WebTV).
   The last two images are bumped to the next row at this window size.

5. Set the window size to 600 × 300 (640 × 480, Maximized).
This setting is better, but still not wide enough.

6. Set the window size to 760 × 420 (800 × 600, Maximized).
At this setting, the window size is wide enough to accommodate the images without wrapping.

7. Save and close the file.

Assessments

Assessment 2.1   Modify an HTML Document

In this exercise, you will copy text from a text-only file and paste it into an HTML document. Then, you will modify the HTML document page properties to produce the final page shown at the end of the exercise.

1. Open grandmas.htm and grandmas.txt from the review_02 folder.

```
Even as the neighborhood gentrifies around it, Grandma's House maintains
its down-home atmosphere and excellent food. The chicken is crispy and juicy
and always hot. Corn bread, sweet potatoes, and collard greens are scrumptious.
Be sure to stop by and chat with owner/chef, Grandma Quebedeaux, the undisputed
Creole queen  of the Desert. She's usually perched close to the entrance
to meet and greet hungry patrons.

Order from the menu or graze the buffet, where you can choose from a large
variety of mouth-watering dishes including: beans, seafood gumbo, jambalaya,
macaroni and cheese, ribs, baked and fried chicken, fish, fried okra, mashed
and sweet potatoes, gravy, salad bar, and a variety of desserts. Grandma's
House is not the place to begin your low carb diet.
```

grandmas.txt

PALM SPRINGS DINING

» Grandma's House

grandmas.htm

2. Copy and paste all of the text in grandmas.txt to grandmas.htm, directly below the second heading Grandma's House.

3. Save the HTML file and close the text file.

4. Compose a descriptive title for the page.

5. Set the window size to 760 × 420 (800 × 600, Maximized).

6. Change the page font.

7. Add a background image (the following illustration uses bg_stripe.gif).
   All images are located in the images folder. All background image filenames are preceded by bg_ for easy identification.

8. Adjust the left margin to move the text away from the background image. *Your file should resemble the following illustration:*

PALM SPRINGS DINING

» Grandma's House

Even as the neighborhood gentrifies around it, **Grandma's House** maintains its down-home atmosphere and excellent food. The chicken is crispy and juicy and always hot. Corn bread, sweet potatoes, and collard greens are scrumptious.

Be sure to stop by and chat with owner/chef, Grandma Quebedeaux, the undisputed Creole queen of the Desert. She's usually perched close to the entrance to meet and greet hungry patrons.

Order from the menu or graze the buffet, where you can choose from a large variety of mouth-watering dishes including: beans, seafood gumbo, jambalaya, macaroni and cheese, ribs, baked and fried chicken, fish, fried okra, mashed and sweet potatoes, gravy, salad bar, and a variety of desserts. Grandma's House is not the place to begin your low carb diet!

9. Save and close the file.

Assessment 2.2   Work with the Tag Selector, Properties, and Views

In this exercise, you will use the Tag Selector to identify HTML tags of selected Web page elements, the Properties panel to identify text and graphic properties, and Split view to observe the HTML code of selected Web page elements.

Use the Tag Selector

1. Open sports_bars.htm from the review_02 folder.

2. Use pen and paper to write down the HTML tags that appear on the Tag Selector as you select each of the following Web page elements:

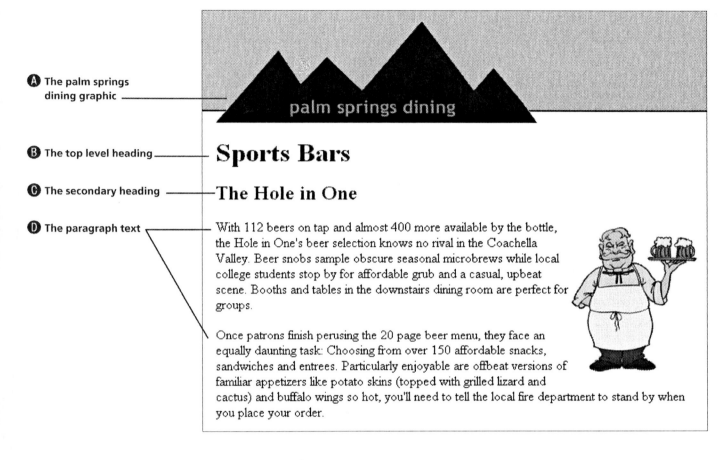

A The palm springs dining graphic

B The top level heading

C The secondary heading

D The paragraph text

Use the Properties Panel

3. Write down the width and height of the image of the man carrying the two frothy mugs.

4. Write down the format used in the heading text Sports Bars.

Use Split View

5. Switch to Split View (Code and Design views).

6. In Design view, click on the Palm Springs Dining image at the top of the page.

7. In Code view, observe the HTML code for the selected image.

8. In Code view, select the text beer snobs in the first paragraph, second sentence.

9. Observe the text selection in Design view.

10. Switch to Design view, and then close the file.

Critical Thinking

Critical Thinking 2.1   On Your Own

The St. James Restaurant is going online! The purpose of the site is to showcase the restaurant and reduce the number of calls from people requesting menu and wine choices, banquet facilities, and location. The Web design dream team has asked you to use a text editor (Notepad, Simple Text, etc.), or pen and paper, to establish a naming convention and title for these pages:

!TIP! *You might want to review the Naming HTML Documents section before you begin.*

Titles

- homepage (The Web hosting service uses index.htm for the homepage name.)
- wine list
- menu
- banquet facilities
- contact us

Once you have established a name and title for each page, write down your choice for the following page design criteria.

Page Properties

- Background color
- Background image (all background image names are preceded by bg_ and are located in the images folder)
- Top margin (30 pixels recommended for this exercise)
- Font

Document Window (Consider the target audience for these settings)

- Choose a document window size
- Choose an Internet connection speed

Critical Thinking 2.2   **With a Group**

The choice of background color or background images varies from person to person. This is what makes the Web such a wonderful avenue for self expression. Your group assignment is to design the St. James homepage based on the criteria set in the previous exercise. The filename that contains the text for the homepage is index.htm, which is located in the review_02 folder. Feel free to experiment with various background colors, background images, and margin settings.

Preview your page designs in a Web browser and make notes that compare and contrast the readability of different colors and background images. Reach a consensus regarding which page design works best, and why. The following illustration is an example of what the page might look like:

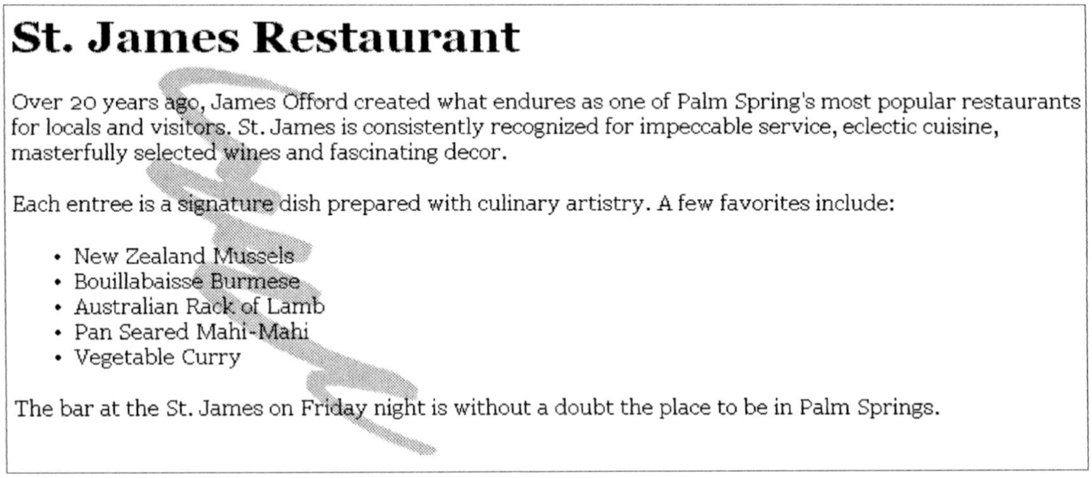

St. James Restaurant

Over 20 years ago, James Offord created what endures as one of Palm Spring's most popular restaurants for locals and visitors. St. James is consistently recognized for impeccable service, eclectic cuisine, masterfully selected wines and fascinating decor.

Each entree is a signature dish prepared with culinary artistry. A few favorites include:

- New Zealand Mussels
- Bouillabaisse Burmese
- Australian Rack of Lamb
- Pan Seared Mahi-Mahi
- Vegetable Curry

The bar at the St. James on Friday night is without a doubt the place to be in Palm Springs.

LESSON 3

Working with Text

In this lesson, you will learn how to organize and format your Web pages. Web pages containing large blocks of text are more difficult to read than their printed counterparts. This is because computer screen resolution is much lower than the resolution of a printed page. For this reason, you should organize information on your Web pages into well-structured logical units so your readers can scan the page without having to read large blocks of text. Multiple headings, paragraphs, and lists are used for this purpose. Once the content is organized, you apply formatting to make the pages pretty.

Case Study

Janet has come a long way since she and Justin fired up Dreamweaver for the first time. She's now ready to tackle the job of gathering and organizing content for the Editor's Choice page, which she plans to update weekly. Organizing information into logical units that readers can easily scan is a crucial step in structuring the page content. Janet uses headings, short and descriptive paragraphs, line breaks, lists, and a horizontal rule to separate sections of the page for easy scanning. She also chooses a consistent page font and color scheme to format the page.

PALM SPRINGS DINING

»Editor's Choice

Simba's House of Ribs
190 N. Sunrise
Palm Springs, CA

Simba's House of Ribs is famous for its down-home atmosphere and quality comfort food. The fried chicken is crispy, juicy, and always hot. Corn bread, sweet potatoes, and collard greens are scrumptious.

Order from the menu or graze the buffet, where you can choose from a large variety of mouth-watering *Cajun and Southern favorites*, and a wide variety of homemade desserts. **Simba's is not the place to begin your low carb diet!**

Simba's Collard Greens Recipe

Ingredients

- 1 Pound fresh collard greens
- 4 Smoked ham hocks
- Crushed red pepper
- Hot pepper sauce
- Salt and pepper

Directions

1. Cut and thoroughly wash greens.
2. Place in large pot with ham hocks, crushed red pepper and enough water to cover.
3. Simmer slowly for about two hours (until greens are tender).
4. Add salt, pepper, and hot pepper sauce, to taste.
5. Serve with sliced Vidalia onion for garnish.

© 2005 Palm Springs Dining

Formatting Headings and Paragraphs

Headings are the best means of letting a reader know what your Web page has to offer. Depending upon the complexity of your content, various levels of headings may be needed to organize and subdivide it. The primary heading, called Heading 1, is used to describe the page contents at a high level. A subheading or a supporting paragraph typically follows.

 TIP! *Since the first heading on a page describes the page content, it's a good idea to include the heading text in the page title.*

Formatting Headings

HTML provides six levels of headings. When you format text as Heading 1, the HTML tags <h1> and</h1> are added in Code view. These tags instruct a Web browser to display the text in a level one heading.

```
<h1>Palm Springs Dining</h1>
```

Because some search engines prioritize information based on the page heading and the content that follows, the creation of clear and precise headings is particularly important. Without headings, all text on the page has the same priority, which renders it less useful to speech-based browsers and some search engines.

The Properties panel displays the format of text that is selected on the page. You can change the format by choosing among options in the pop-up menu.

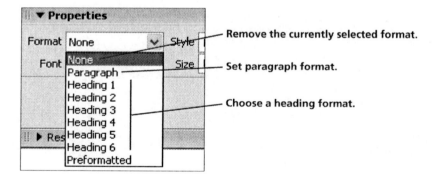

Inserting a New Paragraph

Any new line of text you add to a Web page is formatted as a paragraph until you indicate otherwise by choosing another format, such as a heading, or an item in a list. Each time you insert a new paragraph, the HTML paragraph tags <p></p> are added in Code view.

```
<p>Simba's House of Ribs is a Palm Springs landmark for down-home cooking. The
chicken is crispy and juicy and always hot.</p>
```

Pressing ⌨Enter (Win) or ⌨Return (Mac) creates a new paragraph.

Inserting a Line Break

A line break starts a new line without a blank line between it and the previous line of text. This forces the text to wrap to the next line. It is the word processing equivalent of a "soft return." To insert a line break, position the insertion point where you want the line break to occur, and then choose Insert→HTML→Special Characters→Line Break from the menu bar.

Line breaks are useful, for example, in addresses.

> Simba's House of Ribs
> 190 North Sunrise
> Palm Springs, CA

Without a line break, (using `Enter` or `Return` at the end of each line), the previous address example would look like:

> Simba's House of Ribs
>
> 190 North Sunrise
>
> Palm Springs, CA

When you insert a line break, the HTML break tag <br> tag is added in Code view.

```
<p>Simba's House of Ribs<br>
190 North Sunrise<br>
Palm Springs, CA</p>
```

 ## Hands-On 3.1   Apply Headings and Insert Paragraphs

In this exercise, you will start at the top of a long page and work your way down to apply headings and insert paragraphs and line breaks.

1. Open index.htm from the lesson_03 folder.
   The unformatted page is difficult to read. Let's format it.

Format Headings

2. Click anywhere in the text Palm Springs Dining.

3. Use the Format pop-up menu on the Properties panel to apply Heading 1 to this text.

4. Click anywhere in the text Editor's Choice.

5. Use the Format pop-up menu on the Properties panel to apply Heading 2 to this text.

6. Repeat this process to apply a Heading 3 to the text Simba's Collard Greens Recipe, and Directions.

Insert a Line Break

7. Position the insertion point to the left of the text 190, and then choose Insert→HTML→Special Characters→Line Break from the menu bar.
This moves the text to the next line without creating a paragraph.

8. Position the insertion point to the left of the text Palm Springs, CA, and then press (Win) [Shift]+[Enter] or (Mac) [Shift]+[Return].
This line break keyboard shortcut moves the text directly below the street address.

Insert a Paragraph

9. In the long paragraph, beginning with the words, "Simba's House of Ribs is famous..." position the insertion point to the left of the O in Order, and then press [Enter] or [Return].
This creates a new paragraph.

10. Save the file but keep it open.

Formatting Lists

We often make lists to organize our day: to-do lists, shopping lists, things we can put off lists, etc. On Web pages, lists are ideal for presenting groups of related items that can be easily scanned. HTML offers formatting options for both lists with bullets (unordered lists) and lists with numbers (ordered lists).

 TIP! *Regardless of the type of list you are creating, each item in the list must be contained in its own paragraph (pressing [Enter] or [Return] after each item) for the list to be formatted correctly.*

Unordered Lists

Unordered lists are ideal for listing items than can appear in any sequence. A bullet precedes each item in the list.

> • Blackberry Pie
> • Raspberry Mousse
> • Chocolate Decadence

The HTML code begins with the unordered list tag <ul>, followed by a series of list item tags <li>, which format each item in the list with a bullet.

```
<ul>
  <li>Blackberry Pie</li>
  <li>Raspberry Mousse</li>
  <li>Chocolate Decadence</li>
</ul>
```

Ordered Lists

Ordered lists are ideal for listing items that appear in a numbered sequence. A number precedes each item in the list.

> 1. Scoop out a huge spoonful of ice cream.
> 2. Place the spoon in your mouth.
> 3. Call your cardiologist.

The HTML code for an ordered list begins with the ordered list tag <ol> and is followed by a series of list item tags <li>, which format each item in the list with a number.

```
<ol>
   <li>Scoop out a huge spoonful of ice cream.</li>
   <li>Place the spoon in your mouth.</li>
   <li>Call your cardiologist.</li>
</ol>
```

The Properties panel provides options to create ordered and unordered lists as well as nested lists (a list within a list). The position of an item in a list can be altered by demoting (move to sublevel) or promoting (move to primary level) the item in a nested list.

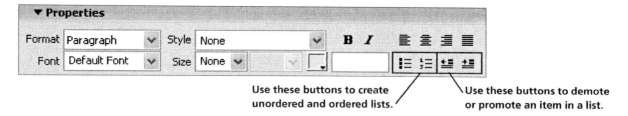

Use these buttons to create unordered and ordered lists.

Use these buttons to demote or promote an item in a list.

To create a nested list, select the list items you want to nest and choose Text→Indent from the menu bar, or use the Text Indent button in the Properties panel.

> 1. Fish
>   ◦ Catfish
>   ◦ Trout
>   ◦ Pompano
> 2. Shellfish
>   ◦ Crawfish
>   ◦ Shrimp
>   ◦ Oysters

QUICK REFERENCE: FORMATTING UNORDERED AND ORDERED LISTS

Task	Procedure
Format an Unordered List	■ Select the series of paragraphs you want to use in the list. ■ Click the Unordered List button on the Properties panel or choose Text→List→Unordered List from the menu bar.
Format an Ordered List	■ Select the series of paragraphs you want to use in the list. ■ Click the Ordered List button on the Properties panel or choose Text→List→Ordered List from the menu bar.
Return an ordered/ unordered list to regular paragraphs	■ Drag the insertion point over all of the items in the list to select them, and then choose Text→List→None from the menu bar.
Promote a list item	■ Click inside the list item, and then click the Text Indent button on the Properties panel.
Demote a list item	■ Click inside the list item, and then click the Text Outdent button on the Properties panel.

Hands-On 3.2   Format Unordered and Ordered Lists

In this exercise, you will format an unordered and ordered list.

Before you begin: The index.htm file should still be open.

1. Select the five lines between the text Ingredients and Directions.

2. Click the Unordered List 🔲 button on the Properties panel.
   This creates a bulleted list.

3. Select the remaining five lines under the text Directions.

4. Click the Ordered List 🔲 button on the Properties panel.
   This creates a numbered list.

5. Position the insertion point at the end of the last list item, garnish, and press Enter or Return.
   Notice that this extends the list.

6. Press Enter or Return again.
   This creates a new paragraph below the list.

7. Save the file but keep it open.

Aligning Text

The default text alignment for HTML documents is left. You can choose other alignment options (right, center, justify) from the Properties panel.

WARNING! *While it's tempting to use different alignment options, it is best to align text using CSS. You will learn how to do this in Lesson 9, Working with Styles.*

Applying Character Formatting

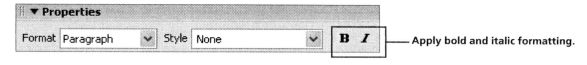

FROM THE KEYBOARD

To apply bold or italic:

WIN ONLY
Ctrl + B
Ctrl + I

MAC ONLY
⌘ + B
⌘ + I

When you need to add emphasis to text on a Web page, you can use the Properties panel to quickly apply bold or italic formatting.

You may recall from Lesson 1, Getting Started that you set general preferences to use <strong> and <em> (instead of <b> and <i>). That's because the <strong> tag replaced the obsolete <b> tag, and the <em> tag replaced the obsolete <i> tag.

The following example shows the code for each tag:

```
<strong>This text is bold.</strong>
<em>This text is italicized.</em>
```

 Hands-On 3.3   Apply Character Formatting

In this exercise, you will apply bold and italic formatting to text on a Web page.

1. Select the text "Cajun and Southern favorites," which is located in the second paragraph.

2. Click the Italic $\boldsymbol{I}$ button on the Properties panel.

3. With the text still selected, observe the Tag Selector.
   The HTML emphasis tag <em> is highlighted to identify the current selection on the page.

4. Select the text "Simba's is not the place to begin your low carb diet," which is located in the last sentence of the second paragraph.

5. Click the Bold **B** button on the Properties panel.

6. With the text still selected, observe the Tag Selector.
   The HTML strongly emphasized tag <strong> is highlighted to identify the current selection on the page.

7. Save the file but keep it open.

Inserting HTML Elements

Dreamweaver provides a special command for inserting HTML elements, such as horizontal rules and special characters, to help distinguish the copy on your page. Both of these elements are available from the Insert menu and the Insert bar.

Inserting a Horizontal Rule

A horizontal rule is a thin line that extends across the width of the page, dividing the text of your document into sections. When you insert a horizontal rule, the default width is 100% and the height is 2 pixels. These properties can be modified with the Properties panel.

The HTML horizontal rule tag <hr> is added in Code view when you insert a horizontal rule.

Inserting Special Characters

Often documents require characters that aren't available from the keyboard, such as the copyright © symbol. Special characters are represented in HTML by a name or a number, referred to as a character entity. Dreamweaver uses the entity name. Entities are not HTML tags.

- To display the © symbol, use the © character entity.

- To display a » symbol, use the » character entity.

If the special character you need doesn't appear in the Special Characters list (such as »), you can choose Insert→HTML→Special Characters→Other to open the Insert Other Character dialog box.

When you click on a character...

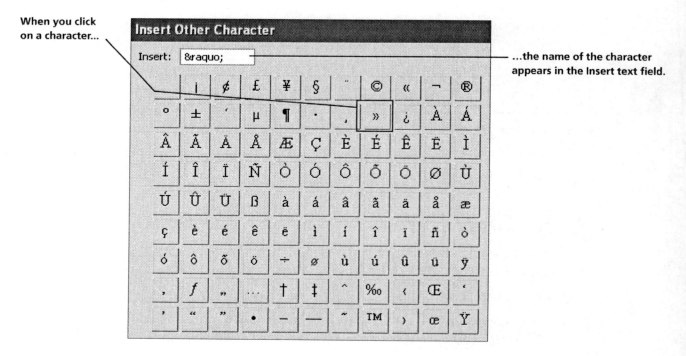

...the name of the character appears in the Insert text field.

QUICK REFERENCE: INSERTING HTML ELEMENTS

Task	Procedure
Insert a line break	■ Choose Insert→HTML→Special Characters→Line Break or position the insertion point to the left of the text, then press `Shift` + `Return` or `Shift` + `Enter`.
Insert a horizontal rule	■ Choose Insert→HTML→Horizontal Rule.
Insert a copyright symbol	■ Choose Insert→HTML→Special Characters→Copyright.
Insert other special characters	■ Choose Insert→HTML→Special Characters→Other.
	■ Make a selection from the Insert Other Character dialog box.

Hands-On 3.4   Insert HTML Elements

In this exercise, you will insert a horizontal rule and two special characters.

1. Position the insertion point directly below the ordered list.

Insert a Horizontal Rule

2. Choose Insert→HTML→Horizontal Rule.
   A horizontal rule is inserted at the bottom of the page.

3. With the horizontal rule still selected, observe the Tag Selector.
   The HTML tag <hr> is highlighted to indicate the currently selected element on the page.

4. Click anywhere below the horizontal rule.
   This is where you'll insert a copyright © symbol.

Insert Special Characters

5. Choose Insert→HTML→Special Characters→Copyright.
   This inserts the copyright symbol.

6. Add a space after the copyright symbol, and then type **2005 Palm Springs Dining.**

7. Scroll to the top of the page and position the insertion point directly to the left of the heading Editor's Choice.

8. Choose Insert→HTML→Special Characters→Other.

9. From the Insert Other Character dialog box, choose » (») and click OK.
   You should see ». This is a popular, but optional, Web page symbol you can use to draw attention to a topic or identify the current page.

10. Save the file but keep it open.

TIP! *To insert a horizontal rule from the Insert Bar, choose the HTML category; to insert a special character, choose the Text category.*

Setting Page Properties

In Lesson 2, Working with HTML Documents, you got a sneak preview of how to set basic CSS appearance properties. You learned how to change the font, apply background color, insert a background image, and set the page margins. Now it's time to delve a little deeper into CSS to learn more about font properties, such as how to choose a font grouping, and the difference between using relative and absolute values for font sizes.

The two most basic ways to set CSS font properties are:

- Page Properties dialog box—Sets global properties to *all* text on the page

- Properties panel—Sets local properties to *selected text* on a page

The following illustration shows why you might want to use one method over the other.

The font properties were set globally using the Page Properties dialog box. All of the formatting is consistent and the text is easy to read.

The font properties were set locally, using the Properties panel. The fonts are inconsistent and the text is difficult to read.

 TIP! *Local properties override global properties, and they're much more difficult to manage if overused.*

Choosing a Font Grouping

The Font menu on both the Page Properties dialog box and the Properties panel contains a grouping of similar fonts.

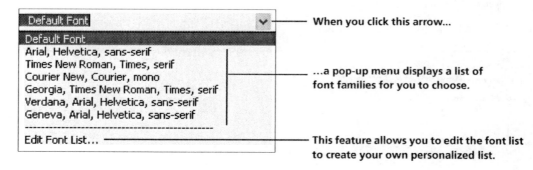

When you click this arrow...

...a pop-up menu displays a list of font families for you to choose.

This feature allows you to edit the font list to create your own personalized list.

A browser displays text using the font it finds first on users' computers. If none of the specified fonts are available, the Web browser uses the default font based on the font classification, which is the last item in each font family (sans-serif, serif, or mono).

Serifs are the fine lines (or "little feet") used to finish off a stroke in a letter. They help guide readers through text on printed pages.

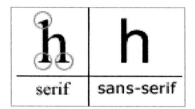

 TIP! *Sans-serif fonts such as Verdana, Arial, Helvetica, and Geneva are the best choices for text displayed on computer screens. Serif fonts are a better choice for print media.*

Choosing a Font Size

The Size pop-up menu on both the Properties panel and the Page Properties dialog box provides a variety of preset font sizes.

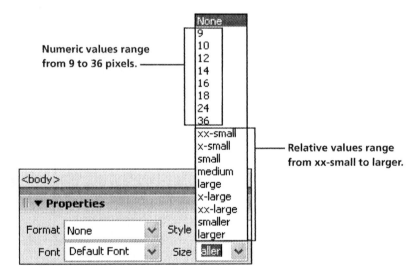

Numeric Compared to Relative Font Sizes

Choosing a numeric (absolute) value gives you more control as a designer, but it gives less flexibility to the user because the text size cannot be scaled (increased or decreased in size) in a Web browser. Choosing relative size settings reverses this control because the user can scale the size of text on the page.

This illustration shows the same text displayed at small, medium (the default), and largest using View→Text Size commands from the (Win) Internet Explorer menu bar.

Small	Medium	Largest
The text in this row uses a relative font size. The text is scalable in a browser. →	Simba's House of Ribs 190 N. Sunrise Palm Springs, CA	Simba's House of Ribs 190 N. Sunrise Palm Springs, CA	**Simba's House of Ribs 190 N. Sunrise Palm Springs, CA**
The text in this row uses a numeric font size. The text is not scalable in a browser. →	Simba's House of Ribs 190 N. Sunrise Palm Springs, CA	Simba's House of Ribs 190 N. Sunrise Palm Springs, CA	Simba's House of Ribs 190 N. Sunrise Palm Springs, CA

 TIP! *It's up to you to apply size settings in a manner that balances your need to control the design with the user's need to control readability.*

Choosing a Font Color

When choosing a font color, use as much contrast as possible between the foreground (text color) and background color of the page. Background and foreground color can dramatically enhance or detract from the usability of a Web page.

Nice contrast—It is easy to read on black and white computer screens used by some people with visual impairments. →

> When using color, ensure that the foreground (text color) and background color combinations provide sufficient contrast for users who are colorblind or who have black and white computer screens.

Nice contrast—It is easy to read on all computer screens. →

> When using color, ensure that the foreground (text color) and background color combinations provide sufficient contrast for users who are colorblind or who have black and white computer screens.

Poor contrast—It is difficult to read because the colors are too similar and do not provide enough contrast. →

> When using color, ensure that the foreground (text color) and background color combinations provide sufficient contrast for users who are colorblind or who have black and while computer screens.

 TIP! *If you aren't a graphic artist, you can spend all day trying to come up with a color scheme that works. When in doubt, use a white background with black text.*

 QUICK REFERENCE: SETTING APPEARANCE PAGE PROPERTIES

Task	Procedure
Make appearance settings for the current page	■ Display the page for which you wish to set CSS appearance properties. ■ Choose Modify→Page Properties from the menu bar. ■ Choose the Appearance category. ■ Make the desired appearance settings.

Choosing Heading Properties

FROM THE KEYBOARD

To display the Page Properties dialog box:

WIN ONLY
Ctrl + J

MAC ONLY
⌘ + J

Dreamweaver has six different sizes, or levels, of headings. The properties for each level are set by default, but you can customize them. Depending on your page design and personal tastes, you may wish to use a different font type, size, and color for the headings on the page. To do this, access the Headings category of the Page Properties dialog box.

The Headings category is chosen.

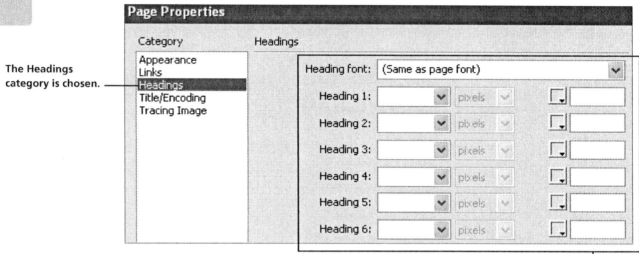

Headings properties are displayed here.

 QR **QUICK REFERENCE: SETTING HEADINGS PAGE PROPERTIES**

Task

Make headings settings for the current page

Procedure

- Display the page for which you wish to set CSS appearance properties.
- Choose Modify→Page Properties from the menu bar.
- Choose the Headings category.
- Make the desired headings settings.

Hands-On 3.5   Set Page Properties

In this exercise, you will set CSS appearance and headings properties.

Before you begin: The index.htm file should still be open.

1. Choose Modify→Page Properties from the menu bar.

Set CSS Appearance Properties

2. Follow these steps to set CSS Appearance properties:

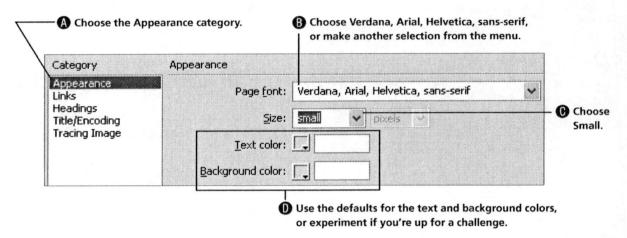

Ⓐ Choose the Appearance category.

Ⓑ Choose Verdana, Arial, Helvetica, sans-serif, or make another selection from the menu.

Ⓒ Choose Small.

Ⓓ Use the defaults for the text and background colors, or experiment if you're up for a challenge.

3. Click Apply. Do NOT click OK.
Review the new page format. Continue to choose different settings until you have achieved the look you want. Do NOT click OK.

Set CSS Headings Properties

4. Choose the Headings category.
The page contains a Heading 1, a Heading 2, and a Heading 3.

5. Follow these steps to set CSS headings property options:

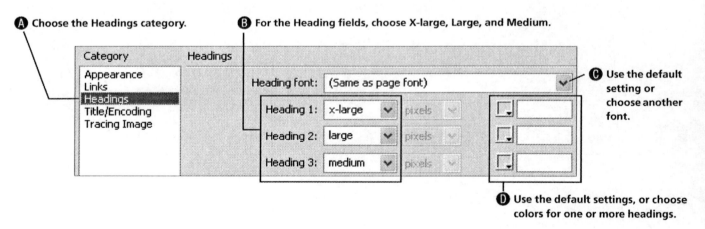

Ⓐ Choose the Headings category.

Ⓑ For the Heading fields, choose X-large, Large, and Medium.

Ⓒ Use the default setting or choose another font.

Ⓓ Use the default settings, or choose colors for one or more headings.

6. Click Apply.
Review the formatting changes to the document and make changes as necessary to provide contrast between the text and background color.

7. Click OK.

8. Save the file but keep it open.

Test the Font Size for Scalability

9. Tap `F12` to open the file in your default browser.

10. (Win) Internet Explorer users choose View→Text Size→Larger (Mac) Internet Explorer users choose View→Text Zoom→150%.
    Observe that your use of relative font sizes makes all of the text on the page scalable for people with visual challenges. Explore different text sizes if you wish.

11. Set the text size back to medium or 100%.

12. Close your browser, and then return to the Document window.

13. Leave the file open.

Observing Internal CSS Styles

In the last exercise, you used the Page Properties dialog box to set CSS appearance and headings properties for all of the text on a page. When you did this, Dreamweaver inserted a series of CSS styles in the head of your document in Code view. The styles redefined the body and heading tags based on the properties you set. The internal styles apply only to the current document.

In Lesson 5, Working with Anchors and Links, you'll learn how to export internal styles to create an external CSS style sheet to which you can link multiple pages in your site. In Lesson 9, Working with Styles, you'll learn how to create and manage custom styles using the CSS Styles panel.

 Hands-On 3.6   **Observe Internal CSS Styles**

In this exercise, you will use the Tag Selector and Code view to explore the internal CSS styles generated in the last exercise.

1. Click once on the <body> tag, which appears on the Tag Selector.
   This selects every element on the page.

2. Click the Code button on the Document toolbar.

3. Observe the contents of the <style> tag that appears directly above the <body> tag.
   It is not important that you understand the CSS code yet, but you are probably able to recognize almost all of the HTML tag names and the properties you set in the last exercise.

4. Click the Design button.

5. Leave the file open.

Removing Internal CSS Styles

When you first begin working with CSS styles, chances are you'll create a lot of extraneous internal styles that just add bulk to your document. When this happens, you can wipe the CSS slate clean by removing all or some of the internal styles.

QUICK REFERENCE: REMOVING INTERNAL STYLES

Task	Procedure
Remove internal styles	■ Choose Manage Styles from the Style pop-up menu on the Properties panel or choose Text→CSS Styles→Manage Styles from the menu bar.
	■ Select the style you want to remove.
	■ Click the Remove button on the \<style\> dialog box.

Hands-On 3.7   Remove Internal CSS Styles

In this exercise, you will remove the internal CSS styles from the current document.

Before you begin: The index.htm file should still be open.

Remove Internal CSS Styles

1. Find the Style pop-up menu on the Properties panel.

2. Follow these steps to remove the internal CSS styles:

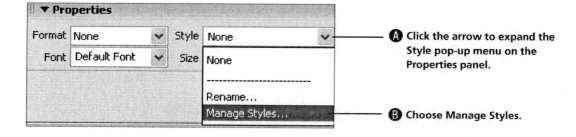

Ⓐ Click the arrow to expand the Style pop-up menu on the Properties panel.

Ⓑ Choose Manage Styles.

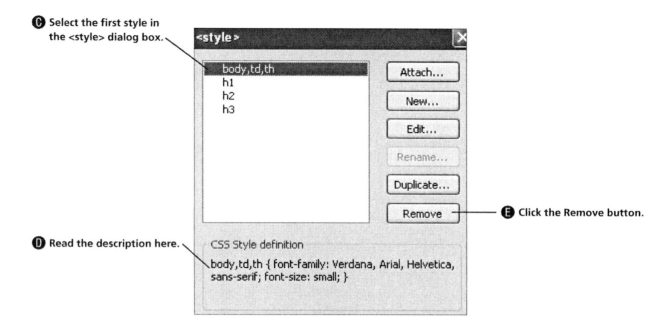

C Select the first style in the <style> dialog box.

D Read the description here.

E Click the Remove button.

<style>

body,td,th
h1
h2
h3

Attach...
New...
Edit...
Rename...
Duplicate...
Remove

CSS Style definition

body,td,th { font-family: Verdana, Arial, Helvetica, sans-serif; font-size: small; }

3. Repeat this process until all of the styles are removed.

4. Click Done.
The internal styles are removed from the document.

5. Save and close the file.

Concepts Review

True/False Questions

1. The first heading on a Web page should describe the page content.   TRUE   FALSE

2. The HTML tags <b> and <i> were replaced with <strong> and <em>.   TRUE   FALSE

3. You should use the Properties panel to set the font for all text on a page.   TRUE   FALSE

4. It's a good idea to edit the font list on the Properties panel and add several fonts such as Braggadocio, Egyptian Hieroglyph, and Botox Rocks.   TRUE   FALSE

5. Sans-serif fonts are the best choice for text display on a computer screen.   TRUE   FALSE

6. Numeric font sizes are scalable in most Web browsers.   TRUE   FALSE

7. When choosing a font color, you should use as much contrast as possible between the text color and background color of the page.   TRUE   FALSE

8. You use the Page Properties dialog box to set CSS appearance and headings properties for all of the text on a page.   TRUE   FALSE

9. Local CSS font properties override global CSS font properties.   TRUE   FALSE

10. An entity, such as   is one of the new HTML tags.   TRUE   FALSE

Multiple Choice Questions

1. Which of the following HTML elements describe the page contents at the highest level?

   a. Paragraph

   b. Line break

   c. Heading 1

   d. Unordered list

2. You can insert a line break by _____.

   a. Pressing Shift + Enter (Win) or Shift + Return (Mac)

   b. Choosing Insert→HTML→Special Characters→Line Break

   c. Pressing Enter, and then pressing Backspace

   d. Both a and b

3. Which of the following statements best describes a horizontal rule?

   a. It is the opposite of a vertical rule.

   b. It is a lazy rule.

   c. It is a thin line that extends across the width of the page.

   d. None of the above

4. Which of the following HTML tags is not used to define the document structure?

   a. <h1>

   b. <strong>

   c. <p>

   d. <ol>

Skill Builders

Skill Builder 3.1   Format Headings and Lists

In this exercise, you will format headings and lists. Then, you will insert a horizontal rule and the copyright symbol.

1. Open guide.htm from the review_03 folder.

2. Format the text with the following styles:

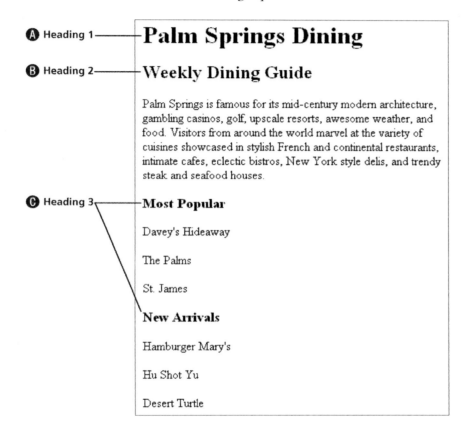

Format Lists

3. Follow these steps to format an unordered and ordered list:

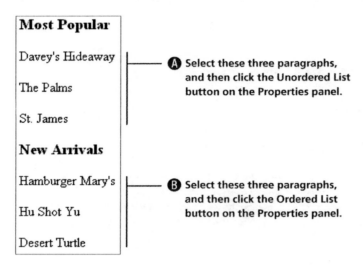

Most Popular

Davey's Hideaway

The Palms

St. James

A Select these three paragraphs, and then click the Unordered List button on the Properties panel.

New Arrivals

Hamburger Mary's

Hu Shot Yu

Desert Turtle

B Select these three paragraphs, and then click the Ordered List button on the Properties panel.

Insert HTML Elements

4. Position the insertion point below the ordered list.

5. Choose Insert→HTML→Horizontal Rule.

6. Position the insertion point below the horizontal rule.

7. Choose Insert→HTML→Special Characters→Copyright.

8. Add a space after the copyright symbol, and then type **2005 `Palm Springs Dining`**.

9. Save the changes but keep the file open.

Skill Builder 3.2   Format CSS Properties

In this exercise, you will format CSS font, size, background color, margins, and headings properties. The margins are designed for a window size of 760 × 420 (800 × 600, maximized).

Format CSS Appearance Properties

1. Choose Modify→Page Properties from the menu bar.

2. Follow these steps to format CSS Appearance properties:

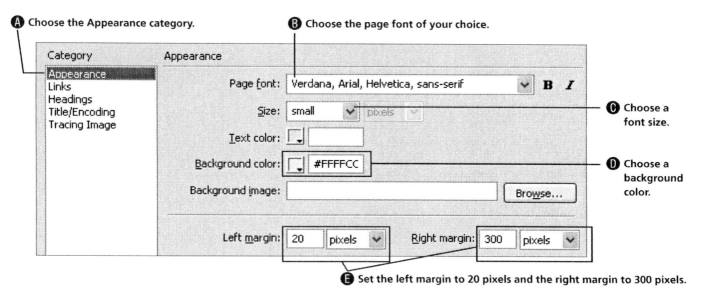

Ⓐ Choose the Appearance category.

Ⓑ Choose the page font of your choice.

Ⓒ Choose a font size.

Ⓓ Choose a background color.

Ⓔ Set the left margin to 20 pixels and the right margin to 300 pixels.

Format CSS Headings Properties

3. Follow these steps to format CSS headings:

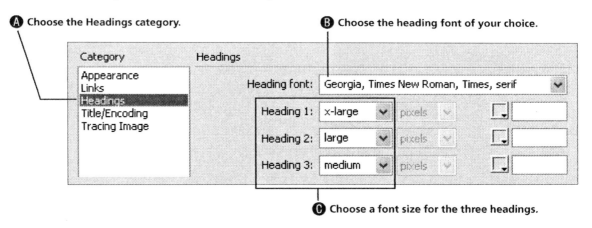

Ⓐ Choose the Headings category.

Ⓑ Choose the heading font of your choice.

Ⓒ Choose a font size for the three headings.

4. Click Apply.
Review the formatting changes and make modifications if necessary.

5. Click OK.

6. Save the changes but keep the file open.

Skill Builder 3.3   Remove Internal CSS Styles

In this exercise, you will remove the internal CSS styles.

Before you begin: The guide.htm file should still be open.

1. Choose Text→CSS Styles→Manage Styles.
   This is another way to open the <style> dialog box.

2. Select the first style that appears in the list, and then click Remove.

3. Continue to click Remove until all of the styles are removed from the <style> list.

4. Click Done.
   All of the internal styles are removed from the document.

5. Save and close the file.

 **Assessments**

Assessment 3.1   Format a New Page

In this exercise, you will create and format the Editor's Choice Web page, which you will create from scratch.

1. Follow these guidelines to create the document shown in the following illustration:

   - Create a new, blank HTML document named **editors_choice.htm** and save it in the review_03 folder.
   - Set the window size to 760 × 420 (800 × 600, Maximized).
   - Set the left margin to 20 pixels and the right margin to 320 pixels.
   - Type, and then format the text shown in the illustration.
   - Type a descriptive title in the Title Text field on the Document toolbar.
   - Choose a page font and size and a background color.
   - Choose a font type, size, and color for the headings.
   - Insert the » special character to the left of the text Editor's Choice, and the © special character to the left of the year 2005.

PALM SPRINGS DINING

» Editor's Choice

Simba's House of Ribs
190 N. Sunrise
Palm Springs, CA

Simba's House of Ribs is a Palm Springs landmark for down-home cooking. The chicken is crispy and juicy and always hot. Order from the dinner menu, or belly up to the buffet table.

Southern Favorites

- Collard Greens
- Barbeque Ribs
- Fried Chicken
- Yams

Rules for Successful Fried Chicken

1. Soak the chicken in buttermilk for 4 hours
2. Place chicken parts in hot oil and a little butter
3. Don't crowd the chicken
4. Turn pieces every ten minutes
5. Cover the last 5 minutes
6. Drain chicken on the Picayune Times

© 2005 Palm Springs Dining

---

2. Save and close the file.

Assessment 3.2   Format a Nested List

In this exercise, you will create a new document and format a nested list.

1. Follow these guidelines to create the Web page shown in the following illustration:
   - Create a new, blank HTML document named **nested_list.htm** and save it in the review_03 folder.
   - Type the text and format the list as shown.
   - Compose a descriptive title.

   A. Fish
       1. Catfish
       2. Trout
       3. Redfish
       4. Pompano
   B. Shellfish
       1. Crawfish
       2. Shrimp
       3. Oysters
       4. Crab

2. Save and close the file.

Critical Thinking

Critical Thinking 3.1   On Your Own

Mary Ellen is a passionate cook; she always has been. She and her family left the tiny town of Turkey Creek, Louisiana when she was six years old and moved to New York. For many years she returned to Turkey Creek to spend the summer with her grandparents, Elmer and Myrtle Ray. One of her fondest childhood memories is sitting in the big swing on Grandma Ray's back porch singing church songs and shelling black-eyed peas. Always, singing the last stanza of "Shall We Gather at the River" meant heading for the kitchen and scribbling notes about each dish Grandma was preparing for supper.

While organizing her New York kitchen, Mary Ellen ran across a crumpled grease- and flour-stained piece of brown paper bag that her tiny fingers had used many years ago to transcribe the recipe for Shrimp Etouffee, Grandpa Ray's favorite dish. In honor of her grandmother, Mary Ellen wants to post the recipe on her cooking club's Website.

Guidelines:

- Create a new, blank HTML document named **grandmothers_recipe** and store it in the review_03 folder.
- Type the ingredients and directions shown in the following illustration.
- Compose a descriptive title for the page.
- Format the page with headings and paragraphs and use line breaks to format the ingredients.
- Use CSS appearance and headings properties to format the page.

Grandmother's Shrimp Etouffee

Ingredients

1 pound peeled and deveined shrimp
1 stick butter
1/2 cup chopped red onion
1/2 cup chopped red bell pepper
1/2 cup chopped green bell pepper
1 tablespoon minced garlic
1 tablespoon worcestershire sauce
3 tablespoons flour
1 tablespoon paprika
2 cups water
1 tablespoon creole seasoning
salt and pepper to taste
dash of cayenne pepper

Directions

Melt the butter in a dutch oven or large pot. Add the paprika. Season shrimp with creole seasoning and salt and pepper. Saute' the shrimp for about 5 minutes and then remove from pot. Add the onions, bell pepper, garlic to the pot. Saute' about 10 minutes. Put the cooked shrimp back in the pot and add the worcestershire sauce and water. Cook over medium heat for about 20 minutes.

Dissolve 3 tablespoons of flour in 1/4 cup of water. When mixed well (no lumps), add to the pot. Cook for another 20 to 25 minutes until thickened. Serve over rice.

Critical Thinking 3.2   On Your Own

Your Dreamweaver skills have landed you an audition for a summer job at Palm Springs Dining! The job entails formatting pages before they're uploaded to the remote site. Janet and Justin hand you a copy of the page shown in the following illustration which would scare away anyone with less skills.

Guidelines:

- Open audition.htm from the review_03 folder.
- Reformat the document using CSS appearance and headings properties.
- Save the file as **weekly_guide.htm** in the review_03 folder.
- Save and close the file.

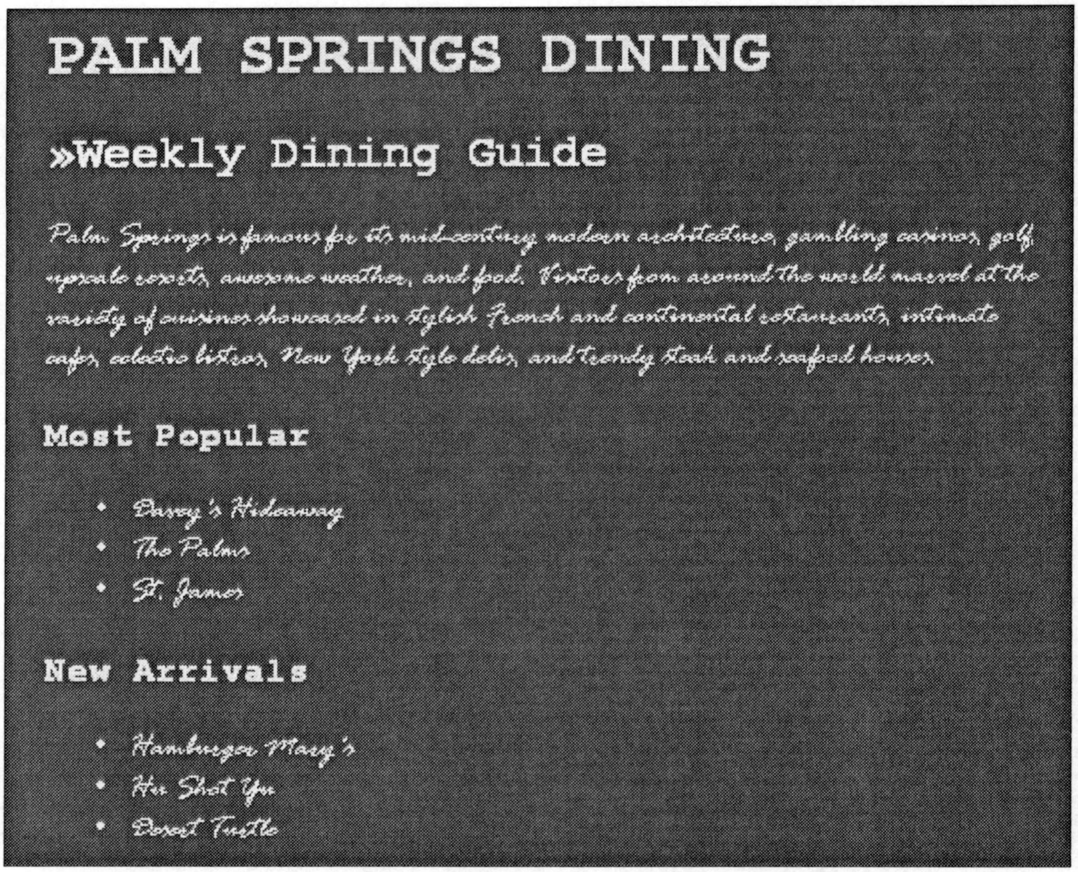

PALM SPRINGS DINING

»Weekly Dining Guide

Palm Springs is famous for its mid-century modern architecture, gambling casinos, golf, upscale resorts, awesome weather, and food. Visitors from around the world marvel at the variety of cuisines showcased in stylish French and continental restaurants, intimate cafes, eclectic bistros, New York style delis, and trendy steak and seafood houses.

Most Popular

- Davey's Hideaway
- The Palms
- St. James

New Arrivals

- Hamburger Mary's
- His Shot Ya
- Desert Turtle

Critical Thinking 3.3 **With a Group**

Roger Bambenek is president of Seattle Chain Gang, a popular biking club. This summer the club is sponsoring a marathon from Seattle to Southwest desert locations in California, Arizona, and Nevada—where average daytime temperatures soar into triple digits. The event is staged to draw attention to breast cancer and to help raise money for research. The event attracts biking club members from around the world. Roger, aware that biking in desert locations can be very dangerous to unsuspecting bikers from cooler climates, wants to prepare a page of "bike smart" safety tips to post to the Chain Gang Web site. He naturally asks you for assistance.

Guidelines:

- Brainstorm with your group to determine the content of the page.
- Use headings, paragraphs, and bulleted lists to organize the information so that readers can easily scan the important topics.
- Format the page to your liking.
- Save the completed document as **bike_smart.htm** in the review_03 folder.

Critical Thinking 3.4 **Web Research**

Oahn Dang works as a travel agent for Wind Energy Systems, a private corporation that conducts business throughout the United States, Canada, Mexico, and Europe. The numerous phone calls and emails from employees seeking information on California hiking and biking trails, museums, adventure parks, aquariums, boat tours, and other points of interest have prompted her to create a site on her corporate intranet. Oahn has great ideas, including the site name "Go with the Wind," but she just doesn't have the skill to put the site together. Will you offer your services?

Guidelines:

- Use your favorite search engine to locate points of interest that Oahn's associates might seek.
- Create a new Web page and use it to organize your research results. Apply CSS appearance and headings properties to make the page pretty.
- Save the completed document as **go_wind.htm** in the review_03 folder.
- Save and close the file.

LESSON 4

Working with Images

One of the main attractions of Web authoring is the ability to combine text and images to create a unique visual display. Images and other forms of multimedia play a significant role in capturing the attention of your audience and communicating the intended message of your site. In this lesson, you will learn about popular graphic file formats used on the Web; how to insert, resize, crop, and resample images; and how to align images with text. You will also learn how to make your images accessible to speech-based (non-visual) browsers.

IN THIS LESSON

Case Study

George Garcia is the junior layout artist for Palm Springs Dining. His duties include laying out text and images on the homepage and the Restaurant Review page. Amy, the graphic artist, is still working on the logo design but she has already provided George with the width and height of the final image. Armed with this information, George inserts an image placeholder the correct size and continues with the page layout. When the logo is ready for prime time, George will replace the image placeholder with the final image.

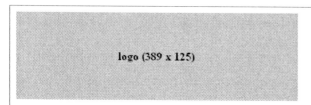

Home ~ Most Popular~ New Restaurants ~ Reviews

Weekly Dining Guide

Palm Springs is famous for mid-century modern architecture, gambling casinos, golf courses, upscale resorts, awesome weather, and **food**. Visitors from around the world marvel at the variety of cuisines showcased in stylish French and continental restaurants, intimate cafes, eclectic bistros, New York style delis, and trendy steak and seafood houses.

One of the toughest decisions you may ever have to make in the Palm Springs Desert Resorts is where to dine. With nearly 700 restaurants available throughout the area, your plate will always be full of excellent choices.

On the Weekly Dining Guide page, George inserts a 389 x 125 image placeholder that he will replace with the logo when the final design is completed.

On the Restaurant Review page, George crops an area away from one large image to form a single image, which he then resizes and re-samples.

Restaurant Review

The French Revolution
383 North Palm Canyon Drive
Palm Springs, CA

The French Revolution
like steamed lobster u
rack of lamb with a pir
appetizers, entrees an

The Napoleon Room

The new Napoleon din
fantasy land setting fo
meat, game, seafood

He aligns the image to create a text wrap. To finish the page, he adds space to the left and right of the image.

Understanding Graphic File Formats

The two most commonly used file formats for graphics on the Web are GIF (Graphic Interchange Format) and JPG (Joint Photographic Experts Group). GIF (pronounced "gif" or "jiff") images contain blocks of solid, flat colors (256 or fewer) with little or no blending of colors. GIF images support background transparency and animation. JPG (pronounced "jaypeg") are photographic quality images that contain a wide tonal range of millions of colors. JPG images do not support background transparency or animation.

A third file format, PNG (Portable Network Graphics), is also used on the Web; however, this format is not supported by older browsers. The graphics used in this book are either GIF or JPG.

 TIP! *When choosing a file format, always aim for the highest image quality and the lowest possible file size.*

 Hands-On 4.1 **Identify Graphic File Formats**

In this exercise, you will open a file that contains a GIF and a JPG image. You will observe the color differences between the two images.

1. Open graphic_file_formats.htm from the lesson_04 folder.
   The document contains a JPG and a GIF image.

2. Observe the difference in the color quality of each image.
   The JPG image is a high quality digital photograph; the GIF image is simple computer generated art that uses large, solid blocks of the same color.

3. Close the file without saving.

Inserting Images on the Page

FROM THE KEYBOARD

To insert an image:

WIN ONLY
[Ctrl]+[Alt]+[I]

MAC ONLY
[⌘]+[Option]+[I]

You can insert an image by choosing Insert→Image from the menu bar or by dragging the Image button on the Insert bar to the insertion point on the page. Either of these actions will open the Select Image Source dialog box, which provides options for locating and previewing images in your local site, or anywhere on your file storage location. You can also drag an image filename from the images folder directly to the insertion point on the page.

When you insert an image, Dreamweaver writes this HTML code, which is used by the browser to define the page layout and enhance the downloading speed of graphics.

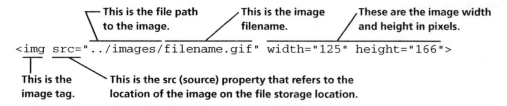

QUICK REFERENCE: INSERTING AN IMAGE

Task	Procedure
Insert an image	■ Choose Insert→Image from the menu bar, or
	■ Click the Image button on the Insert bar, or
	■ Drag the Image button to the insertion point on the page.

Hands-On 4.2   Insert an Image

In this exercise, you will insert two images into a Web page.

1. Open pasta_tip.htm from the Lesson_04 folder.

2. Position the insertion point in front of the first word in the first paragraph, To.

3. Choose Insert→Image from the menu bar.
   This opens the Select Image Source dialog box.

4. (Win) Follow these steps to insert the first new image on the page:

Ⓐ Navigate to the images folder on your local site.

Ⓒ Notice that the image preview, width and height, file size, and download time appear here.

Ⓑ Click once on happy_chef.gif to select it.

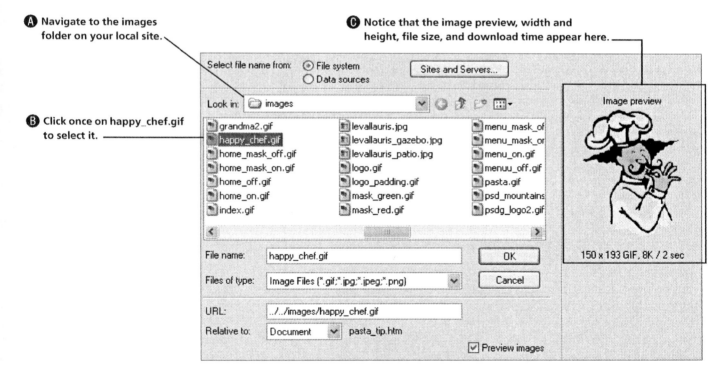

5. (Mac) Follow these steps to insert the first new image on the page:

A Navigate to the images folder on your local site.

C Notice that the image preview, width and height, file size, and download time appear here.

B Click once on happy_chef.gif to select it.

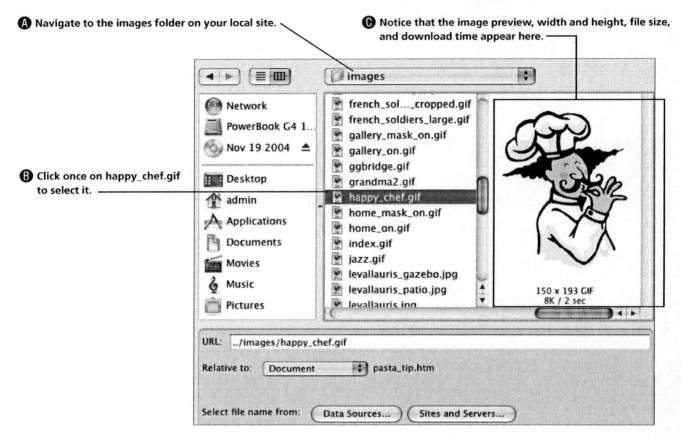

6. Click OK (Win) or Choose (Mac).
The image appears to the left of the text.

7. Position the insertion point directly above the horizontal rule.
This is where you will insert the logo graphic for the fictional Assaggi Ristorante.

8. Choose Insert→Image from the menu bar.

9. Navigate to the images folder on your local site.

10. Click once on assaggi.gif to select it.

11. Click OK (Win) or Choose (Mac).

12. Save the file but keep it open.

The two graphics you inserted should now appear in the locations shown in the following illustration:

Aligning Images with Text

Adjusting the placement of an image allows you to create a more visually appealing Web design by controlling the amount of white space (open space) between the image and surrounding text or images. Image alignment refers to the location of the image in relation to text or other images on the page.

The Align menu on the Properties panel lists nine align properties you can use. Of these, Left and Right are used to wrap multiple lines of text around an image. The other seven properties are used to align an image with a single line of text.

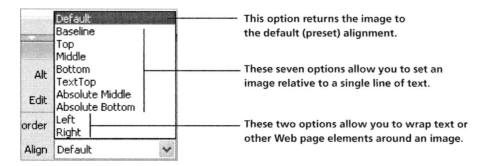

Wrapping Text Around an Image

Wrapping text around an image is a great way to conserve horizontal space and to create interesting visual effects.

When the image is left aligned, the text flows to the right margin.

When the image is right aligned, the text flows to the left margin.

 Hands-On 4.3   Wrap Text Around an Image

In this exercise, you will practice using the left and right align properties to wrap text around an image.

Before you begin: The pasta_tip.htm file should be open.

1. Set the window size to 760 × 420 (800 × 600, Maximized). If you don't remember how to do this, then see The Window Size Menu section of Lesson 2 (page 38).
   This sets the window size small enough for you to see the text wrap more clearly when it occurs.

2. Select the happy chef image.

3. Choose Right from the Align menu on the Properties panel. Do NOT deselect the image.
   This aligns the image to the right and the text flows to the left margin.

4. Choose Left from the Align menu.
   This aligns the image to the left and the text flows to the right margin.

Aligning an Image to a Single Line of Text

When you need to align an image with a single line of text (not two or more lines), Dreamweaver provides seven alignment options.

ALIGNING AN IMAGE TO A SINGLE LINE OF TEXT	
Alignment Option	**Description**
Baseline	This option aligns the baseline (bottom) of the text or other element in the same paragraph to the bottom of the selected image. It is normally the browser default alignment setting.
Top	This option aligns the image with the top of the tallest item in the line. That item may be text or a larger image.
Middle	This option aligns the baseline of the text with the middle of the image.
Bottom	This option is the same as Baseline.
Text Top	This option aligns the top of the image with the top of the tallest character in the text line.
Absolute Middle	This option aligns the middle of the image with the middle of the text.
Absolute Bottom	This option aligns the bottom of the image with the lowest point of the text line, including descenders (lowercase letters that extends below the base line, such as "g," "j," or "p").

 NOTE! *Baseline, Text Top, Absolute Middle, and Absolute Bottom are not part of the official HTML standard and only work in some browsers. Keep it simple. Stick with Top, Middle, and Bottom, which are the defaults.*

 Hands-On 4.4   Align an Image to a Single Line of Text

In this exercise, you will align an image relative to a single line of text.

1. Select the image of the plate of pasta at the bottom of the page.
   The image appears in the same line as the short text block.

2. Set the Align property on the Properties panel to Top.
   This aligns the text with the top of the image.

3. Set the Align property to Middle.
   This aligns the text with the middle of the image.

4. Set the Align property to Default.
   This aligns the text with the bottom of the image.

5. Save the file but keep it open.

Composing Alternative Text

Computers cannot interpret images and present them in a meaningful alternate format if the image cannot display. For this reason, alternative text (description of image) gives the computer something to present to:

- Readers with visual impairments
- Text-based browsers
- People who have turned off image loading in their browsers
- Search engines

When an image cannot display in a browser, the alternative text appears in an image place-holder, which is the same size as the image.

Speech-based browsers read the alternative text to blind users. When composing alternative text, imagine that you're describing the image to someone over the telephone.

To add alternative text to an image, select the image and type a description in the Alt box on the Properties panel. You may choose the <empty> setting on the Properties panel for images that are not important to the content of the page. Speech-based browsers ignore all images set to <empty>. It is important to note that leaving the Alt text box blank is not the same as using the <empty> setting. Speech and text-based browsers attempt to locate alternative text if the Alt text box is blank.

 TIP! *Always compose alternative text for important images and use the <empty> setting for all less important images.*

The following illustration shows the same image in three various states when loaded in the Internet Explorer browser. If you'd like to see a demonstration of this first hand, you can open alt_text_demo.htm from the lesson_04 folder and preview the file in your browser.

The image displays in visual browsers and the alternative text is spoken in non-visual browsers.

The image cannot display. The alternative text appears in visual browsers and the alternative text is spoken aloud.

The image cannot display in visual browsers and there is no alternative text to describe the image. Non-visual browsers ignore the image and continue processing the rest of the page.

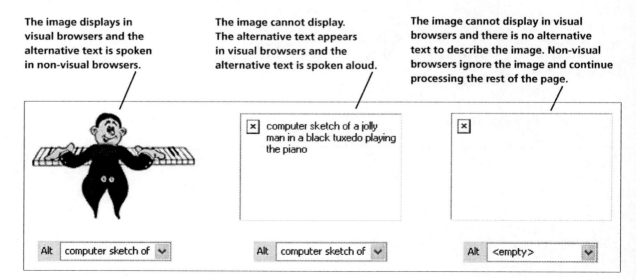

Hands-On 4.5 **Compose Alternative Text**

In this exercise, you will compose alternative text for the most important image on the page and use the <empty> setting for the two less important images.

Before you begin: The pasta_tip.htm file should be open.

1. Select the Assaggi logo graphic at the top of the page.
   This is the most important image on the page.

2. Click in the Alt text box on the Properties panel and type **Assaggi – Ristorante Italiano**.

3. Tap [Enter] or [Return].

4. Select the happy chef image.
   This image is used for decoration only.

5. Choose <empty> from the Alt pop-up menu.

6. Select the plate of pasta image.

7. Choose <empty> from the Alt pop-up menu.

8. Save the file but keep it open.

Adding an Image Border

Border [1]   A border defines the boundaries of an image. To add a border, select the image and type a number in the Border text field on the Properties panel.

 Hands-On 4.6   **Add an Image Border**

In this exercise, you will add a 1 pixel border around an image.

Before you begin: The pasta_tip.htm file should be open.

1. Select the happy chef image again.

2. Click in the Border text field on the Properties panel and type **1**.

3. Tap [Enter] or [Return].

4. Click anywhere off the image to deselect it.
   A 1 pixel black border appears around the image.

5. Select the image.

6. Click twice in the Border text field and type **0**.

7. Tap Enter or Return.

8. Click anywhere off the image.
   The border is removed.

9. Save the file but keep it open.

Adding Space Around an Image

Sometimes you need to add a few pixels of vertical space (above and below), and/or horizontal space (left and right) to move an image away from text or other elements on the page. To add space, select the image and then type a number in the V Space and/or H Space text box on the Properties panel.

When you add vertical or horizontal space, Dreamweaver highlights the image and shows the amount of added space in black to provide a visual representation of the space you are adding. When you deselect the image, the highlighting disappears and the space is added to the image.

Twenty pixels of vertical space appear above and below the image.

Twenty pixels of horizontal space appear to the left and right of the image.

Ten pixels of space appear on all sides of the image.

 Hands-On 4.7   Add Space Around an Image

In this exercise, you will add a few pixels of vertical and horizontal space to an image.

1. Select the happy chef image.

2. Type **20** in the V Space text box on the Properties panel and tap Enter or Return.
   The image background is highlighted and 20 pixels of space are added above and below the image.

3. Type **20** in the H Space text box on the Properties panel and tap [Enter] or [Return].
For both the left and right of the image, 20 pixels of space has been added.

4. Select the text you typed in the V Space text box, tap [Delete], and then tap [Enter] or [Return].
This removes the vertical space around the image and returns the vertical space to the default setting.

5. Deselect the image.
The background highlight disappears and horizontal space is kept around the image.

6. Save the file but keep it open.

Resizing and Refreshing Images

Dreamweaver allows you to manipulate and edit images in a variety of ways. For example, when you insert an image that may not be the right size for the page you're creating, you can resize (change height and width) the image without permanently changing the dimensions. This allows you to see how the new size affects your page layout. You can then refresh the image and return it to its original size, or you can resample the image and change its size permanently. You will learn how to resample an image later in this lesson. Here we explore how to resize and refresh an image.

When you insert an image, the image appears with three selection handles. You can drag the handles to resize the image proportionally or non-proportionally.

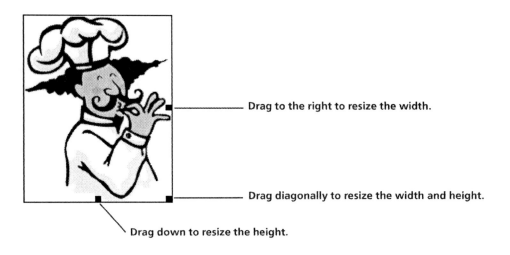

Drag to the right to resize the width.

Drag diagonally to resize the width and height.

Drag down to resize the height.

It is almost always better to resize an image proportionally so the width and height change by the same factor. Non-proportionally scaled images appear distorted on the page. Hold down the [Shift] key while you drag the image's corner selection handle to constrain the proportions of the image. This will keep the image's current proportions.

This is the original image

The image was scaled proportionally by holding down the [Shift] key and dragging the corner sizing handle.

The image was scaled non-proportionally by dragging the bottom sizing handle.

Refreshing an Image

When you resize an image by dragging a selection handle, the width and height properties update automatically and the new dimensions appear bold in the Properties panel. Also, the Refresh icon appears next to the width and height text boxes. When you click the Refresh icon, the image is restored to its original size and the Refresh icon disappears.

The bold text is a visual indicator that the image has been resized. ———

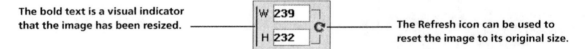

——— The Refresh icon can be used to reset the image to its original size.

 Hands-On 4.8   Resize and Refresh an Image

In this exercise, you will use the resize handles on an image to resize it proportionately and non-proportionately. You will then use the Refresh icon to return the image to its original size.

1. Click once on the happy chef image to select it.

Resize an Image Proportionally

2. Click the handle on the corner of the image, hold down the [Shift] key, and then drag to the right until the image is approximately 50% larger.

3. Click the Refresh ⟳ button on the Properties panel.
This restores the image to its original size.

Resize an Image Non-Proportionally

4. Click the center-right handle, and then click and drag directly to the right.
This shows the picture stretched non-proportionally.

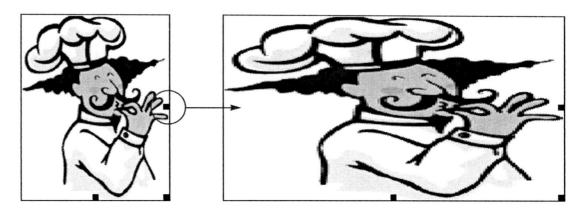

5. Click the Refresh ⟳ button on the Properties panel.
This restores the image to its original size.

6. Save and close the file.

Editing Images in Dreamweaver

Dreamweaver MX 2004 provides basic image editing features that allow you to edit images without switching between Dreamweaver and any other image editing program.

The Resample tool adds/subtracts pixels to/from a resized JPG or GIF image.

The Brightness and Contrast tool is used to modify the amount of light and dark in an image.

The Crop tool cuts unwanted areas from an image.

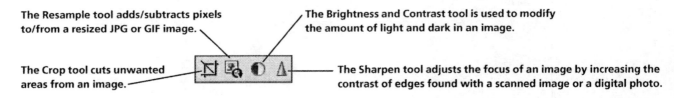

The Sharpen tool adjusts the focus of an image by increasing the contrast of edges found with a scanned image or a digital photo.

The two most useful tools are Crop and Resample because they fix the two most common problems with images: unwanted areas and file size.

Cropping an Image

When an image contains more content than you need, you can crop the area you don't want. If you crop an area and then decide you'd like to revert to the original image, you should undo any changes immediately or the action will permanently alter the image.

When you select an image and click the Crop button on the Properties panel, eight grab handles surround the image.

Click on and drag any grab handle to frame the area of the image you want to keep. Dreamweaver dims the area of the image you're cropping.

When you click the Crop button or tap [Enter] or [Return], the excessive areas are cropped.

Resampling an Image

After resizing an image, you can resample it to accommodate its new dimensions. When an image is resampled, pixels are added to or removed from it. Resampling an image to a higher resolution (based on decreasing the image size) typically causes little loss of quality. Resampling an image to a lower resolution (based on increasing the image size) always causes data loss and usually a drop in quality.

 TIP! *Resampling an image reduces an image's file size, resulting in improved download performance.*

It's a good idea to use a copy of an important image, such as a logo or any other images you use on multiple pages, to practice cropping and resampling. Cropping and resampling an image permanently resizes the image unless you undo the action immediately. If you use the same image on other pages in your site, they will appear at the new dimensions when you open the page in Dreamweaver or a Web browser.

 Hands-On 4.9   **Crop, Resize, and Resample an Image**

In this exercise, you will crop, resize, and resample an image. If you make a mistake during this exercise, immediately choose Edit→Undo from the menu bar.

1. Open reviews.htm from the lesson_04 folder.
   The file contains an image of three French soldiers.

Crop an Image

2. Select the image and click the Crop ⬜ button on the Properties panel.
   An alert box appears with a warning that the action you are about to perform is permanent.

3. Read the warning carefully, and then click OK.
   A selection area appears inside the image, indicated by the dashed line (Win) or solid black lines (Mac). Grab handles are located on the corners and centers of each side of the selection area.

4. Adjust the size of the crop area so that it fits snugly against the soldier on the right, as shown in the following illustration:

5. Click the Crop ⬜ button on the Properties panel.
   This crops the unwanted area. Do NOT deselect the image.

6. Notice that the Resample 🔲 button on the Properties panel is dimmed.
   This is because you didn't drag the image to change its dimensions; you merely cropped an unwanted area.

Resize an Image

7. While holding down the [Shift] key, drag the right corner sizing handle slowly up and to the left until the image is approximately 10% smaller. Do NOT deselect the image.

8. Notice that the Resample 🔲 button is now available.

Resample an Image

9. Click the Resample button on the Properties panel.

10. Read the warning that appears, and then click OK.
    Because you decreased the size of the image, resampling it added pixels to match the appearance of the original image as closely as possible.

11. Align the image to the left or right if you wish.

12. Save and close the file.

Working with Image Placeholders

An image placeholder is a temporary graphic you can use until final artwork is ready to be added to a Web page. When the final graphic becomes available, you use it to replace the image placeholder.

Inserting an Image Placeholder

To insert an image placeholder, place the insertion point where you would want the final graphic and choose Insert→Image Objects→Image Placeholder from the menu bar. This opens the Image Placeholder dialog box. After you insert an image placeholder, you can view or modify the image placeholder properties in the Properties panel.

QUICK REFERENCE: SETTING IMAGE PLACEHOLDER DIALOG BOX OPTIONS

Setting	Description
Name	The placeholder name is optional; leave the text box blank if you do not want a label to appear. If you use a name, it must begin with a letter and can contain only letters and numbers. Spaces and high ASCII characters (foreign language accents, math symbols, and trademark and copyright symbols) are not allowed.
Width/Height	If you don't know the width and height dimensions of the final image, you can estimate.
Color	This setting lets you specify an optional color for the placeholder.
Alternative Text	This text appears in a Web browser.

 Hands-On 4.10   **Insert Image Placeholders**

In this exercise, you will insert an image placeholder and set the name, width and height, and alternative text properties.

1. Open index.htm from the lesson_04 folder.

2. Position the insertion point in the blank space above the heading at the top of the page.

3. Choose Insert→Image Objects→Image Placeholder from the menu bar.
   This opens the Image Placeholder dialog box.

4. Follow these steps to set image placeholder properties:
   The width and height settings are from the estimated size of the final image.

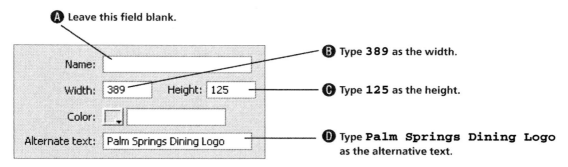

A Leave this field blank.

Name:

Width: 389   Height: 125

Color:

Alternate text: Palm Springs Dining Logo

B Type **389** as the width.

C Type **125** as the height.

D Type **Palm Springs Dining Logo** as the alternative text.

5. Click OK.
   The image placeholder appears at the top of the page. The width and height appear in the center of the placeholder. The alternative text will only show when the page is displayed in a Web browser.

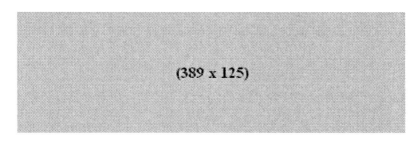

(389 x 125)

6. Save the file but keep it open.

Replacing an Image Placeholder

When the final image becomes available, you use it to replace the image placeholder. You can use this same technique to replace one image with another.

QUICK REFERENCE: WORKING WITH IMAGE PLACEHOLDERS

Task	Procedure
Insert an image placeholder	■ Choose Insert→Image Objects→Image Placeholder from the menu bar.
Replace an image placeholder	■ Double-click the image placeholder.
	■ Select an image from the Select Image Source dialog box.

Hands-On 4.11   Replace an Image Placeholder

In this exercise, you will replace the image placeholder with the final image. You will then insert a background image on the page.

1. Double-click the image placeholder.
   This opens the Select Image Source dialog box.

2. Select psdg_logo2.gif from the images folder.

3. Click OK.
   The placeholder has been replaced by the final image.

4. Choose Modify→Page Properties from the menu bar.
   This opens the Page Properties dialog box.

5. Click the Background Image Browse button.
   This opens the Select Image Source dialog box.

6. Select bg_home11.gif from the images folder.

7. Click OK twice.
   This closes both dialog boxes, and the background image fills the page background.

8. Save and close the file.

 **Concepts Review**

True/False Questions

1. When you resize an image but don't resample it, the original image is resized and the file size changes.   TRUE   FALSE

2. The Refresh icon is used to restore an image to its original size if you resize the image but don't resample it.   TRUE   FALSE

3. To wrap text to the left of an image, set the image align property to Right.   TRUE   FALSE

4. Leaving the Alt box on the Properties panel blank is the same as choosing the <empty> option.   TRUE   FALSE

5. You should compose short descriptive text for all important images on a page and set the ones used for visual purposes only to <empty>.   TRUE   FALSE

6. When you resize an image to a smaller size and then resample it, pixels are subtracted from the image.   TRUE   FALSE

7. When you crop an image, the action is permanent unless you undo the action immediately.   TRUE   FALSE

8. You can add horizontal space to the left or to the right of an image by setting the H Space property.   TRUE   FALSE

9. When you resize and resample an image, all pages that use the same image are affected.   TRUE   FALSE

10. The only difference between a GIF and JPG image is the file size.   TRUE   FALSE

Multiple Choice Questions

1. The most widely used graphic file formats on the Web are:
   a. JPG
   b. BMP
   c. GIF
   d. Both a and c

2. Which key is used to resize an image proportionally while dragging the corner sizing handle?
   a. Shift
   b. Alt
   c. Backspace
   d. F2

3. A GIF image is limited to _____ colors.
   a. 256 or fewer
   b. thousands of
   c. millions of
   d. 216

4. Which of the following techniques is used to insert an image on the page?
   a. Choose Insert→Image.
   b. Click the Images button on the Common category of the Insert bar.
   c. Drag and drop the image filename from the Images folder to the Document window.
   d. All of the above

Skill Builders

Skill Builder 4.1   Insert Images and Set Image Properties

In this exercise, you will insert two images on the page and modify their properties.

1. Open levallauris_insert.htm from the review_04 folder.

Insert Images

2. Position the insertion point in the blank space above the top heading, The Roberson House.

3. Choose Insert→Image from the menu bar.

4. Select levallauris.jpg from the images folder.

5. Position the insertion point in front of the first word in the first sentence, Built.

6. Now insert levallauris_patio.jpg.
   The page should now look like this illustration:

The Roberson House

Built in 1924, the Roberson House is a major historical landmark. Th
Roberson, son of the famous Nellie Coffman. According to Marjorie Bell Bright, Nellie Coffma
feminist, arrived in Palm Springs in 1909, where the survey shows only a few residents, no

Resize and Resample an Image

7. Select the last image you inserted, levallauris_patio.jpg.

8. While holding down the [Shift] key, drag the corner sizing handle up and to the left until the image is approximately 104 × 157.
   The width and height boxes on the Properties panel show the size of the image while you are dragging the resize handles. Do NOT deselect the image.

9. Click the Resample button on the Properties panel.
   Dreamweaver matches the resized image as closely as possible to the original image. Do NOT deselect the image.

Add a Border

10. Type **2** in the Border text field on the Properties panel and tap [Enter] or [Return].

11. Click anywhere off the image to deselect it.
    A 2 pixel black border appears around the image.

Align an Image

12. Set the window size to 760 × 420 (800 × 600, Maximized).
    This setting will enable you to observe the text wrap more clearly.

13. While the image is selected, choose Left from the Align menu on the Properties panel.
    This aligns the image to the left and the text wraps around the image. Do NOT deselect the image.

Add Horizontal Space

14. Type **10** in the H Space text box on the Properties panel and tap [Enter] or [Return].
    This adds 10 pixels of space to the left and right of the image.

Compose Alternative Text

15. Select the first image.
    This is the most important image on the page.

16. Click in the Alt text box on the Properties panel and type **Photographs of the Le Vallauris restaurant dining rooms.**

17. Select the second image.

18. Choose <empty> from the Alt menu on the Properties panel.

19. Save and close the file.

Skill Builder 4.2   Insert an Image Placeholder

In this exercise, you will insert an image placeholder, and then you will replace it with an image.

1. Open levallauris_placeholder.htm from the review_04 folder.

2. Place the insertion point to the left of the word They, which is located in the fourth paragraph.

3. Choose Insert→Image Objects→Image Placeholder.

4. Follow these steps to complete the options in the Image Placeholder dialog box:

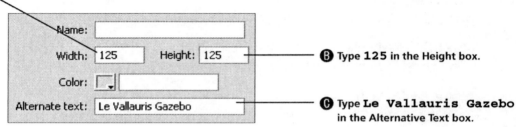

Ⓐ Type **125** in the Width box.

Ⓑ Type **125** in the Height box.

Ⓒ Type **Le Vallauris Gazebo** in the Alternative Text box.

5. Click OK.

Replace an Image Placeholder

6. Click twice on the image placeholder.
   This opens the Select Image Source dialog box.

7. Select levallauris_gazebo.jpg from the images folder.

8. Click OK.

9. Align the image to the right.

10. Save and close the file.

Assessments

Assessment 4.1   Insert and Modify Images

In this exercise, you will insert and modify images. All images are located in the images folder.

1. Open sports_bars.htm from the review_04 folder.
   The page contains two headings, several paragraphs, but no images.

Insert the Images

2. Follow these guidelines to redesign the page:

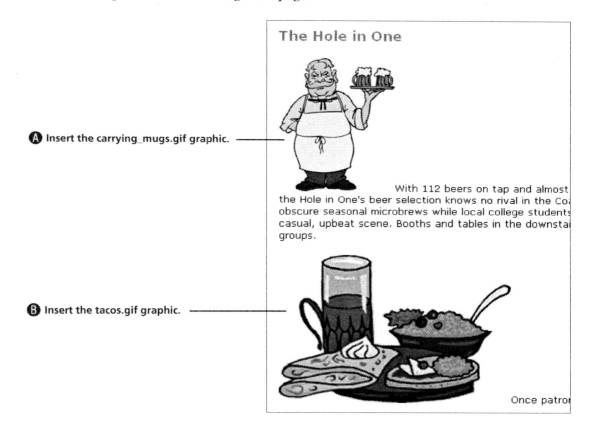

Ⓐ Insert the carrying_mugs.gif graphic.

Ⓑ Insert the tacos.gif graphic.

The Hole in One

With 112 beers on tap and almost
the Hole in One's beer selection knows no rival in the Co
obscure seasonal microbrews while local college students
casual, upbeat scene. Booths and tables in the downstai
groups.

Once patror

Align the Images

3. Align the first image to the right.

4. Align the second image to the left.

Resize and Resample the Images

5. Resize the first image to approximately 130 × 154.

6. Resize the second image to approximately 148 × 96.

7. Resample both of the images.

Add Horizontal Space

8. Add 10 pixels of horizontal space to each image.

Compose Alternative Text

9. Use the Properties panel to compose alternative text for the first image. Use the alternative text of your choosing.

10. Set the alternative text for the second image to <empty>.

11. Compare your page with the final design shown in the following illustration:

Sports Bars

The Hole in One

With 112 beers on tap and almost 400 more available by the bottle, the Hole in One's beer selection knows no rival in the Coachella Valley. Beer snobs sample obscure seasonal microbrews while local college students stop by for affordable grub and a casual, upbeat scene. Booths and tables in the downstairs dining room are perfect for groups.

Once patrons finish perusing the 20 page beer menu, they face an equally daunting task: Choosing from over 150 affordable snacks, sandwiches and entrees. Particularly enjoyable are offbeat versions of familiar appetizers like potato skins (topped with grilled lizard and cactus) and buffalo wings so hot, you'll need to tell the local fire department to stand by when you place your order.

For something more offbeat, try a grilled shark sandwrich served with banana-beer ketchup. Diners looking for a filling dinner can't do better than the popular taco platter.

12. Save and close the file.

Assessment 4.2   Replace Image Placeholders

In this exercise, you will replace image placeholders to display the images shown in the following illustration. You will also add a background image.

1. Open street_fair.htm from the review_04 folder.

2. Follow these guidelines to replace the image placeholders shown in the following illustration:

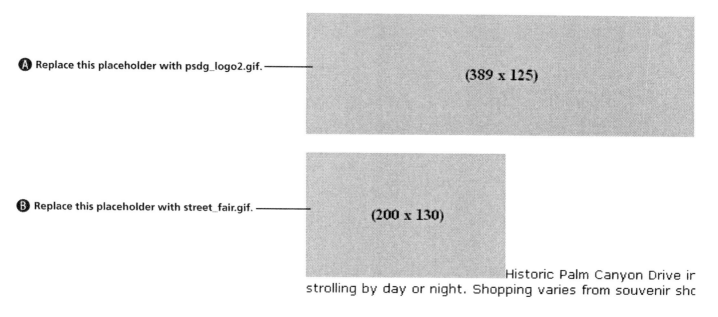

A Replace this placeholder with psdg_logo2.gif.

(389 x 125)

B Replace this placeholder with street_fair.gif.

(200 x 130)

Historic Palm Canyon Drive ir
strolling by day or night. Shopping varies from souvenir shc

3. Align the second image to the left.

4. Use the Page Properties dialog box to set the background image to bg_home8.gif.
Your page should resemble the following illustration:

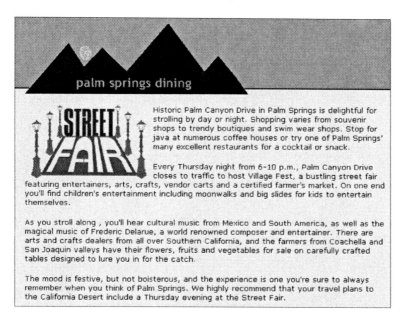

5. Save and close the file.

Assessment 4.3   Crop, Scale, Resample, and Align Images

In this exercise, you will insert, crop, scale, resample, and align images. You will also add space as needed, compose alternative text for important images, and set the Alt property to <empty> for less important images.

1. Open rhythm.htm from the review_04 folder.

2. Insert the Palm Springs Dining logo, named psdg_logo2.gif, at the top of the page.

3. Add the background image bg_home11.gif.

4. Insert drumbeat_large.gif directly to the left of the text This, which is located in the first paragraph.

5. Crop the large image to remove the two small drum images.

6. Resize and resample the cropped image.

7. Add space around images as needed.

8. Compose alternative text for each image or set the Alt property to <empty>.

9. Align the drum image and the two mask images, as shown in the following illustration:

10. Save and close the file.

Critical Thinking

Critical Thinking 4.1   On Your Own

As a layout artist apprentice for Palm Springs Dining, your first assignment is to spruce up the Piano Bars page.

Follow these guidelines to get the job done:

- Open piano_bars.htm from the review_04 folder.

- Insert the images shown in the following illustration.

- Resize and resample the images. Add space as necessary.

- Include alternative text for the images you consider the most important and use the <empty> option for less important graphics.

A The filename is logo.gif.

B The filename is piano_bar.gif.

PALM SPRINGS DINING

Piano Bars

During their heyday in the 1940s, piano bars were glamorous destinations for the 'fast crowd' to savor a martini and a cigarette while listening to ripped off renditions of Frank Sinatra and Duke Ellington. Today, while most piano bars have lost the charm and drama, one piano bar in Palm Springs keeps the glamorous piano-playing tradition going strong.

The Painted Cactus

This popular piano bar lends sophistication to the elegantly appointed dining room. Expect Sinatra, but don't be surprised to hear Billy Joel or Elton John. With many dishes prepared tableside, there's ample opportunity for the talented staff to impress.

Enduring classics mingle with, and sometimes outshine a roster of contemporary favorites. Start with a Grey Goose Vodka martini, garnished with Gorgonzola stuffed Jalapeno olive. For an appetizer, try the Painted Cactus Seafood Tower, a chilled mountain of lobster, shrimp, king crab, and Ahi tuna. Be sure to save room for the Steak Diane, flamed tableside to buttery tenderness; or filet mignon, with a charbroiled exterior set off by a delicate mushroom-port demi-glace. Choose from an extensive wine list, or order by the glass. The Ecco Domani merlot goes well with steaks.

C The filename is cocktail.gif.

Critical Thinking 4.2   **On Your Own**

Bonnie Bedelia is president of the Voyagers Travel Club, a local travel agency that provides reduced rate travel services to Las Wages College students and faculty in Lodi, California. The club encourages travel to develop professional and social skills. Bonnie has offered you a free five-day trip if you will lay out the graphics she needs to post on her Web site for the next tour. She gives you this page (vacation.htm), which isn't much help, you might think.

The body text is written in Lorem Ipsum, a non-existent language that has been used for many years to simulate the English Language because the letter spacing is so similar. Lipsum (for short) serves as a text placeholder you can use to lay out your page until you have the final content. You can copy and paste to create more text. Because you can't read the text, you can concentrate on the layout, not the content.

Voyager Travel Club

Massa sit amet, consectetuer adipiscing elit. Phasellus lobortis mi a wisi. Nullam facilisis pellentesque sapien. Cras luctus, sem ac pellentesque porttitor, sem dui tempus eros, in fermentum enim metus non turpis. Pellentesque libero. Ut non nunc id lacus luctus ornare.

Quisque metus. Nulla tempor nisl eget arcu. Mauris sit amet nisl eget arcu laoreet iaculis. Praesent nonummy, tortor non venenatis ullamcorper, magna pede condimentum nulla, eget dictum est massa vitae augue. Integer ligula augue, tristique quis, luctus sed, auctor vitae, velit.

Follow these guidelines to win that free trip:

- Open vacation.htm from the review_04.

- Use your skills to lay out the page using images from the images folder. The image names are ggbridge.gif, lighthouse.gif, and beach.gif.

- Assign alternative text to important images and use the <empty> property for all images that are used for decoration.

- Resize, crop, and resample the images as necessary.

- Modify the page properties to your satisfaction.

- Define a descriptive page title.

Try to beat the layout shown in the following illustration:

Voyager Travel Club

San Francisco

 Massa sit amet, consectetuer adipiscing elit. Phasellus lobortis mi a wisi. Nullam facilisis pellentesque sapien. Cras luctus, sem ac pellentesque porttitor, sem dui tempus eros, in fermentum enim metus non turpis. Pellentesque libero. Ut non nunc id lacus luctus ornare.

Quisque metus. Nulla tempor nisl eget arcu. Mauris sit amet nisl eget arcu laoreet iaculis. Praesent nonummy, tortor non venenatis ullamcorper, magna pede condimentum nulla, eget dictum est massa vitae augue. Integer ligula augue, tristique quis, luctus sed, auctor vitae, velit.

Point Reyes Lighthouse

Nulla sit amet quam a dui tristique pharetra. Fusce rutrum orci ac sapien. Donec laoreet quam nec mauris malesuada consequat. Sed tristique risus at nisl. Mauris ut quam at orci sagittis commodo. Vivamus mi nibh, placerat id, porttitor ac, consectetuer quis, massa. Ut vehicula ligula sit amet ante.

Sed arcu. Donec scelerisque augue non magna. Fusce metus. Maecenas ac erat. Aenean sem. Nullam ligula diam, auctor eu, tincidunt sed, placeNullam facilisis pellentesque sapien. Cras luctus, sem ac pellentesque porttitor, sem dui tempus eros, in fermentum enim metus non turpis. Pellentesque libero. Ut non nunc id lacus luctus ornare.

Laguna Beach

 Quisque metus. Nulla tempor nisl eget arcu. Mauris sit amet nisl eget arcu laoreet iaculis. Praesent nonummy, tortor non venenatis ullamcorper, magna pede condimentum nulla, eget dictum est massa vitae augue. Integer ligula augue, tristique quis, luctus sed, auctor vitae, velit.

Vivamus mi nibh, placerat id, porttitor ac, consectetuer quis, massa. Ut vehicula ligula sit amet ante. Sed arcu. Donec scelerisque augue non magna. Fusce metus. Maecenas ac erat. Aenean sem.

Working with Anchors and Links

You began your Web page design journey by setting up a local site to store the project files used in this book. You've learned how to use the Dreamweaver design workspace to create and modify HTML documents, to define the document structure, to make the pages pretty by applying CSS appearance and headings properties, and to insert and modify graphics. You're nearing the countdown to the main event—publishing a local site to a remote location—which occurs in the next lesson! In this lesson, you will learn how to create hyperlinks using both text and images so users can jump to any location in your local site or to any location on the Internet.

Case Study

Kylie Anderson is the Web production manager at Palm Springs Dining. She is responsible for creating and maintaining all of the links in the site. Kylie sets CSS link color and text underline properties and then exports the internal styles to create an external style sheet. Finally, she links all of the other pages in the site to the external style sheet.

A graphic link leads to the homepage.

A text navigation section links all top-level pages in the site.

Several links lead to resources on the Internet.

This link jumps to an invisible anchor at the top of the page.

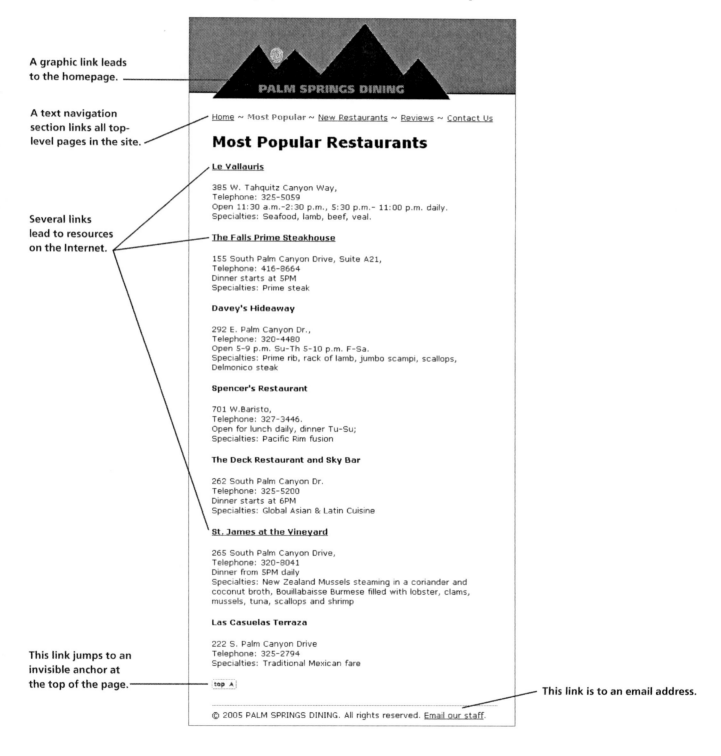

This link is to an email address.

Understanding Absolute and Relative File Paths

When you begin adding links to pages within your site, or to someone else's site, Dreamweaver provides a unique file path for either type of link.

- A document relative path tells the browser where to find the linked resource relative to the current page within the site. Links within your site are called relative links.

- An absolute path, on the other hand, provides the complete URL for a given page that is on someone else's site. Links outside your site are called absolute links.

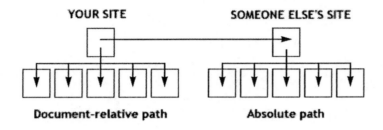

YOUR SITE   SOMEONE ELSE'S SITE

Document-relative path   Absolute path

IDENTIFYING ABSOLUTE AND RELATIVE FILE PATHS

Path Type	Example	Description
Document relative	menus/caesar_salad.htm	This path leads to a file located in a folder on your site. Document relative paths work much the same way they do on your computer.
Absolute	http://www.labpub.com	This path leads to a file that is not part of your site.

 NOTE! *Dreamweaver also provides a site-relative path option for large sites that use several servers or one server that hosts several different sites. This is not used for exercises in this book.*

Working with Absolute Links

The most straightforward type of link is a link to a page on someone else's site. These links are easy to create, as long as you know the site's URL. To create an absolute link, you use the Link text field on the Properties panel.

Linking with the Link Text Field

The Link text field is primarily used to enter an absolute path to a file outside your site. Here's how the process works:

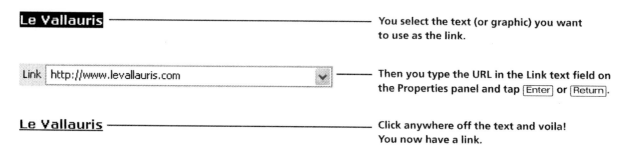

You select the text (or graphic) you want to use as the link.

Then you type the URL in the Link text field on the Properties panel and tap [Enter] or [Return].

Click anywhere off the text and voila! You now have a link.

 TIP! *If you are connected to the Internet, you can preview the file in your browser and click the link to jump to the location specified in the URL.*

Each time you create a new link, the path is stored in the Link pop-up menu in case you need to use it later. When you close Dreamweaver, the link history list is cleared.

 TIP! *When you first create a text link, the text appears bright blue and underlined. You'll learn how to control the appearance of various link states near the end of this lesson.*

 Hands-On 5.1   Link to an Internet Resource

In this exercise, you will create a link to a file that is outside of your site.

1. Open most_popular.htm from the lesson_05 folder.
   The CSS appearance and headings properties are set for this page.

2. Select the text Le Vallauris.
   Have you ever noticed that the more difficult a restaurant name is to pronounce, the more expensive it is?

3. Type **http://www.labpub.com/learn/dw04/web/vallauris.htm** in the Link box on the Properties panel and press [Enter] or [Return].

4. Deselect the text.
   The text appears bright blue and underlined. This visual cue identifies the text as a link.

5. Save the file, and then preview it in your browser.

6. Click the link to Le Vallauris.
   The page that opens is a simulation of the Le Vallauris homepage.

7. Leave your browser window open and return to the Document window. Keep the file open.

Reading Absolute File Paths

When you created the link to Le Vallauris, Dreamweaver inserted this HTML code in Code view. The code begins with the anchor <a> tag. HTML uses the anchor <a> tag to create a link to another document. An anchor can point to any resource on the Web: an HTML page, an image, a sound file, a movie, etc.

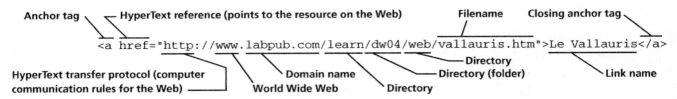

The text you use for a link name should accurately describe the link. Never use words like Click Here. Some search engines use hypertext as keywords to help potential visitors find information in your site. Most importantly, readers with visual imparities rely on accurate link names to navigate Internet resources.

Linking to an Email Address

When you want to encourage your visitors to email you, provide them with an email link on one or more of your pages. When someone clicks an email link, their email program launches automatically (provided they have an email account and email software) and a new message opens with your email address already in the To field.

The Email Link ▣ button on the Common tab of the Insert bar makes it easy to add an email link. You can also choose Insert→Email link from the menu bar. To create an email link manually, select the link text or graphic and type mailto: followed by an email address in the Link text box on the Properties panel. For example:

⚠ **WARNING!** *Be aware that putting a link to your email on a Web page invites spammers who troll the Web looking for mailto links.*

QR▶ **QUICK REFERENCE: MAKING LINKS**

Task	Procedure
Make an absolute link	■ Select the text or graphic you want to use as a link.
	■ Enter the URL in the Link text field on the Properties panel.
Link to an email address	■ Select the text or graphic you want to use as a link.
	■ Click the Email Link button on the Common Category of the Insert Bar, or
	■ Choose Insert→Email Link from the menu bar.

Hands-On 5.2   Link to an Email Address

In this exercise, you will link to an email address.

Before you begin: The most_popular.htm file should be open.

1. Scroll to the bottom of the page and select the text directly below the horizontal rule, Email our staff.

2. Click the Email Link ⊞ button on the Common tab of the Insert bar or choose Insert→Email Link from the menu bar.
This opens the Email Link dialog box.

3. Follow these steps to link to your email address:

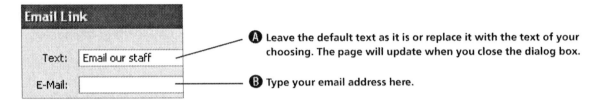

A Leave the default text as it is or replace it with the text of your choosing. The page will update when you close the dialog box.

B Type your email address here.

4. Click OK.
Observe the link in the Link text box on the Properties panel.

5. Save the file, and then preview it in your browser.
If your browser is set up to send email, the email application will open when you click the link. If not, the link will not work.

6. Leave your browser window open and return to the Document window. Keep the file open. ■

Working with Relative Links

A relative link lets you jump to a document located anywhere within your site by specifying the path through the folder hierarchy from the referring document (current document) to the destination document (linked document). When you click a link in the referring document, you are taken to the destination document.

Dreamweaver provides two options on the Properties panel to assist you in creating relative links to pages within your site.

Point to File—Drag this icon to the destination file to create a link.

Browse for File—Use this icon to open the Select File dialog box and navigate to the destination file location.

⚠**TIP!** *You could type a path in the Link text field, but this is not recommended because one mistyped word will result in a broken link.*

Linking with Browse for File

When using Browse for File, you simply select the text or graphic you want to use as a link and then use the Browse for File icon on the Properties panel to locate and select the destination file.

 TIP! *Always save a file before adding relative links.*

 Hands-On 5.3   Link Local Files with Browse for File

In this exercise, you will create a link to index.htm. The referring file and the destination file are in the same folder. You will preview the file in your browser and test the link.

Before you begin: *The most_popular.htm file should be open.*

1. Select the text Home, which is located directly below the graphic at the top of the page.

2. Follow these steps for your version of Dreamweaver to create a link using Browse for File.

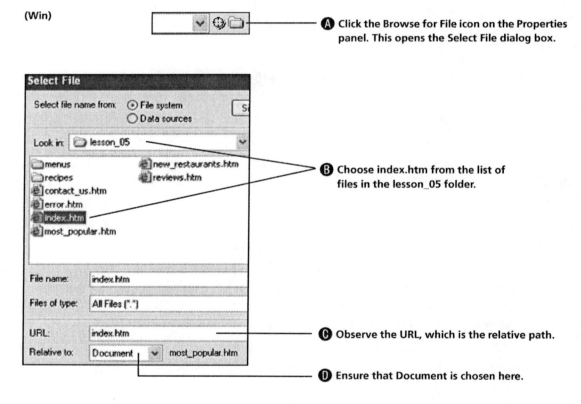

(Win)

A Click the Browse for File icon on the Properties panel. This opens the Select File dialog box.

B Choose index.htm from the list of files in the lesson_05 folder.

C Observe the URL, which is the relative path.

D Ensure that Document is chosen here.

(Mac)

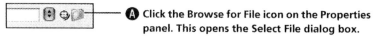

A Click the Browse for File icon on the Properties panel. This opens the Select File dialog box.

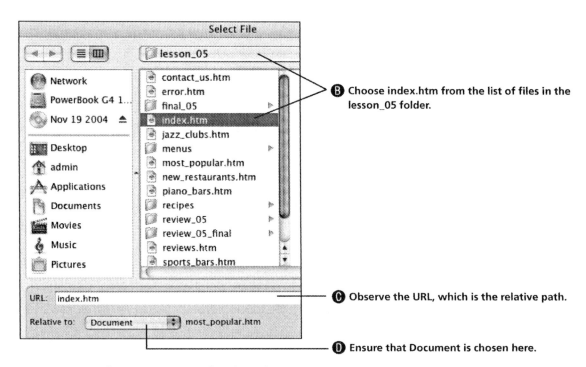

B Choose index.htm from the list of files in the lesson_05 folder.

C Observe the URL, which is the relative path.

D Ensure that Document is chosen here.

3. Press OK or Choose. Do NOT deselect the text.

4. Notice the Link text field on the Properties panel.
The relative path is shown. Since both documents are in the same folder, only the filename is used.

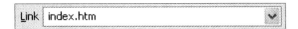

5. Deselect the text.
The text is now bright blue and underlined.

6. Save the file, and then preview it in your browser.

7. Click the Home link.
This opens the homepage in the browser. The homepage is not formatted, but you will fix this later. Note the Most Popular link.

8. Click the Most Popular link.
This takes you back to where you started. Notice that the color of the link Home has changed. That is because the state of the link has changed from "unvisited" to "visited." Never leave a site visitor stranded. Always provide a link back to the previous page.

9. Leave your browser window open and then return to the Document window. Keep the file open.

Linking with Point to File

The Point to File linking option is a huge timesaver when you need to quickly link multiple pages within your site. To use Point to File, select the text or graphic you want to use as a link, and then drag the Point to File icon to the destination file in the Files panel.

QUICK REFERENCE: LINKING FILES WITHIN YOUR SITE

Task	Procedure
Link with Browse for File	■ Select the text or graphic you want to use as a link.
	■ Click the Browse for File 📁 icon on the Properties panel.
	■ Make a selection from the Select File dialog box.
Link with Point to File	■ Select the text or graphic you want to use as a link.
	■ Drag the Point to File 🎯 icon on the Properties panel to the destination file in the Files panel. (You can point the icon to a closed folder and it automatically opens to display its contents.)

 Hands-On 5.4   **Link with Point to File**

In this exercise, you will use Point to File to link to several pages.

Before you begin: The most_popular.htm file should be the active page.

1. Select the text New Restaurants, which appears in the text navigation section below the graphic at the top of the page.

2. Drag the Point to File 🎯 icon on the Properties panel to new_restaurants.htm and release the mouse button.

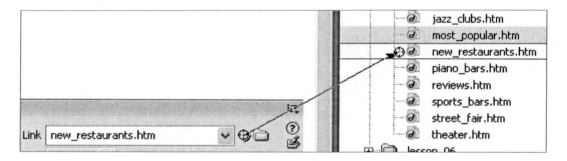

3. Select the text Reviews.

4. Drag the Point to File 🎯 icon on the Properties panel to reviews.htm and release the mouse button.

5. Repeat this process to create a link to contact_us.htm.

6. Save the file, and then test the links in your browser.

7. Return to Dreamweaver. Keep the file open.

Making Graphic Links

Creating graphic links is just as easy as creating text links. You select the graphic and then use Browse for File or Point to File.

 Hands-On 5.5   Make a Graphic Link

In this exercise, you will create a link from a graphic.

1. Click once on the Palm Springs Dining logo at the top of the page.
   It is common practice to have a site logo link to the homepage.

2. Use Browse for File or Point to File 🌐 to link to the index.htm file.
   If you use Point to File, make sure to drag the link Point to File icon, not the Src Point to File icon.

3. Save the file, and then preview it in your browser.

4. Click anywhere on the graphic.
   The homepage will now be displayed.

5. Leave your browser window open and return to the Document window. Keep the file open.

⚠️**TIP!** *If your graphic has a border and you use it as a link, the border will appear bright blue to identify it as a link. If this happens, select the graphic and then use the Properties panel to set the border to zero.*

Reading Relative File Paths

When you created your first relative link, you used most_popular.htm as the referring page and index.htm as the destination page. Both files are in the same folder. Dreamweaver added this HTML code in Code view.

```
<a href="index.htm">Home</a>
```
When the referring and destination documents are in the same folder, only the destination document's filename is used.

When you begin linking pages within your site, chances are the two files are not always going to be in the same location. To help you understand how pathnames work, here are several examples. These illustrations represent the file structure for lesson_05.

The referring and destination document are in the same folder. The path is most_popular.htm.

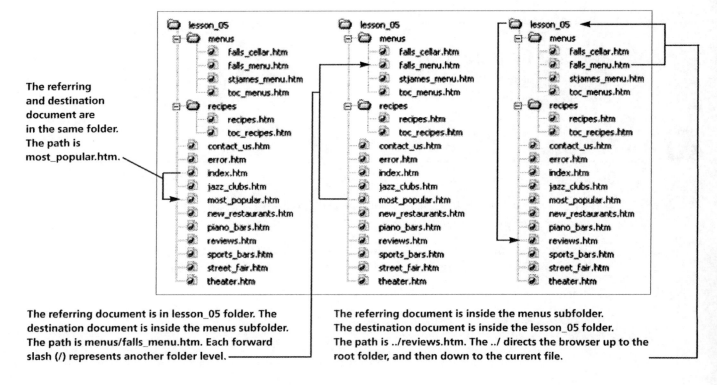

The referring document is in lesson_05 folder. The destination document is inside the menus subfolder. The path is menus/falls_menu.htm. Each forward slash (/) represents another folder level.

The referring document is inside the menus subfolder. The destination document is inside the lesson_05 folder. The path is ../reviews.htm. The ../ directs the browser up to the root folder, and then down to the current file.

You may be wondering why you need to understand path structures since Dreamweaver does all the coding behind the scenes. Well, broken links happen! When they do, you can fix them effortlessly using the skills you develop in this lesson. If you really want to impress your friends or boss, just fix their broken links!

WARNING! *When you move, delete, or rename linked files within Dreamweaver, you are given the option of having all relevant links updated automatically. Performing any of these actions outside of Dreamweaver will result in broken links.*

Creating and Linking to a Named Anchor on the Same Page

Throughout this lesson Dreamweaver has been using the anchor <a> tag and the href attribute to create links. The anchor tag has another attribute called "name" that you can use to create an invisible marker on your page. Then you can provide a link to that invisible marker, which Dreamweaver calls a named anchor. In long documents that require a lot of vertical scrolling, it's a good idea to provide a link back to the top of the page. Here's how the process works:

First, insert an anchor at the top of the page...

...then type an anchor name in the Named Anchor dialog box.

Finally, select the text or image you want to use as a link to the named anchor and type # followed by the anchor name in the Link text field on the Properties panel.

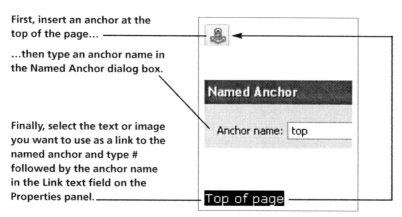

You can also create a link to a named anchor by selecting the text or graphic link and dragging the Point to File icon to the anchor symbol.

 WARNING! *Anchor names are case-sensitive. If you use lowercase letters (recommended) to name an anchor, you must use lowercase letters when you link to the anchor.*

Creating and Linking to a Named Anchor on Another Page

You can insert a named anchor in one page and then create a link to the anchor in another page. This allows you to jump to specific locations in any page in your site.

 TIP! *(Win) When you link to an anchor in another page, open both pages and tile the windows vertically. (Mac) Simply position both pages side-by-side. This way, you can select the text or graphic link on one page, and then drag the Point to File icon to the anchor symbol on the other page.*

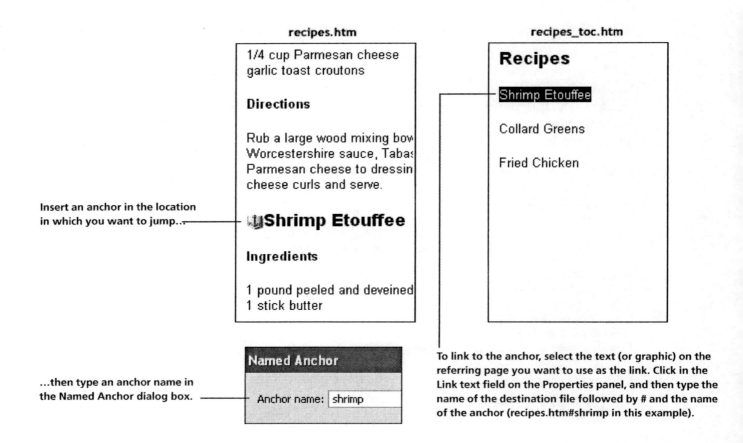

recipes.htm

1/4 cup Parmesan cheese
garlic toast croutons

Directions

Rub a large wood mixing bow
Worcestershire sauce, Taba:
Parmesan cheese to dressin
cheese curls and serve.

Shrimp Etouffee

Ingredients

1 pound peeled and deveined
1 stick butter

recipes_toc.htm

Recipes

Shrimp Etouffee

Collard Greens

Fried Chicken

Insert an anchor in the location in which you want to jump...

...then type an anchor name in the Named Anchor dialog box.

Named Anchor

Anchor name: shrimp

To link to the anchor, select the text (or graphic) on the referring page you want to use as the link. Click in the Link text field on the Properties panel, and then type the name of the destination file followed by # and the name of the anchor (recipes.htm#shrimp in this example).

TIP! *This technique is useful when you have a table of contents page and you want to provide links to specific topics on another page. If you use multiple anchors on the same page, each anchor name must be unique.*

FROM THE KEYBOARD

To Show/Hide all invisible elements:

WIN ONLY

 Ctrl + Shift + I

MAC ONLY

 ⌘ + Shift + I

Invisible Elements

Invisible elements are those you insert on your Web pages that are for internal purposes only. They aren't designed to be seen by the final audience. For example, the named anchor symbol is an invisible element. The symbol for the named anchor appears on a Web page while you are designing it but not in a browser. To show or hide marker icons for invisible elements, choose View→Visual Aids→Invisible Elements from the menu bar.

TIP! *Showing invisible elements lets you select them and change their properties in the Properties panel; hiding them lets you see the page closer to the way it will appear in a browser.*

Hands-On 5.6   Insert and Link to a Named Anchor

In this exercise, you will insert a named anchor at the top of a page and then create a link to the anchor. You will also test the link in your browser.

Before you begin: *Make sure most_popular.htm is the active page.*

1. Select the Palm Springs Dining graphic, and then press the ⎡Home⎤ key on your keyboard.
   This moves the insertion point to the left of the graphic and to the top of the page.

Insert a Named Anchor

2. Click the Named Anchor ⚓ button in the Common category of the Insert Bar or choose Insert→Named Anchor.
   This opens the Named Anchor dialog box.

3. Type **top** as the anchor name.

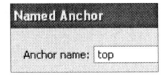

4. Click OK.
   You should see the anchor symbol at the top of the page.

5. If you do not see the anchor symbol, choose View→Visual Aids from the menu bar and make sure a checkmark appears next to Invisible Elements.

Link to the Named Anchor

6. Scroll to the bottom of the page and click once on ⎡top ▲⎤.

7. Click in the Link text field on the Properties panel and type **#top.**
   This creates a link to the named anchor.

Test the Link in Your Browser

8. Save the file, and then open the page in your browser.

9. Scroll to the bottom of the page and click on the graphic link to the top of the page.
The link takes you back to the top of the page.

10. Leave your browser open and return to the Document window. Keep the file open.

Reading a Named Anchor File Path

When you insert an anchor, you are prompted to define a unique name for the anchor. Dreamweaver adds the name to the anchor tag in Code view. In this example, the name of the anchor is "top."

```
<a name="top">
```

Once you insert an anchor, you then create a link to the anchor. In Code view this would read:

```
<a href="#top">Top of Page</a>
```

The pound (#) sign to the left of the anchor name is a unique identifier browsers use to find named anchors. Only use the pound sign in links to named anchors.

 TIP! *If you could give verbal instructions to your browser to make this link work, you'd say, "When someone clicks on the hypertext named Top of Page, jump to a location named top."*

In the following example, a named anchor is located in one file and a link to the named anchor is located in another file. Both files are in the same folder. The name of the anchor is shrimp. The name of the destination file is recipes.htm.

```
<a name="shrimp">
<a href="recipes.htm#shrimp">Shrimp Etouffee</a>
```

A click on the hypertext Shrimp Etouffee in the referring files jumps to the anchor named shrimp in the destination file.

 TIP! *Let's talk to that browser again. "When someone clicks on the hypertext named Shrimp Etoufee, open a file named recipes.htm and then jump to a location named shrimp."*

Targeting a Link to a New Browser Window

By default, all of your links open in the current browser window. This allows your site visitors to browse your links and then use the Back button on their browser to return to their previous location. Targeting a link means directing it to open in a location other than the current browser window. For example, you target a link to open in a new browser window. When your site visitor browses the contents, she can close the new window and return to her previous location in your site.

Be aware that opening a link in a new browser window can lead to confusion for some unsuspecting users who may not understand that a new browser window has opened and they cannot use the Back button to get back to their previous location.

If you want a link to open the destination document in a new window, go to the Target pop-up menu on the Properties panel and choose the _blank option. (The other options are used to control Frame content. You will learn how to create frames-based pages in Lesson 10, Working with Frames.)

This option makes the link open in a new browser window.

 QUICK REFERENCE: TARGETING A LINK TO A NEW BROWSER WINDOW

Task	Procedure
Target a link to a new browser window	■ Select the text or graphic link.
	■ Choose _blank from the Target pop-up menu on the Properties panel.

 Hands-On 5.7   Target a Link to a New Browser Window

In this exercise, you will target a link to open in a new browser window.

Before you begin: Make sure most_popular.htm is the active page.

1. Scroll down the page and select the hypertext St. James at the Vineyard.
   The link has already been created for you.

2. Choose _blank from the Target pop-up menu on the Properties panel.

3. Save the file, and then open the file in your browser.

4. (Win) Maximize the browser window. (Mac) Drag the resize box in the lower-right corner of the browser to fully expand the browser window.
   This enables you to see the new browser window when it opens.

5. Click the link to St. James at the Vineyard.
The link opens in a new browser window. The Back button is dimmed and you cannot use it to get back to your page.

6. Close the new browser window.
You are returned to the Most Popular page.

7. Leave your browser open and return to the Document window. Keep the file open.

Modifying a Link

At some point, you may need to modify a link because the URL you are linking to has changed or you simply no longer need it. Dreamweaver can help with modifying a link, but in some cases you need to modify a link the old fashioned way—by hand.

Changing a Link's Destination

When you link to pages in someone else's site, you always run the risk that their site may change or the page may no longer exist. You have no control over how files are managed on someone else's server; you can, however, change your link's destination to point to the new file location. You may also need to occasionally change a link on your own site to point to a different page. In both of these cases, you must change the links on your Web pages by hand.

 Hands-On 5.8   Change a Link's Destination

In this exercise, you will modify an absolute link to change the link's destination. The new link destination will bypass a Flash introduction and take you directly to the homepage.

1. Select or click anywhere inside the hypertext St. James at the Vineyard.
The current path reads http://www.labpub.com/learn/dw04/web/sj.htm.

2. Double-click the Link text field on the Properties panel to select the existing path. Type **http://www.labpub.com/learn/dw04/web/sjhome.htm** and tap ⌈Enter⌉ or ⌈Return⌉.

3. Save the file, and then open the file in your browser.

4. Click the link to St. James at the Vineyard.
The new link takes you directly to the homepage, which is a simulation of the real homepage.

5. Leave your browser window open and return to the Document window. Keep the file open.

Removing a Link

FROM THE KEYBOARD

To remove a link:

WIN ONLY

[Ctrl]+[Shift]+[L]

MAC ONLY

[⌘]+[Shift]+[L]

Sometimes you may want to remove a link from a page but leave the link text intact. To remove a link, select the text or graphic link and clear the Link field on the Properties panel, or choose Modify→Remove Link from the menu bar.

QUICK REFERENCE: MODIFYING A LINK

Task	Procedure
Change an absolute link destination	■ Click anywhere inside a text link or select a graphic link.
	■ Double-click the Link text field on the Properties panel to select the old URL and type the new link destination.
Change a relative link destination	■ Click anywhere in a text link or select a graphic link.
	■ Use Point to File or Browse for file and choose another file.
Remove a link	■ Click anywhere inside a text link or select a graphic link.
	■ Choose Modify→Remove Link.

 Hands-On 5.9   Remove a link

In this exercise, you will remove a link from a page.

1. Scroll to the top of the page and click anywhere in the hypertext Reviews.

2. Choose Modify→Remove Link.
   The link is removed and the text is left intact.

3. Save the file but keep it open.

Setting Link Color and Underline Style Properties

FROM THE KEYBOARD

To open the Page Properties dialog box:

WIN ONLY

[Ctrl]+[J]

MAC ONLY

[⌘]+[J]

We've mentioned that, by default, a link that has not yet been visited appears underlined and blue. And you have likely noticed that the color of a link changes once it has been used. Have you also noticed that some links change their appearance when you roll your mouse pointer over them? These conditions are called link states. These and other link properties can be modified by overriding default settings in the Links category of the Page Properties dialog box.

 TIP! *When changing default link color and underline style properties, focus on ensuring consistent design and navigation throughout your site.*

Hands-On 5.10 Set Link Style Properties

In this exercise, you will set link rollover color and underline style properties.

1. Choose Modify→Page Properties.
   This opens the Page Properties dialog box.

2. Choose the Links category.

3. Follow these steps to set Links properties:

Ⓐ Type **#CC660C** in the Rollover Links text box. (This is the color code used in the site logo, which you could select from the color options in the adjacent box.)

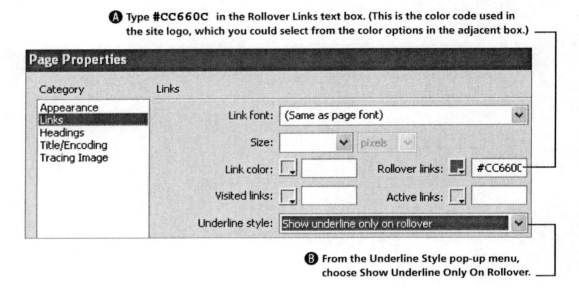

Ⓑ From the Underline Style pop-up menu, choose Show Underline Only On Rollover.

4. Click OK.

5. Save the file, and then preview it in your browser.
   The links that have not been clicked should appear as bright blue normal text; visited links (links that you have clicked) should appear as purple normal text.

6. Roll the mouse pointer over the links on the page.
   The color changes to the rollover color and the text is underlined.

7. Click the Contact Us link.
   The Contact Us page contains the default page and link property settings.

8. Close your browser and return to the Document window. Keep the file open.

Exporting Styles

Linking can do more than just help a visitor jump from one place in your site to another. Linking can also connect a style sheet to selected pages.

You already know that when you set page properties in the Page Properties dialog box or in the Properties panel, Dreamweaver adds internal CSS styles that apply to only the current page. While this is a great way to quickly spruce up a page, it's not very efficient when you want to apply these new styles to other pages in your site. A much better approach is to export the internal styles to create an external CSS style sheet.

When you choose File→Export→CSS Styles, Dreamweaver prompts you to name the new CSS file and specify a storage location. Dreamweaver then creates a new style sheet from the internal styles and stores the file in the specified location in the Files panel. Then, you can link one or more pages in your site to the external style sheet.

Even though you export internal styles, the styles remain in your document until you delete them. This can create potential style conflicts. You'll learn how to delete internal styles later in this lesson.

 QUICK REFERENCE: EXPORTING INTERNAL STYLES

Task	Procedure
Export internal styles	■ Open the page that contains the internal styles you want to export.
	■ Choose Text→CSS Styles→Export or File→Export CSS Styles.
	■ Specify a filename and storage location.

 Hands-On 5.11   Export Internal Styles

In this exercise, you will export internal styles to create an external CSS style sheet.

Before you begin: Make sure most_popular.htm is the active page.

1. Choose File→Export→CSS Styles.
   This opens the Export Styles as CSS File dialog box.

2. Save the file as **psd** in the lesson_05 folder.
   Dreamweaver adds the .css extension and stores the file in the specified location. If you don't see the style sheet, you may need to click the Refresh button on the Files panel menu bar to update the files list.

Linking to an External Style Sheet

Now that you have an external style sheet, you can link one or more HTML documents to it. That way, all of the linked pages share the same appearance, headings, and link properties. When you make a change to the external style sheet, all of the documents linked to it update automatically when you open them in Dreamweaver or in a Web browser. Having all of your styles in one place dramatically reduces style management tasks throughout your entire site. There are several methods you can use to attach external style sheets but we're going to cut to the chase and call out "The Terminator," the CSS Styles panel.

Using the CSS Styles Panel

FROM THE KEYBOARD
To open the Styles panel:

WIN AND MAC
[Shift]+[F11]

The CSS Styles panel is used to manage styles in much the same way the Files panel is used to manage files. You use the CSS Styles panel to create, edit, and delete CSS styles, as well as to attach external style sheets. To open the CSS Styles panel, choose Window→CSS Styles. The CSS Styles panel is a member of the Design panel group. In Lesson 9, Working with Styles, you will create and manage advanced styles with the CSS Styles panel.

 TIP! *Unless you have a very large monitor, you may want to close the Files panel to create more room to work in the CSS Styles panel.*

The CSS Styles panel is chosen.

The internal styles for the current document are shown here.

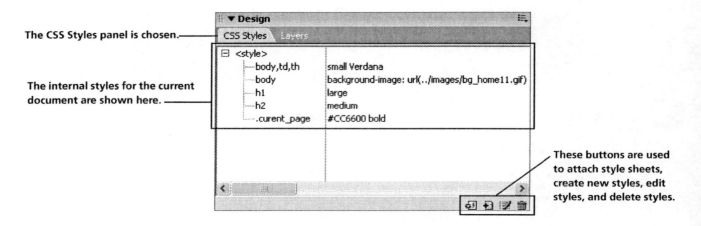

These buttons are used to attach style sheets, create new styles, edit styles, and delete styles.

Deleting Internal Styles

Before attaching an external style sheet to your page, you should delete the internal styles. You could use one of several dialog boxes to accomplish this, but as we stated earlier, we're going for "The Terminator" feature provided by the CSS Styles panel.

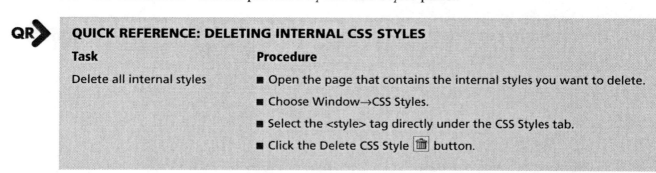

QR **QUICK REFERENCE: DELETING INTERNAL CSS STYLES**

Task	Procedure
Delete all internal styles	■ Open the page that contains the internal styles you want to delete.
	■ Choose Window→CSS Styles.
	■ Select the <style> tag directly under the CSS Styles tab.
	■ Click the Delete CSS Style 🗑 button.

QUICK REFERENCE: DELETING INTERNAL CSS STYLES (CONTINUED)

Task	Procedure
Delete selected styles	■ Open the page that contains the internal styles you want to delete.
	■ Choose Window→CSS Styles.
	■ Select the style from the list.
	■ Click the Delete CSS Style button.

 QUICK REFERENCE: ATTACHING AN EXTERNAL STYLE SHEET

Task	Procedure
Attach an external style sheet	■ Open the page you want to link to the external style sheet.
	■ Choose Window→CSS Styles.
	■ Click the Attach Style Sheet 🔗 button.

 Hands-On 5.12   **Link to an External Style Sheet**

In this exercise, you will delete internal styles and then link the external style sheet to the active page and to other pages in the lesson_05 folder.

Before you begin: Make sure most_popular.htm is the active page.

1. Choose Window→CSS Styles.
   This opens the CSS Styles panel.

Delete Internal Styles

2. Follow these steps to delete the internal styles from the current page:

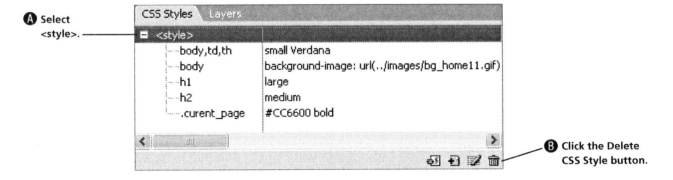

This deletes the <style> tag and all of the internal styles in the current document and clears the list of styles in the CSS Styles panel.

3. Follow these steps to attach the external style sheet:

A Click the Attach Style Sheet button to open the Attach External Style Sheet dialog box.

B Type **psd.css** in the File/URL text field or click the Browse button to locate the file in the lesson_05 folder.

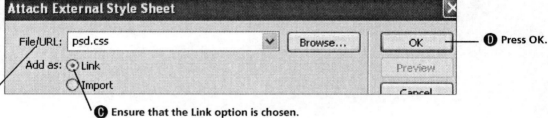

D Press OK.

C Ensure that the Link option is chosen.

4. Save and close the file.

Attach the Style Sheet to Other Pages

5. If the Files panel is closed, tap [F8] to reopen it.

6. Open index.htm, new_restaurants.htm, reviews.htm, and contact_us.htm from the lesson_05 folder.
These files do not contain internal styles.

7. Use the technique outlined in step 3 to individually link each file to the external style sheet.

8. Close the CSS Styles panel.

9. Save each file individually after linking it to the external style sheet.
Until you are more experienced with Dreamweaver, it is better to save files individually than using the Save All command.

10. Open most_popular.htm in your browser.

11. Follow the links on each page to make sure they work.

12. Close your browser. Return to the Document window, and then close all files.

Reading the Link Tag

In the last exercise, you linked several pages to an external CSS Style sheet. Each time you did this, the HTML <link> tag was added in Code view. Let's take a look at the code.

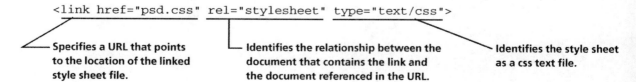

```
<link href="psd.css" rel="stylesheet" type="text/css">
```

Specifies a URL that points to the location of the linked style sheet file.

Identifies the relationship between the document that contains the link and the document referenced in the URL.

Identifies the style sheet as a css text file.

Concepts Review

True/False Questions

1. Links to pages within your site should use document relative paths. **TRUE   FALSE**

2. You can easily identify a document relative link because the file path always uses http and www. **TRUE   FALSE**

3. You can use Point to File or Browse for File to create an absolute link. **TRUE   FALSE**

4. Click Here is a perfect link name when you can't think of anything else to use. **TRUE   FALSE**

5. When the referring document and the destination document are in the same folder, only the destination document's filename is used in a relative link. **TRUE   FALSE**

6. Invisible elements can be shown or hidden. **TRUE   FALSE**

7. Href is the protocol used to access Web pages over the Internet. **TRUE   FALSE**

8. When creating a link to email, it's OK to leave a space after mailto: and the email address. **TRUE   FALSE**

9. Anchors and links can be used together to provide navigation to a specific location within the same page or to another page within your site. **TRUE   FALSE**

10. When you remove a link from a page, the link name is also removed. **TRUE   FALSE**

Multiple Choice Questions

1. Which of the following examples are relative paths?
   a. index.htm
   b. ../index.htm
   c. resources/index.htm
   d. All of the above

2. Which protocol is used to send and receive email?
   a. mailto
   b. http
   c. mailto:
   d. getmail:

3. Which of the following examples are absolute paths?
   a. http://www.yahoo.com
   b. /jewelry/ebay.com
   c. ../credit_cards/nordstrom.htm
   d. None of the above

4. An anchor is named "features". Which of the following link names can be used to link to the anchor in the same page?
   a. features
   b. /features
   c. #features
   d. ../features

 **Skill Builders**

Skill Builder 5.1   Create Links

In this exercise, you will add two missing links on the same page and then add a link to an email address.

1. Open toc_menus.htm from the review_05/menus folder.

2. Locate the text Home and Contact Us.
   Our goal is to link the toc_menus page to these two pages.

3. Select the text Home.

4. Click the Browse for File 🗁 icon on the Properties panel.
   This opens the Select File dialog box.

5. Select index.htm from the review_05 folder.

6. Select the text Contact Us.

7. Drag the Point to File 🎯 icon to contact_us.htm, which is also located in the review_05 folder.

8. In the copyright section at the bottom of the page, select the text Email our Staff.

9. Choose Insert→Email Link from the menu bar or click the Email button on the Common tab of the Insert bar.
   This opens the Email Link dialog box.

10. Type your email address in the E-Mail text box and click OK.

11. Save and close the file.

Skill Builder 5.2   Create and Link to a Named Anchor

In this exercise, you will insert a named anchor and then link to it.

1. Open stjames_menu.htm from the review_05/menus folder.

2. Place the insertion point at the top of the page.
   This is where you will insert a named anchor.

3. Choose Insert→Named Anchor from the menu bar or click the Named Anchor ⚓ button on the Common tab of the Insert bar.
   This opens the Named Anchor dialog box.

4. Use **top** as the anchor name and click OK.
   This inserts the named anchor symbol at the top of the page. If you do not see the symbol, choose View→Visual Aids. Make sure there is a checkmark next to Invisible Elements.

5. Scroll to the bottom of the page and select the purple graphic called "top".

6. Click the Link text field on the Properties panel and type **#top**.

7. Save the file, and then open it in your browser.

8. Test the new link to make sure it works.

9. Leave your browser open and return to the Document window.

10. Save and close the file.

Skill Builder 5.3   Link to a Style Sheet

In this exercise, you will attach a page to an external CSS style sheet.

1. Open jazz_clubs.htm from the review_05 folder.

2. Choose Text→CSS Styles→Manage Styles or click the Style menu on the Properties panel and choose Manage Styles.
   This opens the Edit Style Sheet dialog box. This is another way to attach a style sheet.

3. Click Attach.
   This opens the Attach External Style Sheet dialog box.

4. Click the Browse button and navigate to the review_05 folder.

5. Select psd.css from the list of files and then click OK (Win) or Choose (Mac).

6. Ensure that the option Add as Link is chosen in the Attach External Style Sheet dialog box.

7. Click OK, and then click Done.

8. Save and close the file.

 **Assessments**

Assessment 5.1 Add and Modify Links

In this exercise, you will add graphic and text links, set link color and underline style properties.

1. Open piano_bars.htm from the review_05 folder.
   The navigation section at the top of the page is missing links to the top-level pages in the site.

2. Follow these steps to add links to pages located in the review_05 folder:

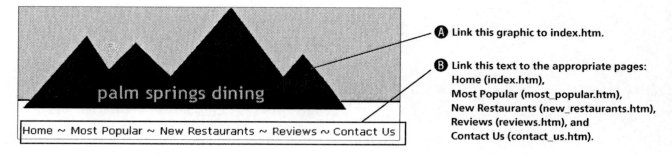

A Link this graphic to index.htm.

B Link this text to the appropriate pages:
Home (index.htm),
Most Popular (most_popular.htm),
New Restaurants (new_restaurants.htm),
Reviews (reviews.htm), and
Contact Us (contact_us.htm).

3. Remove the links to Frank Sinatra and Duke Ellington.

4. Set the link color and the text underline properties to your specifications.

5. Save the file but leave it open.

Assessment 5.2 Export and Remove CSS Styles

In this exercise, you will export styles, remove internal CSS styles, and link to an external style sheet.

Before you begin: The piano_bars.htm file should be open.

1. Export the CSS styles to the review_05 folder and name the CSS style sheet **piano_bars.css**.

2. Delete all of the internal styles.

3. Attach the file to the piano_bars.css file you created in step 1.

4. Save and close the file.

Assessment 5.3 Link to an Anchor on a Different Page

In this exercise, you will insert an anchor and link it to another page.

1. Open recipes.htm and toc_recipes.htm from the review_05/recipes folder.

2. Tile the windows vertically (Win) so that you can see the pages side-by-side or manually position the windows side-by-side (Mac).

3. Follow these guidelines to insert a named anchor in the recipes.htm file and a link to the anchor in the toc_recipes.htm file:

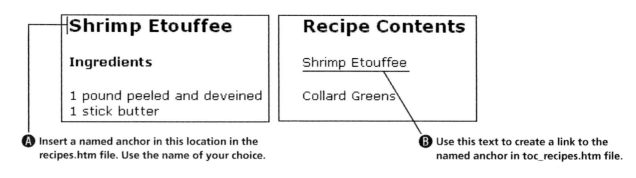

A Insert a named anchor in this location in the recipes.htm file. Use the name of your choice.

B Use this text to create a link to the named anchor in toc_recipes.htm file.

4. Choose File→Save All from the menu bar.

5. Open toc_recipes.htm in your browser and test the link to make sure it works.

6. Leave your browser open and return to the Document window.

7. Choose File→Close All from the menu bar.

# Critical Thinking

Critical Thinking 5.1   On Your Own

Justin and Janet are almost ready to make the Palm Springs Dining site available to the public. They understand that one of the fastest ways to drive people away from their site is to have links that don't work and pages that do not provide a way to get back to the previous page or to the homepage.

Your expertise in linking pages prompted Janet to give you the job of testing and completing the links on the site. In return, you get a free dinner for two at Le Vallauris, St. James at the Vineyard or The Falls Prime Steak House.

Follow these guidelines to complete this project:

- Open index.htm from the review_05 folder.

- Open the file in your browser and follow all of the linked pages.

- Make a written list of the pages that need to be linked to other pages and pages that need formatting.

- Use your list to add the links. You will fix the formatting problems in the next exercise.

Critical Thinking 5.2   On Your Own

Now that you have the links working, it's time to make the pages pretty. Follow these guidelines to delete internal styles and link to an external style sheet:

- Use the list you created in the last exercise to track down all of the pages that need formatting.

- Delete the internal styles in all pages that contain them.

- Link all of the unformatted pages to psd.css, which is located in the review_05 folder.

When you have finished, call Janet and tell her which restaurant you've chosen for dinner!

Critical Thinking 5.3   Web Research

There are numerous free clip art resources on the Web. Use your favorite browser and search engine to find clip art images that you can download legally and add to the images folder in the Palm Springs Dining site. Be forewarned that most free things on the Internet come with a price tag. For example, you may have to wade through numerous pop-up ads, blinking text, and flying objects before you find a resource you'd like to recommend to others.

Write down the URL of all acceptable sites and create short notes about what to expect to find on the site. When you have enough resources, use the following guidelines to add a new page to the Palm Springs Dining site:

- Save any page (except index.htm) in the review_05 folder as **resources.htm**.

- Change the heading on the page to **Clip Art Resources** or the text of your choice.

- Change the page title.

- Type a brief description of each site.

- Add a link to each site.

- Add a link in the contents area on the homepage (index.htm) to the Resources page.

- Target each link to a new browser window.

LESSON 6

Working with Site Management

It's show time! In this lesson, you will learn how to set up and transfer files to another location on your computer using local/network access. If you're ready to publish your site to a Web server using Dreamweaver's FTP feature, you'll learn how to do that too! You will also learn how to use Dreamweaver's site management features to help you update linked files when you move, rename, or delete them. You will also use the Link Checker to track down and fix broken links in your site and will then run Site Reports to help you make your site more accessible to people with physical disabilities.

Case Study

Janet is ready to upload the files for her Palm Springs Dining site to a remote location. Before making the site available to others, she spends time organizing files and folders, and deleting files she no longer needs. Janet understands that broken links will quickly drive away visitors, so she uses Dreamweaver's Link Checker to find and fix all broken links and then runs an HTML Site Report to locate untitled pages and images without alternative text.

The Link Checker tab on the Results panel...

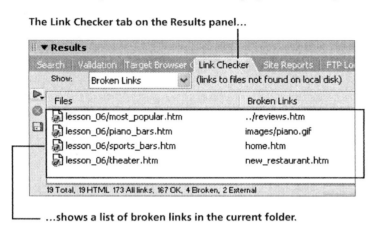

...shows a list of broken links in the current folder.

The Site Reports tab on the Results panel...

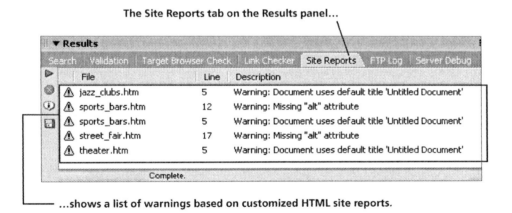

...shows a list of warnings based on customized HTML site reports.

When Janet is confident that the site is ready for prime time, she uses Dreamweaver's site management tools to set up a remote site and then transfers selected files and folders to the remote location. When Janet makes modifications to files in the local site, she uses the Synchronize Files feature to compare files between the local and remote sites to determine which site contains the most recent version of a file.

Setting Recommended Site Preferences

FROM THE KEYBOARD

To open the Preferences dialog box:

WIN ONLY
Ctrl + U

MAC ONLY
⌘ + U

Before continuing, you should review a few site preferences settings in the Files Panel to ensure that Dreamweaver is configured properly for this lesson and the remaining lessons in this book.

 Hands-On 6.1   Set Recommended Site Preferences

In this exercise, you will set site preferences for this and future lessons.

1. (Win) Choose Edit→Preferences from the menu bar. (Mac) Choose Dreamweaver→Preferences from the menu bar.

2. Follow these steps to set recommended site preferences:

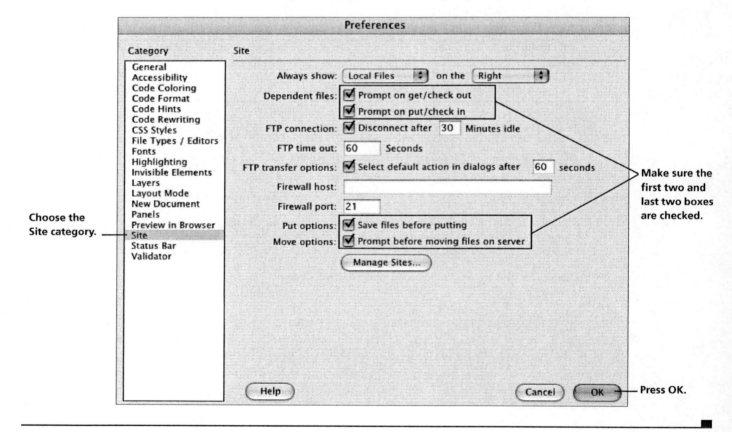

Choose the Site category.

Make sure the first two and last two boxes are checked.

Press OK.

Setting Up Remote Information for Local/Network Access

Normally you perform site management and maintenance tasks before transferring files to a remote location. Until you have a remote server to store your files, you can upload them to an alternate location to your file storage location. For this lesson, the alternative location will be referred to as the "remote site." To provide you with lots of hands-on practice, you'll upload files to the alternate location and then make changes to the original, local files. At the end of this lesson, you will learn how to keep the files on your alternate (remote) site synchronized with the files on your local site.

NOTE! *If you're ready to upload files to a server, see Appendix B on the Web page for this book for instructions on how to set up the remote information and how to use Dreamweaver's FTP feature.*

In Lesson 1, Getting Started you used the Basic tab of the Site Definition dialog box to set up a local site. To define a remote site, you begin from the Advanced tab, choosing an option from the Access pop-up menu to specify how you are going to connect to the remote location. In this lesson, we will use Local/Network access.

REMOTE INFO OPTION SETTINGS FOR LOCAL/NETWORK ACCESS

Setting	Description
Access	Choose Local/Network if you are accessing a network folder or if you are running a Web server on your local computer.
Remote Folder	Use the folder icon to browse to and select a remote root folder for your site.
Refresh Remote File List Automatically	For increased speed when copying files to the remote location, do NOT select this option.
Automatically Upload Files to Server on Save	Choosing this option will slow down the upload process when publishing files to a remote server and can result in incomplete Web pages. It's best to upload a page when you're finished with it, not each time you save it. Do NOT select this option.
Enable File Check In and Check Out	Do NOT select this option unless you are collaborating with a design team and all members are using Dreamweaver.

QUICK REFERENCE: SETTING UP REMOTE INFO FOR LOCAL/NETWORK ACCESS

Task	Procedure
Set up remote information for local/network access	■ Create a new folder in your file storage location. Use the name of your choosing.
	■ Choose Site→Manage Sites.
	■ Choose your local site name in the Manage Sites dialog box.
	■ Click Edit to open the Site Definition dialog box.
	■ Ensure that the Advanced tab is chosen.
	■ Ensure that the Remote Info category is chosen.
	■ Choose Local/Network from the Access pop-up menu.
	■ Click the Remote folder icon to locate and select the folder in your file storage location.
	■ Leave all checkboxes unchecked.

 Hands-On 6.2   Set Up Remote Info

In this exercise, you will set up remote info for local/network access using the location of your choosing on your local storage device.

1. Use Windows Explorer or Macintosh Finder to create a new folder named **unit1_remote** in your file storage location.

2. Launch Dreamweaver and ensure that the unit1 local site is open in the Files Panel Local view.

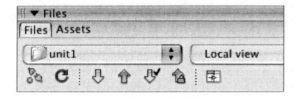

3. Choose Site→Manage Sites from the menu bar.
   This opens the Manage Sites dialog box.

4. Choose unit1 and click Edit.
   This opens the Site Definition dialog box for the current site.

5. Choose the Advanced tab (Win) or click the Advanced button (Mac).

6. Follow these steps to set up a remote location:

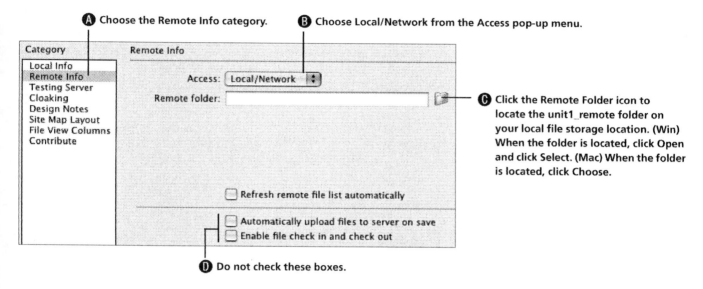

Ⓐ Choose the Remote Info category.

Ⓑ Choose Local/Network from the Access pop-up menu.

Ⓒ Click the Remote Folder icon to locate the unit1_remote folder on your local file storage location. (Win) When the folder is located, click Open and click Select. (Mac) When the folder is located, click Choose.

Ⓓ Do not check these boxes.

7. Click OK to close the Site Definition box.

8. Click Done to close the Manage Sites dialog box.

Uploading Files to a Remote Location

Now that you have a remote storage location, you are ready to upload files. Dreamweaver allows you to pick and choose just the files and folders you want to upload. If you're ready to go live with your own site, you can select the local root folder and upload the entire site. For simplicity, we're going to upload only the lesson_06 folder and the dependent files.

Dependent Files

Dependent files are those referenced in an HTML document that browsers need when loading pages. Some examples of dependent files are images and external style sheets. The dependent files feature uploads only the images used in files you're uploading and puts them in a separate images folder.

Remote Location Uploading

To upload files to and download files from a remote location, you use the Get and Put files buttons on the Files panel.

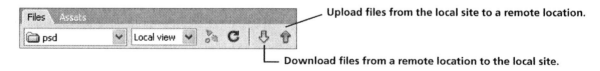

Upload files from the local site to a remote location.

Download files from a remote location to the local site.

Hands-On 6.3 **Upload Files to a Remote Location**

In this exercise, you will upload the lesson_06 folder and its dependent files.

1. Select the lesson_06 folder in the Files panel.

2. Click the Put File(s) ⬆ button on the Files panel.
   This opens the Dependent Files dialog box.

3. Click Yes.
   After a brief status message appears, a copy of all of the files and folders in the lesson_06 folder are uploaded to the remote location on your computer.

Modifying Linked Files

Performing routine daily tasks such as moving, renaming, and deleting files is about as much fun as cleaning house—and the result is pretty much the same. You feel so much better afterward, and you can probably find things faster.

Moving and Renaming Linked Files

When you move or rename a linked file, the Update Files dialog box shows you a list of all links that will be updated; it doesn't, however, give you a chance to cancel the operation so you must choose Update or Don't Update.

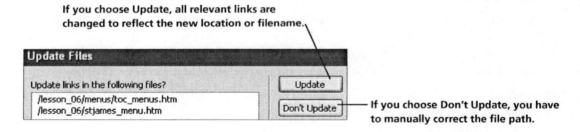

If you choose Update, all relevant links are changed to reflect the new location or filename.

If you choose Don't Update, you have to manually correct the file path.

Deleting a Linked File

Keeping the files in your site tidy and compact will make maintenance much easier as your site gets larger. You should delete files you aren't using or move them to a location outside of Dreamweaver. When you delete a linked file, the following warning appears.

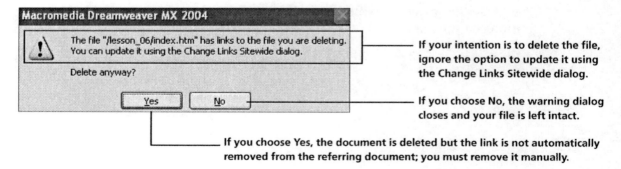

If your intention is to delete the file, ignore the option to update it using the Change Links Sitewide dialog.

If you choose No, the warning dialog closes and your file is left intact.

If you choose Yes, the document is deleted but the link is not automatically removed from the referring document; you must remove it manually.

Hands-On 6.4   Move, Rename, and Delete Linked Files

In this exercise, you will practice using the Files panel to move, rename, and delete linked files. First, you will ensure that a general preference you set in Lesson 1, Getting Started is still in place.

Check General Preferences

1. (Win) Choose Edit→Preferences. (Mac) Choose Dreamweaver Preferences from the menu bar.

2. In the General category, ensure that Prompt is chosen in the menu next to Update links when moving files. Click OK.
   This option gives you an opportunity to see the links that will be updated when you move a linked file.

Move a Linked File

3. In the Files panel, ensure that the lesson_06 folder is expanded.

4. Observe that the lesson_06 folder contains a series of HTML files and two subfolders.

5. In the lesson_06 folder, drag and drop the file stjames_menu.htm into the menus subfolder.
   The Update Files dialog box shows the links that will update.

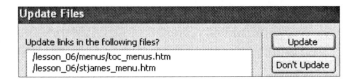

6. Click Update.
   The links in stjames_menu.htm and toc_menus.htm update to reflect the new file path.

Rename a Linked File

7. In the lesson_06/menus folder, rename menu_falls.htm to **falls_menu.htm**.
   The Update Files dialog box shows the link that will update.

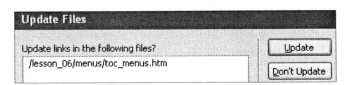

8. Click Update.
   The link in toc_menus.htm updates to reflect the new filename.

Delete a Linked File

9. In the lesson_06 folder, select coffee_houses.htm and press ⌈Delete⌋.
   A warning message shows the name of the file that has links to the file you are deleting.

The file "/lesson_06/index.htm" has links to the file you are deleting.
You can update it using the Change Links Sitewide dialog.

Delete anyway?

10. Click Yes.

The file is deleted, resulting in a broken link in index.htm. You will find and fix the broken link later.

11. Click once on the lesson_06 folder and press the Refresh **C** button or [F5].

This Refresh button prompts Dreamweaver to recheck the list of files.

⚠️**WARNING!** *Always refresh the Files panel after modifying linked files. Failing to do this can result in erroneous results when you check for broken links.*

──

Performing Routine Site Maintenance

FROM THE KEYBOARD
To open the Results panel group:
WIN AND MAC
[F7]

Publishing a page to your site that contains spelling and grammatical errors is embarrassing but publishing pages with broken links, untitled pages, and no alternative text for images can be extremely frustrating. Dreamweaver provides all the tools you need to find and fix potential problems in your site.

FROM THE KEYBOARD
To open the Link Checker tab on the Results panel group:
WIN AND MAC
[Shift]+[F8]

Using the Link Checker

Dreamweaver's Link Checker can help you track down broken links in your entire site, in the current document, or in selected files and folders. There are a number of ways to use the Link Checker. The approach we use here is to choose Window→Results to open the Results panel group and choose the Link Checker tab.

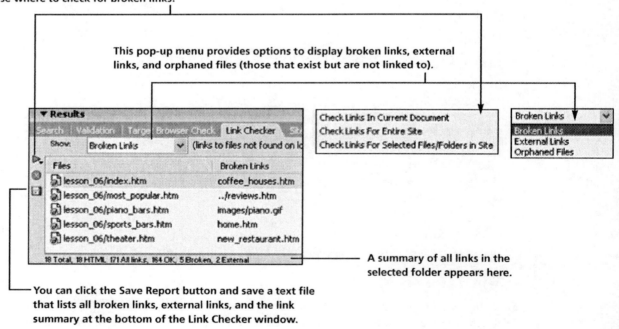

This tiny arrow opens a pop-up menu for you to choose where to check for broken links.

This pop-up menu provides options to display broken links, external links, and orphaned files (those that exist but are not linked to).

A summary of all links in the selected folder appears here.

You can click the Save Report button and save a text file that lists all broken links, external links, and the link summary at the bottom of the Link Checker window.

The only links that Dreamweaver verifies are links to documents within your site (relative links). Dreamweaver compiles a list of external links (absolute links) that appear in the selected document or documents, but does not verify them.

NOTE! *Dreamweaver uses the term "link" to refer to a linked document and the paths to dependent external files, such as images, CSS style sheets, and Flash movies. For example, if a graphic is missing or in the wrong location, it will be reported as a broken link.*

Hands-On 6.5   Find Broken Links

In this exercise, you will use the Link Checker to find broken links in the lesson_06 folder. You will also save a report that lists all broken links and the number of external links and their location in the site.

1. In the Files panel, click once on the lesson_06 folder to select it.

2. Choose Window→Results or press F7.
   This opens the Results panel group.

3. Follow these steps to find broken links in the selected folder:

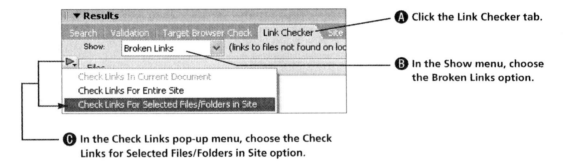

A Click the Link Checker tab.

B In the Show menu, choose the Broken Links option.

C In the Check Links pop-up menu, choose the Check Links for Selected Files/Folders in Site option.

4. Follow these steps to observe the broken links and to save a report:

A Click the Save Report button and save the file as **broken_links.txt** in the lesson_06 folder.

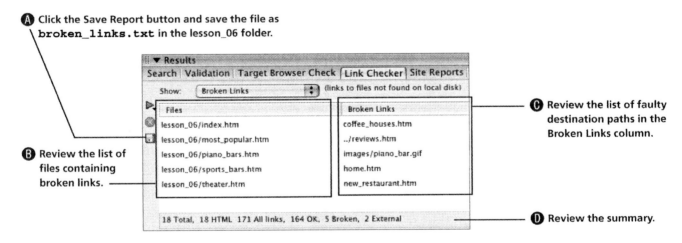

B Review the list of files containing broken links.

C Review the list of faulty destination paths in the Broken Links column.

D Review the summary.

5. Leave the Link Checker open.

The Link Checker Report

The link checker report is a text file that provides details on broken and external links. This report can be a useful reference if you don't have time to fix the broken links right away or to hand off to someone else to troubleshoot.

Fixing Broken Links

The Link Checker provides several ways to fix broken links:

Click a broken link and you have the option of typing in the correct link or browsing to locate the filename. Remember, incorrectly typing the path will create another error.

Double-click the filename, and the page will open with the link highlighted.

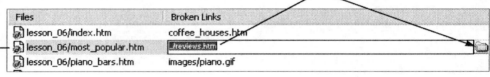

Files	Broken Links
lesson_06/index.htm	coffee_houses.htm
lesson_06/most_popular.htm	./reviews.htm
lesson_06/piano_bars.htm	images/piano.gif

QUICK REFERENCE: FINDING AND FIXING BROKEN LINKS

Task	Procedure
Check links within the current document	■ Open the file you want to check. ■ Choose File→Check Page→Check Links. ■ The Broken Links results appear in the Link Checker panel of the Results panel group.
Check links within a portion of a local site	■ Select the files or folders to check. ■ Click the green arrow on the Results panel and choose Check Links for selected files/folders in site from the pop-up menu.
Check links in the entire site	■ Click the green arrow on the Results panel and choose Check Links for entire site.

 Hands-On 6.6   Fix Broken Links

In this exercise, you will fix two broken links. You will leave the other broken links as they are, then fix them in the Concepts Review section at the end of this lesson.

Before you begin: Be sure the broken links still appear in the Link Checker window of the Results panel group.

1. In the Link Checker window, double-click the lesson_06/index.htm file.
   This opens the homepage in Design view and the broken Coffee Houses link is highlighted. If necessary, move the Results panel to the right in order to see the highlighted text.

2. Ensure that the link is selected and tap Delete to remove the text and the link.
   You are removing the link because you deleted the file earlier.

3. Double-click the lesson_06/most_popular.htm file.
   This opens the Most Popular page in Design view and the broken Reviews link is highlighted at the top of the page. Do NOT deselect the text link.

4. Observe the path to the file in the Link text field on the Properties panel.
   The two files are in the same folder so the ../ is not used.

5. Drag the Point to File icon on the Properties panel to reviews.htm in the lesson_06 folder in the Files panel.
   This fixes the broken link.

6. Choose File→Save All from the menu bar.
   The filenames are removed from the broken link list.

7. Close the Results panel group.

8. Choose File→Close All from the menu bar.

Running Reports

Dreamweaver's site reporting feature helps you identify HTML problems, such as untitled documents, missing alternative text for images, and problems that might make your pages less accessible to users with visual impairments. You can run site reports for the current document, selected files, or the entire site.

TIP! *Unlike broken links, which are actually non-functional, Site Reports show warnings only. However, you should heed the warnings and correct the potential problems.*

To run a Site Report, choose Site→Reports from the menu bar to open the Reports dialog box.

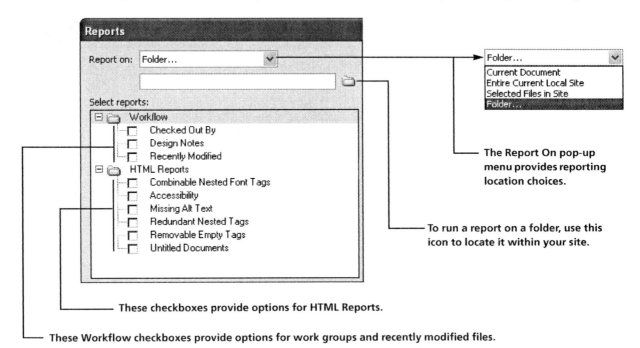

The Report On pop-up menu provides reporting location choices.

To run a report on a folder, use this icon to locate it within your site.

These checkboxes provide options for HTML Reports.

These Workflow checkboxes provide options for work groups and recently modified files.

When you run a report, the results are displayed in the Site Reports tab on the Results panel group.

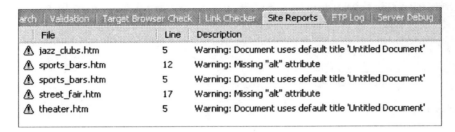

 Hands-On 6.7   Run a Site Report

In this exercise, you will run a site report to locate missing alternative text (for images) and untitled documents. Later you will learn how to fix these warnings.

1. Choose Site→Reports.
   This opens the Reports dialog box.

2. Follow these steps to setup an HTML report:

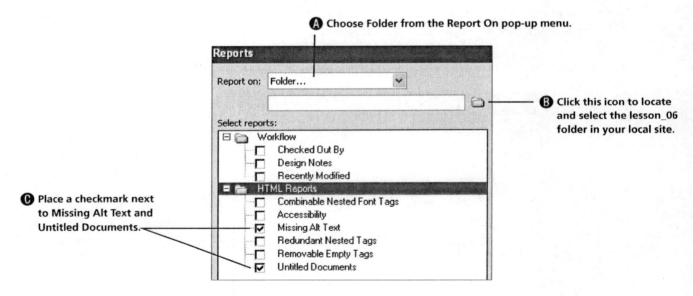

Ⓐ Choose Folder from the Report On pop-up menu.

Ⓑ Click this icon to locate and select the lesson_06 folder in your local site.

Ⓒ Place a checkmark next to Missing Alt Text and Untitled Documents.

3. Click Run.
   The results are shown in the Site Reports tab on the Results panel group.

4. Keep the report open.

Fixing Warnings in Site Reports

The Site Reports tab on the Results panel group provides all the information you need to locate and fix warnings.

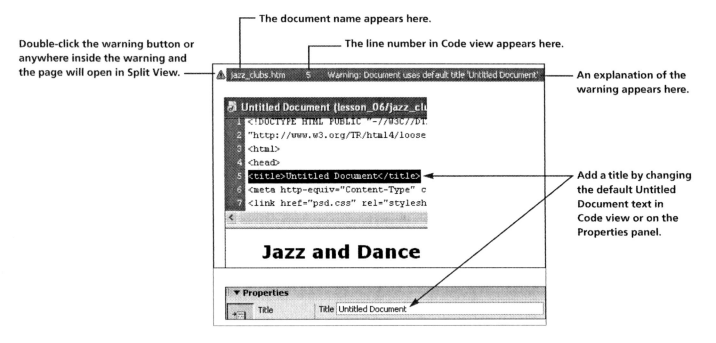

Double-click the warning button or anywhere inside the warning and the page will open in Split View.

The document name appears here.

The line number in Code view appears here.

An explanation of the warning appears here.

Add a title by changing the default Untitled Document text in Code view or on the Properties panel.

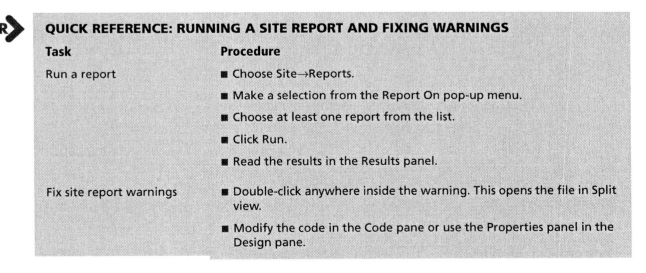

QUICK REFERENCE: RUNNING A SITE REPORT AND FIXING WARNINGS

Task	Procedure
Run a report	■ Choose Site→Reports.
	■ Make a selection from the Report On pop-up menu.
	■ Choose at least one report from the list.
	■ Click Run.
	■ Read the results in the Results panel.
Fix site report warnings	■ Double-click anywhere inside the warning. This opens the file in Split view.
	■ Modify the code in the Code pane or use the Properties panel in the Design pane.

Hands-On 6.8   Fix Warnings

In this exercise, you will fix two warnings shown in the Site Report.

Fix an Untitled Document Warning

1. Follow these steps to locate the warning on the Jazz Clubs page:

A Ensure that the Site Reports tab is chosen.

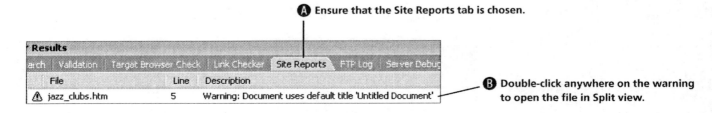

B Double-click anywhere on the warning to open the file in Split view.

2. Follow these steps to fix the warning:

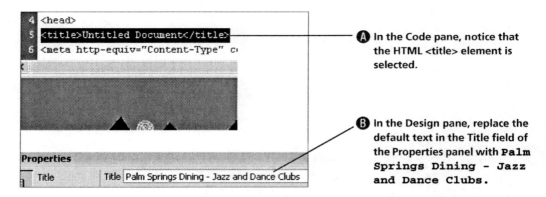

A In the Code pane, notice that the HTML <title> element is selected.

B In the Design pane, replace the default text in the Title field of the Properties panel with **Palm Springs Dining - Jazz and Dance Clubs.**

3. Click the Design View button.
   The new page title appears in the Title text field on the Document toolbar.

4. Save and close the file.
   The warning is not removed from the Site Reports list until you run another report.

Fix a Missing "Alt" Attribute Warning

5. Double-click anywhere on the second warning to open sports_bars.htm in Split view.
   The HTML image tag is selected in the Code pane and the image is selected in the Design pane.

6. Click the Alt menu on the Properties panel, type **Palm Springs Dining logo,** and then press ⌈Enter⌋ or ⌈Return⌋.
   The alt attribute is added to the image tag in Code view.

7. Click the Design view button.

8. Save and close the file.

9. Close the Results panel group.

Synchronizing Local and Remote Files

When you're developing your site, managing a large number of files may be one of your greatest challenges, especially if more than one person is working on the site. A question that you'll probably ask yourself many times is, "Where is the most recent file?" Fortunately, you can use Dreamweaver's Synchronize Files feature to compare files between the local and remote site to determine which site contains the most recent version of a file. If the latest version is on the local site, Dreamweaver will upload that file to the remote site.

If you were to upload the lesson_06 files to your remote location without synchronizing them the file you deleted and the file you renamed in the beginning of this lesson would remain on your remote site.

 TIP! *Removing unused and out of date files on your remote site makes your site much easier to maintain.*

File synchronization can also delete files on either the local or remote site if the file doesn't appear in both versions of the site. You can apply the synchronize command to selected files and folders or apply it to the entire site.

SITE SYNCHRONIZE DIALOG BOX OPTIONS

Option	Description
Synchronize	Entire Site—Synchronize all of the files in the entire site
	Selected Files Only—Synchronize only selected files and/or folders
Put Newer Files to Remote	This option uploads all local files that have more recent modification dates than their remote counterparts.
Get Newer Files from Remote	This option downloads all remote files that have more recent modification dates than their local counterparts.
Get and Put Newer Files	This option places the most recent versions of all files on both the local and the remote sites.
Delete remote files not on local drive	This option deletes all of remote files that are no longer a part of the local site.

 WARNING! *Choose the option to delete remote files not on your local drive with great caution. This action cannot be undone.*

 Hands-On 6.9   Synchronize Local and Remote Files

In this exercise you will synchronize the files in the lesson_06 folder.

1. In the Files panel, right-click or control-click the lesson_06 folder and choose Synchronize from the context menu.
    This opens the Synchronize Files dialog box.

2. Follow these steps to synchronize the local and remote files:

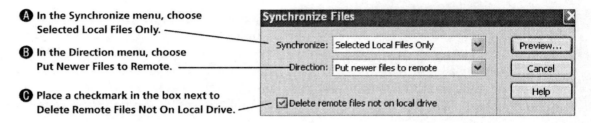

Ⓐ In the Synchronize menu, choose Selected Local Files Only.

Ⓑ In the Direction menu, choose Put Newer Files to Remote.

Ⓒ Place a checkmark in the box next to Delete Remote Files Not On Local Drive.

3. Click Preview.

A summary of files to be deleted and updated appear in the Preview window.

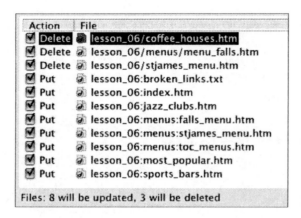

4. Click OK.

Dreamweaver displays a prompt that asks if you really want to delete the selected file(s).

5. Click Yes.

Three files are deleted and eight files are updated.

6. The Synchronization status dialog box opens.

The Save Log option allows you to save the verification information as a text file in your local site. You might want to do this if you are working with a team or if you want to keep track of updated and/or deleted files.

7. Click Close.

Concepts Review

True/False Questions

1. Dependent files aren't considered links so they cannot be located and fixed with the Link Checker.   TRUE   FALSE

2. A remote site can be created in your file storage location, network drive, or Web server.   TRUE   FALSE

3. You use the Put Files button to upload files to the remote location.   TRUE   FALSE

4. The Link Checker report is a text file that provides details on broken external links.   TRUE   FALSE

5. The Link Checker can find and fix broken links in your entire site, the current document, or selected files and folders.   TRUE   FALSE

6. You should leave a few broken links on your site to challenge visitors.   TRUE   FALSE

7. The most efficient way to fix a broken link is to click the broken link name in the Link Checker and type a new path name.   TRUE   FALSE

8. When you delete a linked page, the link in the referring document is automatically removed.   TRUE   FALSE

9. The Synchronize Files feature compares files between the local and remote site to determine which site contains the most recent version of a file.   TRUE   FALSE

10. You should delete or move files you are not using to a location outside of Dreamweaver.   TRUE   FALSE

Multiple Choice Questions

1. What should you do after deleting linked files?
   a. Create a new link.
   b. Close the Files panel.
   c. Click the Refresh button on the Files panel.
   d. Close the Link Checker.

2. You can open the Link Checker by _____.
   a. Tapping [F7] and clicking the Link Checker tab
   b. Choosing Window→Results and clicking the Link Checker tab
   c. Opening a page and pressing [Shift]+[F8] to go directly to the Link Checker tab
   d. All of the above

3. Which of the following examples are dependent files?
   a. Graphics
   b. Linked style sheets
   c. HTML files
   d. Both a and b

4. Which of the following statements best describe a few of the Link Checker's capabilities?
   a. Verifying that all external links work
   b. Verifying that all external and internal links work
   c. Verifying that all internal links work
   d. Both b and c

 # Skill Builders

Skill Builder 6.1   Fix Broken Links and Run a Report

In this exercise, you will perform all of the necessary steps to find and fix broken links, missing Alt text, and untitled documents. You will also synchronize files in the remote location.

1. Open index.htm from the review_06 folder.

2. Choose Window→Results or tap [F7] to open the Results panel.

Find Broken Links

3. Follow these steps to find broken links:

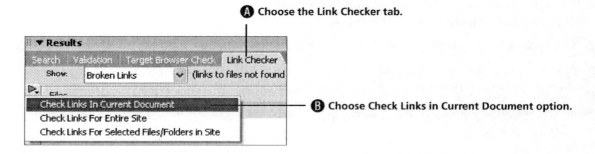

Ⓐ Choose the Link Checker tab.

Ⓑ Choose Check Links in Current Document option.

4. Observe the broken links in the document.
   There are two broken links.

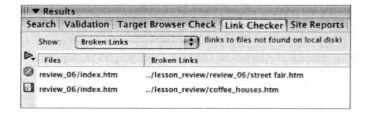

Fix Broken Links

5. Click once on the first broken link in the Broken Links column.
   This highlights the broken link, and a folder icon appears to the right of the broken link text.

6. Click the folder icon.
   This opens the Select File dialog box.

7. Use the Select File dialog box to locate and select street_fair.htm from the list of files in the review_06 folder, and then click OK or Choose.

8. Click anywhere in the white space below the remaining broken link.
   This updates the Link Checker and the broken link to the Street Fair file is removed.

9. Repeat steps 5 and 6.

10. Use the Select File dialog box to locate and select coffee_houses.htm from the list of files in the review_06 folder, and then click OK or Choose.

11. Click anywhere in the white space below the broken link.
This updates the Link Checker and the broken link to the Coffee Houses file is removed.

12. Close the Results panel.

13. Save the file but keep it open.

Run a Report on Selected Files

14. Choose Site→Reports.
This opens the Reports dialog box.

15. Follow these steps to run a report:

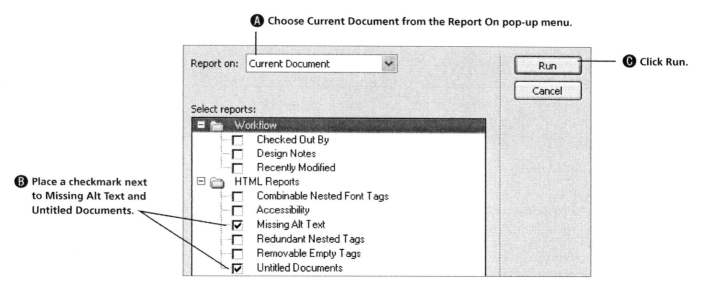

16. Observe the warnings.
There are two warnings in the current document.

Fix the Warnings

17. Double-click on the first warning.
    This opens the page in Split view. The selected image is missing the Alt attribute.

18. Click the Alt text field on the Properties panel, type **Palm Springs Dining logo**, and then press [Enter] or [Return].
    The filename remains in the Site Report list until you save the file and run another report.

19. Double-click on the second warning.
    This opens the page in Split view. The page uses the default title Untitled Document.

20. Select the Title text field on the Properties panel, type **Palm Springs Dining – Weekly Dining Guide**, and then press [Enter] or [Return].
    This replaces the default title with a title that describes the page contents.

21. Close the Results panel.

22. Click the Design button to return to Design view.

23. Save and close the file.

Skill Builder 6.2 Synchronize Local and Remote Files

In this exercise, you will use file synchronization to compare files on your local site with the files on your remote site. Then, you will upload the files you modified in the last exercise.

1. Right-click or control-click the review_06 folder and select Synchronize.
   This opens the Synchronize dialog box.

2. Follow these steps to synchronize the local and remote files:

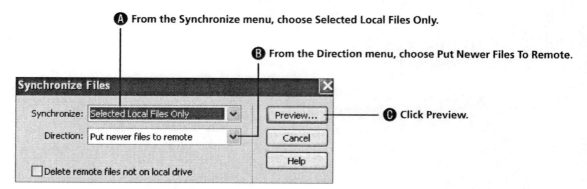

A From the Synchronize menu, choose Selected Local Files Only.

B From the Direction menu, choose Put Newer Files To Remote.

C Click Preview.

3. Preview the files to be processed.

Action	File
☑ **Put**	review_06:broken_links.txt
☑ Put	review_06:coffee_houses.htm
☑ Put	review_06:contact_us.htm
☑ Put	review_06:error.htm
☑ Put	review_06:falls_cellar.htm
☑ Put	review_06:falls_menu.htm
☑ Put	review_06:index.htm
☑ Put	review_06:jazz_clubs.htm
☑ Put	review_06:menus
☑ Put	review_06:menus:stjames_menu.htm
☑ Put	review_06:menus:toc_menus.htm
☑ Put	review_06:most_popular.htm
☑ Put	review_06:new_restaurants.htm
☑ Put	review_06:piano_bars.htm
☑ Put	review_06:psd.css
☑ Put	review_06:recipes
☑ Put	review_06:recipes:recipes.htm
☑ Put	review_06:recipes:toc_recipes.htm
☑ Put	review_06:reviews.htm
☑ Put	review_06:sports_bars.htm
☑ Put	review_06:street_fair.htm
☑ Put	review_06:theater.htm

Files: 22 will be updated

4. Click OK.
The files are updated in the remote location and the Synchronization log dialog box opens.

5. Click Close.

 **Assessments**

Assessment 6.1   Fix Links, Run a Report, and Synchronize Files

In this exercise, you will perform basic site maintenance tasks such as finding and fixing broken links, running a report, and synchronizing files.

Find Broken Links

1. Open recipes.htm from the review_06/recipes folder.

2. Use the Link Checker to check for broken links in the current document.
   You should find two broken links.

3. Fix the broken links.

4. Save the file, and then run the Link Checker again to make sure the broken links are fixed.

Run a Report

5. Run a report on the recipes.htm file to locate missing Alt attributes and untitled documents.

6. Fix the warnings.

7. Run the same report again to make sure the warnings are fixed.

8. Save and close the file.

Assessment 6.2   Synchronize Local and Remote Files

In this exercise, you will synchronize local files and remote files.

1. Synchronize the files in the review_06 folder.

2. Preview the files to be updated on the remote site.
   There are still broken links in the review_06 folder. You will find and fix all of these links next.

Critical Thinking

Critical Thinking 6.1   On Your Own

Janet and Justin have found and fixed several broken links and warnings on the Palm Springs Dining site, but they need to devote more time plotting their strategy to enhance the site and spend less time performing management and maintenance chores. They've asked you to assume the responsibility of modifying local files, checking for broken links, and running reports before uploading files to the remote location.

Follow these guidelines to prepare the review_06 files for publication to the remote location:

- Delete jazz_clubs.htm from the review_06 folder.

- Move falls_cellar.htm and falls_menu.htm into the menus folder and update the links.

- Run the Link Checker to find all broken links in the review_06 folder.

- Fix all of the broken links.

- Run a report on the review_06 folder to find missing Alt text and untitled documents.

- Fix all of the warnings in the report.

Critical Thinking 6.2   On Your Own

In the last exercise, you made modifications to several files in the review_06 folder. Follow these guidelines to ensure that the local files and the remote files are synchronized:

- Synchronize the review_06 folder.

- Update and delete files that should no longer be on the remote site.

- Take the rest of the day off!

Unit 2

Beyond the Basics

The capabilities of Dreamweaver MX 2004 far exceed the basics of plain HTML Web pages, allowing you to design data tables and page layout tables. In this unit, you will learn how to import, sort, and export data; to insert and modify tables; to insert images into table cells; and to design page layouts for different window sizes. You will also learn how to use Cascading Style Sheets (CSS) to format your pages, design frames to display three or more pages in separate windows, and use features such as templates, library items, and snippets to help dramatically reduce your production time.

Lesson 7: Working with Data Tables

Lesson 8: Working with Page Layout Tables

Lesson 9: Working with Styles

Lesson 10: Working with Frames

Lesson 11: Working with Automation Tools

Working with Data Tables

In this lesson, you will learn how to create and modify tables, copy and paste table cells, and set table, row, and cell properties. You will also learn how to import tabular data from an Excel spreadsheet, sort a table, and export tabular data as a text file. Doubtless, you already appreciate that tables are useful for organizing information. You will be happy to know that not only can you build tables in Dreamweaver, but you may also populate them with data imported from a spreadsheet program. What you may not appreciate is that

tables are an indispensable tool for designing Web pages. Tables are used to define the layout of a page—to control where on the page text and graphics fall. Understanding how to create and arrange the cells of a table and change the table's dimensions to suit your content and design is a skill you'll absolutely need to have in your Web design toolbox.

Case Study

Dixie Miller is a liberal arts major at College of the Desert. Her expertise in Dreamweaver has landed her a job with the Palm Springs Dining Web development team. She is responsible for maintaining the Editor's Choice Nominees page, which has a data table. Dixie keeps the data in an Excel spreadsheet because the data is needed in other applications. She saves the spreadsheet as a tab-delimited text file and then imports it into Dreamweaver, where she formats, sorts, and displays the new nominees in a well-organized table on the Palm Springs Dining site.

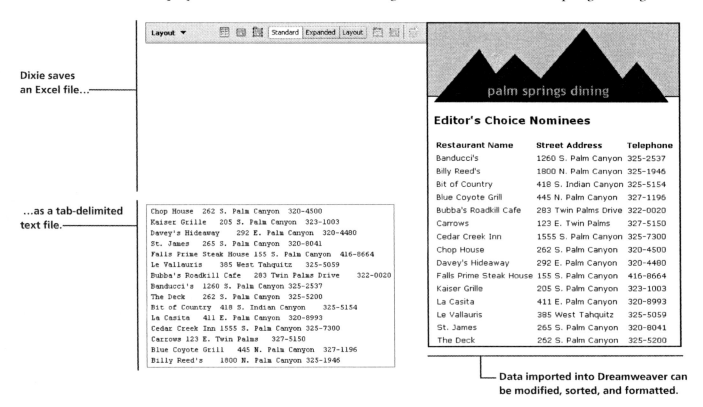

Dixie saves an Excel file...

...as a tab-delimited text file.

Data imported into Dreamweaver can be modified, sorted, and formatted.

Getting Started with Tables

This lesson explores data tables and provides lots of hands-on exercises to show you how tables work. Nailing down these skills will prepare you for using tables for page layout in Lesson 8, Working with Page Layout Tables.

Data Tables

Data tables are similar to simple spreadsheets (databases). A table is a grid of rows and columns that intersect to form cells. In the following illustration, the first row is formatted with a table header tag <th> to make the column headings stand out.

Restaurant Name	Street Address	Telephone
Banducci's	1260 S. Palm Canyon	325-2537
Billy Reed's	1800 N. Palm Canyon	325-1946
Bit of Country	418 S. Indian Canyon	325-5154
Blue Coyote Grill	445 N. Palm Canyon	327-1196
Bubba's Roadkill Cafe	283 Twin Palms Drive	322-0020
Carrows	123 E. Twin Palms	327-5150
Cedar Creek Inn	1555 S. Palm Canyon	325-7300

Tools for Creating Tables

Dreamweaver provides three viewing modes: Layout, Standard, and Expanded Tables mode. You select the viewing mode on the Layout category of the Insert bar. In Layout mode, you use cells and tables to format your page before adding content. In Standard mode, you insert a table and specify the number of rows and columns. Then, you add text and images to table cells the same way you add these elements outside of a table. This is the approach we will use in this lesson. Expanded Tables mode will be explained in Lesson 8, Working with Page Layout Tables.

The Layout Category of the Insert Bar

⚠️ **NOTE!** *The Insert bar will be dimmed (not available) until a document is open in the Document window.*

FROM THE KEYBOARD

To display the Insert bar:

WIN ONLY
[Ctrl]+[F2]

MAC ONLY
[⌘]+[F2]

The Layout category of the Insert bar provides options for inserting a table in Standard and Expanded Tables modes, and for drawing tables and table cells in Layout mode.

The Layout category is chosen.

The Table button is used to insert a table.

The Standard mode is chosen.

The Tabular Data button is used to import table data.

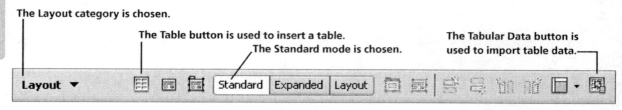

When you insert a table, Dreamweaver opens the Insert Table dialog box, which is divided into three sections: Table Size, Header, and Accessibility. The following table describes the various table dialog box settings.

TABLE DIALOG BOX SETTINGS

Setting	Option	Description
Table Size	Rows	Determines the number of rows to add to the table
	Columns	Determines the number of columns to add to the table
	Table Width	Specifies the width of the table in pixels or as a percentage of the browser window's width
	Border Thickness	Specifies the width, in pixels, of the table's border
	Cell Padding	Determines the number of pixels between a cell's border and its contents
	Cell Spacing	Determines the number of pixels between adjacent table cells
Header	None	Does not enable column or row headings for the table
	Left	Makes the first column of the table a column for headings so that you can enter a heading for each *row* of the table
	Top	Makes the first row of the table a row for headings so that you can enter a heading for each *column* of the table
	Both	Enables you to enter column and row headings in the table
Accessibility	Caption	Provides a table title that displays outside of the table
	Align Caption	Specifies where the table caption appears in relation to the table
	Summary	Provides a table description (speech-based browsers read the summary text)

Visual Aids for Tables

Dreamweaver provides two visual aids for working with tables: table widths and table borders. Both of these visual aids are on by default.

Visual Aids for Table Widths

The first thing you will notice when working with tables is the table widths visual aid, which shows a light gray horizontal bar across the top or bottom of a selected table. The location of the visual aid depends on the location of the table. To show or hide table widths visual aids, choose View→Visual Aids→Table Widths.

In the following illustration, the number 300 represents the width of the table in pixels. Clicking the tiny triangle next to the table size opens a menu that provides options for working with the table.

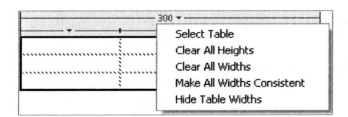

In the following illustration, you see three triangles that appear above each column. Clicking any of these triangles opens a menu that provides options for working with columns.

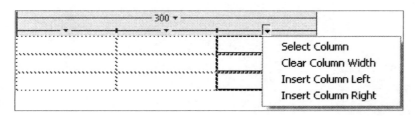

Visual Aids for Table Borders

The table borders visual aid is used to display gridlines that show the boundaries of table cells. (This visual aid will not hide a border that you've set with the Properties panel.) To show or hide table borders, choose View→Visual Aids→Table Borders.

This illustration shows the default gridlines that surround each table cell.

Restaurant Name	Street Address
Banducci's	1260 S. Palm Canyon
Billy Reed's	1800 N. Palm Canyon
Bit of Country	418 S. Indian Canyon

This illustration shows the table borders visual aid turned off so you can see how the table will appear in a Web browser.

Restaurant Name	Street Address
Banducci's	1260 S. Palm Canyon
Billy Reed's	1800 N. Palm Canyon
Bit of Country	418 S. Indian Canyon

 NOTE! *The more familiar you become with tables, the more likely you are to rely on table widths visual aids. Feel free to turn them on or off. However, note that you cannot modify a table with the table border visual aid turned off.*

Inserting a Table

Perhaps the best way to get started with tables is to insert one in a Web page and explore its architecture. We will begin by choosing the Layout category on the Insert bar.

 Hands-On 7.1   Insert a Table

In this exercise, you will insert a table and set basic table properties. Then you will view the HTML table code in Code view.

1. Make sure the Document toolbar is displayed. If you do not see it, choose View→Toolbars→Document from the menu bar.

2. Choose View→Visual Aids and ensure that a checkmark appears next to Table Borders.

3. Open editors_choice.htm from the lesson_07 folder.

4. Place the insertion point directly below the Editor's Choice Nominees text.

5. On the Insert bar, choose the Layout category.

6. Choose the Standard mode.

Insert a Table and Set Table Size Properties

7. Click the Table button on the Insert bar or choose Insert→Table from the menu bar. *This opens the Table dialog box.*

8. Choose the settings shown in the following illustration:

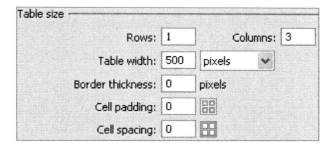

You will set the border thickness, cell padding, and cell spacing properties later.

9. Click OK.
   A one-row, three-column (1 × 3) table is inserted on the page. Do NOT deselect the table.

Switch to Code View

10. Click the Code view button on the Document toolbar.
Review the HTML tags and the   entity in each table cell. An explanation follows.

11. Save the file and keep it open. Remain in Code view.

■

The HTML Table Tags

When you inserted a table in the last exercise, Dreamweaver added the following HTML tags in code view:

The <table> tag contains the properties set in the Table dialog box.

The table row <tr> tag starts a new table row.

Table content is housed inside individual table data <td> cells. The entity   is a non-breaking space.

```
<table width="500" border="0" cellspacing="0" cellpadding="0">
   <tr>
      <td> </td>
      <td> </td>
      <td> </td>
   </tr>
</table>
```

 TIP! *You will find it helpful to commit these table tags to memory.*

Non-Breaking Spaces

A non-breaking space is a single space produced by the   character entity. Non-breaking spaces are used to prevent browsers from collapsing empty table cells. Dreamweaver automatically removes non-breaking spaces when content is inserted into a table cell.

 TIP! *You first learned about character entities in the Inserting Special Characters section of Lesson 3 (page 74).*

Populating a Table

You can populate (fill) a table by typing text, inserting graphics, copying and pasting cells from other tables, and even inserting a table within a table. Typing text inside table cells is similar to entering data into a spreadsheet program (like Microsoft® Excel) or into tables produced by a word processing program (like Microsoft Word).

 QUICK REFERENCE: INSERTING A TABLE

Task	Procedure
Insert a table	■ Place the insertion point where you want to insert a table and choose Insert→Table or press the Table button on the Insert bar (Layout category).
	■ Set the desired Table dialog box options.

 **Hands-On 7.2**   **Enter Data for a Table**

In this exercise, you will work in Design view as you type text in each table cell.

1. Switch to Design view.

2. Position the insertion point in the first table cell and type **Restaurant Name**.

3. Press ⎡Tab⎤.
   This moves the insertion point to the next table cell.

4. Type **Street Address** and press ⎡Tab⎤.
   This moves the insertion point to the next table cell.

5. Type **Telephone** and press ⎡Tab⎤.
   This advances the insertion point to the next cell, which in this case adds a new row to the table.

6. Click below the last empty row to position the insertion point in a new paragraph directly below the table.
   Your page should now resemble the following illustration:

Editor's Choice Nominees

Restaurant Name	Street Address	Telephone

7. Save the file but keep it open.

Importing Tabular Data

Many academic, government, and business Web sites rely on tables to present data from a spreadsheet or database. It's convenient to maintain and update data in one place, and then import it into different applications as needed. For example, say you maintain information in a spreadsheet or database program, but want to display it (or part of it) in a table on your site. You don't have to copy and paste the information into Dreamweaver; you can import it as tabular data, and then customize it.

Importing data from a spreadsheet such as Excel involves saving the file as a tab- or comma-delimited text file. A delimiter is a space or character such as a tab, slash, comma, or semicolon used to separate individual entries so the data can be imported into another program and still be formatted correctly. In this lesson, the text file has already been created for you.

The Import Tabular Data dialog box in Dreamweaver provides options to specify the source of the data file, the delimiter you used when saving the file, and to specify format options for the table that will be created using that data.

To display the Import Tabular Data dialog box, use the Tabular Data 🔳 button on the Layout category of the Insert bar or choose Insert→Table Objects→Import Tabular Data.

IMPORT TABULAR DATA DIALOG BOX SETTINGS

Setting	Description
Data File	This is the name of the data file to import. Use Browse to select a file.
Delimiter	This specifies the delimiter used in the file you're importing.
Table Width	Fit to Data makes each column wide enough to fit the longest text string in the column. Set specifies a fixed width in pixels or as a percentage of the width of the browser window.
Cell Padding	This refers to the number of pixels between a cell's content and the cell boundaries.
Cell Spacing	This refers to the number of pixels between adjacent table cells.
Format Top Row	This option provides formatting options for the first table row.
Border	This refers to the number of pixels for the table's border.

QUICK REFERENCE: IMPORTING TABULAR DATA

Task	Procedure
Save an Excel file as text	■ Open a file in Excel. ■ Choose File_Save As. ■ In the Save as Type list, choose Text (Tab delimited) (*.txt). ■ Click OK to close all prompts.
Import tabular data from text file	■ In Dreamweaver, place the insertion point where you want the table to appear. ■ Choose File_Import_Tabular Data or use the Tabular Data button in the Layout category of the Insert bar. ■ Type the name and location of the text file or click the Browse button on the Import Tabular Data dialog box to locate the file. ■ In the Import Tabular Data dialog box, enter the information about the text file containing your data.

Hands-On 7.3   Import Tabular Data

In this exercise, you will import a tab-delimited text file directly below the table.

Before you begin: The editors_choice.htm file should still be open.

1. Ensure that the insertion point is directly below the small table.

2. Click the Tabular Data ▦ button on the Insert bar or choose File→Import→Tabular Data. *This opens the Import Tabular Data dialog box.*

3. Click the Browse button and select editors_choice.txt from the lesson_07/text folder.

4. Choose the settings shown in the following illustration:
These settings ensure that the table for the imported data will be the same size as the small table previously created on this page.

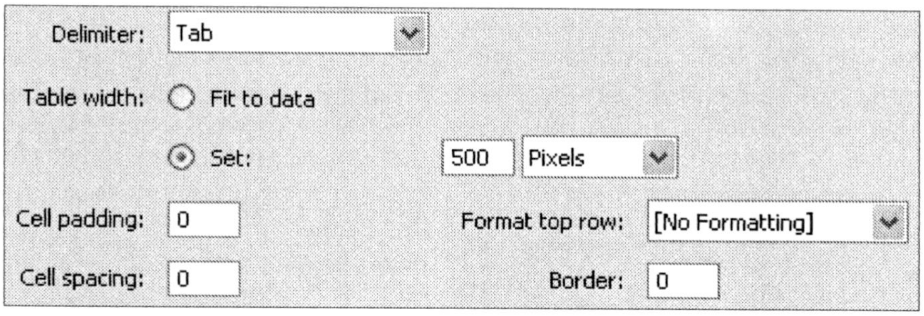

Delimiter:	Tab			
Table width:	◯ Fit to data			
	⦿ Set:	500	Pixels	
Cell padding:	0	Format top row:	[No Formatting]	
Cell spacing:	0	Border:	0	

5. Click OK.
The imported data appears below the small table on the page.

Restaurant Name	Street Address	Telephone
Chop House	262 S. Palm Canyon	320-4500
Kaiser Grille	205 S. Palm Canyon	323-1003
Davey's Hideaway	292 E. Palm Canyon	320-4480
St. James	265 S. Palm Canyon	320-8041
Falls Prime Steak House	155 S. Palm Canyon	416-8664
Le Vallauris	385 West Tahquitz	325-5059
Bubba's Roadkill Cafe	283 Twin Palms Drive	322-0020
Banducci's	1260 S. Palm Canyon	325-2537
The Deck	262 S. Palm Canyon	325-5200
Bit of Country	418 S. Indian Canyon	325-5154
La Casita	411 E. Palm Canyon	320-8993
Cedar Creek Inn	1555 S. Palm Canyon	325-7300
Carrows	123 E. Twin Palms	327-5150
Blue Coyote Grill	445 N. Palm Canyon	327-1196
Billy Reed's	1800 N. Palm Canyon	325-1946

6. Save the file but keep it open.

Copying and Pasting Table Cells

You now have two tables. The first table contains the headings for each column and the second table contains the data. You can combine the two tables by copying and pasting the contents of the second table into the first empty cell in the first table. This technique only works if both tables have the same structure. You cannot, for example, paste a four column table into a three column table. You also cannot cut or copy table cells that do not form a rectangular (contiguous) region.

Restaurant Name	Street Address
Chop House	262 S. Palm Canyon
Kaiser Grille	205 S. Palm Canyon
Davey's Hideaway	292 E. Palm Canyon

These cells form a contiguous region.

Restaurant Name	Street Address
Chop House	262 S. Palm Canyon
Kaiser Grille	205 S. Palm Canyon
Davey's Hideaway	292 E. Palm Canyon
St. James	265 S. Palm Canyon

These cells do not form a contiguous region.

 Hands-On 7.4   Copy and Paste Table Cells

In this exercise, you will copy and paste the cells in the second table to the first table.

Copy Table Cells

1. Follow these steps to select the table cells in the second table:

Ⓐ Click anywhere inside the first table cell.

Chop House	262 S. Palm Canyon	320-4500
Kaiser Grille	205 S. Palm Canyon	323-1003
Davey's Hideaway	292 E. Palm Canyon	320-4480
St. James	265 S. Palm Canyon	320-8041
Falls Prime Steak House	155 S. Palm Canyon	416-8664
Le Vallauris	385 West Tahquitz	325-5059
Bubba's Roadkill Cafe	283 Twin Palms Drive	322-0020
Banducci's	1260 S. Palm Canyon	325-2537
The Deck	262 S. Palm Canyon	325-5200
Bit of Country	418 S. Indian Canyon	325-5154
La Casita	411 E. Palm Canyon	320-8993
Cedar Creek Inn	1555 S. Palm Canyon	325-7300
Carrows	123 E. Twin Palms	327-5150
Blue Coyote Grill	445 N. Palm Canyon	327-1196
Billy Reed's	1800 N. Palm Canyon	325-1946

Ⓑ Drag across the table to the last cell of the last row. This selects the table cells, not the table.

2. Choose Edit→Copy or press ⌃Ctrl+Ⓒ or ⌘+Ⓒ.
   This copies the table cells.

Paste Table Cells

3. Click once inside the first empty cell in the second row in the top table.

4. Choose Edit→Paste or press ⌃Ctrl+Ⓥ or ⌘+Ⓥ.

All of the cells from the second table are inserted into the first table. The first table should now match the following illustration:

Restaurant Name	Street Address	Telephone
Chop House	262 S. Palm Canyon	320-4500
Kaiser Grille	205 S. Palm Canyon	323-1003
Davey's Hideaway	292 E. Palm Canyon	320-4480
St. James	265 S. Palm Canyon	320-8041
Falls Prime Steak House	155 S. Palm Canyon	416-8664
Le Vallauris	385 West Tahquitz	325-5059
Bubba's Roadkill Cafe	283 Twin Palms Drive	322-0020
Banducci's	1260 S. Palm Canyon	325-2537
The Deck	262 S. Palm Canyon	325-5200
Bit of Country	418 S. Indian Canyon	325-5154
La Casita	411 E. Palm Canyon	320-8993
Cedar Creek Inn	1555 S. Palm Canyon	325-7300
Carrows	123 E. Twin Palms	327-5150
Blue Coyote Grill	445 N. Palm Canyon	327-1196
Billy Reed's	1800 N. Palm Canyon	325-1946

5. Save the file but keep it open.
   You will delete the second table in the next exercise.

Selecting a Table and Its Parts

FROM THE KEYBOARD
To select a table:

WIN ONLY
Ctrl+A, A

MAC ONLY
⌘+A, A

To select a single cell:

WIN ONLY
Ctrl+A

MAC ONLY
⌘+A

In order to delete or modify a table, row, or column, you must first select the table element you want to modify. Dreamweaver provides numerous methods for selecting tables, table rows, columns, and individual cells.

 Hands-On 7.5   **Select a Table and Its Parts**

In this exercise, you will select a table, rows, columns, and cells. You will also delete the second table.

Before you begin: *The editors_choice.htm file should be open.*

1. Click anywhere in the second table and click the <table> tag on the Tag Selector.
   This selects the table and highlights the tag for the currently selected table.

<body> <table> <tr> <td>

2. Tap [Delete].
This deletes the table.

3. In the remaining table, click anywhere in the last empty row and then click the table row <tr> tag on the Tag Selector.
This highlights the row and the tag for the currently selected row.

4. Press [Delete].
This deletes the empty row.

5. Follow these steps to select one or more rows:

Ⓐ **Click anywhere inside a table cell in the starting row...**

Chop House	262 S. Palm Canyon	320-4500
Kaiser Grille	205 S. Palm Canyon	323-1003
Davey's Hideaway	292 E. Palm Canyon	320-4480

Ⓑ **...and drag the mouse pointer down to the final row, last cell.**

6. Follow these steps to select a column:

Ⓐ **Click anywhere inside a table cell in the starting column...**

Ⓑ **...and drag the mouse pointer to the last cell in the same column.**

Name	Street
Chop House	262 S. Palm Canyon
Kaiser Grille	205 S. Palm Canyon
Davey's Hideaway	292 E. Palm Canyon
St. James	265 S. Palm Canyon
Falls Prime Steak House	155 S. Palm Canyon
Le Vallauris	385 West Tahquitz

 NOTE! *Unlike table rows and table cells, there is no HTML tag for table columns. Therefore, when you select a column, you will not see an HTML tag on the Tag Selector that identifies the column.*

7. Click anywhere inside the table, and then click the table data <td> tag on the Tag Selector.
This highlights the tag to identify the currently selected cell.

8. Hold down the [Ctrl] or [⌘] key and click inside individual cells.
This technique is used to select non-contiguous cells.

Restaurant Name	Street Address
Chop House	262 S. Palm Canyon
Kaiser Grille	205 S. Palm Canyon
Davey's Hideaway	292 E. Palm Canyon
St. James	265 S. Palm Canyon

9. Save the file but keep it open.

Adjusting the Table Size

You can adjust the table size and appearance by increasing or decreasing the height and width of the entire table, as well as the size of the columns and rows within it. In the beginning of this lesson, you inserted a table and set the width to 500 pixels. Here, we explore several ways to adjust the table size, starting with dragging the selection handles.

Dragging the Selection Handles

When you select a table, the table appears with three selection handles which you can drag to resize the table vertically, horizontally, or both.

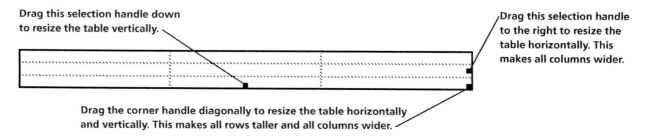

Drag this selection handle down to resize the table vertically.

Drag this selection handle to the right to resize the table horizontally. This makes all columns wider.

Drag the corner handle diagonally to resize the table horizontally and vertically. This makes all rows taller and all columns wider.

 TIP! *Hold down the* [Shift] *key while dragging the corner selection handle to constrain the proportions of the table.*

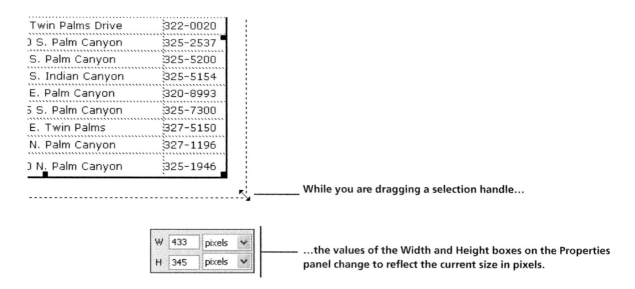

While you are dragging a selection handle...

...the values of the Width and Height boxes on the Properties panel change to reflect the current size in pixels.

Dragging Columns and Rows

When you move the insertion point over a table border, the pointer will turn into a double-headed arrow. You can then click and drag the arrow to the left or right or up or down to resize an individual cell. This is very easy to do by accident!

WARNING! *If you accidentally resize a cell, Dreamweaver adds new width and height values inside each <td>or <th> tag that has been modified. This can produced unexpected results, especially when designing advanced tables. When this occurs, you should choose Edit→Undo.*

Clearing Column Widths and Row Heights

There will undoubtedly be times when you need to clear all column widths or row heights in a table. There are two obscure buttons located on the Properties panel you can use to erase the settings and start over again. The buttons appear when a table is selected.

This button clears columns widths. ─────────────────

─── **This button clears row heights.**

Hands-On 7.6   Resize a Table

In this exercise, you will drag selection handles to resize a table. Then you will clear the column widths and row heights.

Before you begin: The editors_choice.htm file should still be open.

1. Click anywhere inside the table and choose Modify→Table→Select Table.

2. Click and drag the side selection handle to the right until the Width box on the Properties panel reads approximately 600 pixels.

3. Place the insertion point on the border of any cell and drag the double arrow up or down or to the left or right approximately ½ inch.

4. While the table is still selected, click the Clear Columns Widths button on the Properties panel and then click the Clear Row Heights button.
   This removes all column widths and row heights from the table and table cells. Now the table is just wide enough to accommodate the table data.

5. Save the file but keep it open.

Setting the Table Width

When setting the table width you can use two units of measure: pixels or percentage. Specifying the width in pixels (an absolute value) produces a fixed-width table that doesn't resize in the browser window. Specifying percentage (a relative value) produces a flexible table that resizes relative to the width of the browser window.

Hands-On 7.7   Set the Table Width

In this exercise, you will set the table width to a relative value, and then to an absolute value. After each change, you will open the file in your browser and observe the difference between the two settings.

1. Select the table.

Set the Table Width to a Relative Value

2. Follow these steps to set the table width:

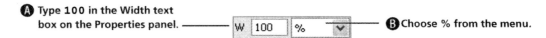

Ⓐ Type **100** in the Width text box on the Properties panel. ⎯⎯ W 100 % ⎯⎯ Ⓑ Choose % from the menu.

Preview the Table in Your Browser

3. Save the file

4. Press F12 to open the file in your primary browser.

5. (Win) Maximize your browser window or (Mac) drag the resize area at the bottom-right corner of the browser to expand the browser window as wide as possible.
   The table flows from the left margin to the right margin.

6. (Win) Restore down the browser window and then slowly resize the browser window to the left or (Mac) slowly drag the resize area of the browser to the left.
   Observe how the table remains 100% wide, relative to the size of the browser window.

7. Leave your browser window open and return to the Document window.

Set the Table Width to an Absolute Value

8. Select the table.

9. Follow these steps to set the table width in pixels:

Ⓐ Type **500** in the Width text box. ⎯⎯ W 500 pixels ⎯⎯ Ⓑ Choose pixels from the menu.

10. Repeat steps 3–7.
    Observe that the table width remains a fixed width and does not resize with the browser window.

11. Keep the file open.

Adding and Deleting Rows and Columns

FROM THE KEYBOARD

To add a single row above the current table row:

WIN ONLY

`Ctrl`+`M`

MAC ONLY

`⌘`+`M`

To add a column to the left of the current table column:

WIN ONLY

`Ctrl`+`Shift`+`A`

MAC ONLY

`⌘`+`Shift`+`A`

Chances are you will frequently need to modify a table by inserting or deleting new rows or columns, or making other adjustments. There are several techniques you can use and your choice will largely depend on whether you want to add single or multiple rows and columns.

Adding Single Rows or Columns

To add a single row or column, click the table cell where you want to add a new row or column and choose Insert→Table Objects. Select from one of four options.

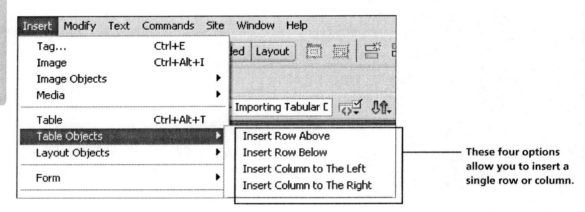

These four options allow you to insert a single row or column.

Adding Multiple Rows or Columns

When you need to add multiple rows or columns, click in the cell where you want to add multiple rows or columns, and then choose Modify Table→Insert Rows or Columns. This opens the Insert Rows or Columns dialog box.

To Insert Rows:

This option specifies what to insert.

This menu specifies the number of rows to insert.

This option specifies the location for the new rows.

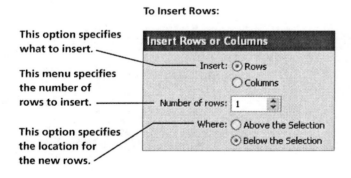

To Insert Columns:

This option specifies what to insert.

This menu specifies the number of columns to insert.

This option specifies the location for the new columns.

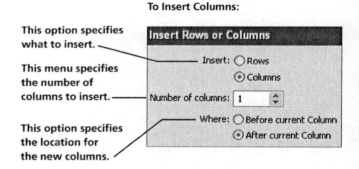

Deleting Rows or Columns

FROM THE KEYBOARD

To delete a table row:

WIN ONLY

`Ctrl`+`Shift`+`M`

MAC ONLY

`⌘`+`Shift`+`M`

To delete a table column:

WIN ONLY

`Ctrl`+`Shift`+`-`

MAC ONLY

`⌘`+`Shift`+`-`

To delete a row or column, click inside the row or column you want to delete. Then, choose Modify→Table and make a selection from the list.

Hands-On 7.8   Add and Delete Rows and Columns

In this exercise, you will practice adding and deleting rows and columns.

Before you begin: The editors_choice.htm file should still be open.

1. Click inside the first table cell in the first row.

2. Choose Insert→Table Objects→Insert Column to the Left from the menu bar.
   A new column is added to the left of the table.

3. Choose Modify→Table Objects→Delete Column from the menu bar.
   This deletes the new column you inserted in step 2.

4. Click anywhere in the last table row.

5. Choose Modify→Table→Insert Rows or Columns from the menu bar.

6. Choose the settings shown in the following illustration:
   This adds four new rows at the bottom of the table.

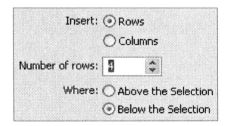

7. Select the four new rows.

8. Choose Modify→Table→Delete Row.
   This deletes the selected rows.

9. Save the file but keep it open.

Formatting a Table Header

Perhaps the most important aspect of table formatting is setting the table header. A table header identifies categories of information in a tabular table. This type of formatting is especially useful for speech-based browsers that assist visually impaired readers in keeping track of how the data is organized. When you format a table header, Dreamweaver replaces the <td> tag with the table header <th> tag in your HTML code.

When you insert a table, Dreamweaver provides placement options for table header text: None, Left (row heading), Top (column heading), or Both. In the next exercise, you will format the top row with a table header.

Aligning a Table Header

By default, table header text is center aligned. You can change the alignment by choosing another setting from the Horizontal pop-up menu on the Properties panel.

 Hands-On 7.9   Format and Align a Table Header

In this exercise, you will select the first row in the table and apply a table header. Then, you will align the text to the left.

Before you begin: The editors_choice.htm file should still be open.

1. Place the insertion point in any cell in the first row and click the <tr> tag on the Tag Selector.
   This selects the first row.

2. Follow these steps to format and align a table header:

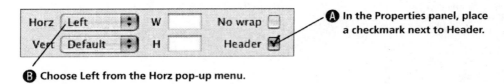

Ⓐ In the Properties panel, place a checkmark next to Header.

Ⓑ Choose Left from the Horz pop-up menu.

3. Deselect the table.
   The first row is formatted as a table header row.

4. Save the file but keep it open.

Setting Border and Spacing Properties

 NOTE!

HTML provides a border property for tables, but not for table cells. To add a border to a table cell, you must use CSS.

There's more to formatting tables than setting the number of rows and columns, the width of the columns, and the height of the rows. You can customize the appearance of your tables by setting border and spacing properties, background and border colors, and alignment on the page. Here, we explore adding a table border and adjusting table spacing.

Adding a Table Border

It is sometimes helpful to put borders around tables. To add a border around the table, select the table and then enter a value inside the Border box on the Properties panel. The value will determine the width of the border. When you want to remove a border, select the table and set the border value to zero.

 TIP! *Leaving the Border box empty is not the same as typing zero. Set the Border to 0 to ensure that older browsers will not use a default border for tables.*

Adjusting Table Spacing

Controlling the space between elements in a table is crucial for data tables and tables you use for page layout. You control this space with two very important table properties: cell padding and cell spacing. Cell padding is the amount of space between the walls of the cell and the content within them. Cell spacing is the amount of space between the table cells, not including the border. The following illustration shows the same table with various cell padding and cell spacing settings.

Examples of cell padding and cell spacing settings

 TIP! *If you do not want to use cell padding or cell spacing, set the value of each property to zero to ensure that browsers do not use their default values.*

 Hands-On 7.10 Set Border and Spacing Properties

In this exercise, you will select the table and then use the Properties panel to add a thin border to the table and to add cell padding to each cell in the table.

Before you begin: The editors_choice.htm file should still be open.

Add a Border

1. Select the table.

2. Type **1** in the Border text box on the Properties panel and tap Enter or Return.
   A 1 pixel border is added to the table. Do NOT deselect the table.

Add Cell Padding

3. Type **4** in the CellPad box on the Properties panel and tap Enter or Return.
   This adds 4 pixels of space between the walls of the cell and the content within them. Do NOT deselect the table.

Add Cell Spacing

4. Type **10** in the CellSpace box and tap Enter or Return.
   This adds 10 pixels of space between the table cells, not including the border. This space is for demonstration purposes only.

5. Set the cell spacing value back to **0**.

6. Save the file but keep it open.

Sorting a Table

You can perform a simple sort on the contents of a single column, or you can perform a more complex sort on the contents of two columns. You cannot perform a sort on a table that does not form a rectangle or square. To sort a table, select the table and choose Commands→Sort Table. This opens the Sort Table dialog box.

SORT TABLE DIALOG BOX SETTINGS

Setting	Description
Sort By	Determines which column will be used to sort the table rows
Order	Determines whether the contents should be sorted alphabetically or numerically, and whether the data should be sorted in ascending or descending order
Then By	Determines the sorting order for a secondary sort on a different column
Sort Includes the First Row	Determines whether the first row should be included in the sort (if the first row contains a table header, leave this box unchecked)
Sort Header Rows	Determines whether to sort the table header row
Sort Footer Rows	Determines whether to sort the table footer row
Keep All Row Colors the Same After the Sort Has Been Completed	Determines whether to move colors associated with a row when the data in the row is sorted

QUICK REFERENCE: SORTING A TABLE

Task	Procedure
Sort a table	■ Select the table.
	■ Choose Commands→Sort Table.
	■ Set sort options in the dialog box.

 Hands-On 7.11 Sort a Table

In this exercise, you will sort the table to arrange the restaurant names alphabetically in ascending order.

Before you begin: The editors_choice.htm file should still be open.

1. Select the table.

2. Choose Commands→Sort Table.
   This opens the Sort Table dialog box.

3. Use the default settings shown in the following illustration:

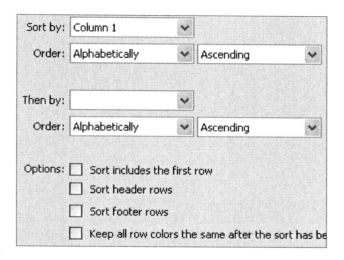

4. Click OK.

The data in the first column is sorted alphabetically in ascending order.

5. Save the file but keep it open.

Exporting Tabular Data

If you need the data in a Dreamweaver table for use with a spreadsheet, database, word processing, or page layout program, you cannot just copy the table and paste it into another application. You can, however, export the data and specify tab, space, comma, colon, or semi-colon as the delimiter. When you export a table, the entire contents of the table are exported; you cannot select portions of a table to export.

 TIP! *If you need to export only some of the data in a table, select the rows that contain the data and copy and paste them outside the current table. Then, you can export the new table data.*

To export table contents, choose File→Export→Table. This opens the Export Table dialog box, which you can use to specify the delimiter and line breaks for your operating system.

EXPORT TABLE DIALOG BOX SETTINGS	
Setting	**Description**
Delimiter	Specifies the delimiter character used to separate items in the exported file
Line Breaks	Specifies the operating system you will use to open the file: Windows, Macintosh, or UNIX

QUICK REFERENCE: EXPORTING TABLE DATA

Task	Procedure
Export table from Dreamweaver	■ In Dreamweaver, place the insertion point anywhere in the table.
	■ Choose File→Export→Table.
	■ Specify options for exporting the table.
	■ Click Export.
	■ Enter a name for the new file.
	■ Click Save.

Hands-On 7.12 Export Table Data

In this exercise, you will export the table to the lesson_07/text folder.

1. Click anywhere in the table.

2. Choose File→Export Table.
   This opens the Export Table dialog box.

3. Choose Tab from the Delimiter menu.

4. Choose the operating system for your version of Dreamweaver from the Line Breaks menu.

5. Click Export.
   This opens the Export Table dialog box.

6. Save the file as **editors_choice_export.txt** in the lesson_07/text folder.

7. Save and close the file.

Concepts Review

True/False Questions

1. Formatting a table header in boldface is the same as using the Header checkbox on the Properties panel. **TRUE**   **FALSE**

2. When you select a table row, the <tr> tag is highlighted on the Tag Selector. **TRUE**   **FALSE**

3. You can add a table cell border by selecting a cell and typing a value in the Border box on the Properties panel. **TRUE**   **FALSE**

4. Copying and pasting table cells into another table only works if both tables have the same structure. **TRUE**   **FALSE**

5. Dreamweaver replaces non-breaking spaces when you enter data within a table cell. **TRUE**   **FALSE**

6. Only cells that form a rectangular region can be copied. **TRUE**   **FALSE**

7. If you need the data in a Dreamweaver table for use in a spreadsheet, you can simply copy the table and paste it into another application. **TRUE**   **FALSE**

8. The <th> tag and the <td> tag can be used interchangeably. **TRUE**   **FALSE**

9. To add a new table row, place the insertion point inside the last table cell in the last row and tap Tab. **TRUE**   **FALSE**

10. You should always set cell padding, cell spacing and border properties to zero if you do not want a browser to use its default values for these properties. **TRUE**   **FALSE**

Multiple Choice Questions

1. Which of the following methods is used to delete a table row?
   a. Select the row and press Delete.
   b. Click anywhere inside the row and choose Modify→Table→Delete Row.
   c. Click anywhere inside the row and press Delete.
   d. Both a and b

2. Which of the following HTML tag sets are not parts of a table?
   a. <th>, <td>
   b. <table>, <tr>
   c. <tr>, <column>, <th>
   d. <table>, <tr>, <td>

3. Which of the following entities appears in each table cell when you insert a table?
   a. »
   b. ©
   c.
   d. &tbsp;

4. If you do not want a table to flow from margin to margin, which unit of measure should you use for the width?
   a. Picas
   b. Pixels
   c. %
   d. Centimeters

Skill Builders

Skill Builder 7.1   Import Tabular Data

In this exercise, you will import tabular data from a text file to create a new table. Then you will insert a new row and populate each cell in the new row with text.

1. Open cuisine.htm from the review_07 folder.

2. Place the insertion point directly below the California Cuisine text.

Import Tabular Data

3. Choose File→Import Tabular Data.
   This opens the Import Tabular Data dialog box.

4. Click the Browse button.

5. Locate and select california_cusine.txt from the review_07/text folder.

6. Choose the settings shown in the following illustration:
   This is a quick way to size the table and set spacing and border properties.

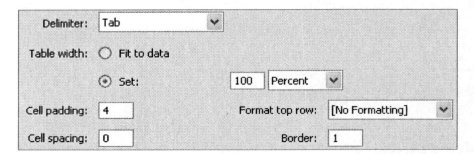

7. Click OK.

Insert a New Row

8. Click anywhere in the first row.

9. Choose Insert→Table Objects→Insert Row Above from the menu bar.

10. Use the following illustration to populate the table cells in the new row:

Restaurant	Location	Telephone

11. Save and close the file.

Skill Builder 7.2   Modify a Table

In this exercise, you will insert new rows and columns, copy and paste table cells from one table into another table, delete a table, format and align a table header, and add cell padding.

1. Open cuisine2.htm from the review_07 folder.
   The page contains a large table and a small table. The width of the large table is set to 100%.

Insert Columns and Rows

2. Place the insertion point in the second cell of the first row of the large table.

3. Choose Insert→Table Objects→Insert Column to the Right.
   This inserts a new column. Leave the insertion point inside the first cell of the new column.

4. Choose Insert→Table Objects→Insert Row Above.
   You should now have an empty column and a new empty row at the top of the table.

5. Use the following illustration to populate the cells in the new table row:

Restaurant	Location	City	Telephone

6. Locate the small table shown in the following illustration:
   You will use this data to populate the new City column.

Palm Springs
Palm Desert
Palm Springs
Palm Desert
Rancho Mirage
Cathedral City
Palm Desert
Palm Springs

Copy and Paste Table Cells

7. Click in the first cell of the small table and drag the insertion point to the bottom of the table.
   This selects the table cells, not the table.

8. Choose Edit→Copy.

9. Position the insertion point in the first empty cell in the second row of the large table.

10. Choose Edit→Paste.

11. Delete the small table.

Format and Align a Table Header

12. Select the first row.

13. Place a checkmark next to Header on the Properties panel.
Do NOT deselect the row.

14. Choose Left from the Horizontal pop-up menu on the Properties panel.

Add Cell Padding

15. Select the table, type **4** in the CellPad box on the Properties panel, and then press ⌈Enter⌉ or ⌈Return⌉.
The table should now resemble the following illustration:

Restaurant	Location	City	Telephone
Blue Coyote Grille	445 N. Palm Canyon	Palm Springs	327-1196
Kaiser Grille	205 S. Palm Canyon	Palm Desert	323-1003
Kaiser Grille	74-255 Highway 111	Palm Springs	779-1988
The Chop House	262 S. Palm Canyon	Palm Desert	320-4500
Dakota Bar & Grill	73-260 El Paseo	Rancho Mirage	346-0744
Jovanna's	74-063 Highway 111	Cathedral City	568-1315
Randy's Cafe	73-560 Highway 111	Palm Desert	340-3036
Davey's Hideaway	292 E. Palm Canyon	Palm Springs	320-4480
The Grill	1600 N. Indian Canyon	Palm Springs	778-6670

16. Save the file but keep it open.

Skill Builder 7.3　Sort and Export Table Data

In this exercise, you will sort and export a table.

Before you begin: The cuisine2.htm file should be open.

1. Click anywhere in the table.

2. Choose Commands→Sort Table.

3. Sort the table using the default Sort Table dialog box options and press OK.

4. Choose File→Export Table.

5. Choose Tab for the delimiter and choose the Line Breaks option for your operating system.

6. Press Export.

7. Save the file as **cuisine.txt** in the review_07/text folder.

8. Close the file.

Assessments

Assessment 7.1   Insert and Format a Table

In this exercise, you will create and format a table.

1. Create a new blank HTML document.

2. Save the file as **appetizers.htm** and store it in the review_07 folder.

3. Follow these guidelines to create the table shown in the following illustration:

   - Insert a table with **10** rows and **2** columns.
   - Set the table width to **310** pixels.
   - Set the cell padding to **4**.
   - Set the cell spacing to **0**.
   - Set the table border to **0**.
   - Format the first row as a table header.
   - Align the table header to the left.

Appetizers	Price
Ahi Tuna Tartar	14.5
Eggplant Enchiladas	9.75
Blue Lump Crab Cake	12.5
Grilled Gulf Shrimp	14
New Zealand Mussels	10.5
Main Lobster Salad	14.75
Seared Sea Scallops	12.5
Hudson Valley Foie Gras	22.5
Duck Confit and Mache Salad	10.75

4. Save the file, and then preview it in your browser.

5. Leave your browser window open and return to the Document window.

6. Close the file.

Critical Thinking

Critical Thinking 7.1   On Your Own

Mike Dooms' dad was an avid CD collector for many years. His eclectic musical taste ranged from Country to 17th Century Italian Baroque. Mike inherited the collection, but he doesn't listen to CDs and he certainly doesn't listen to Bach, Hank Williams, or Billie Holiday. He's decided to sell the collection on the Internet and use the money to upgrade his MP3 player and the sound system in his 1975 Mustang.

Mike catalogued a small portion of the collection in Excel and saved the spreadsheet as a tab-delimited text file. Mike has offered you 10% of the profit if you'll use your Dreamweaver skills to import the data into a table, and then format and sort it.

Follow these guidelines to create a table:

- Create a new page named **cd_collection.htm** and save it in the review_07 folder.

- Import the tabular data from cd_collection.txt, which is located in the review_07/text folder.

- Format and sort the table as shown in the following illustration.

- Save the file when completed, and then close it.

Title	Artist	Genre
Tocatta and Fugue in D minor	Daniel Chorzempa	Classical
Chopin Nocturnes	Vlado Perlemuter	Classical
Vivaldi 9 Concertos	I Musici	Classical
Fandango	Rafael Puyana	Classical
Concerto for Orchestra	Concertgebouw Orchestra	Classical
Always Never the Same	George Strait	Country
Killin' Time	Clint Black	Country
Reba	Reba McEntire	Country
Did I Shave My Legs for This?	Deana Carter	Country
Everywhere We Go	Kenny Chesney	Country
A Lot About Livin'	Alan Jackson	Country
Easy Come Easy Go	George Strait	Country
Sampler for Aids Relief 2	Various	Jazz
Songs for Distingue Lovers	Billie Holiday	Jazz
The Johnny Mercer Songbook	Ella Fitzgerald	Jazz
The Songbooks	Ella Fitzgerald	Jazz
December	George Winston	New Age
Soaring with the Angels	Frederic Delarue	New Age
Some Peoples Lives	Bette Midler	Pop
Stronger than Pride	Sade	Pop
New Land	Bernardo Rubaja	Pop
Greatest Hits	Linda Ronstadt	Pop
South Pacific	Rogers and Hammerstein	Show
Famous Swing Classics	Bert Kaempfert	Swing

Critical Thinking 7.2　　**Web Research**

Paula Gray is a librarian by day and a food critic by night. Her moonlighting has added two inches to her waist, so she's decided to join a local gym and get started on a new diet to lose the weight before her fiancé returns from his overseas trip.

She's heard about the popular diets that are advertised on the Internet. Paula has asked you to work with her to research, evaluate, and compare the most popular diet crazes. You, being a Dreamweaver guru, suggest to Paula that she publish her findings on the Web. To do this, you'll need to create a table that lists the following criteria:

- Diet Name
- Overview
- The Diet Creator
- Medical Studies
- Additional Resources

Use your browser and favorite search engine to research the latest diet crazes and record your results in a new Dreamweaver table. Save the file as **diet.htm** in the review_07 folder.

Working with Page Layout Tables

In this lesson, you will learn how to use images, background color, and advanced table properties to design fixed-width and flexible page layouts. If you want to design great Web pages today, you need to know how to work with page layout tables. When Tim Berners-Lee invented the Web to help fellow scientists exchange particle physics documents, he never dreamed that one day the Web would compete with the sophisticated design of newspapers, magazines, and television ads. As the Web and its users matured, however, the design of Web pages became increasingly important. Designers battling for control over page layout found their primary weapon in the HTML <table> tag. Tables, originally designed to display only data, became the tool of choice for ensuring precise page layout.

Case Study

Justin Timberland's hard work helping Janet get the Palm Springs Dining Guide online has paid off. He's started his own company, building Web sites for local businesses and non-profit organizations. His company, Just in Time Design, is working on a remake of the Web site for St. James at the Vineyard, an enchanting restaurant in Palms Springs, California. Justin created a series of tables, and filled the cells with exotic graphics and vibrant color that capture the mystique of the restaurant's interior design. Justin presented his client with two versions of the same page. The first version is a "frozen" design; the page does not change size, regardless of the browser window size.

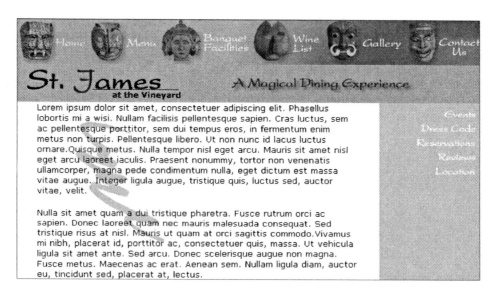

The second version is a "liquid" design that changes size when a site visitor resizes the browser window.

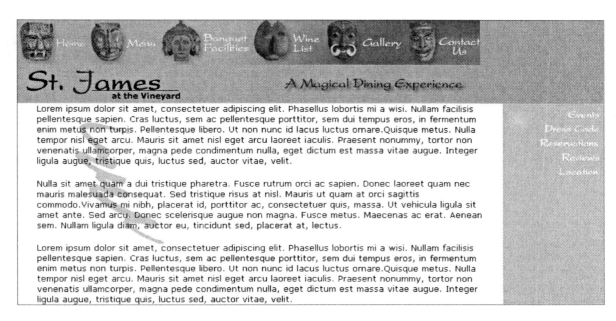

Inserting Images in Table Cells

You have undoubtedly noticed that table cells expand or contract based on their content. This is especially apparant when you insert an image in a table cell. For example, the height of a table row is determined by the tallest element in that row. Similarly, the width of all of the cells in a column is determined by the widest element in that column.

This image determines the height of this row.

This image determines the width of this column.

A picture is worth a thousand words, so we begin this lesson by adding an image to a table cell. Understanding how table cells expand and collapse based on content will make it easier for you to plan your table based page layout design.

 Hands-On 8.1   Add an Image to a Table Cell

In this exercise, you will insert an image inside a table cell.

1. Open table_align.htm from the lesson_08 folder.

   A 1 × 2 table appears at the top of the page. The first table cell contains a small amount of Lipsum (placeholder text) and the other table cell is propped open by a single non-breaking space.

2. Place the insertion point inside the blank table cell.

   The non-breaking space will be replaced when you insert an image in the next step.

3. Choose Insert→Image from the menu bar.

   This opens the Select Image Source dialog box.

4. Select swing.jpg from the images folder and click OK or Choose.

   This inserts the image in the table cell. The row height increases to accommodate the image. If you accidentally inserted the image outside the table cell, you can drag and drop it into the table cell.

5. Save the file but keep it open.

Aligning Tables

When you insert a table, it aligns with the left side of the page by default. Other elements on the page will be either above or below it. Three alignment options available on the Properties panel allow you to center the table on the page or wrap text or other Web page elements to the left or right. Having selected the table, you will see these options:

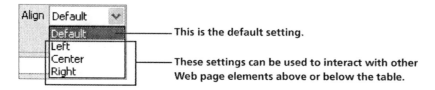

— This is the default setting.

— These settings can be used to interact with other Web page elements above or below the table.

The following four images illustrate how the four alignment options differ.

The table aligns to the left margin.

Text appears below the table and is aligned with the left margin.

Mauris sit amet nisl eget arcu laoreet iaculis.

Lorem ipsum dolor sit amet, consectetuer adipiscing elit. Phasellus lobortis mi a wisi. Nullam facilisis pellentesque sapien. Cras luctus, sem ac pellentesque porttitor, sem dui tempus eros, in fermentum enim metus non turpis.

The Default alignment option is chosen.

The table aligns to the left margin.

Mauris sit amet nisl eget arcu laoreet iaculis.

Lorem ipsum dolor sit amet, consectetuer adipiscing elit. Phasellus lobortis mi a wisi. Nullam facilisis pellentesque sapien. Cras luctus, sem ac pellentesque porttitor, sem dui tempus eros, in fermentum enim metus non turpis.

— The paragraph wraps around the table. The text is still left aligned.

The Left alignment option is chosen.

Text wraps around the table, aligning with the left margin. ——

Lorem ipsum dolor sit amet, consectetuer adipiscing elit. Phasellus lobortis mi a wisi. Nullam facilisis pellentesque sapien. Cras luctus, sem ac pellentesque porttitor, sem dui tempus eros, in fermentum enim metus non turpis.

Mauris sit amet nisl eget arcu laoreet iaculis.

——**The table aligns on the right margin.**

The Right alignment option is chosen.

The table is centered on the page. ——

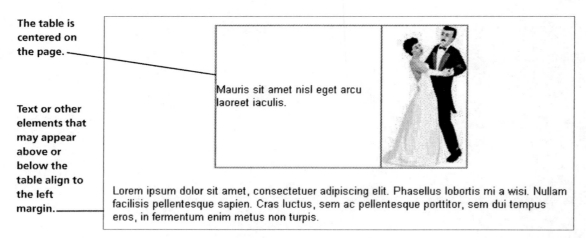

Mauris sit amet nisl eget arcu laoreet iaculis.

Text or other elements that may appear above or below the table align to the left margin. ——

Lorem ipsum dolor sit amet, consectetuer adipiscing elit. Phasellus lobortis mi a wisi. Nullam facilisis pellentesque sapien. Cras luctus, sem ac pellentesque porttitor, sem dui tempus eros, in fermentum enim metus non turpis.

The Center alignment option is chosen.

 NOTE!   *Throughout this course, you have been encouraged to use the Tag Selector to identify the currently selected element on a Web page. The use of this tool becomes more critical as you begin to work with page layout tables.*

 ## Hands-On 8.2   Align a Table

In this exercise, you will practice aligning a table.

***Before you begin:** The table_align.htm file should be open.*

1. Click anywhere in the table and click the <table> tag on the Tag Selector.
   This selects the table.

2. Observe the Align menu on the Properties panel.
   The Default setting is chosen. The table sits at the left margin and two paragraphs sit below the table. Do NOT deselect the table.

Align the Table

3. Choose Left from the Align menu.

   This aligns the table to the left and the two paragraphs that were below the table now wrap around the table.

4. Choose Right from the Align menu.

   This aligns the table to the right and the two paragraphs now wrap around the table.

5. Choose Center from the Align menu.

   This aligns the table to the center of the page and disrupts the flow of the two paragraphs that appear below the table.

Return the Table Alignment to the Default Setting

6. Choose Default from the Align menu.

   This aligns the table back to the left margin.

7. Save and close the file.

Aligning Table Cells

Table cells have their own properties, separate from table properties. The properties of rows can be independently set as well. When you click inside a cell, the Properties panel is partitioned to display text and cell formatting properties.

The top half of the Properties panel displays the cell's text formatting properties.

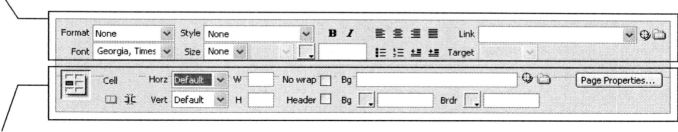

The bottom of the panel shows the cell's formatting properties.

By default, any content in a table data cell is horizontally aligned to the left and vertically aligned to the middle of the cell.

The image in this cell uses the default horizontal and vertical alignment settings.

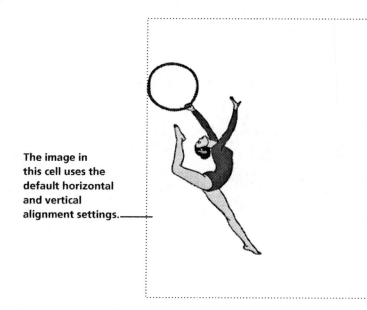

Lorem ipsum dolor sit amet, consectetuer adipiscing elit. Phasellus lobortis mi a wisi. Nullam facilisis pellentesque sapien. Cras luctus, sem ac pellentesque porttitor, sem dui tempus eros, in fermentum enim metus non turpis.

Pellentesque libero. Ut non nunc id lacus luctus ornare. Quisque metus. Nulla tempor nisl eget arcu. Mauris sit amet nisl eget arcu laoreet iaculis.Praesent nonummy, tortor non venenatis ullamcorper, magna pede condimentum nulla, eget dictum est massa vitae augue. Integer ligula augue, tristique quis,Lorem ipsum dolor sit amet, consectetuer adipiscing elit.

Lorem ipsum dolor sit amet, consectetuer adipiscing elit. Phasellus lobortis mi a wisi. Nullam facilisis pellentesque sapien. Cras luctus, sem ac pellentesque porttitor, sem dui tempus eros, in fermentum enim metus non turpis

The text in this cell determines the height of the table row.

 ## Hands-On 8.3   Set Table Row and Cell Alignment Properties

In this exercise, you will set table row and individual cell alignment properties.

1. Open cell_align.htm from the lesson_08 folder.

   There are two tables on the page. The first table contains an image and text; the second table contains only text.

Align a Table Cell Containing an Image

2. Click in the first table cell. Do NOT click on the image.

3. Click the <td> tag on the Tag Selector.

   This selects the first table cell.

4. Observe the default horizontal and vertical alignment settings on the Properties panel. Do NOT deselect the table cell.

   The image is horizontally aligned to the left and vertically aligned in the middle of the table cell.

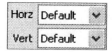

5. Set the horizontal and vertical alignment properties shown in the following illustration:

6. Practice using other alignment options or set the horizontal and vertical properties back to Default.

Align a Table Cell Containing Text

7. Locate the second table and observe the text in the first cell.
   This cell determines the row height.

8. Click inside the second table cell.

9. Click the <td> tag on the Tag Selector.
   This selects the second table cell.

10. Observe the default horizontal and vertical alignment settings on the Properties panel.
   The text is horizontally aligned to the left, and vertically aligned in the middle of the cell.

11. Set the horizontal and vertical alignment properties shown in the following illustration:

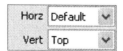

12. Practice using other alignment options or set the horizontal and vertical properties back to Default.

13. Save and close the file.

 TIP! *If your intention is to use the default alignment, set the property to Default. If you set the alignment to Left and it is the default alignment, you're adding extra HTML code that a Web browser has to read.*

Merging and Splitting Cells

FROM THE KEYBOARD

To merge cells:

WIN ONLY
Ctrl + Alt + M

MAC ONLY
⌘ + Option + M

To split cells:

WIN ONLY
Ctrl + Alt + S

MAC ONLY
⌘ + Option + S

Seldom is a simple table capable of satisfying your page layout requirements. You will often need to merge cells to form a single cell that spans multiple columns or rows. You can merge any number of adjacent cells—as long as the entire selection is rectangular or square—to produce a single cell that spans several columns or rows. Merging cells allows you to create complex page layouts. To merge table cells, select a contiguous (adjacent) range of cells and choose Modify→Table→Merge Cells from the menu bar.

This cell spans 2 columns				
	This cell spans 3 rows		This cell spans 2 columns and 2 rows	

You can also split a cell into any number of rows or columns. To split a cell, click in the cell and choose Table→Modify→Split Cell from the menu bar.

The cells below are split into 3 rows	The cells below are split into 3 columns		

You can also use the Merge Cells and Split Cells button on the Properties panel to merge and/or split cells.

The Merge Cells button is active only when you've selected multiple cells. ———

Cell

——— The Split Cell button appears only when you select a single cell or click in a cell.

 NOTE! *Merging and splitting numerous table cells can produce an overly complex table that is difficult to manage. In this lesson, we will use nested tables instead of splitting table cells.*

QR **QUICK REFERENCE: MERGING AND SPLITTING CELLS**

Task	Procedure
Merge cells	■ Select the cells you want to merge. The selected cells must be contiguous and in the shape of a rectangle or square.
	■ Choose Modify→Table→Merge Cells or click the Merge Cell button on the Properties panel.
Split cells	■ Click in the cell or select the cell.
	■ Choose Modify→Table→Split Cell or click the Split Cell button on the Properties panel.

 Hands-On 8.4   Merge Table Cells

In this exercise, you will merge two cells to form one cell. Then, you will insert three images and align the table row. The images are located in the images folder.

1. Open cell_merge.htm from the lesson_08 folder.
   The page contains a 2 × 2 table that is 566 pixels wide.

2. Click anywhere in the second row and click <tr> on the Tag Selector.
   This selects the entire row.

3. Choose Modify→Table→Merge Cells from the menu bar.

   This merges the two cells into a single cell.

4. Insert chain_left.gif into the first table cell in the first row.

   This image sets the height of the first row.

5. Insert chain_right.gif into the second table cell in the first row.

   Observe how the image is vertically aligned in the table cell.

6. Insert chain_bottom.gif into the cell in the second row.

   This image is 566 pixels wide, the same size of the table.

7. Select the first table, and then choose Bottom from the Vertical align menu on the Properties panel.

   This switches the default alignment and ensures that the content of both cells align to the bottom of each cell. Your page should look like the following illustration:

8. Save and close the file.

Coloring Tables, Rows, and Cells

Now it's time to get the crayons out of your Web design toolkit and let your inner child come forward. Tables don't have to be boring—especially tables used for page layout. You can apply color to tables, cells, and rows. Before you start using those crayons, you need to understand the order of color formatting precedence in HTML.

Color Formatting Precedence in HTML

When you apply background color to a page, every element on the page inherits the color, including all default tables, rows, and cells. You can override the page background color by applying a background color to a table. When you do this, all rows and cells inherit the table background color. You can then override the table background color by applying color to an entire row or to individual table cells. So, the order of color formatting precedence begins with the lowest element and ends with the highest element:

1. Cell

2. Row

3. Table

4. Page

Choosing a Color

When working with tables, the Properties panel provides three color boxes. The top portion of the panel contains the Text Color box; the bottom half contains Background Color and Border Color boxes. A table must have the border property set to at least 1 pixel for the border color to show.

To choose a color, expand the color box and use the Color Picker. When you choose a color, the hexadecimal equivalent of the color appears in the Color hex field. If you're a genius and can remember hexadecimal color values, you can type the value in the color hex field to the right of the color box.

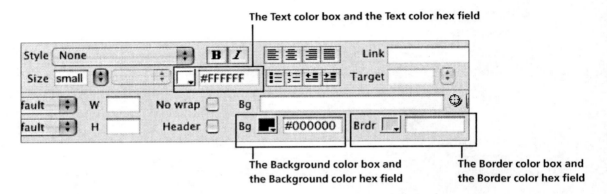

The Text color box and the Text color hex field

The Background color box and the Background color hex field

The Border color box and the Border color hex field

 ## Hands-On 8.5   Apply Table Background Color

In this exercise, you will apply background color to a table row and individual cells.

1. Open color.htm from the lesson_08 folder.
   Yikes! The bright aqua background color overpowers the content. The color flows from the page to the table, rows, and cells.

2. Click in the first table cell, and then click <tr> on the Tag Selector.
   This selects the first row. This row spans the two columns below it.

3. Follow these steps to apply background and text color to the first row:

A Type #333333 (dark gray) inside the background hex field. Or, choose a color from the Color Picker.

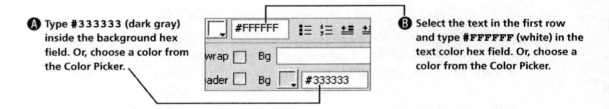

B Select the text in the first row and type #FFFFFF (white) in the text color hex field. Or, choose a color from the Color Picker.

4. Click in the first table cell in the second row and click <td> on the Tag Selector.

5. Set the background color to **#CCCCCC** (light gray) or use the Color Picker to choose a color.

6. Click in the second table cell in the second row and click <td> on the Tag Selector.

7. Set the background color to **#FFFFFF** or use the Color Picker to choose a color.

The table should now resemble this illustration, without the color of course:

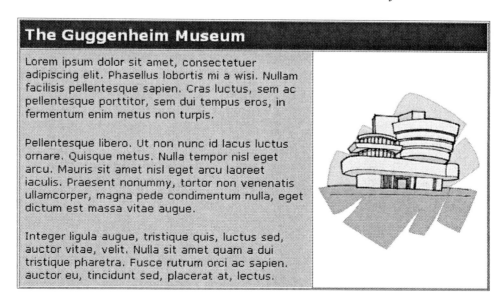

8. Save and close the file.

Using Expanded Tables Mode

FROM THE KEYBOARD

To switch in and out of Expanded Tables mode:

WIN AND MAC

F6

Sometimes a cell is so tiny that it's awkward to position the insertion point. In such situations you may need to switch to Expanded Tables mode. When you switch from Standard mode to Expanded Tables mode, Dreamweaver temporarily adds quite a bit of cell padding and spacing so you can easily place the insertion point or see an expanded view of each table cell. You will use Expanded Tables mode in the next exercise to insert tiny transparent images in table cells!

 NOTE! *Expanded Tables mode is not meant for editing purposes. Once you make your selection or place the insertion point, return to the Standard mode to make your edits. Some visual operations, such as resizing, will not give expected results in Expanded Tables mode.*

 QR **QUICK REFERENCE: SWITCHING IN AND OUT OF EXPANDED TABLES MODE**

Task	Using the Menu Bar	Using the Insert Bar
Switch to expanded tables mode	Choose View→Table Mode→Expanded Tables Mode	In the Layout category of the Insert Bar, click the Expanded Tables Mode button.
Switch out of expanded tables mode	Choose View→Table Mode→Expanded Tables Mode	In the Layout category of the Insert Bar, click the Standard Mode button.

Using Spacer GIFs

Table cells behave like tiny rubber bands; they expand when you add content and collapse when they're empty. To keep cells from collapsing, insert an invisible image. Called a spacer GIF, a 1 × 1 pixel transparent image can be inserted in a cell and resized to reserve whatever cell real estate you may need. This little trick can give you a lot of control over the actual size of the cell and can be used for such purposes as setting an exact amount of space between columns, collapsing an empty table row down to 1 pixel, or increasing the row height to x number of pixels. Spacers can be any size you need. When you insert a spacer, you set the desired width and height in the Properties panel. Spacers are generally set to be invisible but they don't have to be, as you will see in the following exercise.

 NOTE! *If you don't have a spacer image, Dreamweaver can create one for you. (Win) Choose Edit→Preferences or (Mac) choose Dreamweaver→Preferences. In the Layout Mode category, press Create, and then specify a storage location for the spacer GIF. While this feature is available, it's a lot easier to use the spacer GIFs provided for you in this lesson.*

 QUICK REFERENCE: INSERTING SPACER GIFS

Insert spacer GIFs	■ Click in an empty cell.
	■ Choose Insert→Image and browse to a transparent 1 × 1 pixel GIF previously created to serve as a spacer.
	■ While the transparent GIF is selected, use the Properties panel to change its dimensions to reflect the width or height of the cell space you are trying to preserve.
	■ Set the Alt property to <empty>.

 ## Hands-On 8.6   Insert Spacers

In this exercise, you will switch to Expanded Tables mode and insert three spacer images to serve as "control" rows. The spacers are red so you can clearly see them once you increase the width and height.

1. Open spacers.htm from the lesson_08 folder.
   The page contains a 600 pixel wide table. The first, third, and last table rows are merged to span five columns. You will insert a spacer inside each of these rows.

2. Choose View→Table Mode→Expanded Tables mode from the menu bar or use the Expanded Tables Mode button on the Layout category of the Insert bar.

3. Read the message in the Getting Started in Expanded Tables mode and press OK.
   All of the table cells are temporarily expanded.

4. Click inside the table cell in the first row.

5. Choose Insert→Image, navigate to the images folder, and then select spacer_red.gif.
   This image is identical to a regular spacer image, except you can see it. Do NOT click anywhere on the page or you will deselect the image which is barely visible.

6. Type **600** in the Width box on the Properties panel and press ⌈Enter⌉ or ⌈Return⌉.
   Do NOT click anywhere on the page or you will deselect the image.

7. Set the Alt property on the Properties panel to <empty>.

   Spacer images wreck havoc on blind readers when this property is not set properly.

8. Using the same technique you used in steps 4–6, insert the same spacer in the third and last row of the table. Set width to 600 and the alternative text property to <empty>.

9. Choose View→Table Mode→Standard Mode from the menu bar or use the Standard Mode button on the Layout category of the Insert bar.

   The default non-breaking spaces were replaced by the spacers, and the rows are now only 1 pixel high.

10. Save the file.

11. Preview the file in your browser.

12. Leave your browser open, and return to the Document window.

13. Close the file.

 TIP! *Sometimes you may be working on multiple versions of the same file though the files are stored in different locations in your site. If you have a question about where to save the current file, choose Site→Locate in Site and Dreamweaver will jump to the location from which the file was opened.*

Breaking Up Large Tables

When planning your page layout, keep in mind that large, complex tables may take a while to display in a Web browser. This is because a browser cannot display anything inside a table until it encounters the close table </table> tag. For some page layouts, it's much better to break up large tables to form multiple small tables. The following illustration shows three separate tables that were cut from one large table. Each table is separated by a paragraph space for demonstration purposes.

Table 1 is a single cell that contains an image and a paragraph of text. ————

Table 2 is a copy of the table you worked with in the last exercise. ————

Table 3 has 16 pixels of cell padding (white space) around the copy. ————

Note that only Table 3 has cell padding. Making this block of copy a separate table allowed us to apply this formatting. If the three tables were a single table, adding 16 pixels of cell padding would destroy the page design. In a moment, we're going to remove the space between the three tables to give the illusion of one large table.

 TIP! *If you're pulling out your hair because your tables aren't behaving the way you want, select the problem table, cut it to the Clipboard, and paste it in an isolated section on the page for troubleshooting purposes.*

 ## Hands-On 8.7   Combine Multiple Tables

In this exercise, you will remove the space between three separate tables to see how much easier it is to work with a few smaller tables instead of one large one.

1. Open xtreme_ice_busted.htm from the lesson_08 folder.
   The page contains three separate tables.

2. Position the insertion point in the blank space below the first table, and then press Backspace (Win) or Delete (Mac).
   This removes the paragraph space and the two tables appear as one.

3. Position the insertion point in the blank space below the second table, and then press Backspace (Win) or Delete (Mac).
   Your page should now resemble the following illustration:

4. Save the file.

5. Preview the file in your browser.

6. Leave your browser open and return to the Document window.

7. Leave the file open.

Nesting Tables

The process of inserting a table inside another table is called nesting. In the next exercise, we're going to create another table and then copy and paste three tables inside the new table. The Xtreme Ice page would look better if the tables were center aligned. Also, it would be pretty cool to have a single thin border surround all three tables.

This lesson would not be complete without at least one table trick. Well, get ready!

 ## Hands-On 8.8   Outline and Nest Tables

In this exercise, you're going to insert a 1 × 1 table, set the background color to black, set the cell padding to 1, and center align the table. Then, you'll select the three tables from the last exercise, cut them to the Clipboard, and then paste them into the outer table. Finally, you will use the Tag Selector to explore the hierarchy of each table.

Before you begin: The xtreme_ice_busted.htm file should be open.

Insert a New Table

1. Place the insertion point below the last table on the page.

2. Choose Insert→Table from the menu bar.

3. Set the table properties shown in the following illustration:

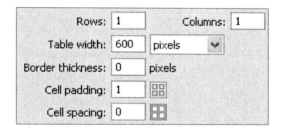

4. Click OK. Do NOT deselect the table.

   Notice how the new table "snaps" to the table above. Make sure the <table> tag is highlighted on the Tag Selector.

Set Additional Table Properties

5. Open the BG Color box on the Properties panel and use the Color Picker to select Black. Do NOT deselect the table.

   Note the hex color code for black is #000000. The 1 pixel of cell padding combined with the black background table color will provide the outline we're looking for.

6. Set the Align property on the Properties panel to Center.

Cut and Paste Tables

7. Click to the right of the third table (the one with the text paragraph and 16 pixels of padding) and drag the mouse pointer up and to the left of the first table.

   This selects all three tables.

8. Choose Edit→Cut from the menu bar.

This cuts the selection to the Clipboard, leaving only the new table.

9. Click in the new table and choose Edit→Paste from the menu bar.

This pastes the three tables inside the new table.

Explore the Table Hierarchy

10. Click in the table that contains the Xtreme Ice banner (the top table) and notice the <table> tags that appear on the Tag Selector.

The first <table> tag represents the outer table. The second <table> tag represents the table you just clicked inside.

11. Click the far right <table> tag on the Tag Selector.

This selects the current table.

12. Use the same technique for each table on the page.

The Tag Selector is extremely useful for identifying and selecting tables and table elements, especially when you're working with nested tables.

13. Save the file.

14. Preview the file in your browser.

The page should resemble the following illustration:

15. Leave your browser open and return to the Document window.

If you would like to experiment further on your own, you can change the table outline color by selecting the outer table and choosing another color and make the border larger by selecting the outer table and increasing the cell padding.

16. Close the file.

Designing for Different Window Sizes

Designing an HTML page to fit different window sizes and screen resolutions—and still control the placement of content—is one of the biggest challenges you'll face in Web design. Not everyone uses a high resolution monitor and not everyone works with their window maximized. A surefire way to lose site visitors is to design pages that look great on your computer without bothering to check how they may look on someone else's computer.

In Lesson 2, Working with HTML Documents, you learned how to use the Window Size pop-up menu to test your pages at various window sizes and screen resolutions. As a refresher, please refer to the following illustration:

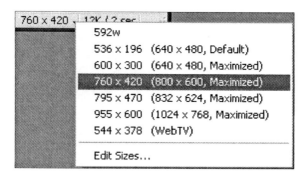

The Window Size Settings

The Window Size pop-up menu is located on the Status bar at the bottom-right corner of the Document window. Macintosh users always have the Window Size pop-up menu available when a document is open. Windows users, however, must restore down the document window because Dreamweaver disables this feature when the window is maximized.

The Window Size pop-up menu can be used to determine the optimal window size based on various screen resolutions. A window size of 760 × 420 is used with a screen resolution of 800 × 600 to compensate for the "chrome" (menu bar, address bar, toolbars, etc.) that each browser uses. If you ensure that all tables and their contents are less than 760 pixels wide, you can be fairly assured that users viewing your page at 800 × 600 resolution will not have to scroll horizontally.

The following illustrations show the same page set at three different window sizes. The page was designed for an optimal window size of 760 × 420.

In this illustration, the window size is 600 × 300 (640 × 480, maximized). The window is not large enough to display the entire content and a horizontal scroll bar appears at the bottom of the window and a vertical scroll bar appears at the right of the window.

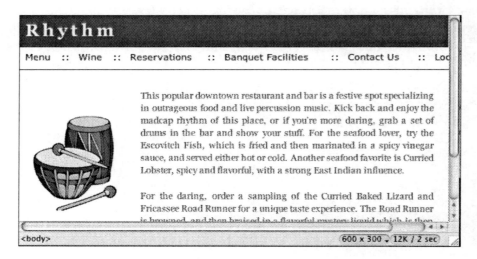

In this illustration, the window size is 760 × 420 (800 × 600, maximized). All of the content displays and the scroll bars are hidden.

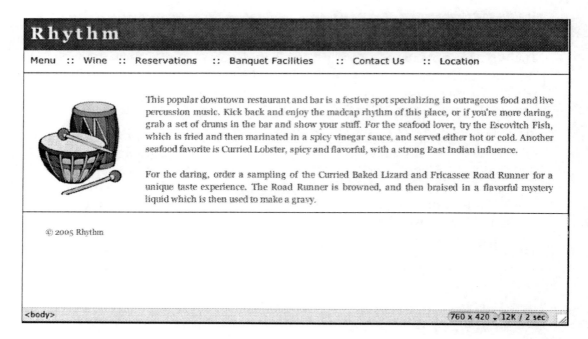

In this illustration, the window size is 955 × 600 (1024 × 768, maximized.) All of the content shows and there is excessive white space below the content.

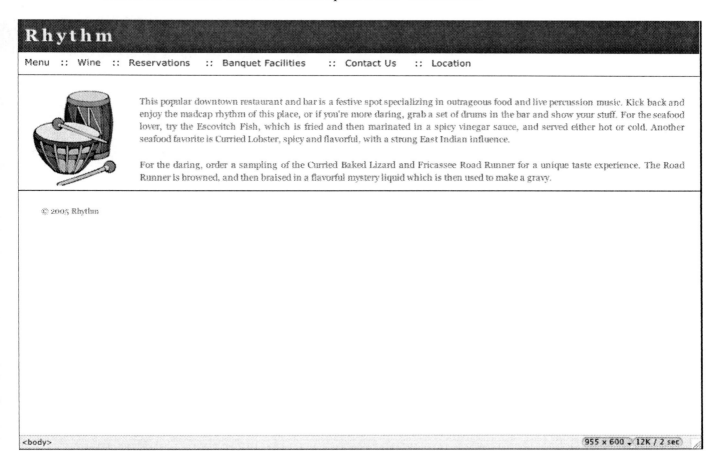

Currently, approximately 50% of Web users have their screen resolution set to 1024 × 768 (or higher) and 35% use a screen resolution of 800 × 600 pixels. Only a small percentage of users still have their screen resolution set to 640 × 480. To accommodate the widest audience, it makes sense to design your pages so that they look good at 800 × 600 or higher. That's the middle road!

Once you've chosen a window size, you need to decide whether you want the content to fit inside a fixed pixel width table or whether the entire page should flow from the left to the right margin when the page is opened in a browser.

TIP! *A fixed width page layout is often called a "frozen design" because the page doesn't resize with the browser window. A flexible width page layout is often referred to as a "liquid design" because the page contents resize with the browser window.*

Designing Fixed Width Tables

With a fixed width approach, you lay out your entire page in one table. This table is then set to a fixed width and (optionally) centered. This is the approach we used in the last exercise. When the user resizes the browser window, the table is frozen on the page. The width of the table should be set low enough to display at the most widely used resolution (800 × 600). Centering the table splits the excess space around it when viewed at higher resolutions.

Designing Flexible Width Tables

A table set to a percentage will expand and contract along with the width of the user's screen. A common technique is to lay out your entire page in one table and set its width to 100%. This means the table will occupy the entire width of the browser window.

 Hands-On 8.9   **Observe Frozen and Liquid Tables**

In this exercise, you will open two versions of the same page. One page uses frozen design; the other page uses liquid design.

1. Open st_james_liquid.htm, and then open st_james_frozen.htm from the lesson_08 folder.

2. Preview st_james_frozen.htm in your browser.

3. Resize the browser window by making it more narrow and as wide as possible.
   Observe that the table is "frozen" on the page—it doesn't resize with the browser window.

4. Return to the Document window.

5. Preview st_james_liquid.htm in your browser.

6. Resize the browser window by making it more narrow, and then as wide as possible.
   Observe that the page content stretches to occupy 100% of the browser window.

7. Leave your browser open and return to the Document window.

8. Choose File→Close all from the menu bar.

Planning a Flexible Width Table

Let's take a close look at st_james_liquid.htm and explore how liquid page design works. You might be surprised at how easy it really is to make your pages work in any size browser window.

The page in the following illustration consists of five tables, as follows:

1. The outer table—This is identical to the outline table you created on the Xtreme Ice page, except that the background color is different and the width is set to 100%.

2. A fixed width table—This contains 12 images. The total width of all the images is 696 pixels. The table is set to a fixed width of 696 pixels to keep the images from shifting.

3. **A fixed width table**—This table is also 696 pixels wide and contains two cells. Each cell contains one image. The first cell is aligned to the left; the second cell is aligned to the right.

4. **The main content table**—This is set to 100% so the content flows all the way across the page. The second table cell contains a background image. There are several invisible spacer GIFs in the last row of this table (which, of course, you can't see). We'll look more closely at this row in Expanded Tables mode.

5. **A small table of graphic links**—This will be cut and pasted into the far right cell in the main content table.

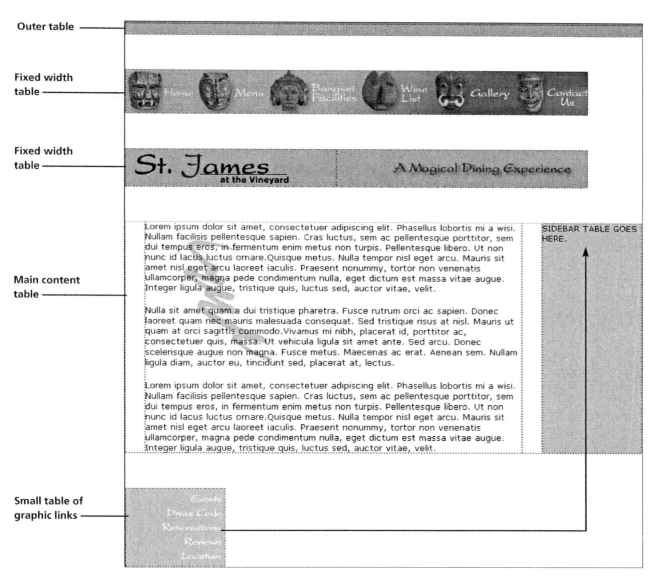

Get comfortable; we're going to now take a closer look at how this liquid page was built.

Hands-On 8.10   Analyze and Reassemble a Liquid Table Design

In this exercise, you will analyze and reassemble a liquid table design.

1. Open st_james_hack.htm from the lesson_08 folder.

   This is a disassembled version of the St. James page. The page margins are all set to 0. You can check this by choosing Modify→Page properties from the menu bar.

2. Notice the five tables, one after another, on the page.

3. Choose View→Table Mode→Expanded Tables mode from the menu bar.

   The extra spacing and padding in this mode will help you understand the layout much better.

4. Observe that in the second table each of these images appears in an individual table cell.

5. Scroll down to the bottom row of the main content area shown in the following illustration:

A A 30 x 1 pixel spacer is inside this cell. This creates a 30 pixel wide column of white space.

| | ullamcorper, magna pede condimentum nulla, eget dictum est massa vitae augue. Integer ligula augue, tristique quis, luctus sed, auctor vitae, velit. | | |

B A 200 x 1 pixel spacer is inside this cell. This stops the text from wrapping when the browser is resized too narrow.

C A 30 x 1 pixel spacer is inside this cell. This creates a 30 pixel wide column of white space.

D A 150 x 1 pixel spacer is inside this cell. This ensures that this cell will remain at a fixed width once the small table is inserted.

6. Locate the small table shown in the following partial illustration:

   The spacer image is selected to show you its width and height. The width is the same width as the table; the height is 30 pixels, which expands the height of the table cell to provide extra white space above the table.

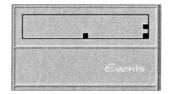

7. Switch back to Standard mode.

8. Delete the text in the main content table that reads, SIDEBAR TABLE GOES HERE.

9. Select the small table at the bottom of the page and cut it to the Clipboard.

10. Paste the table inside the cell whose text you just deleted.

11. Place the insertion point directly below the second table and press [Delete] or [Backspace] to remove the space.

12. Place the insertion point directly below the third table and press [Delete] or [Backspace] to remove the space.

13. Click above the second table and carefully drag down to select the tables below.

    Be careful not to extend the selection below the last table on the page.

14. Cut and paste the three tables inside the table at the top of the page.

    If necessary, remove any extra space between the tables. The page should now resemble the following illustration:

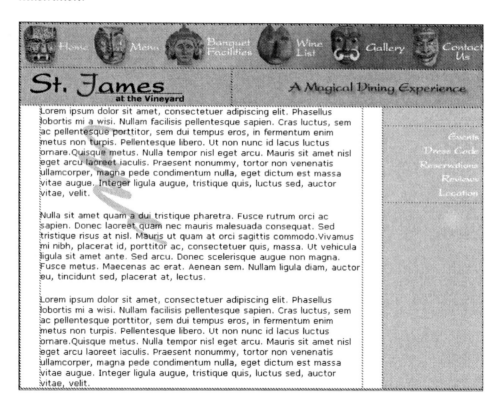

15. Preview the file in your browser.

16. Resize the browser window to make it narrow and then wide.

17. Leave the browser window and return to the Document window.

18. Close all files.

Concepts Review

True/False Questions

1. Tables were originally designed to anchor text and graphics on a Web page. TRUE FALSE

2. The default horizontal alignment for table data cells is left. TRUE FALSE

3. You can merge any number of adjacent cells as long as the entire selection is rectangular or square. TRUE FALSE

4. A table cell with the widest content determines the width of the entire column. TRUE FALSE

5. If you create a 600 pixel wide table and you insert a 650 pixel wide image, the table remains 600 pixels wide. TRUE FALSE

6. A table set to a percentage will expand and contract along with the width of the browser window. TRUE FALSE

7. When using spacers, you should always use a cool name for the alternative text. TRUE FALSE

8. Expanded Tables mode is not intended for editing purposes. TRUE FALSE

9. Nested tables are tables that appear inside other tables. TRUE FALSE

10. If you are designing a fixed width page layout for 800 × 600 screen resolution, all tables on the page should be 800 pixels wide. TRUE FALSE

Multiple Choice Questions

1. Which of the following best describes Lipsum (Lorem Ipsum)?
   a. An ancient roman scholar
   b. Pig Latin
   c. A combination of Latin and Greek
   d. Placeholder text

2. When adding background color to a table, rows, and cells, which element has the highest priority?
   a. Table
   b. Cell
   c. Row
   d. Page

3. A table can contain which of the following elements?
   a. Text
   b. Hypertext
   c. Graphics
   d. All of the above

4. When you are having difficulty selecting a 1 pixel spacer GIF, which option should you choose?
   a. Try to locate it in Code view.
   b. Switch to Layout mode.
   c. Switch to Expanded Tables mode.
   d. Use the Properties panel.

Skill Builders

Skill Builder 8.1   Align and Populate Table Cells

In this exercise, you will design a basic page layout and use Expanded Tables mode, insert images, set cell alignment, add spacers, and set page and table background color.

1. Open entertainment.htm from the review_08 folder.
   The page contains a five row, five column table that is set to 100% wide.

2. Choose View→Table Mode→Expanded Tables mode from the menu bar or tap ⬚F6.
   It will be much easier to insert images in this mode.

3. Insert jazz.gif into the second cell in the second row and set the Alt property to the text of your choosing.

4. Insert piano_bar.gif into the second cell in the fourth row and set the Alt property to the text of your choosing.

5. Save the file.
   Your page should resemble this illustration:

6. Preview the file in your browser.
   The text flows all the way across the page because the table width is set to 100%.

7. Resize the browser window from left to right and observe how the text wraps.

8. Leave the browser open and return to the Document window.
   Remain in Expanded Tables mode and keep the file open.

Skill Builder 8.2   Insert Spacers

In this exercise you will modify the document you developed in the last exercise. The page layout of the document has several flaws. The text is too close to the graphics so when the browser window is too narrow, the heading wraps to the next line. You will add a few spacers to prevent the excessive text wrap. You will also set the Alt property of each spacer to <empty> immediately after you change the width.

1. Follow these steps to add four spacers to cells in the last row:

    The widths of the four spacers total 480 pixels. The width of each image in the second column is 150 pixels. The combined widths total 630 pixels, which is within the range of a window size of 760 × 420. Be sure to set the Alt property of each spacer to <empty>.

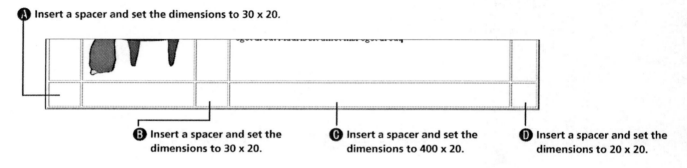

Ⓐ **Insert a spacer and set the dimensions to 30 x 20.**

Ⓑ **Insert a spacer and set the dimensions to 30 x 20.**

Ⓒ **Insert a spacer and set the dimensions to 400 x 20.**

Ⓓ **Insert a spacer and set the dimensions to 20 x 20.**

2. Choose View→Table Mode→Standard mode on the menu bar or tap F6 to return to Standard mode.

3. Use the Window Size pop-up menu to set the window size to 760 × 420 (800 × 600, Maximized).

    Ensure that a horizontal scroll bar doesn't appear at the bottom of the document window. If you see a horizontal scroll bar, you need to do the math to ensure that the total width of all spacers doesn't exceed 480 pixels.

4. Preview the file in your browser.

5. Resize the browser window to the left just before the horizontal scroll bar appears at the bottom of the page and observe that the spacers prevent the text from wrapping when the browser encounters the spacers, which are propping open the table cells.

6. Leave the browser open and return to the Document window.

7. Save the file but keep it open.

Skill Builder 8.3   Add Background Color

In this exercise, you will apply background color to the page and to table cells. Optionally, you can add a border to the table and practice adding border colors to table cells.

1. Select the table and use the BG Color box on the Properties panel to set the background color for the table.

   Feel free to color each row or any individual table cell instead of having the table appear in one color.

2. (Optional) Add at least a 1 pixel border to the table.

3. (Optional) Select a table cell or a series of table cells and use the Brdr (Border Color) box on the Properties panel to apply border color.

   To select a series of table cells, use Ctrl *or* ⌘ *-click in each cell.*

4. Choose Modify→Page Properties.

5. Choose a page font type, font size, and background color. Then set the page margins.

6. Tweak the colors and margin settings until you are satisfied with the color scheme and layout.

7. Save and close the file.

Skill Builder 8.4   Merge Table Cells

In this exercise, you will merge table cells, set cell properties, and insert images to create a basic page layout.

1. Open empowerment.htm from the review_08 folder.

   The page contains a 4 × 3 table. Text for one of the table cells appears below the table.

2. Merge the table cells as shown in the following illustration. Select the cells, and then choose Modify→Table→Merge Cells, or press M (Mac and Win).
   This is an undocumented shortcut to merge table cells.

3. Insert empower.gif in the cell that forms the first row.

4. Insert spacer_red.gif in the cell that forms the second row and set the dimensions to 560 × 1.
   Use Expanded Tables mode if you wish for this step. Don't forget to set the Alt property to <empty>.

5. Cut the text to the Clipboard and paste it into the empty merged cell in the third row (the cell that spans two rows).

6. Click outside the table.

This allows Dreamweaver to readjust the table based on the new contents.

7. Follow these steps to insert the final images:

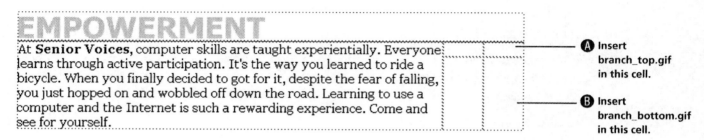

Ⓐ Insert branch_top.gif in this cell.

Ⓑ Insert branch_bottom.gif in this cell.

8. Select the cell that contains the branch bottom image and set the vertical alignment to Top.

9. Set the alternative text property for the empowerment image and the two branches to <empty> or to the text of your choosing.

10. Save the file, and then preview it in your browser.

Your file should match this illustration:

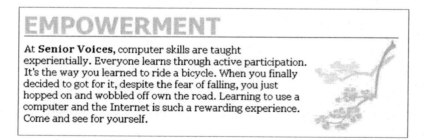

11. Leave your browser open and return to the Document window.

12. Close the file.

Assessments

Assessment 8.1   Design a Basic Page Layout

In this exercise, you will design a page with a nested table.

1. Create a new HTML document and save it as **tango.htm**. Store the file in the review_08 folder.

2. Insert a table and set the following properties:

Rows	5
Columns	4
Table Width	100%
Border, Cell Padding, and Cell Spacing	0

3. Insert tango_logo.gif into the third cell of the second row.

4. Open tango.txt from the review_08/text folder. Copy and paste the text into the third cell of the third row, and then close the text file.

5. Insert tango.gif in line with the text in the location of your choosing.

6. Set the image alignment property to left or right.

7. Set the vertical alignment property of the first cell in the third row to top.
This cell will contain a small nested table.

8. Switch to Expanded Tables mode.

9. Insert a new table with these properties into the first cell in the third row:

Rows	5
Columns	3
Table Width	115 pixels
Border, Cell Padding, and Cell Spacing	0

10. Populate the table, as shown in the following illustration, and follow these guidelines to insert spacer GIFs in the last row:

Remember to set the Alt property for all spacers to <empty>.

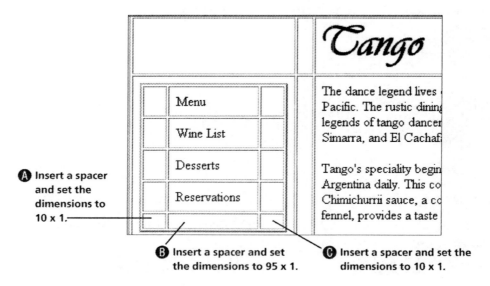

Ⓐ Insert a spacer and set the dimensions to 10 x 1.

Ⓑ Insert a spacer and set the dimensions to 95 x 1.

Ⓒ Insert a spacer and set the dimensions to 10 x 1.

11. Switch to Standard mode.

12. Set the Alt property for the tango and dancer graphics.

Use the text of your choosing. Your file should resemble the following illustration:

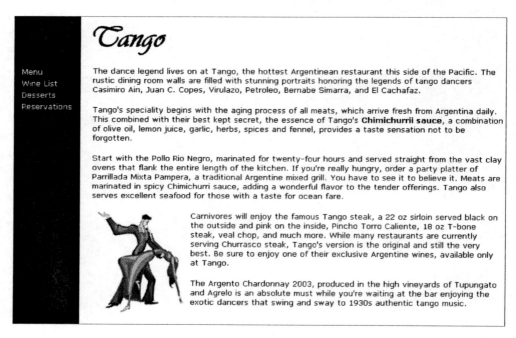

13. Save the file but keep it open.

Assessment 8.2   Format a Page Layout Table

In this exercise, you will format the Tango page you designed in the last exercise. Page layout is subjective. Feel free to experiment with different font groupings, text and link colors, and page background colors.

1. Select the text in the first small table cell, type **#** in the Link text field on the Properties panel, and press Enter or Return.

   The pound (#) sign creates a link placeholder that enables you to test link state colors and underline style properties. Placeholder links behave like real links, except they don't jump anywhere.

2. Repeat step 1 for the remaining text in the table.

3. Click inside the first table cell in the first row, and then drag straight down to select the entire row and the nested table.

4. Set the background color to **#000000** (black).

5. Click in the content table (the main table on the right) and click the <table> tag on the Tag Selector.

6. Set the background color to **#FFFFFF** (white).

   The layout should now resemble the following illustration:

7. Choose Modify→Page Properties from the menu bar.

8. Set the page font, background color, link colors, and underline style properties as you like. The following property settings are merely suggestions:

Appearance Category	
Page Font	Veranda, Arial, Helvetica, sans-serif
Size	Small
Background Color	#FFFFFF
Links Category	
Link Color	#FFFFFF
Rollover Links	#DA1707
Visited	#666666
Underline Style	Never Underline

9. Save and close the file.

Critical Thinking

Critical Thinking 8.1   On Your Own

Just in Time Design is recruiting new employees to help them with their demanding Web design schedule. Justin distributes a picture of a Web page to your Dreamweaver class and asks anyone interested to recreate the liquid page layout design. The winner will receive a $500 hiring bonus and an extra week of paid vacation.

Using the details shown in the following illustration, design this Web page layout. All the files can be found in the review_08 folder. All the images are in the images folder.

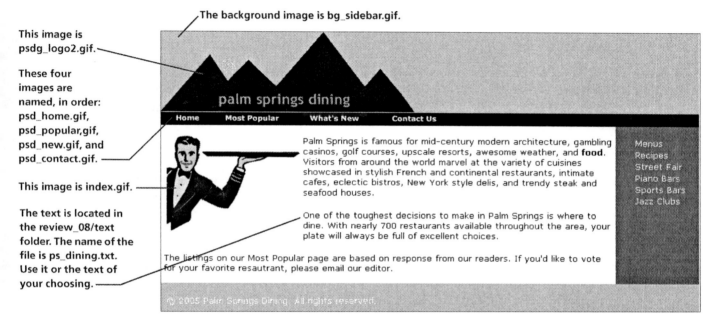

The background image is bg_sidebar.gif.

This image is psdg_logo2.gif.

These four images are named, in order: psd_home.gif, psd_popular.gif, psd_new.gif, and psd_contact.gif.

This image is index.gif.

The text is located in the review_08/text folder. The name of the file is ps_dining.txt. Use it or the text of your choosing.

palm springs dining

Home   Most Popular   What's New   Contact Us

Palm Springs is famous for mid-century modern architecture, gambling casinos, golf courses, upscale resorts, awesome weather, and **food**. Visitors from around the world marvel at the variety of cuisines showcased in stylish French and continental restaurants, intimate cafes, eclectic bistros, New York style delis, and trendy steak and seafood houses.

One of the toughest decisions to make in Palm Springs is where to dine. With nearly 700 restaurants available throughout the area, your plate will always be full of excellent choices.

The listings on our Most Popular page are based on response from our readers. If you'd like to vote for your favorite resautrant, please email our editor.

Menus
Recipes
Street Fair
Piano Bars
Sports Bars
Jazz Clubs

© 2005 Palm Springs Dining. All rights reserved.

When you are finished, save the file as **palm_springs_dining.htm** in the review_08 folder, and then close it.

Working with Styles

In this lesson, you will learn more about how to use styles in cascading style sheets. CSS has taken the World Wide Web to a new level of sophistication with formatting capabilities that were once available only in print media. Web designers now have more precise control over page layout, fonts, colors, backgrounds, and other typographical effects. Now there is a way to update the appearance and formatting of an unlimited number of pages by modifying just one document. New advancements allow for compatibility across browsers and platforms, less code, smaller pages, and faster download times. This lesson covers what CSS styles are, where they reside, how they are created and modified, the three types of CSS selector styles, and how external style sheets are created and linked to other pages in your site.

Case Study

Just in Time Design has a new client, Lillian, who is Justin's mom. Lillian is the founder of Senior Voices, a senior citizens group that gets together several times a week to learn and share computer and Internet skills. Lillian has persuaded Justin to share his knowledge with her group so they may build and post a Web site dedicated to empowering seniors in their community. As he contemplates how this Web site might be designed, Justin considers how many seniors have vision problems and other special needs, so he chooses a design that has scalable font sizes and well-organized headings. Justin has been experimenting with CSS and thinks, "Hmm, maybe this is the page I should design before unleashing my CSS skills to paying clients." Lillian, naturally proud of her son, shares the finished page with her group.

A heading with a border on the left and top, and letter spacing increased to improve readability

Senior Voices

Self-Empowerment Through Learning

Welcome to **Senior Voices**. It is never too late to learn. If you doubt it for a moment, ask anyone attending our computer workshops. Our youngest student is 71, and our oldest is 93. When we opened our doors a few months ago, most of our students didn't know how to type. Some had never used an electronic keyboard; most had never seen the Internet. In fact, one Senior Voice's member thought the Internet was a subversive spy ring like the CIA. Today, we're writing about issues that are important to us, and sharing that information with others. Through the generous donation of a major computer company, we now have a state-of-the-art computer room and everyone has their own mouse!

At Senior Voices, computer skills are taught experientially. Everyone learns through active participation. It's the way you learned to ride a bicycle. When you finally decided to got for it, despite the fear of falling, you just hopped on and wobbled off down the road. Learning to use a computer and the Internet is such a rewarding experience. Come and see for yourself.

Courses:

- Introduction to the Internet
- How to Choose an Internet Service Provider
- How to Configure Email
- Using Dreamweaver MX 2004

A background image centered precisely on the page

Schedule:

Day	Time	Instructor
Monday	9-12	Bill
Wednesday	9-10:30	Jill
Friday	9-12	Jill

Paragraph text that displays differently, but only when the paragraph is inside a table cell

New classes are being added each month. Watch the bulletin board for announcements.

We live in the Communication Age. At home or at a senior center, with the help of a computer and the Internet, you have limitless access to Health Care Information, Financial Services, Social Services, and a lot more! Join the 21st Century. Join Senior Voices!

© 2005 Senior Voices

247

Getting Started with CSS

Cascading style sheets (CSS) is a universal, text-based language that any computer can read. A style sheet is a group of styles. Each style in the style sheet has specific formatting instructions, called rules. A rule to format all of the text on the page in the Verdana font would look like this in CSS:

```
body { font-family: Verdana }
```

A Web browser could use this rule to apply the Verdana font to all text elements on a Web page. Styles are most commonly used to format text, but they also include formatting properties for tables, layers, images, and other page layout elements.

Here we explore style storage locations, the three types of styles, and how styles are applied in a "cascading" order.

Understanding Style Storage Locations

As you create styles for your site, they are stored internally, in the Web page itself, or in another file called an external style sheet. External styles are stored in a style sheet file along with your other Web page documents. External style sheets are a good choice for multiple pages because you can use them to maintain design consistency throughout all of the pages in your site. When you want to update the look of your site, open the external style sheet and make changes. All of the pages linked to the style sheet are then updated automatically when opened in a browser.

Internal styles appear in the head of your page in Code view. They apply to a single document and are not shared with any other pages. Internal styles are a good choice when you have a single page that you want to format differently from other pages in your site. You have already created many internal styles. You've also learned how to export internal styles to create an external style sheet.

Inline styles are those that appear inside an HTML tag. This type of style is used to modify a single occurrence of a tag. This example changes the font of a single paragraph:

```
<p style="font-family: Verdana">When displayed in a Web browser, this text
will appear in the Verdana font.</p>
```

Inline styles used for formatting purposes, as shown in the previous example, are rarely used because they must be hand coded and are difficult to maintain. The reason they're mentioned here is because one day you may have to reformat a page that contains this type of style.

Dreamweaver creates inline styles only when you draw a layer and position it on a Web page. You will learn more about inline styles and layers in Lesson 14, Working with Layers.

Understanding Style Types

When you begin to create CSS styles from scratch, you need to determine the type of styles you're going to need. Dreamweaver provides three CSS style types: class selectors, tag selectors, and advanced selectors. A selector is merely the type of the style that you're defining.

A class selector is a custom style you can attach manually to HTML elements, such as paragraphs, text, headings, table cells, list items, etc. For example, if you want your copyright text to be displayed in bold and dark green, you can create a class selector style named "copyright" with boldface and dark green text formatting. You would then select your copyright text on the page and apply the copyright style.

A tag selector is a style created to redefine the appearance of all elements that share the same HTML tag. For example, if you want all of your paragraph text to be displayed in the Georgia font and dark gray, you would create a tag selector style using the paragraph tag <p> and specify the Georgia font and dark gray color. All paragraph text on a page would automatically appear in that style because you've redefined the style for the paragraph tag.

 TIP! *When you want one or more paragraphs on the same page to display in a different font and a smaller font size, simply define a class selector style and apply it to the selected paragraphs.*

Advanced selectors fall into three categories: ID, contextual selectors, and pseudo-classes. They will be covered later in this lesson.

Understanding the Cascading Order

The term "cascading" refers to the order in which styles are applied to a Web page. Let's say that you've specified the following formatting instructions for all paragraphs on the same page:

- External style sheet—font family Verdana

- Internal style sheet—font family Arial

- Inline style—font family Helvetica

When a Web browser loads the page, it has to figure out the order of the styles in order to apply them correctly. Which style wins? The style closest to the element being modified by the style, and that would be the inline style.

Generally speaking, the order of precedence (top priority) is:

1. Inline styles

2. Internal styles

3. External styles

Number 1 has the highest priority, which means that it will override any conflicting internal or external style sheet.

 TIP! *If you carefully plan your styles and know how to read them, you can avoid the complexity of troubleshooting style conflicts that may occur when you use both internal and external styles.*

Before we continue with this lesson, let's make sure that the recommended CSS Styles preferences are set on your computer.

 Hands-On 9.1   Set CSS Styles Preferences

In this exercise, you will set CSS Styles preferences.

1. Choose Edit→Preferences (Win) or Dreamweaver→Preferences (Mac).

2. Choose the Category CSS Styles.

3. Use the following illustration to set CSS Styles preferences:

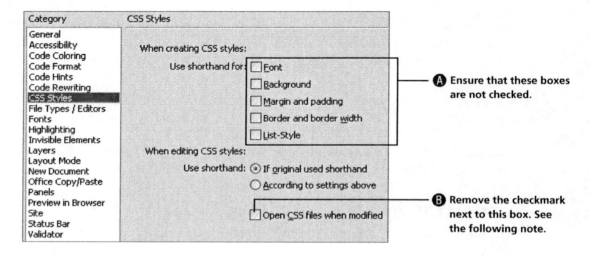

NOTE! *When this box is checked, the external style sheet file is automatically opened when styles are modified. New web designers might find this feature distracting.*

Exploring the Anatomy of a Style

Browsers are programmed to translate all Web based languages. If only we had those multilingual capabilities and that speed! We poor humans have to take our time and read code very carefully, line by line, if we are to truly understand what's going on behind the scenes.

Reading Internal Style Code

When you use the Page Properties dialog box or the Properties panel to create the first CSS style on a new page, Dreamweaver automatically adds a pair of style tags <style> </style> and a comment tag <!-- --> in Code view. (You will learn more about the comment tag in Lesson 15, Working with HTML.)

Modern browsers ignore the comment and process the CSS code that appears inside the comment tags; older browsers that do not support CSS ignore the styles altogether and continue processing the page. The following example is an internal style used to format all paragraph text on a Web page:

```
<style type="text/css">
<!--
p { font-family: Verdana }
-->
</style>
```

Now, let's look at just the CSS style to make it easier to read. This example is a tag selector style.

```
p { font-family: Verdana }
```

The style begins with p, which is a paragraph tag selector. Following the tag selector is a single rule, which is enclosed in a pair of curly braces { }. The rule describes the formatting the browser should apply to all paragraphs on the page.

The rule consists of a style property and its value. The combination of the property and the value is called a declaration. In the following example, the style tells a Web browser that all paragraph text on the page should be formatted in the Verdana font.

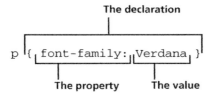

Now, let's review the following class selector style example. A class selector style begins with a period and is followed by a name that you supply. The style in the following example has two rules: one that specifies the font size and another that specifies the text color. The two rules are separated by a semicolon. The style tells a Web browser that any text that uses this style should be 12 pixels tall and gray, as designated by the hex code #CCCCCC.

```
.copyright { font-size: 12px; color: #CCCCCC }
```

Reading External Style Code

External styles look almost identical to internal styles, but do not contain HTML code. In the following example, notice the absence of the style and comment tags.

```
ul { list-style-type: square }
```

This tag selector style tells a Web browser that any list item element that appears in an unordered list (bulleted list) should be formatted with a square. (You learned about unordered and ordered lists in Lesson 3, Working with Text.)

Creating Styles from Scratch

The Page Properties dialog box and the Properties panel only offer limited CSS capabilities and, as you've seen, all of the styles you create with these tools are stored internally. When you use the CSS Styles panel to create styles from scratch, you have access to **all** of the CSS formatting properties. You also have an opportunity to store the new styles internally or externally.

Using the CSS Styles Panel

FROM THE KEYBOARD

To open the CSS Styles panel:

WIN AND MAC

Shift + F11

The following illustration serves as a refresher on how to use the CSS Styles panel. To open the Styles panel, choose Window→CSS Styles.

Selectors appear in the left column; properties and values appear in the right column.

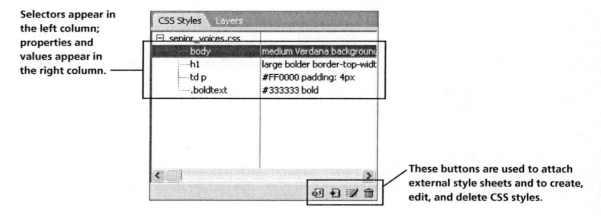

These buttons are used to attach external style sheets and to create, edit, and delete CSS styles.

Using the New CSS Style Dialog Box

When you choose Text→CSS Styles→New from the menu bar or click the New CSS Style button at the bottom of the CSS Styles dialog box, the New CSS Style dialog box opens. The New CSS Style dialog box allows you to choose among three selector types and two storage locations for the new styles. The pop-up menu at the top of the dialog box changes names based on the selector type you choose.

In the following illustration, the Class Selector Type is chosen and the pop-up menu above Selector Type reads Name. This selector type allows you to create your own class styles that can be applied to one or more elements on the page. To create a new class, replace the default name (.unnamed1) in the Name box and precede the style name with a period. If you forget the period, Dreamweaver will add it for you.

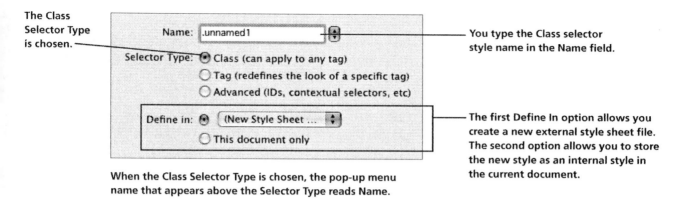

The Class Selector Type is chosen.

When the Class Selector Type is chosen, the pop-up menu name that appears above the Selector Type reads Name.

You type the Class selector style name in the Name field.

The first Define In option allows you create a new external style sheet file. The second option allows you to store the new style as an internal style in the current document.

In the following illustration, the Tag Selector Type is chosen and the pop-up menu reads Tag. The Tag Selector Type allows you to specify an HTML tag as the tag that will be redefined by the new style. The default appearance of the tag becomes modified by the style.

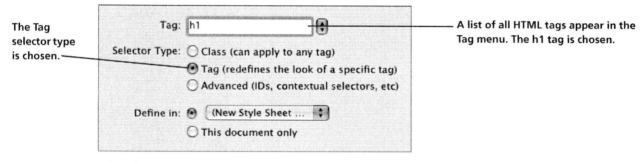

The Tag selector type is chosen.

When the Tag selector type is chosen, the pop-up menu name that appears above the Selector Type reads Tag.

A list of all HTML tags appear in the Tag menu. The h1 tag is chosen.

The Advanced selector type allows you to create styles that provide additional control in particular situations, including styles for link states and those that only work in a certain context. When you choose this option and expand the pop-up menu, the four link states (pseudo-classes) appear in a list: a:link, a:visited, a:hover, and a:active. To choose any of the other options (ID, contextual selectors), you type the name in the Selector field.

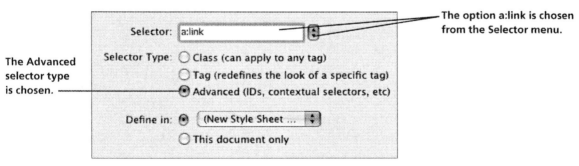

The Advanced selector type is chosen.

When the Advanced selector type is chosen, the pop-up menu that appears above the Selector Type reads Selector.

The option a:link is chosen from the Selector menu.

Using the CSS Style Definition Dialog Box

The CSS Style dialog box opens when you specify which selector type you're creating in the New CSS Style dialog box. This dialog box provides 8 categories and 67 properties you can use to style your Web pages. You will explore many of these categories and properties in this lesson.

The Type category is chosen.

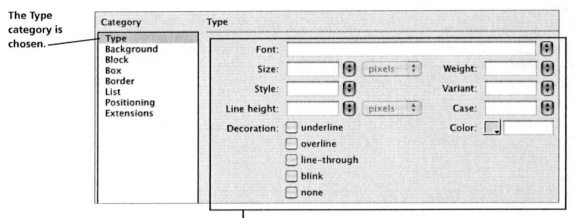

The property settings for the current category are shown here.

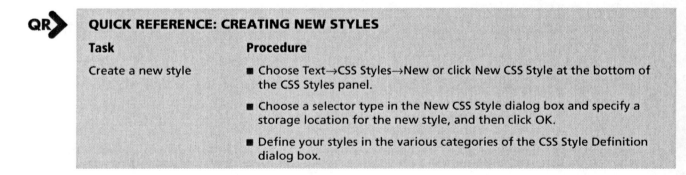

QUICK REFERENCE: CREATING NEW STYLES

Task	Procedure
Create a new style	■ Choose Text→CSS Styles→New or click New CSS Style at the bottom of the CSS Styles panel.
	■ Choose a selector type in the New CSS Style dialog box and specify a storage location for the new style, and then click OK.
	■ Define your styles in the various categories of the CSS Style Definition dialog box.

Hands-On 9.2   Create Tag and Class Selector Styles

In this exercise, you will use Code view to explore the anatomy of a style as you create it.

1. Open dixie.htm from the lesson_09 folder.
    The document doesn't contain a single style.

2. Choose Window→CSS Styles from the menu bar.
    This opens the CSS Styles panel.

3. Choose View→Code or click the [Code] button on the Document toolbar.
    It is not important that you understand the tags that appear in the head of the document.

4. Locate <title>Dixie Miller Presents</title> near the top of the page. This tag identifies the page title.
    The internal style will automatically appear below the title when you set a page property for this document. You don't have to worry about the position of the insertion point.

5. Click the New CSS Style ⬛ button at the bottom of the CSS Styles panel or choose Text→CSS Styles→New from the menu bar.
   This opens the New CSS Style dialog box.

6. Set the options in the New CSS Style dialog box fields according to the following table:

Selector Type	Tag
Tag	h1 (choose it from the pop-up menu)
Define In	This Document Only

7. Click OK.
   The CSS Style Definition dialog box opens.

8. Move the CSS Style Definition dialog box away from the head of the document so you can easily see the code each time you add a new style.

9. In Code view, note the <style></style> tags that appear below the <title></title> tags. Also, note the light gray HTML comment tag.
   Dreamweaver color codes the tags to help you easily locate the styles within the tags.

10. In the CSS Style Definition dialog box, ensure that the Type category is chosen.

11. From the Font pop-up menu, choose Verdana, Arial, Helvetica, Sans-Serif. Click Apply.
    Dreamweaver updates the style to show the first style rule for the h1 selector.

12. From the Size pop-up menu, choose X-large and click Apply.
    Continue to observe the styles each time you click Apply.

13. Click the Color box and use the Color Picker to select a dark gray or type **#333333** in the Color hex box located to the right of the Color box. Click Apply.
    You should now have three separate rules for the h1 style.

14. Click OK.

15. Choose View→Design or click the 🔲 Design button on the Document toolbar.
    Observe the change to the page Heading.

16. Save the file but leave it open.

Creating and Applying Class Selector Styles

What do you do when you need to create a new style but there is no HTML tag for the style? You start from the beginning to create a class selector style. If you've used the Properties panel to format a Web page element, you've already created a class style. The first style you create with the Properties panel is automatically named .style1 and is added to the <style> tag in the head of your HTML document.

```
.style1 { font-size: small; }
```

When you create a class style from scratch, you must name it and then apply it to one or more elements on the page. Use short, descriptive names that begin with a period. If you forget to type the period when you're defining the style, Dreamweaver adds it for you. This is an example of the class style you'll define in the next exercise.

```
.dixie { font-size: x-small; color: #333333; }
```

When you apply the dixie class style to a paragraph tag, Dreamweaver adds the class property to the paragraph tag. When the style is applied, the period that precedes the style name is not used.

```
<p class="dixie">
```

If you apply the class style to a selection that isn't a tag, for example a single word, or a text selection that doesn't include an entire paragraph, Dreamweaver wraps the selection within a <span> tag like this:

```
<span class="dixie">Dixie Miller</span>
```

The <span> tag applies a style to a span of text that can't be identified by an HTML tag.

 ## Hands-On 9.3   Create a Class Selector Style

In this exercise, you will create a class selector style.

Before you begin: The dixie.htm file should still be open.

1. Choose View→Code or click the ◇ Code button on the Document toolbar.
2. Locate the h1 style you created in the previous exercise.
3. Choose Text→CSS Styles→New from the menu bar or click the New CSS Style button on the CSS Styles panel.
4. Set the options in the New CSS Style dialog box fields according to the following table:

Selector Type	Class
Name	**.dixie**
Define In	This Document Only

5. Click OK.
   The CSS Style Definition dialog box opens.
6. Note that the new class selector style appears below the h1 style.
7. Click the Color box and use the Color Picker to select Red or type **#FF0000** in the color hex box located to the right of the Color box. Click Apply.
8. Click OK.
9. Choose View→Design or click the ⬚ Design button on the Document toolbar.
10. Save the file but leave it open.

Applying a Class Selector Style

To apply a class style, select an element on the page and use the Style or Class menu on the Properties panel. The Properties panel displays the Style menu when the selection is text; it displays the Class menu when the selection is any object other than text (images, tables, etc.).

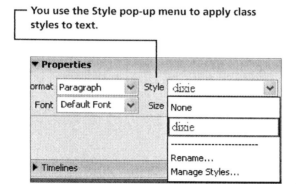

You use the Style pop-up menu to apply class styles to text.

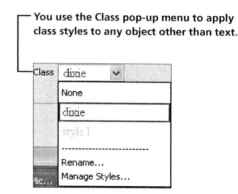

You use the Class pop-up menu to apply class styles to any object other than text.

 Hands-On 9.4   Apply a Class Style

In this exercise, you will apply the dixie style to selected text on the page.

Before you begin: The file dixie.htm should still be open.

1. Select the text Dixie Miller in the first paragraph.

2. Choose dixie from the Style pop-up menu on the Properties panel.
   This applies the style to the selected text. Do NOT deselect the text.

3. Note the tag <span.dixie> on the Tag Selector.

4. Switch to Code view and observe how the <span> tag and class attribute (property) are tied to form the style.
   The <span> tag is used because you applied the style to a text selection, not an HTML tag.

5. Switch back to Design view.

6. Select the entire last paragraph on the page.

7. Apply the dixie style to the paragraph. Do NOT deselect the text.

8. Note the <p.dixie> tag on the Tag Selector.
   The <p> tag is used because you applied the style to an HTML element, not a text selection.

9. Save the file but leave it open.

Detaching Class Styles

As you saw in the previous exercise, when you apply a class style, Dreamweaver add the class attribute to an HTML element. To change the class style, either apply another class style to the selection to override the style or detach it. You will undoubtedly need to detach class styles at some point, especially when you inherit Web pages from clients or co-workers.

Hands-On 9.5   Detach Class Styles

In this exercise, you will detach class styles and delete internal styles.

1. Select the last paragraph of text on the page.

2. Switch to Code view.
   You don't have to be in Code view to detach a style, but it provides a visual guarantee that the class attribute is indeed detached.

3. Choose None from the Style pop-up menu on the Properties panel.
   This detaches the class attribute from the paragraph tag.

4. Switch to Design view.

5. Save and close the file.

 TIP! *To detach all class styles in a page, in Design view, choose Edit→Select All, and then choose None from the Styles menu on the Properties panel.*

Creating Advanced Selector Styles

You may recall from the beginning of this lesson that Dreamweaver lumps three selector styles into the advanced selector type category: ID, contextual selectors, and pseudo-classes. This section focuses on two advanced selector types: contextual selectors and pseudo-classes.

Creating Contextual Selector Styles

A contextual selector (also called a descendent selector) is one that must appear in a specific situation for a style to be applied. Say you have multiple paragraphs that appear inside and outside of table cells. You'd like to be able to format only the paragraphs that appear inside the table cells with a different color and some padding. You could create a contextual selector style such as the one shown in the following example:

```
td p { color: #FF0000; padding: 20px; }
```

This code talks to the browser, saying, "Format only paragraph text that appears inside a table data (<td>) cell red and add 20 pixels of padding to the top, bottom, left, and right."

Creating Pseudo-Class Selector Styles

You'll be relieved to know that pseudo-classes are merely styles for the four link states (a:link, a:visited, a:hover, and a:active). To ensure that these pseudo-class styles work properly, they must be defined in the order in which they appear in the New CSS Style dialog box. There are four pseudo-class selector styles:

- a:link—A link that has not been clicked

- a:visited—A link that has been clicked

- a:hover—The link as the mouse pointer rolls over it

- a:active—The link that's being clicked at this moment

 Hands-On 9.6   Create Advanced Selectors

In this exercise, you will create a contextual selector and four pseudo-class selectors.

1. Open advanced_selectors.htm from the lesson_09 folder.
   The file contains two headings, three paragraphs, and two tables.

2. Choose Text→CSS Styles→New from the menu bar or click the New CSS Style button in the CSS Styles panel.

Create a Contextual Selector

3. Set the options in the New CSS Style dialog box according to the following table:

Selector Type	Advanced
Selector	td p
Define In	This Document Only

4. Click OK.

5. Choose the Type category.

6. Click the Color box and use the Color Picker to select Red.

7. Click Apply, and then click OK.
   Only the paragraph text inside the table at the top of the page is red.

8. Choose Text→CSS Styles→New from the menu bar or click the New CSS Style button in the CSS Styles panel.

Create Pseudo-Class Selectors

9. Set the options in the New CSS Style dialog box according to the following table:

Selector Type	Advanced
Selector	a:link (choose it from the pop-up menu)
Define In	This Document Only

10. Click OK.

11. Choose the Type category.

12. Set the following properties:

Decoration	Place a checkmark next to None
Color	Type #0000FF in the Color hex field

13. Click OK.

14. Use the technique in steps 8–13 to set the remaining link colors.
    Use the decoration and link color of your choosing.

15. Save the file, and then preview it in your browser.

16. Use your mouse pointer to test each link state.

17. Leave your browser open and return to the Document window.

18. Close the file.

Exploring More CSS Style Categories

You've had the opportunity to use the Type category of the CSS Style Definition dialog box. Here, we explore four more categories: Background, Block, Box, and Border. Because you realistically would probably never use all of the properties in each of these categories on a single page, we provide an HTML document you can use to explore a variety of these properties in the following Hands-On exercises.

Setting Background Properties

You use the Background category of the CSS Style Definition dialog box to define background settings for a CSS Style. The Background category is used to set the background color and image for a page, table, or text block. You can also specify whether an image tiles horizontally or vertically, or not at all.

 ## Hands-On 9.7   Explore Background Properties

In this exercise, you create a class selector style to work with background color and a background image.

1. Choose Window→CSS Styles (if necessary) to open the Styles panel.

2. Open css_categories.htm from the lesson_09 folder.
   This page contains an internal style that defines the page and Heading 1 font.

3. Choose Text→CSS Styles→New from the menu bar or click the New CSS Style button on the CSS Styles panel.

4. Set the options in the New CSS Style dialog box according to the following table:

Selector Type	Class
Name	.bg
Define In	This Document Only

5. Click OK.

6. Choose the Background Category.

7. Set the following properties:

Background Color	Type **#FFFFCC** in the Background Color hex field.
Background Image	Click the Browse button, select baby.gif from the images folder, and then press Choose or OK.

8. Click OK to close the Style Definition dialog box.

9. Select all of the text that appears between the Background and Block headings.

10. From the Style pop-up menu on the Properties panel, choose bg, and then click anywhere outside the selected text.
    The image tiles horizontally and vertically, repeating as many times as it can in the text block.

11. Select the .bg style in the CSS Styles panel. If you don't see the style, you may need to click the arrow next to <style> to expand it. Then click the Edit Style button at the bottom of the panel.
    This opens the CSS Style Definition dialog box.

12. Choose the Background category.

13. From the Repeat pop-up menu, choose Repeat-X and click Apply.
    The image repeats horizontally across the text block.

14. Use the technique in step 13 to choose Repeat-Y and click Apply.
    The image repeats vertically down the text block.

15. Use the technique in step 13 to choose No-Repeat and click Apply.
    The image appears one time only in the upper left portion of the text block.

16. From the Horizontal Position pop-up menu, choose Center. Click Apply.
    This centers the background image in the center of the text block.

17. From the Vertical Position pop-up menu, choose Bottom. Click Apply.
    The background image is positioned at the bottom of the text block.

18. Practice the other Horizontal and Vertical Position properties and position the baby image in the location of your choosing. Click OK.

19. Save the file but leave it open.

Setting Block Properties

You use the Block category of the CSS Style Definition dialog box to define spacing and alignment settings. This category controls the alignment of text and images in a selected element. Word spacing and letter spacing settings allow you to increase the amount of white space between words or individual letters. Vertical alignment positions selected text or images in a table or layer. The Text Align property sets how text is aligned within an element.

Hands-On 9.8   Explore Block Properties

In this exercise, you will explore block properties.

Before you begin: The css_properties.htm file should be open.

1. Choose Text→CSS Styles→New from the menu bar or click the New CSS Style button on the CSS Styles panel.

2. Set the options in the New CSS Style dialog box according to the following table:

Selector Type	Class
Name Field	`.block`
Define In	This Document Only

3. Click OK.

4. Choose the Block category.

5. Set the following properties:

Letter Spacing	Type **2**, and then choose pixels from the Letter Spacing pop-up menu.
Text Indent	Type **30**, and then choose pixels from the Text Indent pop-up menu.

6. Click OK.

7. Select the text directly below the Block heading.

8. From the Style pop-up menu on the Properties panel, choose block.
The letter spacing is increased by 2 pixels and the first line of text is indented 30 pixels from the left margin.

9. Save the file but leave it open.

Setting Box Properties

You use the Box category of the CSS Style Definition dialog box to define settings that control the placement of elements on the page. Padding sets the space between an element and its border or the margin. Margin sets the amount of space around the outer edge of an element. Float places an element on the left or right margin so that other elements wrap around it. Clear determines whether text, for example, can appear to the left, right, or on neither side of a floating element.

Setting Border Properties

You use the Border category of the CSS Style Definition dialog box to define settings—such as width, color, and style—for the borders around elements.

Hands-On 9.9   Explore Box and Border Properties

In this exercise, you will explore box and border properties.

Before you begin: The css_properties.htm file should be open.

1. Choose Text→CSS Styles→New from the menu bar or click the New CSS Style button on the CSS Styles panel.

2. Set the options in the New CSS Style dialog box according to the following table:

Selector Type	Class
Name Field	**.boxandborder**
Define In	This Document Only

3. Click OK.

Set Box Properties

4. Choose the Box category.

5. Set the following properties:

Padding	Ensure that a checkmark appears next to Same for All.
	Type **60** in the Top field, and then choose pixels from the Top pop-up menu.

6. Click Apply. Do NOT close the dialog box.

Set Border Properties

7. Choose the Border category.

8. Set the following properties:

Ensure that a checkmark appears next to Same for All in the Style, Width, and Color columns.	
Style Top	Choose solid from the pop-up menu.
Width Top	Choose medium from the pop-up menu.
Color Top	Type **#0000FF** in the color hex field.

9. Click OK.

10. Select the text below the Border and Box heading.

11. From the Style pop-up menu on the Properties panel, choose boxandborder.
    A bright blue border appears around the text and the text is surrounded on all sides with 60 pixels of padding.

12. Save and close the file.

Creating an External Style Sheet

All of the styles you've created in this lesson have been internal styles. Admittedly, internal styles are the easiest to manage because they apply to a single page. However, the real power of CSS is the ability to create an external style sheet and link multiple pages to it. This way, you only have to modify one page.

We've shown you how to create all three selector types and you've gotten some hands-on practice using advanced CSS properties. In the real world, keep it simple! Of course, it's tempting to add every bell and whistle you can, but don't. Streamlined pages are much easier to manage than complex pages.

In the following exercise, you will use the Senior Voices page and just the styles you need to make the page pretty using CSS. Once the page is designed, you will open another Senior Voices page and attach your external style sheet.

 Hands-On 9.10   Create an External Style Sheet

In this exercise, you will create an external style sheet for use with the Senior Voices page.

1. Open senior_voices.htm from the lesson_09 folder.
   The page is designed for seniors, so your CSS font styles should be scalable to enable viewers to increase or decrease the font size in their browser.

2. Open the CSS Styles panel.

3. Click the New CSS Styles ⊞ button on the CSS Styles panel.

4. Set the options in the New CSS Style dialog box according to the following table:

Selector Type	Tag
Tag	body (choose it from the pop-up menu)
Define In	(New Style Sheet File)

5. Click OK.

6. Save the new style sheet as **senior_voices.css** in the lesson_09 folder.
   The external style sheet is created and the CSS Styles panel shows its name in the left column of the panel. The CSS Style Definition box opens.

Create Font Styles for All Body Text

7. Ensure that the Type category is chosen.

8. Set the following properties, and then click OK:

Font	Veranda, Arial, Helvetica, Sans-Serif
Size	Medium

9. Observe the new style in the CSS Styles panel.
   You may have to click the arrow next to the external style sheet name to see the style.

10. In the CSS Styles panel, select the style you just created for body.
Note that the buttons at the bottom of the Styles panel are available should you need to create a new style, edit an existing style, or delete a style.

11. Click the New CSS Style button in the CSS Styles panel.

12. Set the options in the New CSS Style dialog box according to the following table:

Selector Type	Tag
Tag	h1 (choose it from the pop-up menu)
Define In	senior_voices.css

13. Click OK.

Create a Heading 1 Style

14. Choose the Type category.

15. Set the Size property to Large, and then click Apply.

16. Choose the Block category.

17. Set the Letter Spacing to **5** pixels, and then click Apply.

18. Choose the Box category.

19. Remove the checkmarks next to Padding and Margin.

20. Set the following properties, and then click Apply:

Padding Left	5 pixels
Margin Top	0 pixels

21. Choose the Border category.

22. Remove the checkmarks next to Style, Width, and Color, set the following properties, and then click Apply.

Style Top and Left	Solid
Width Top and Left	Thin
Color Top and Left	#FF0000

23. Click OK to close the dialog box.

Modify a Style to Include a Background Image

24. Select the body style in the CSS Styles panel.

25. Click the Edit Style ▨ button at the bottom of the CSS Styles panel.
This opens the CSS Style Definition dialog box.

26. Choose the Background category.

27. Click the Browse button, select bg_branch.jpg from the images folder, and then click Apply.
The image tiles horizontally across and vertically down the page.

28. Set the following Background properties:

Repeat	No-Repeat
Attachment	Fixed
Horizontal Position	Center
Vertical Position	Center

29. Click OK.

30. Save the file, and then preview it in your browser.

31. Resize your browser window until a vertical scroll bar appears.

32. Use the vertical scroll bar to scroll up and down the page.
Setting the Background Attachment property to Fixed forces the background image to stay in a fixed position in the browser window at all times.

33. Leave your browser open and return to the Document window.

34. Save and close the file.

Attaching an External Style Sheet

Once you've defined styles in an external style sheet, you can use the CSS Styles panel to attach the style sheet to an HTML file. The real power of CSS formatting is that you can have the styles for your entire site stored in one CSS file and link multiple pages to it. Then, when you want to update the styles, you have to only open one file and make modifications. All HTML files attached to the external style sheet automatically update when loaded in a Web browser.

 Hands-On 9.11   Attach an External Style Sheet

In this exercise, you will attach the Senior Voices external style sheet to an HTML document.

1. Open sv_history.htm from the lesson_09 folder.

2. Click the Attach Style Sheet ⊞ button at the bottom of the CSS Styles panel.
This opens the Attach External Style Sheet dialog box.

3. Ensure that the Add as Link radio button is chosen.

4. Click the Browse button, select senior_voices.css from the lesson_09 folder, and then click OK or Choose.
The style sheet is linked to the current document.

5. Click OK to close the Attach External Style Sheet dialog box.

Delete a CSS Style

6. Select senior_voices.css, which appears directly below the CSS Styles panel tab.

7. Click the Delete CSS Style 🗑 button at the bottom of the CSS Styles panel.
This deletes the link to the external style sheet but does not delete the style sheet.

8. Use the technique outlined in steps 2–4 to reattach the external style sheet.

9. Save and close all files.

Concepts Review

True/False Questions

1. Cascading style sheets can control the appearance of a single page, or multiple pages.   TRUE   FALSE

2. Before adding CSS styles to an existing Web page, remove any preexisting formatting.   TRUE   FALSE

3. External styles override internal styles.   TRUE   FALSE

4. Internal styles are embedded within HTML tags, such as headings and paragraphs.   TRUE   FALSE

5. A CSS selector style is always an HTML tag.   TRUE   FALSE

6. A style sheet is a group of CSS styles.   TRUE   FALSE

7. A declaration consists of a style property and its value.   TRUE   FALSE

8. Class selector styles are automatically applied to HTML elements.   TRUE   FALSE

9. If you want to modify the format of any paragraph text that appears inside a table cell, you can use the contextual selector "p td."   TRUE   FALSE

10. The Page Properties dialog box offers the most options for creating and modifying CSS styles.   TRUE   FALSE

Multiple Choice Questions

1. Which of the following are pseudo-class selectors?
   a. <h6>
   b. <p>
   c. a:link, a:visited, a:hover, a:active
   d. Both a and b

2. Which of the following style rules is correctly stated?
   a. body font-family: Arial
   b. h1 { font-size: x-large }
   c. p { font-family Arial, "Sans-Serif" }
   d. style { body: font-family: Arial }

3. Which of the following CSS categories is used to set word and letter spacing?
   a. Type
   b. Box
   c. Block
   d. None of the above

4. When you create a class style, the _____ HTML element is used to apply the style to a text selection.
   a. <div>
   b. <inline>
   c. <span>
   d. <class>

 **Skill Builders**

Skill Builder 9.1   Create CSS Styles

In this exercise, you will create styles for the page body and three link states.

1. Choose Window→CSS Styles from the menu bar to open the CSS Styles panel.

2. Open french_revolution.htm from the review_09 folder.
   The page consists of three tables that have been broken apart to make it easier for you to see how the pieces of the CSS puzzle come together as you work.

3. Click the New CSS Style ⊞ button at the bottom of the CSS Styles panel.

4. Set the options in the New CSS Style dialog box according to the following table:

Selector Type	Tag
Tag	body
Define In	(New Style Sheet File)

5. Click OK.

6. Save the new CSS file as **french_revolution.css** in the review_09 folder.
   The CSS Style Definition dialog box opens.

Set the Margin Properties

7. Choose the Box category.

8. Ensure that a checkmark appears next to Same for All in the Margin section.

9. Type **0** in the Margin Top box, choose Pixels as the unit of measure, and then click Apply.

Set the Page Background Color

10. Choose the Background category, type **#FFFFFF** in the Background Color hex box, and then click OK.
    You should always set the background color for a page to ensure that older browsers don't use their default color.

11. Click the New CSS Style button on the CSS Styles panel.

12. Set the options in the New CSS Style dialog box according to the following table:

Selector Type	Advanced
Selector	a:link
Define In	french_revolution.css

13. Click OK.

Set the Link State Colors

14. Choose the Type category.

15. Set the following properties:

Decoration	None
Color	#333399

16. Click OK.

17. Use the techniques outlined in steps 11–16 to set the remaining link colors for a:visited and a:hover.
Use the decoration and link color of your choosing.

18. Choose File→Save from the menu bar.

19. Preview the French Revolution page in your browser and test the link states.
The links are link placeholders that allow you to test link states without jumping to another page.

20. Leave your browser window open and return to the Document window.

Skill Builder 9.2　Format a Banner and Links

In this exercise, you will work on the banner and the small table of links.

　1. Click the New Style button on the CSS Styles panel.

Create a Banner Class Style

　2. Set the options in the New CSS Style dialog box according to the following table:

Selector Type	Class
Name	.banner
Define In	french_revolution.css

　3. Click OK.

　4. Choose the Background category.

　5. Type **#A01F11** into the Background Color hex box and click Apply.
This adds the background color property to the style and allows you to keep the dialog box open to create additional styles.

　6. Choose the Box category and set the Padding to **10** pixels, Same for All.

　7. Click OK.

Apply the Banner Class Style

8. Click anywhere in the first table cell of the first table on the page, and then click the <td> tag on the Tag Selector.
This is where you will apply the banner style.

9. Choose banner from the Style pop-up menu on the Properties panel.
This style colors the table cell maroon, and adds 10 pixels of padding.

Create the Heading 1 Styles

10. Repeat step 1 to create a new style.

11. Set the options in the New CSS Style dialog box according to the following table:

Selector Type	Tag
Tag	h1
Define In	french_revolution.css

12. Click OK.

13. Choose the Type category.

14. Set the following properties:

Font	Georgia, Times New Roman, Times, Serif
Size	X-large
Weight	Bold
Color Hex	**#FFFFFF**

You're coloring the heading white to ensure its readability against the dark cell background color. Feel free to use another color if you wish.

15. Click Apply.
Since the style you created was a tag style, not a class style, the change in formatting takes place as soon as you click Apply.

16. Choose the Block category, set the Letter Spacing property to **5** pixels, click Apply, and then click OK.
This increases the spacing between the letters by 5 pixels.

Create the Heading 2 Styles

17. Click the New CSS Style button on the Styles panel and choose h2 from the Tag menu.

18. Choose the Type category.

19. Set the following properties:

Font	Georgia, Times New Roman, Times, Serif
Size	Medium
Color Hex	**#A01F11**

20. Click OK.

This colors the level two heading the same color as the banner background.

21. Save the file but leave it open.

Skill Builder 9.3   Format a Table of Links

In this exercise, you will define and apply a class style to spruce up the small table of links. We'll add some padding to give them some breathing room.

  1. Click the New CSS Style button on the Styles panel.

Create a Class Style for the Links

  2. Set the options in the New CSS Style dialog box according to the following table:

Selector Type	Class
Name	**.links**
Define In	french_revolution.css

  3. Click OK.

  4. Choose the Type category, set the Font to Verdana, Arial, Helvetica, Sans-Serif, set the Size to Small, and then click Apply.

  5. Choose the Box category, set the Padding property to **6** pixels, Same for All, and then click OK.

  6. Choose View→Table Mode→Expanded Tables Mode or click the Expanded Tables mode button on the Document toolbar.

Apply the Link Class Style

  7. Click in the first table cell in the second small table of links (Menu) and click the <td> tag on the Tag Selector.

  8. From the Style pop-up menu on the Properties panel, choose links.
This applies the class style to that table cell.

  9. Click inside the next table cell that contains the double colon (::) and drag all the way to the right to select each remaining cell in the row.
The double colon characters serve as visual separators only; they aren't required.

  10. Repeat step 8 to apply the links style to the cell selection.

  11. Choose View→Table Mode→Standard Mode or click the Standard mode button on the Document toolbar.

  12. Save the file but leave it open.

Skill Builder 9.4   Format the Body of a Page

Next, we need to format the main content area. In this exercise, we'll create a class selector style to dress up the text and add some padding.

1. Click the New Style button on the CSS Styles panel.

Create a Class Style for the Main Content Area

2. Set the options in the New CSS Style dialog box according to the following table:

Selector Type	Class
Name	.pad
Define In	french_revolution.css

3. Click OK.

4. Choose the Type category, set the following properties, and then click Apply.

Font	Georgia, Times New Roman, Times, Serif
Size	Small
Color Hex	#666666
Line Height	18 pixels

5. Choose the Box category and set the Padding property to **10** pixels, Same for All.

6. Click OK.

Apply the Class Style to the Main Content Area

7. Click in the main content area of the third table and click the <td> tag on the Tag Selector.

8. Choose Pad from the Style pop-up menu on the Properties panel.
   This applies the style to the main content area.

9. Select the copyright text below the table and apply the pad style.

10. Save the file but leave it open.

Skill Builder 9.5   Finalize the Page

The final phase of this project is designed to put the finishing touches on the page. In this exercise, you will connect the tables, analyze areas that need improvement, and then create another class style, and insert three spacers.

1. Remove all of the space between the three tables.
   The three tables should now look like one. The copyright text sits on its own line below the main content table.

2. Look carefully at the merged cells in rows 2, 4, and 7.
   These three cells contain only a non-breaking space, which we need to replace with a 1 × 1 pixel spacer.

Insert Spacer GIFs

3. Switch to Expanded Tables mode.

4. Click in the first empty cell located directly below The French Revolution.

5. Insert spacer.gif and set the Alt property to <empty>.
   The spacer doesn't have to be more than 1 × 1 so that's why we're not changing its dimensions. Its only purpose is to collapse the table row to 1 pixel in height.

6. Use the technique outlined in step 5 to insert a spacer in rows 4 and 7.

7. Switch back to Standard Tables mode and notice that the three rows have collapsed down to a height of 1 pixel. Switch back to Expanded Tables mode.

8. Click the New CSS Style button on the CSS Styles panel.

Create a Class Background Style

9. Set the options in the New CSS Style dialog box according to the following table, and then click OK:

Selector Type	Class
Name	**.bgblack**
Define In	french_revolution.css

10. Choose the Background category, type **#000000** in the Background Color hex box, and then click OK.

Apply the Class Background Style

11. Click in the second table cell (the cell that contains the first spacer), and then click the <td> tag on the Tag Selector.

12. Choose bgblack from the Styles pop-up menu on the Properties panel.
    This applies the style to the cell, which now has a black background.

13. Use the technique outlined in steps 11 and 12 to apply the style to rows 4 and 7.
    Remember, click the <td> tag on the Tag Selector; otherwise, you'll apply the style to the spacer and this does nothing.

14. Switch to Standard Table mode.

15. Save the file, and then preview it in your browser.
    Your page should now resemble this illustration:

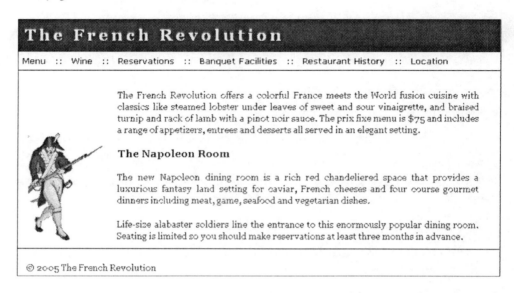

The text in the main content area is pretty light, but you can always modify the style when you return to Dreamweaver and choose a darker color.

16. Leave your browser open and return to the Document window.

17. Continue to modify the file, or close it.

 # Assessments

Assessment 9.1   Create an External Style Sheet

In this exercise, you will use advanced CSS techniques to format a Web page. You'll start by using the CSS Styles panel to create an external style sheet. Then, you will create two custom classes and one tag selector style.

  1. Open psd.htm from the review_09 folder.
     The page is stripped of all formatting and looks pretty dismal.

Create a Banner Class Style

  2. Create a new CSS style and set the options outlined in the following table:

Selector Type	Class
Name	**.banner**
Define in	(New Style Sheet File)

  3. Save the external style sheet as **psd.css** in the review_09 folder.

  4. Choose the Background Category, type **#CCCC99** in the Background Color hex box, and then click Apply.

  5. Choose the Box Category, set the padding to **20** pixels, Same for All, and then click OK.

Create a Title Class Style

  6. Create a new CSS style and set the options outlined in the following table:

Selector Type	Class
Name	**.title**
Define in	psd.css

  7. Choose the Type category, set the following properties, and then click Apply:

Font	Georgia, Times New Roman, Times, Serif
Size	Large
Color	**#666666**

Create a Subtitle Class Style

  8. Choose the Block Category, set Letter Spacing to **2** pixels, and then click OK.

  9. Using the technique in step 2, set the following options in the New CSS Style dialog box and click OK:

Selector Type	Class
Name	**.subtitle**
Define in	psd.css

10. Choose the Type Category, set the following properties, and then click Apply:

Font	Veranda, Arial, Helvetica, Sans-Serif
Size	X-small
Weight	Bold
Case	Uppercase
Color	**#999966**

11. Choose the Block Category, set Letter Spacing to **8** pixels, and then click OK.

Apply the Class Styles

12. Click in the first table cell, and then click the <td> tag on the Tag Selector.

13. Choose banner from the Style pop-up menu on the Properties panel.

14. Select the text Palm Springs Dining and choose title from the Style pop-up menu.

15. Select the text Weekly Dining Guide and apply the subtitle style.

16. Save the file but leave it open.

Assessment 9.2   Format Body Styles and Link States

In this exercise, you will continue to refine psd.htm by defining styles for the body and link states. Be sure to save all new styles in the psd.css external style sheet that you saved in the review_09 folder.

Create a Body Tag Style

1. Create a new style using Body as the Tag Selector.

2. Choose the Background Category, set the background color to **#FFFFFF**, and then click Apply.

3. Choose the Box Category, set all of the page margins to **0**, and then click OK.

Create Pseudo-class Styles

4. Create a new advanced selector type, and choose a:link from the Selector pop-up menu.

5. Choose the Type Category, set the color to **#CC6633**, and then set the Decoration to None.

6. Click OK.

7. Use the technique outlined in steps 4–6 and the following table to set the properties for the visited link state:

Color	#CC6633
Decoration	None

8. Use the technique outlined in steps 4–6 and the following table for the hover link state:

Color	#000000
Decoration	None

9. Save the file, and then preview it in your browser to test the link states.

10. Leave your browser open and return to the Document window.

11. Keep the psd.htm file open for the next exercise.

Assessment 9.3   Create a Class Selector Style

In this exercise, you will create a class selector style to format the cells that contain the links.

Create a Links Class Style

1. Choose Text→CSS Styles→New from the menu bar.

2. Create a new Class selector and type **.links** in the Name box.

3. Define the new style in psd.css.

4. Choose the Type category, set the following properties, and then click Apply:

Font	Veranda, Arial, Helvetica, Sans-Serif
Size	XX-small

5. Choose the Box category, set the following properties, and then click OK:

Top	10 pixels
Bottom	10 pixels
Left	10 pixels

Create a Paragraph Tag Style

6. Create a new style using P as the Tag Selector.

7. Choose the Type Category, set the following properties, and then click OK:

Font	Georgia, Times New Roman, Times, Serif
Size	X-small
Color	#666666
Line Height	18 pixels

Create a New Class Style for the Main Content Area

8. Use the technique outlined in step 1 to create a new class selector and type **.main** in the Name box.

9. Choose the Box Category, set the Padding to **20** pixels, Same for All, and then click OK.

Apply the Custom Styles

10. Switch to Expanded Tables mode.

11. Click in the first table cell in the navigation table that contains the link placeholders, and then click the <td> tag on the Tag Selector.

12. Choose links from the Style pop-up menu on the Properties panel.

13. Click in the next table cell and drag to the end of the row to select all remaining cells.

14. Use the technique outlined in step 12 to apply the links style.

15. Switch back to Standard mode.

16. Click in the main content area (the cell that contains the two paragraphs), and then click the <td> tag on the Tag Selector.

17. Choose main from the Styles pop-up menu on the Properties panel.

18. Save the file but keep it open.

Assessment 9.4   Create and Apply Background Styles

In this exercise, you will work some magic! There are three empty rows that are being propped open by a non-breaking space.

1. Click anywhere in the navigation table (the third row) and observe the Tag Selector.
The navigation table is nested inside another table and the outer table's width is set to 100%. Now we're going to create background color styles for each of the tables.

Create Background Class Styles

2. Create a new class selector style and type **.bgblack** in the Name box.

3. Choose the Background Category, type **#000000** in the Background Color hex box, and then click OK.

4. Create a new class selector style and type **.bggray** in the Name box.

5. Choose the Background Category, type **#CCCCCC** in the Background Color hex box, and then click OK.

6. Switch to Expanded Tables mode.

7. Insert spacer.gif into each of the three empty table cells (rows 2, 4, and 6). Be sure to set the Alt property to <empty>. Use the default dimensions of 1 × 1 pixels.

Apply the Custom Styles

8. Click anywhere in the navigation table, and then click the outer <table> tag on the Tag Selector.
   The outer table contains a 3 × 1 table. The cell in the first row contains the spacer you inserted in step 7. The cell in the second row contains the nested navigation table. The cell in the third row contains the spacer gif.

9. Follow these steps to apply the class styles:

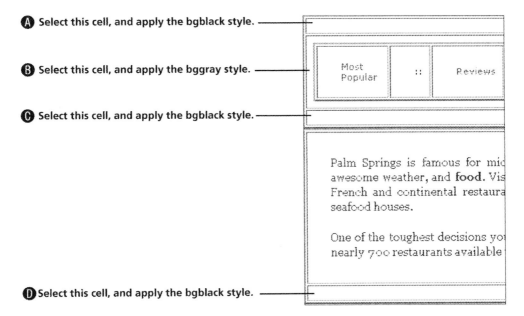

Ⓐ Select this cell, and apply the bgblack style.

Ⓑ Select this cell, and apply the bggray style.

Ⓒ Select this cell, and apply the bgblack style.

Ⓓ Select this cell, and apply the bgblack style.

10. Switch to Standard mode.

11. Your page should now resemble the following illustration:

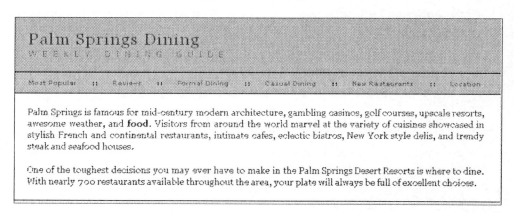

12. Save the file, and then preview it in your browser to test the link states.

13. Leave you browser window open and return to Dreamweaver.

14. Close the file.

Critical Thinking

Critical Thinking 9.1   On Your Own

Khalima Foster won the Web page redesign award at her local community college and landed the job at Just in Time Design. Khalima was chosen not only for her design skills, but also because she's a great troubleshooter. Her final task in the competition was to determine if a document had any leftover styles hanging around that could create nightmares for an unsuspecting worker. Once she located and removed the class styles from the page, she was ready to begin the redesign. Now it's your turn to give troubleshooting a try.

Open rhythm.htm from the review_09 folder. The page is an example of a document that you may inherit from someone else. Class styles are still attached to various elements on the page, but the file is not linked to an external style sheet.

Follow these guidelines, which are merely suggestions, to redesign the page:

- Remove all of the class styles from the page.

- Create a new external style sheet and link it to rhythm.htm.

- Redesign the page using tag, class, and advanced selector types.

- Save the file in the review_09 folder.

Critical Thinking 9.2   With a Group

Now that you've dissected CSS Styles on your own, you're ready to work with a group of teammates to redesign a page from scratch. Open ps_dining.htm from the review_09 folder, and analyze the basic page layout, shown in the following illustration. The page doesn't contain a single CSS Style.

Palm Springs Dining

Weekly Dining Guide

Palm Springs is famous for mid-century modern architecture, gambling casinos, golf courses, upscale resorts, awesome weather, and **food**. Visitors from around the world marvel at the variety of cuisines showcased in stylish French and continental restaurants, intimate cafes, eclectic bistros, New York style delis, and trendy steak and seafood houses.

Main
Most Popular
Reviews
Formal Dining
Casual Dining
New Restaurants

One of the toughest decisions you may ever have to make in the Palm Springs Desert Resorts is where to dine. With nearly 700 restaurants available throughout the area, your plate will always be full of excellent choices.

© 2005 Palm Springs Dining

There are endless ways this page could be redesigned. Divide your design team into small groups and brainstorm the new design. Discuss the color scheme, font types and sizes, navigation scheme, and other styles you will need.

The following illustration represents just one of many possible redesigns of the page using CSS.

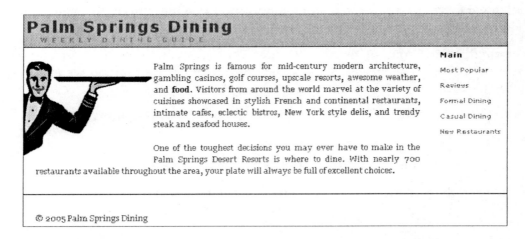

Working with Frames

In this lesson, you will learn how to design a special type of Web page architecture in which pages are displayed in three separate windows, called frames. Dreamweaver provides a variety of templates you can use to get started, or you can design a frameset from scratch. Our frameset will contain one frame that displays a banner page with a graphic, another frame that displays a small table of navigation controls, and a final frame that holds the main site content. You've probably used navigational frames many times. In them, topics are listed as a series of links; when you click a link, the destination page opens in the main content frame but the navigation frame and the banner frames remain the same. This consistency enables users to remain oriented while visiting your site.

Case Study

Frederic Delarue is an international award-winning composer and musician. He built his first Web site four years ago, which he hand coded in HTML. The site showcases his work. Because of his hectic schedule, Frederic enlists the aid of Just in Time Design to makeover his site. Frederic, like many other pioneer novice Web designers, used too many bells and whistles, which he now finds distracting. Justin suggests that Frederic go with an earthy design that reflects his lifestyle and his music. Frederic agrees, and anxiously awaits the makeover.

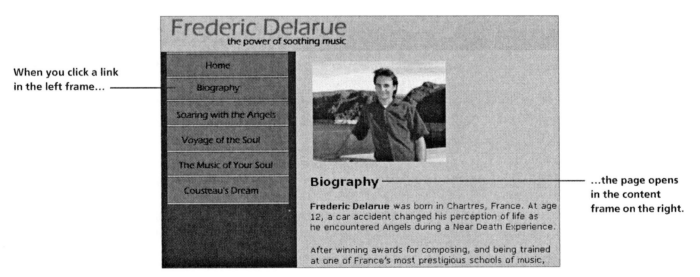

When you click a link in the left frame...

...the page opens in the content frame on the right.

Understanding Frames Terminology

To fully understand frames, you must familiarize yourself with the terminology. You should understand what a frame is and what a frames definition document, known as a frameset, does. To help you, we will explore the rather simple HTML code it uses to direct your Web browser to lay out frames pages.

Frames

A frame is a region in a browser window that displays a single HTML document. The HTML document within a frame exists independently of what is displayed in the rest of the browser window. A frame is really a window or container for the Web page: it is not an actual file.

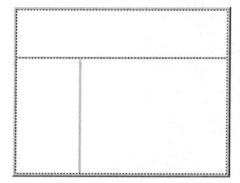

Three blanks frames are shown here.

Here, each frame shows a different HTML document.

The left frame typically provides a table of links; clicking one of these links opens the page in the main frame. The top frame, typically used for the banner of the site, usually does not change as the visitor clicks to new pages. By default, Dreamweaver names each frame. You can always change these names.

Framesets

A frameset is an HTML document that defines the layout and properties of a set of frames, including the number, size, and placement of frames, and the URL of the page that initially loads in each frame. You might think of it as the master plan that describes the layout of your frames-based pages. It describes the spaces into which you'll put content, but it contains no content itself.

You have learned that the <body> tag marks the boundaries of the content in an HTML document. In a Web page based on frames, the <frameset> tag replaces the <body> tag. That's because the <frameset> document doesn't display content; its sole purpose is to let the browser know how to lay out frame pages within the frameset and how to display alternative text in browsers that don't support frames. At the end of this lesson, you will provide alternative text to older and speech-based browsers that don't support frames.

By now, you should be getting pretty good at talking to your browser, which is good because understanding frameset code is vital to using frames. This scaled-down HTML frameset code that tells the browser how to display the two frames shown in the following illustration:

```
<frameset cols="100,*">
   <frame src="left.htm name="leftFrame">
   <frame src="right.htm name="mainFrame">
</frameset>
```

Now, let's translate the code for the browser: "The frameset you are loading has two columns. Make the column in the first frame 100 pixels wide and give the remaining space in the browser window to the frame in the second column, as indicated by the relative value (*). Open a page named left.htm in the frame named leftFrame, and then open a page named right.htm in the frame named mainFrame."

The name of this frame is leftFrame. The column is 100 pixels wide and houses a blank page named left.htm.

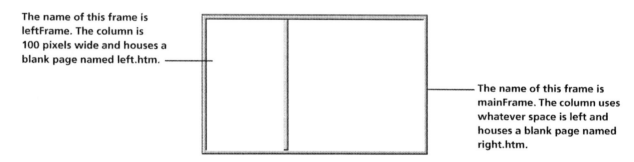

The name of this frame is mainFrame. The column uses whatever space is left and houses a blank page named right.htm.

The frameset file for a site is typically named index.htm. It displays by default if a visitor doesn't specify a filename. This way, the frameset page opens first and the Web browser uses it to arrange the frames content.

So, how many documents does it take to produce a single page composed of two frames, as shown in the previous illustration? The answer is three! Think about it. You need a frameset file, plus two HTML documents—one for each frame.

Nested Framesets

The frameset you will create in this lesson uses nested framesets, meaning that one frameset appears inside another frameset. Unlike table cells, you cannot merge one frame into another to set up a frame than spans multiple columns or rows. Instead, you must insert one frameset inside another. The following illustration shows the architecture of the nested three-frame frameset we will create in this lesson.

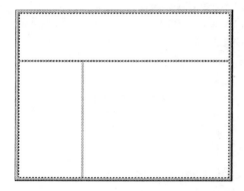

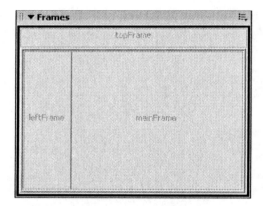

This is the parent frameset (indicated by the heavy border). The frameset contains two rows and one column.

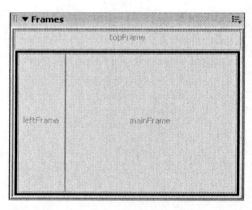

This is the child frameset (indicated by the heavy border). The nested frameset contains one row and two columns.

Let's take a peek at the code that Dreamweaver writes for this type of nested frameset. (This is a simplified version of the code.) Can you imagine having to write this yourself?

```
<frameset rows="56,*" cols="*">
  <frame src="top.htm" name="topFrame">
  <frameset cols="205,*">
    <frame src="nav.htm" name="leftFrame">
    <frame src="content.htm" name="mainFrame">
  </frameset>
</frameset>
```

Now, let's translate the code for the browser: "The frameset you are loading has two rows and one column. Make the first row 56 pixels high and give the remaining space in the browser window to the second row (as indicated by the *) and the column (as indicated by the *).

Open a page named top.htm in the frame named topFrame. Insert another frameset in the second row of the parent frameset and divide the new frameset into two columns. Make the first column 205 pixels wide and give the remaining space to the second column. Open a page named nav.htm in the frame named leftFrame, and then open a page named content.htm in the frame named mainFrame."

Fortunately, Dreamweaver takes care of the nesting and coding details, but it's up to you to know which frameset you're modifying. As you will see, the Tag Selector will help you identify the currently selected frameset.

Creating and Saving Framesets and Frames

Dreamweaver provides two ways to create a frameset: you can design it yourself or choose from a variety of predefined framesets. Until you know what you're doing, we recommend that you use a predefined frameset. To insert a predefined frameset, you must be working in Design view. There are three ways to create a predefined frameset:

- Use the Layout category on the Insert bar.

- Use the New Document dialog box.

- Choose Framesets from the Create from Samples section on the Start page.

Creating a New Frames Page with the Insert Bar

When you already have the content page you want to appear in the main frame, it's easy to insert a predefined frameset from the Layout category of the insert bar. Open the content page and choose a predefined frameset from the frames menu on the Insert bar. The icons for each frameset layout indicate where your current document (shaded area) will display relative to other frames on the page (white areas).

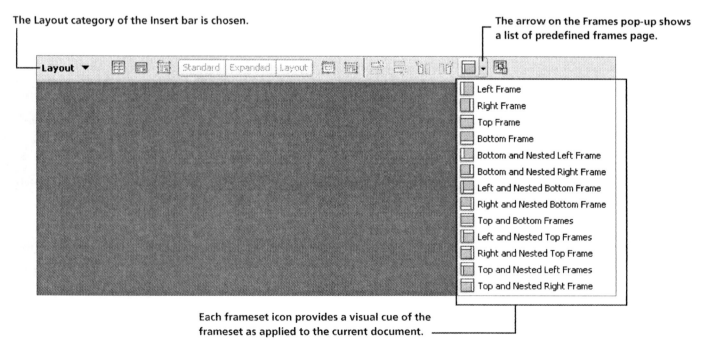

The Layout category of the Insert bar is chosen.

The arrow on the Frames pop-up shows a list of predefined frames page.

Each frameset icon provides a visual cue of the frameset as applied to the current document.

Note that in all the predefined frames, the current HTML document automatically appears in the main frame while all other frames are empty.

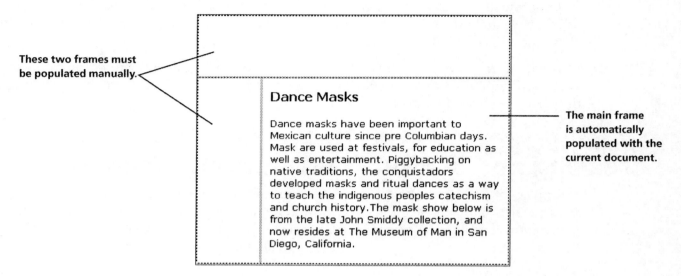

These two frames must be populated manually.

The main frame is automatically populated with the current document.

Dance Masks

Dance masks have been important to Mexican culture since pre Columbian days. Mask are used at festivals, for education as well as entertainment. Piggybacking on native traditions, the conquistadors developed masks and ritual dances as a way to teach the indigenous peoples catechism and church history. The mask show below is from the late John Smiddy collection, and now resides at The Museum of Man in San Diego, California.

 Hands-On 10.1   Create a Predefined Frameset Using Insert Bar

In this exercise, you will open a test page to create a predefined frameset and display an existing document in a frame.

1. Open content_masks.htm from the lesson_10 folder.
   This is a test file you can use to see how the Insert Bar handles predefined framesets.

2. Ensure that the Layout category of the Insert bar is shown. If you do not see the Insert bar, choose View→Toolbars→Insert.

3. Choose View→Visual Aids→Frame Borders from the menu bar and ensure that a check-mark appears next to Frame Borders.
   The borders are visual aids only and do not appear in a browser. Without these visual aids, it would be very difficult to work with frames.

4. Click the tiny arrow next to the frames 🔲▾ button on the Frames pop-up menu on the Layout category of the Insert bar.
   This displays a list of predefined framesets. Observe the blue shaded area on the button. This represents the frame that will house the current document.

5. Choose Top and Nested Left Frames.
   The content_masks page automatically opens in the main frame on the right. Do NOT click anywhere on the page. Observe the <frameset> tag on the Tag Selector. This identifies the outer frameset.

6. Close the file without saving the changes.

Creating Predefined Framesets with the New Document Dialog Box

When you choose File→New, the New Document dialog box opens. The dialog box is divided into two sections: General and Templates. The General section provides a variety of new document options, including Framesets. The Framesets category provides the same selection of predefined framesets offered on the Insert bar but they are named slightly differently and do not show the content frame shaded in blue. Instead, the New Document approach assumes that you are beginning with all of the frames empty. When first learning how to design frames pages, it's easiest to start with an empty frames palette. The following illustration shows the General portion of the New Document dialog box.

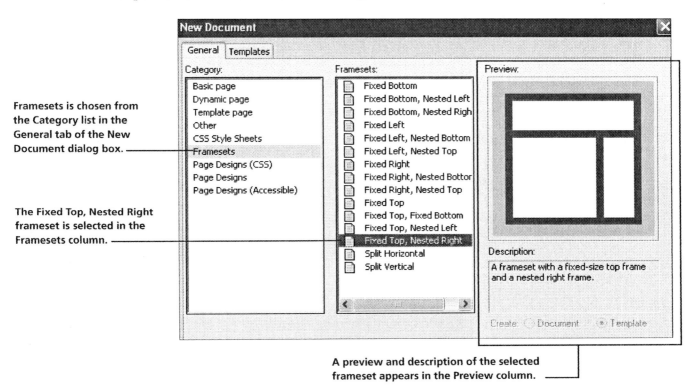

Framesets is chosen from the Category list in the General tab of the New Document dialog box.

The Fixed Top, Nested Right frameset is selected in the Framesets column.

A preview and description of the selected frameset appears in the Preview column.

When you make a selection from the Framesets column, the empty frameset document opens in the Document window.

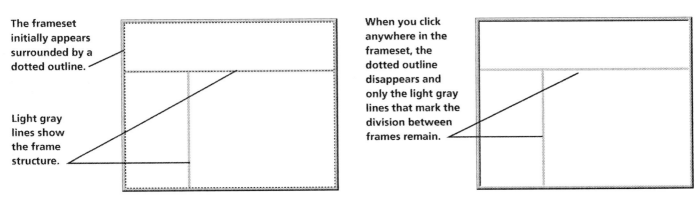

The frameset initially appears surrounded by a dotted outline.

Light gray lines show the frame structure.

When you click anywhere in the frameset, the dotted outline disappears and only the light gray lines that mark the division between frames remain.

Saving Framesets and Frames

As with any other HTML document you create in Dreamweaver, you should save a file immediately after creating it. This helps ensure that any images and links that you add will be directed to the correct location within your site. If you're starting from scratch and don't have the content for any of the frames pages, you can choose File→Save All and Dreamweaver will display a rope border around the frameset document and allow you to name the document and specify a storage location. This process is repeated for each frame in the frameset. What you wind up with is the frameset document and blank HTML documents, one for each frame.

If you already have pages to display in each frame, you can open them within the frame and save them individually. We'll use this process.

 Hands-On 10.2   Create and Save a Frameset

In this exercise, you will create a three-frame frameset. You will use this frameset throughout the remainder of this lesson to design the new Frederic Delarue pages.

1. Choose File→New from the menu bar.
   This opens the New Document dialog box. Ensure that the General tab, not Templates, of the dialog box is chosen.

2. Choose the Framesets category and select Fixed Top, Nested Left from the list of predefined framesets.
   Preview the frameset and read the description.

3. Click Create. Do NOT click anywhere in the document.
   An empty three-frame frameset appears in the new document window. When you save the frameset in the next step, you are saving the frameset file, not a frame file. If you accidentally deselect the frameset, click the border around the edges of the document window.

4. Observe the <frameset> tag on the Tag Selector.
   This identifies the currently selected frameset.

5. Choose File→Save Frameset As from the menu bar.
   This saves the outer frameset.

6. Save the file as **index.htm** in the lesson_10 folder.
   This file becomes the homepage for this project.

NOTE!   *Normally, you would open a page in each of the three empty frames and save them immediately. We are postponing this process because when you're first learning how to use framesets and frames, it's much easier to select these objects when they're empty.*

Selecting Framesets and Frames

To set frame or frameset properties, you begin by selecting the frame or frameset you want to modify. You can select a frame or frameset in the Document window or in the Frames panel. Selecting from the Frames panel is the most straightforward method, so we'll use this approach first.

Selecting Framesets in the Frames Panel

FROM THE KEYBOARD
To open the Frames panel:
WIN AND MAC
Shift + F2

The Frames panel provides a visual representation of each frameset and frame. It shows the frameset architecture in a visual way that may not be apparent in the Document window. To open the Frames panel, choose Window→Frames from the menu bar.

Selecting the Parent Frameset

The parent frame is the outer frame, which consists of a single frame named topFrame. The child frameset is nested in the parent frameset and consists of two frames named leftFrame and mainFrame. (Can you image a parent naming a child leftFrame and mainFrame?!)

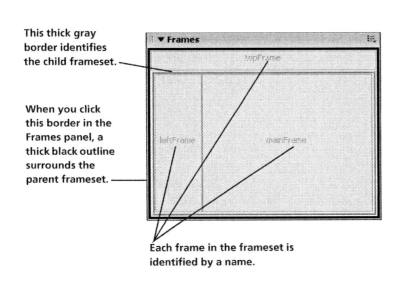

This thick gray border identifies the child frameset.

When you click this border in the Frames panel, a thick black outline surrounds the parent frameset.

Each frame in the frameset is identified by a name.

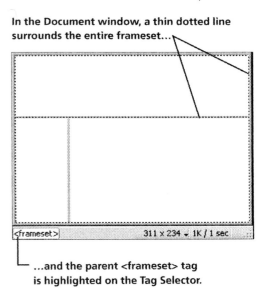

In the Document window, a thin dotted line surrounds the entire frameset...

...and the parent <frameset> tag is highlighted on the Tag Selector.

Selecting the Child Frameset

The child frameset consists of two frames that appear side by side.

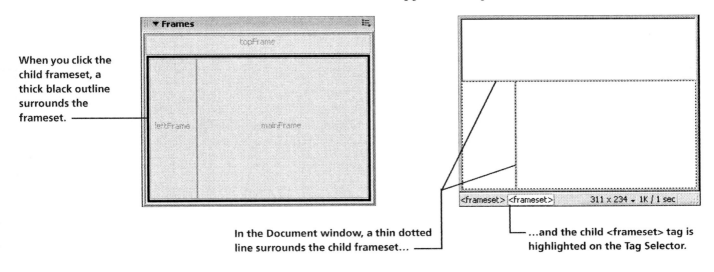

When you click the child frameset, a thick black outline surrounds the frameset.

In the Document window, a thin dotted line surrounds the child frameset...

...and the child <frameset> tag is highlighted on the Tag Selector.

Selecting Frames in the Frames Panel

The following illustrations demonstrate how to select frames in the Frames panel, and how the selected frames are represented visually in the Document window.

When you click inside the top frame in the Frames panel, a solid black outline surrounds the frame.

In the Document window, a dotted outline surrounds the frame...

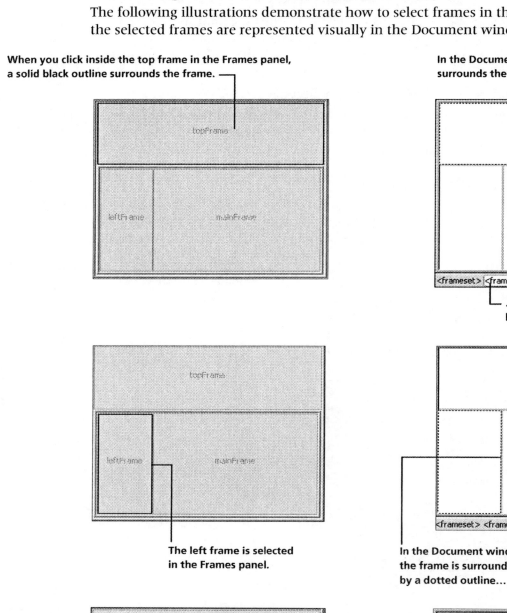

...and the <frame> tag is highlighted on the Tag Selector.

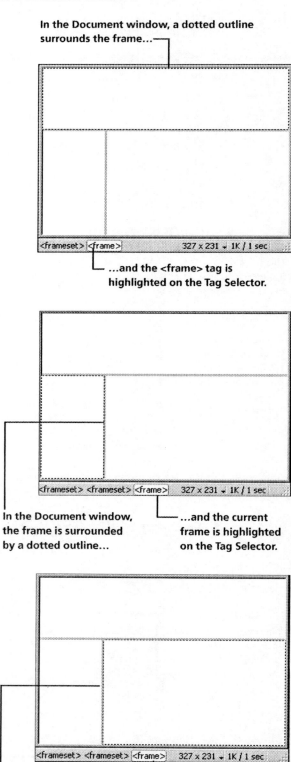

The left frame is selected in the Frames panel.

In the Document window, the frame is surrounded by a dotted outline...

...and the current frame is highlighted on the Tag Selector.

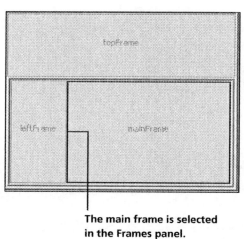

The main frame is selected in the Frames panel.

In the Document window, the frame is surrounded by a dotted outline...

...and the current frame is highlighted on the Tag Selector.

Hands-On 10.3 Select Using the Frames Panel

In this exercise, you will select framesets and frames in the Frames panel. It is vital that you understand which frame is selected before you insert content and begin modifying frame properties.

Before you begin: The index.htm file should still be open.

Select the Parent Frameset

1. If the Frames panel is not already open, choose Window→Frames from the menu bar.

2. Click the top border directly above the frame named topFrame.
   A thick black outline surrounds the frameset.

3. Observe the thin dotted line that surrounds the entire frameset in the Document window.

4. Observe the <frameset> tag on the Tag Selector.
   This identifies the parent frameset.

Select the Child Frameset

5. Click the top gray border directly above the frame named mainFrame.
   A thick black outline surrounds the child frameset.

6. Observe the thin dotted line that surrounds the frameset in the Document window.
   This identifies the child frameset.

7. Observe the child <frameset> tag on the Tag Selector.
   The child frameset appears to the right of the parent frameset.

Select a Frame

8. In the Frames panel, click in the top frame.
   A thin black outline surrounds the top frame.

9. Observe the thin dotted line that surrounds the frame in the Document window.

10. Observe the <frame> tag on the Tag Selector.
    This identifies the currently selected frame.

11. Use the technique outlined in steps 8–10 to select the main frame and the left frame.

12. Leave the file open.

Selecting Framesets in the Document Window

When a frame is selected in the Document window, its borders are outlined with a thin dotted line. When a frameset is selected, all frame borders within the frameset are outlined with a thin dotted line.

When you click this frame border in the Document window, the parent frameset is surrounded by a thin dotted outline...

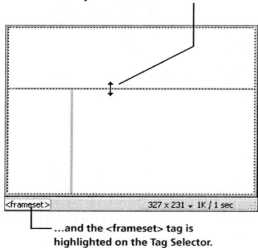

...and the <frameset> tag is highlighted on the Tag Selector.

When you click this border in the Document window, the child frameset is surrounded by a thin dotted outline...

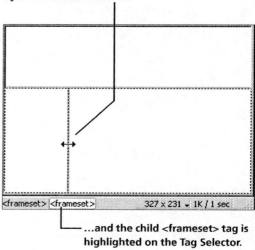

...and the child <frameset> tag is highlighted on the Tag Selector.

Selecting Frames in the Document Window

FROM THE KEYBOARD

To select a frame in the Document window:

WIN ONLY
Alt+Click

MAC ONLY
Shift+Option+Click

Dreamweaver provides numerous options for performing the same tasks. You've already seen how to use the Frames panel to select individual frames. Now, let's explore a reverse technique that lets you select frames in the Document window and observe the selections in the Frames panel. To select a frame from the document window, you must simultaneously press Alt (Win) or Shift + Option (Mac). Otherwise you will be selecting the body of the HTML document.

When you select a frame using the keyboard shortcuts, the frame is surrounded by a dotted line.

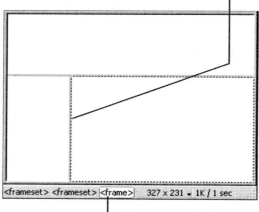

The current <frame> tag is highlighted on the Tag Selector.

The frame is surrounded by a solid black outline in the Frames panel.

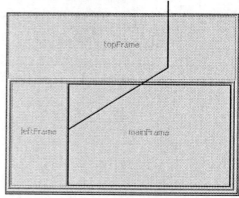

TIP! *The visual cues provided by the Document window and the Frames panel will come in handy when you begin to set properties for framesets and frames.*

Opening a Document in a Frame

Now let's populate the three empty frames. Immediately after you open a document in a frame, you should save it. The following illustration shows how the three documents will appear in each frame at the end of this lesson.

 NOTE! *When you create a frameset, Dreamweaver creates a temporary file for each frame. When you open a page within each frame, and then save the frameset, the temporary file is replaced by the name of each file that appears in each frame.*

The top frame will contain a page with a banner graphic.

The left frame will contain a page with a small table of graphic links.

The main frame will initially contain a page with an image of Frederic Delarue.

To open a file in a frame, position the insertion point in the frame, choose File→Open in Frame, and then navigate to the location that contains the file.

Hands-On 10.4   Open Documents in a Frame

In this exercise, you will populate each frame.

Before you begin: The index.htm file should be open.

1. Click in the top frame to position the insertion point.

2. Choose File→Open in Frame from the menu bar.

3. Open top.htm from the lesson_10 folder.
   The page contains a banner graphic. The background color of the page is set to the background color of the graphic.

4. Repeat this process to open nav.htm in the left frame and content.htm in the right frame.
   The page should resemble the following illustration. Unlike table cells, frames do not expand to accommodate content; they must be resized.

5. Choose File→Save All from the menu bar.
   The temporary filenames are replaced by the name of each file that appears in each frame.

Setting Frameset and Frames Properties

Framesets have their own properties, as do individual frames. Most properties for framesets and frames are set with the Properties panel.

Setting Frameset Properties

Frameset properties control the dimensions of the frames and color and width of the border between frames. The properties you will almost always need to set first are the row height and the column width. You can use the Properties panel if you know the values upfront; otherwise, you can manually resize a frame by dragging the frame border.

When you position the insertion point on a horizontal frame border, the vertical double arrows can be dragged up or down.

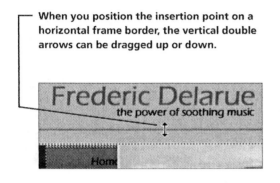

When you position the insertion point on a vertical frame border, the horizontal double arrows can be dragged to the left or right.

To see all of the frameset properties, use the Frames panel to select a frameset and observe the settings on the Properties panel. If you do not see all of the frameset properties shown in the following illustration, click the expander arrow in the lower-right corner of the Properties panel.

These properties control color and width of the border between frames.

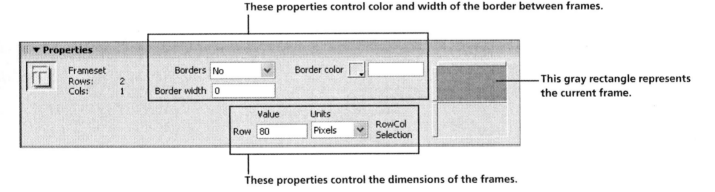

This gray rectangle represents the current frame.

These properties control the dimensions of the frames.

Setting an individual frame property overrides the setting for that property in a frameset. For example, setting border properties in a frame overrides the border properties set in the frameset. When a browser is loading a frameset page, it determines the size and layout of the columns and rows in the following order:

- Pixel measurements are given their space allotment first.

- Columns or rows with percentage measurements are drawn next.

- Frames with relative settings are drawn to fill the rest of the available space.

QUICK REFERENCE: SETTING FRAMESET PROPERTIES

Setting	Description
Borders	This option determines whether borders should appear around frames when the document is viewed in a browser. To display borders, choose Yes; to prevent the browser from displaying borders, choose No. To allow the browser to determine how borders are displayed, choose Default.
Border Width	This option specifies a width for all the borders in the current frameset.
Border Color	This option sets a color for the borders. This setting can be overridden by a border color specified for a single frame.
Value	This option specifies the number of units for the selected row or column.
Units	This option specifies the unit of measure for the selected row or column. ■ Pixels set an exact width or height. When the frameset is loaded in the browser, pixel measurements are followed exactly. ■ Percent refers to a percentage of window (or frameset) size. ■ Relative means that the width or height will be flexible in the frameset, compared to other elements that were given specific pixel or percent measurements.
Row/Col Selection	This option sets frame sizes for rows and columns of the selected frameset. Click a tab on the left side or top of the RowCol Selection area, and then enter a height or width in the Value text box.

 Hands-On 10.5   Set Frameset Properties

In this exercise, you will set frameset properties.

Before you begin: The index.htm file should be open.

1. Click the top border in the Frames panel.
   This selects the parent frameset.

2. Set the frameset properties shown in the following illustration and press ⎡Enter⎤ or ⎡Return⎤. Do NOT deselect the parent frameset.
   The fixed row height of 56 pixels is based on the height of the graphic, which is exactly 56 pixels high. This fixed unit of measure assures that the row will always remain this height.

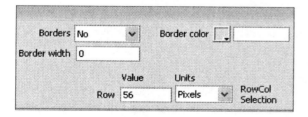

3. Select the default title text Untitled Document on the Document toolbar and type **Frederic Delarue**.
   This sets the title property for the parent frameset. This title will display in the browser title bar and in a list of bookmarks, or favorites.

4. Click the child frameset border on the Frames panel.
This selects the child frameset.

5. Follow these steps to modify the width of the left column. Do NOT deselect the child frameset.
The fixed column width of 205 pixels is based on the width of each graphic "button" in the table plus about 23 extra pixels.

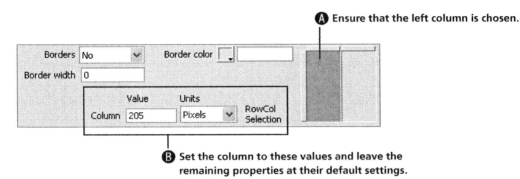

Ⓐ Ensure that the left column is chosen.

Ⓑ Set the column to these values and leave the remaining properties at their default settings.

6. Follow these steps to modify the width of the right column:
The Relative unit of measure allows the browser to make the width of this frame whatever size is necessary based on its contents.

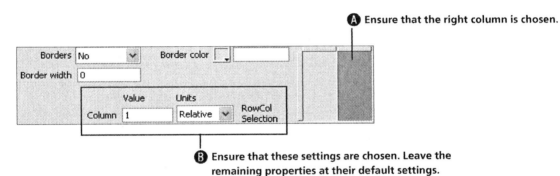

Ⓐ Ensure that the right column is chosen.

Ⓑ Ensure that these settings are chosen. Leave the remaining properties at their default settings.

7. Choose File→Save All from the menu bar.
This shortcut saves all three pages.

8. Press F12 to preview the frameset file in your primary browser.
The links in the document in the left frame have already been created for you to save time.

9. Click any link in the left frame.
The links open each page in the left frame, not in the content (main) frame. That's because they haven't been targeted to that frame.

10. Leave your browser open and return to the Document window.

Setting Frame Properties

Frame properties determine the frame name, source file, borders, and border colors, margins, scrolling, and resizing for individual frames within a frameset.

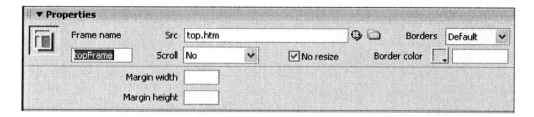

In most cases, you probably do not want borders to show in your frames pages. However, if your page design calls for frame borders, you can set them individually for each frame.

SETTING FRAME PROPERTIES

Setting	Description
Frame Name	This determines the name of the current frame. Don't use spaces or special characters, such as hyphens, etc. A frame name must start with a letter and is case-sensitive. Frame names are NOT the same as page names.
Src	This specifies the source of the document to display in the frame.
Scroll	This determines if scroll bars appear when there is not enough room to display the content of the current frame. Most browsers default to Auto.
No Resize	Check this box to prevent visitors from dragging the frame borders to resize the frame in a browser. This option doesn't prevent you from resizing the frames within Dreamweaver.
Borders	This controls the border of the current frames. The options are Yes, No, and Default. This choice overrides border settings defined for the frameset. Most browsers default to Yes. To turn off a border, all adjacent frames must be set to No (or set to Default with the parent frameset set to No).
Border Color	This sets a border color for all of the frame's borders. This color applies to all borders that touch the frame and overrides the specified border color of the frameset.
Margin Width	This sets the width in pixels of the left and right margins.
Margin Height	This sets the height in pixels of the top and bottom margins.

 Hands-On 10.6   Set Frame Properties

In this exercise, you will name each frame, prevent users from dragging the frame borders, and specify whether scroll bars should appear in each frame when a site visitor resizes the browser window.

Before you begin: The index.htm file should be open.

1. Click in the top frame in the Frames panel.

2. Set the properties shown in the following illustration:
   The name you choose for the frame should accurately describe the frame contents. Setting Scroll to No ensures that scroll bars will not appear in the frame. The No Resize property ensures that visitors cannot resize the frame, and Borders set to No ensures that a Web browser will not display a default border.

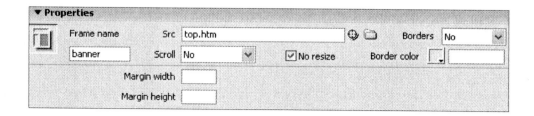

3. Set the same properties for the remaining frames. Name the left frame **navigation** and name the main frame **content**. All other properties are the same as the ones shown in the preceding illustration.

4. Choose File→Save All from the menu bar.

Targeting Links

For content pages to appear in the correct frame, we need to target the links in the navigation frame to the content frame. In Lesson 5, Working with Anchors and Links, you learned how to target an HTML document to a new window by setting the target property on the Properties panel to _blank. We don't want the content pages loading in a new window; we want each page to open in the frame named content.

 ## Hands-On 10.7   Open a Linked Document in Another Frame

In this exercise, you will use the Properties panel to target each link in the navigation frame to open in the content frame.

1. Click once on the graphic named Home, which appears in the first table cell in the Navigation frame.

2. From the Target menu on the Properties panel, choose Content.
   This ensures that this link will open in the frame named content.

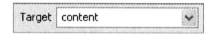

3. Repeat this process to target all of the remaining links in the Navigation frame to the content frame.

4. Choose File→Save All from the menu bar.

5. Press F12 to open the frameset in your browser.

6. Test each link to ensure that the destination page is targeted to the content frame.

7. Leave your browser open and return to the Document window.

Creating No Frames Content

Not everyone who visits your site will have a frames-enabled browser. Very old browsers don't know how to read the <frameset> tag and so they display a blank page. To make your frame pages accessible to the widest audience possible, you can create a fully functional page that is connected with the most important information provided in your frames-based pages. This information should describe the content of the frames on the page. It can consist of long text descriptions or links to frames or other HTML documents. Noframes content does not appear in modern visual browsers but it will be read by screen readers and seen by those using text-based browsers or browsers that do not support frames. Fortunately, Dreamweaver makes this process quite easy.

To modify the frameset to include no frames content, simply open the frameset page, index.htm, and choose Modify→Frameset→Edit NoFrames Content from the menu bar.

 TIP! *No frames pages can be used to improve traffic flow to your site. Many search engine "spiders" search and index no frames content. On your no frames page, include a comprehensive description of your site and keywords that people might use to search for information on your site.*

 ## Hands-On 10.8   Create No Frames Content

In this exercise, you will create a no frames content page, which can be used to prevent older browsers from displaying a blank page.

1. Choose Modify→Frameset→Edit NoFrames Content from the menu bar.
   This opens a new blank area that is part of the <frameset> tag.

2. Open no_frames.text from the lesson_10/text folder.

3. Copy and paste the text in the blank NoFrames Content area.
   This is merely an example of no frames content. You could style this page or add additional content you'd like a visitor to see if their browser doesn't support frames.

4. Choose File→Save All.
   The no frames text is not an HTML file and you won't see it in the Files panel. That's because the content is added to the <frameset> tag in Code view.

5. Choose File→Close All from the menu bar.

Concepts Review

True/False Questions

1. A frameset is an HTML document that defines the layout and properties of a set of frames. TRUE   FALSE

2. A frameset document typically contains text, graphics, and other HTML Web page elements. TRUE   FALSE

3. When one frameset is nested in another frameset, the inner frameset is called the parent. TRUE   FALSE

4. If you already have a content page, you can create a new frames page using the Layout category of the Insert bar. TRUE   FALSE

5. If you're starting from scratch and don't have content for the frames pages, choose File→Save All and Dreamweaver will allow you to name a document for each frame and specify a file storage location. TRUE   FALSE

6. You use the Frames panel to set and modify <frameset> properties. TRUE   FALSE

7. A frame is a region in a browser window that can display one or more HTML documents. TRUE   FALSE

8. In the example, <frameset> <frameset>, the first <frameset> tag is the parent. TRUE   FALSE

9. Frame properties override frameset properties. TRUE   FALSE

10. Framesets are supported by all browsers. TRUE   FALSE

Multiple Choice Questions

1. How many pages are required for a two-frame frameset?
   a. 1
   b. 2
   c. 3
   d. 4

2. A frameset controls which of the following properties?
   a. Borders, border color, and border width
   b. Frame dimensions
   c. The source of the document within the frame
   d. Both a and b

3. Which of the following units of measure sets an exact width or height for a frameset?
   a. Percent
   b. Relative
   c. Pixels
   d. None of the above

4. Which of the following elements are frame properties?
   a. Name
   b. Title
   c. Document title
   d. Width and height

Skill Builders

Skill Builder 10.1 Design a Nested Frameset

In this exercise, you will design a three-frame frameset.

Create the Frameset

1. Choose Window→Frames from the menu bar to open the Frames panel.

2. Choose File→New from the menu bar. Choose the General tab.

3. Choose the Framesets category and select Fixed Top, Nested Left from the list of predefined framesets.

4. Click Create.

5. Choose File→Save Frameset As from the menu bar.

6. Save the file as **grandma.htm** in the review_10/grandma folder.

Populate the Frames

7. Click inside the top frame.

8. Choose File→Open in Frame from the menu bar.

9. Open banner.htm from the review_10/grandma folder.

10. Now open nav.htm in the left frame and content.htm in the right frame.

11. Choose File→Save All from the menu bar.
    Your file should match the following illustration.

12. Keep the documents open.

Skill Builder 10.2 Set Frameset Properties

In this exercise, you will set properties for the two framesets.

1. Click the top border in the Frames panel.

2. Set the Row Value to **68** pixels. Do NOT deselect the frameset.

3. Replace the default title text Untitled Document on the Document toolbar with **Grandma's Recipes**.

4. Click the child frameset border on the Frames panel.

5. Ensure that the left column is highlighted on the Properties panel.

6. Set the Column Value to **170** pixels.
   This makes the column width a little bit wider than the 150 pixel table.

7. Click the right column on the Properties panel.

8. Ensure that the Column Value is set to **1** and Units is set to Relative.

9. Save the documents and keep them open.

Skill Builder 10.3 Set Frame Properties

In this exercise, you will name each frame.

1. Click in topFrame on the Frames panel.

2. Type **banner** to replace the default name on the Properties panel.

3. Click in leftFrame on the Frames panel.

4. Type **navigation** to replace the default name on the Properties panel.

5. Click in mainframe on the Frames panel.

6. Type **recipes** to replace the default name mainFrame.

7. Save the documents and keep them open.

Skill Builder 10.4   Set Frame Properties

In this exercise, you will target the links in the navigation frame to the recipes frame.

1. Click in the Home link in the navigation frame.

2. From the Target pop-up menu on the Properties panel, choose recipes.

3. Now target the remaining two links to the recipes frame.

4. Choose File→Save All from the menu bar.

5. Preview the files in your browser.

6. Test each link to ensure the destination page loads in the right frame, which you named recipes.

7. Leave the browser open, and return to the Document window.

8. Leave the grandma.htm file open.

Skill Builder 10.5   Add a New Content Page

In this exercise, you will add a new page to Grandma's Recipes.

1. Create a new HTML document.

2. Save it in the grandma folder as **hotdogs.htm**.

3. Type **Hot Dog Recipes** and apply a Heading 1 format.

4. On the grandma.htm page, insert another row to the navigation table, and then add a link to your new page.

5. Target the link to open in the recipes frame.

6. Test the new link in your browser.

7. Save and close all files.

Assessments

Assessment 10.1   Insert a New Frameset

In this exercise, you will design a frameset document. You will begin by opening a content page. Then you will use the Layout category to insert a top and nested left frame.

1. Open sv_main.htm from the review_10/senior_voices folder.

2. Use the Frames menu in the Layout category of the Insert bar to insert a top and nested left frame.

3. Save the frameset as **sv_index.htm**. (If you do not see the Save Frameset As command, ensure that the outer frameset is selected.)

4. Open sv_banner.htm in the top frame.

5. Open sv_nav.htm in the left frame.

SENIOR VOICES

Empowerment Thorough Learning

Senior Centers
Library
Social Services
Meals on Wheels
Special Events
Endowment
Wish List

Welcome to **Senior Voices**. It is never too late to learn. If you doubt it for a moment, ask anyone attending our computer workshops. Our youngest student is 71, and our oldest is 93. When we opened our doors a few months ago, most of our students didn't know how to type. Some had never used an electronic keyboard; most had never seen the Internet. In fact, one Senior Voice's member thought the Internet was a subversive spy ring like the CIA. Today, we're writing about issues that are important to us, and sharing that informaton with others. Through the generous donation of a major computer company, we now have a state-of-the-art computer room and everyone has their own mouse!

At **Senior Voices**, computer skills are taught experientially. Everyone learns through active participation. It's the way you learned to ride a bicycle. When you finally decided to got for it, despite the fear of falling, you just hopped on and wobbled off down the road. Learning to use a computer and the Internet is such a rewarding experience. Come and see for yourself.

---

6. Save the documents, but keep them open.

Assessment 10.2   Set Frameset and Frame Properties

In this exercise, you will define two frameset properties.

1. Set the Row Value for the parent frameset.

2. Set the Column Value for the left frame in the child frameset.

3. Set the Column Value for the right frame in the child frameset.

4. Assign each frame a unique name.

5. Save all documents but keep them open.

Assessment 10.3   Target Links to the Content Frame

In this exercise, you will target the links in the left frame to open in the right frame. The first two links point to the correct files in the senior_voices folder; the remaining links are placeholder links.

1. Target the first two links in the left frame to open in the content frame on the right.

2. Save all of the files, and then preview the frameset file in your browser.

3. Test the first two links.
   Both of these links should open the destination page in the right frame.

4. Close any open documents.

Critical Thinking

Critical Thinking 10.1   On Your Own

Jennifer and Mathew Springer made a stay-at-home agreement before they married. Jennifer stayed home with their first child, and now that a second child has arrived, it's Mathew's turn. During his sleepless nights, Mathew made detailed notes about baby care from a new stay-at-home dad's perspective, and felt it would be a great resource for other beginning stay at home dads. He named the site THE FACTS ON SAHD.

Matthew tells his shocking story in the main content page of the frames based pages he's asked you to design so he can share his experiences and resources with other stay-at-home dads. He's already designed the content for each frame but he needs your help making the frames pages work properly.

The following illustration is based on a Left and Nested Top frame design.

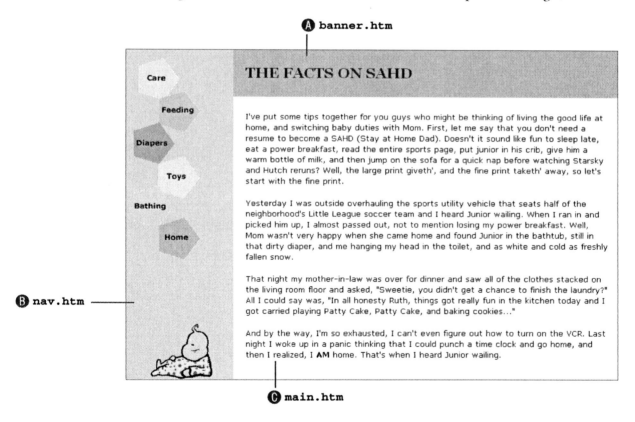

A banner.htm

THE FACTS ON SAHD

I've put some tips together for you guys who might be thinking of living the good life at home, and switching baby duties with Mom. First, let me say that you don't need a resume to become a SAHD (Stay at Home Dad). Doesn't it sound like fun to sleep late, eat a power breakfast, read the entire sports page, put junior in his crib, give him a warm bottle of milk, and then jump on the sofa for a quick nap before watching Starsky and Hutch reruns? Well, the large print giveth', and the fine print taketh' away, so let's start with the fine print.

Yesterday I was outside overhauling the sports utility vehicle that seats half of the neighborhood's Little League soccer team and I heard Junior wailing. When I ran in and picked him up, I almost passed out, not to mention losing my power breakfast. Well, Mom wasn't very happy when she came home and found Junior in the bathtub, still in that dirty diaper, and me hanging my head in the toilet, and as white and cold as freshly fallen snow.

That night my mother-in-law was over for dinner and saw all of the clothes stacked on the living room floor and asked, "Sweetie, you didn't get a chance to finish the laundry?" All I could say was, "In all honesty Ruth, things got really fun in the kitchen today and I got carried playing Patty Cake, Patty Cake, and baking cookies..."

And by the way, I'm so exhausted, I can't even figure out how to turn on the VCR. Last night I woke up in a panic thinking that I could punch a time clock and go home, and then I realized, I **AM** home. That's when I heard Junior wailing.

B nav.htm

C main.htm

The banner, nav, and main pages are located in the review_10/sahd folder. You can open each of the three pages and plot your design strategy before you begin.

Save the frameset file as **index.htm** in the review_10/sahd folder.

Critical Thinking 10.2 On the Web

Now you will finish the SAHD pages by researching and creating Web pages on the following baby topics: care, feeding, diapers, toys, and bathing.

Create five new HTML documents, and save them in the review_10/sahd folder. Use the following filenames:

- **care.htm**
- **feeding.htm**
- **diapers.htm**
- **toys.htm**
- **bathing.htm**

Link each image to the pages you created as a result of your search. Target each of the links to open the destination page in the main frame. The following illustration shows the navigation table with six images.

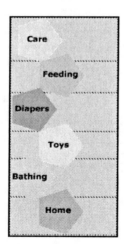

Critical Thinking 10.3 Create No Frames Content

In this exercise, you will create alternative text for old browsers that do not support frames, and a comprehensive site description for search engines. There is no text file for this exercise.

Imagine that someone has landed on THE FACTS ON SAHD homepage and sees a blank page. Describe the site and offer the visitor a fictional link to a NoFrames page they can browse. Type a detailed description of the site services. Add keywords you think someone would type in a search engine to find similar sites.

LESSON 11

Working with Automation Tools

In this lesson, we explore three automation tools that will help reduce your production time: snippets, libraries, and templates. Snippets and library items are sections of code that you can reuse on multiple pages in your site. Library items are linked to pages, snippets are not. A template is a document used as the basis for creating other documents. Template users are allowed to input content in editable regions on the page without fear of destroying the page layout design. When you make a change to the template, you can choose to update all pages based on the template or defer the update to a later time.

Case Study

Bunny Parker is the founder of Dolphin Watch, a non-profit organization that provides a global voice for the protection of dolphins and their environment. Bunny became fascinated with dolphins at age 13 when a dolphin washed ashore near her Malibu home. Her call to 911 saved the dolphin's life and thus began her lifelong journey exploring the dolphin world. Dolphin Watch received a grant for the development of its Web site. Bunny's game plan was to build in as much automation as possible to make it easier for contributors to add content consistent with the page design. She began by creating a snippet of placeholder text that contributors could replace with final content. She included a library item, a tool for tracking references to copyright information that may need to be updated from time to time. And, by saving the page as a template, she made it easy to develop new pages that match. The template guarantees that the site design is flexible, consistent, and easy to update.

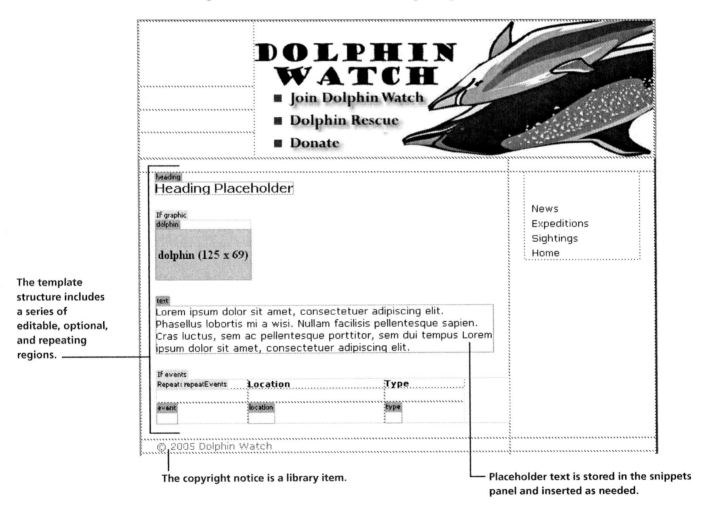

The template structure includes a series of editable, optional, and repeating regions.

The copyright notice is a library item.

Placeholder text is stored in the snippets panel and inserted as needed.

Creating Snippets

A snippet is a simply a piece of text, HTML, CSS, JavaScript, or just about anything else you need to reuse on various pages in your site. Dreamweaver provides a variety of predefined snippets, which you can use as-is or modify to suit your purpose. You can also create your own. For example, if you find yourself creating the same table over and over, you can select the table and turn it into a snippet. When you need it again, you can double-click on its name or drag it onto your page. Snippets can be inserted in the <head> or <body> of an HTML document. The location depends on whether the snippet is a block of code (such as JavaScript) or CSS, text, or an HTML element (such as a table).

The Snippets Panel

FROM THE KEYBOARD
To open the Snippets panel:
WIN AND MAC
Shift + F9

Snippets are stored in the Snippets panel, which is a member of the Code panel group. To open the Snippets panel, choose Window→Snippets from the menu bar.

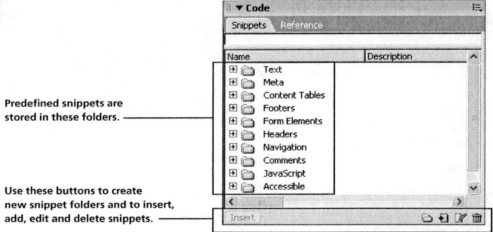

Predefined snippets are stored in these folders. ────

Use these buttons to create new snippet folders and to insert, add, edit and delete snippets. ────

Hands-On 11.1 Create a Lipsum Snippet

In this exercise, you will create a new folder in the Snippets panel and add a new text placeholder snippet to it.

1. Open lipsum.txt from the lesson_11/text folder.
   The file opens in Code view. This is a text file that contains a few paragraphs of Lorem Ipsum (Lipsum).

2. Choose Window→Snippets, or press Shift + F9.
   This opens the Code panel. The Snippets tab is active.

3. Double-click the blue title bar on the Code panel.
   This fully expands the panel.

4. Ensure that all folders are closed and that none are highlighted.
   This ensures that your new folder won't be inserted inside any of the predefined snippet folders.

5. Click the New Snippet Folder 🗀 button on the bottom of the Snippets panel.

6. Name the folder **My Snippets**, and then press ⌈Enter⌉ or ⌈Return⌉.
   The new folder appears in alphabetical order in the Name column of the Snippets panel.

7. Select the My Snippets folder.
   Ensure that the folder is highlighted before you continue.

8. Select all of the text on the page.

9. Click the New Snippet ⊞ button on the bottom of the Snippets panel.
   This opens the Snippet dialog box.

10. Follow these steps to create the snippet:

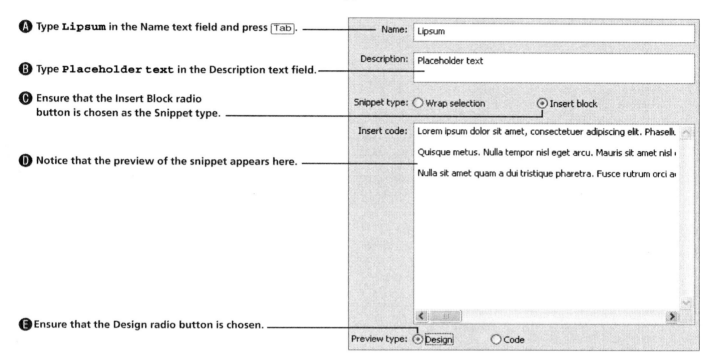

ⓐ Type **Lipsum** in the Name text field and press ⌈Tab⌉.

ⓑ Type **Placeholder text** in the Description text field.

ⓒ Ensure that the Insert Block radio button is chosen as the Snippet type.

ⓓ Notice that the preview of the snippet appears here.

ⓔ Ensure that the Design radio button is chosen.

11. Click OK.
    The snippet is added to the new folder. Notice the icon that identifies snippets in Dreamweaver:

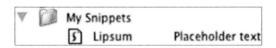

12. Close lipsum.txt.

Inserting a Snippet

You can insert a snippet by dragging and dropping it onto the page or by selecting the snippet and clicking the Insert button at the bottom of the Snippets panel. A snippet inserted onto a page is not linked in any way. If you make changes to the snippet, pages that contain the snippet will not be updated.

QUICK REFERENCE: CREATING AND INSERTING A SNIPPET	
Task	**Procedure**
Create a snippet	■ Choose Window→Snippets from the menu bar.
	■ Create a new folder or select an existing folder in which to store the snippet.
	■ Select the element you wish to turn into a snippet.
	■ Click the New Snippet button in the lower-right corner of the Snippets panel.
	■ Use the Snippet dialog box to set the options for the snippet.
Insert a snippet	■ Choose Window→Snippets from the menu bar.
	■ Position the insertion point where you want the snippet to appear.
	■ Select the snippet from the Snippets panel.
	■ Drag and drop the snippet to the document window or use the Insert button in the lower-left corner of the Snippets panel.

 Hands-On 11.2 **Insert a Snippet**

In this exercise, you will open an HMTL document and insert the snippet you created in the last exercise.

1. Open dolphins.htm from the lesson_11 folder.

2. Position the insertion point below the Introduction text.

3. Choose Window→Snippets, if necessary, to open the Snippets panel.

4. Open the My Snippets folder.

5. Select the Lipsum snippet.

6. Click the [Insert] button in the lower-left corner of the Snippets panel.

7. Select approximately one-third of the text, and then delete it.

8. Break the remaining text into two or more paragraphs.

9. Click anywhere outside the table.
Dreamweaver resizes the table.

10. Close the Code panel.

11. Save the file but leave the document open.
Congratulations! You're one step closer to becoming a Dreamweaver guru.

Managing Your Assets

As your site grows, you will likely accumulate a large number of assets (valuable text, images, etc.) that you use on multiple pages. Keeping track of and managing these assets can be quite a challenge, and that's why Dreamweaver provides the Assets panel. The Assets panel helps you keep most of the components of your site organized and updated. You can easily keep track of and preview several kinds of assets, such as images, colors, URLs, movies, scripts, and links. In the next exercise, you will take a brief tour of the Assets panel to see what assets are available and how the panel is organized. Then, we will explore two special types of assets: library items and templates.

The Assets panel is a member of the Files panel group. To open the panel, choose Window→Assets or, if the Files panel is open, simply click the Assets tab. You can also open the Assets panel by pressing F11.

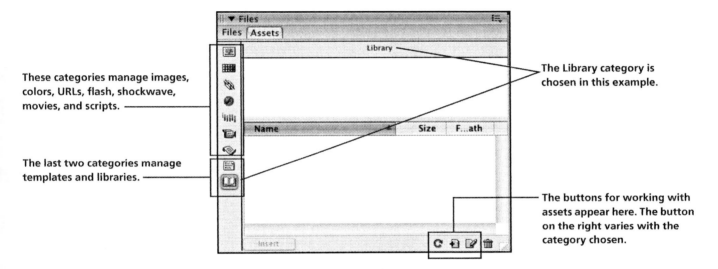

These categories manage images, colors, URLs, flash, shockwave, movies, and scripts.

The last two categories manage templates and libraries.

The Library category is chosen in this example.

The buttons for working with assets appear here. The button on the right varies with the category chosen.

Hands-On 11.3   Tour the Assets Panel

In this exercise, you will take a brief tour of the Assets panel. Then you will add an image to Favorites.

1. Choose Window→Assets from the menu bar.
   This opens the Assets panel.

2. Follow these steps to locate and preview an image in the Images category:

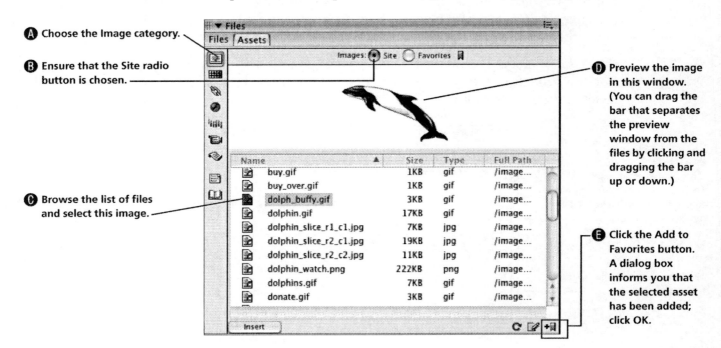

A Choose the Image category.

B Ensure that the Site radio button is chosen.

C Browse the list of files and select this image.

D Preview the image in this window. (You can drag the bar that separates the preview window from the files by clicking and dragging the bar up or down.)

E Click the Add to Favorites button. A dialog box informs you that the selected asset has been added; click OK.

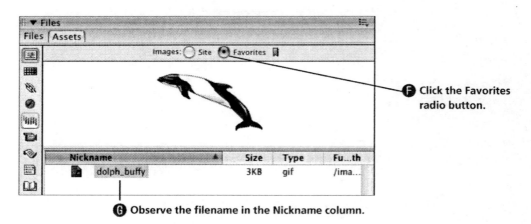

F Click the Favorites radio button.

G Observe the filename in the Nickname column.

Note that when you select the images category, all of the images in the current site are listed, regardless of where they are located. Assets saved to My Favorites can later be inserted or dragged and dropped into the Document window. Adjacent to the Nickname column you'll find three columns that describe the file size, type, and full path.

3. In the Nickname column, click and drag dolph_buffy to the beginning of the first paragraph.

4. Click the Site radio button at the top of the Assets panel.
This switches you back to the site files.

5. Click the Library   button in the Categories list.
This opens the Library window.

6. Leave the Assets panel open.

7. Save the file but keep it open.

Using Library Items

You have undoubtedly noticed that there are several Web page elements throughout your site that may change over time. Two immediate examples are header and footer elements, such as logo and copyright information. Let's consider this scenario: You've created hundreds of pages in your client's site, and the footer of each page contains a copyright notice and a link to the site manager's email address. The site manager leaves the position. How long would it take you to update all those page footers by hand?

If you added the copyright notice as a library item, all you would have to do is edit and save the library file. When you do this, Dreamweaver gives you the option of updating all pages that contain the library item. If you decline the option, you can update the pages later by choosing Modify→Library→Update Pages.

NOTE! *Library items are site specific. Each site you create has its own library, and you cannot share library items between sites.*

Creating a Library Item

Library items are not Web pages; they are document elements that appear within the <body> </body> tags. Library items can be text, forms, tables, images, Java applets, plug-ins, or ActiveX elements.

To create a library item, select the element and choose Modify→Library→Add Object to Library or click the New Library Item button at the bottom of the Assets panel. When you do this, Dreamweaver converts the selection to non-editable content that is linked to the corresponding library item.

Dreamweaver also creates a library folder in the root folder of your local site to store the new item. Library item names use the .lbi extension.

TIP! *You don't have to have the Assets panel open to create a library item. When you make a selection and choose Modify→Library→Add Object to Library, Dreamweaver automatically opens the Assets panel, switches to the Library category, and inserts the item.*

Hands-On 11.4 Create a Library Item

In this exercise, you will select a copyright notice and store it in the library.

Before you begin: The dolphins.htm file should still be open.

1. Select the copyright text at the bottom of the page.

2. Click the New Library Item ⬚ button on the bottom tab of the Assets panel. Read the warning that tells you that this item may not look the same when placed in other documents because the style sheet information is not copied with it. Then, click OK.
   A new, untitled library item is added to the library. Notice that the default name is selected so you can type a new name. Also notice the preview of the library item that appears in the small window above the library items name.

3. Type **copyright** and press ⎵Enter⎵ or ⎵Return⎵.

4. Click in a blank area of the page and observe the copyright notice at the bottom of the page.
   The text now appears in a light yellow background. If you do not see the yellow background, choose View→Visual Aids and ensure that there is a checkmark next to the Invisible Elements option.

5. Click in the small table of links in the right column of dophins.htm, and then click the <table> tag on the Tag Selector (the third <table> tag from the left).
   The table is nested inside two other tables. A class style named .sidebar is applied to the table data tag, which reads <td.sidebar>. Notice that the table data cell contains an unordered list, but the bullets next to each list item don't show. This is because the list is formatted with a CSS style that removes the bullets from each item in the list.

   The links in the table are placeholder links. You will recall that placeholder links contain a pound sign (#), not a path.

6. With the table still selected, use the technique outlined in step 2 to add the table as a library item.

7. Click OK.
   The sidebar table now has a light yellow background. Now you need to name the library item.

8. Type **sidebar** and press ⎵Enter⎵ or ⎵Return⎵.
   This opens the Update Files dialog box.

9. Read the message asking if you want to update links to an item in the library folder. Click Update.
   When you click Update, Dreamweaver adds the new library item named sidebar.lbi to the library folder and the library item appears in the Assets panel.

10. Save and close the file.

11. Open the Files panel, and then open the Library folder.
    You should see the copyright and sidebar library items you created.

12. Close the Library folder.

13. Open library_practice.htm from the lesson_11 folder.
    This page and the page you used to create the two library items are linked to the same external style sheet.

14. Open the Assets panel and ensure that the Library category is chosen.

15. Leave the file open.

Inserting a Library Item

Now you have two library items that you can insert on any page in your site. When you make a change to the library item, you are given the chance to update all of the pages in your site that use the library item.

 Hands-On 11.5   Add Library Items to a Page

In this exercise, you will add the two new library items to the page.

Before you begin: The library_practice.htm file should still be open.

1. Place the insertion point in the first empty cell in the last row.
   This is where you will insert the copyright library item.

2. Select the copyright library item in the Assets panel.

3. Click the ⌈ Insert ⌋ button at the bottom of the Assets panel.
   Observe the tags on the Tag Selector. The last tag reads <mm:libitem>, which identifies the selection as a library item.

4. Click in the large, empty cell to the right of the main content area.
   This is where you will insert the navigation table.

5. Click and drag the sidebar library item to the insertion point.
   The page should now resemble the following illustration:

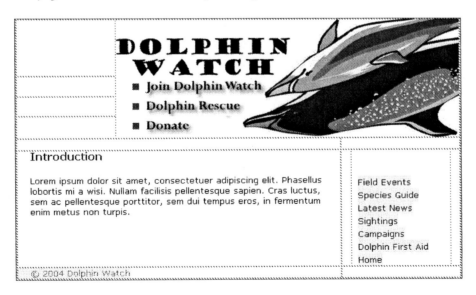

6. Save the file but keep it open.

Editing a Library Item

You'll see the real power of library items when it's time to make a change that affects multiple pages. There are several methods you can use to edit library items. For example, you can select the library item in the Assets panel, and then use the Edit button at the bottom of the panel. However, we're going to use a fast-track approach that doesn't involve switching back and forth from the Files panel to the Assets panel.

When you click a library item that you've inserted on the page, the Properties panel displays useful buttons.

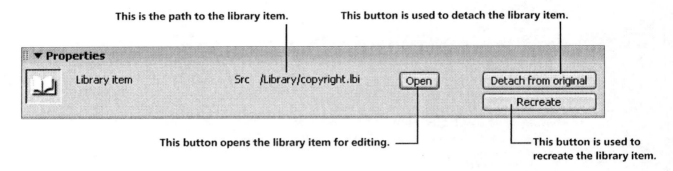

This is the path to the library item.

This button is used to detach the library item.

This button opens the library item for editing.

This button is used to recreate the library item.

 WARNING! *When you want to make a change to a library item, Dreamweaver must open and update (unless you defer this step to a later time) each file that uses it. If the library item is used on hundreds of pages, this could take a significant amount of time because each file must be uploaded to your server. Dreamweaver's Synchronization feature, which you learned to use in Lesson 6, Working with Site Management, can make the uploading much easier.*

QR **QUICK REFERENCE: WORKING WITH LIBRARY ITEMS**

Task	Procedure
Create a library item	Select the Web page element you wish to use as the library item and choose Modify→Library→Add Object to Library. Or, click the New Library Item button at the bottom of the Library category of the Assets panel.
Insert a library item	Place the insertion point in the Document window, select the library item, and then click the Insert button at the bottom of the Assets panel. Or, click and drag the library item to the insertion point in the Document window.
Modify a library item	Select the library item in a document and click the Open button on the Properties panel.
Detach a library file	Select the library item in a document and click the Detach from Original button on the Properties panel. This breaks the link between the selected library item and its source file.
Recreate a library item	Select the library item in a document and click the Recreate a library Item button on the Properties panel. This overwrites the original library item with the current selection.
Delete a library item	Select the library item in the Assets panel, and then click the Delete button at the bottom of the panel or press Delete.

Hands-On 11.6   Edit a Library Item

In this exercise, you will edit the copyright library item.

1. Click once on the copyright library item you inserted in the last exercise.
This highlights the item. The Properties panel changes to provide library item settings.

2. Click the Open button on the Properties panel.
Dreamweaver opens what looks like any other Web page, but isn't. It's a library file, and you can't modify its page properties.

3. Change the year to **2005** and type **All Rights Reserved** after the text Dolphin Watch.

4. Choose File→Save from the menu bar (or press the Save button).
Dreamweaver checks to see if there are any pages that use the library item. If there are, the Update Library Items dialog box opens and shows a list of the pages that will update.

5. Choose Update.

6. Read the information in the Update Pages dialog box, and then click Close.

7. Close the library file.

8. Observe the copyright notice at the bottom of library_practice.htm.
The copyright reflects the changes you made to the library item.

9. Save and close the file.

Detaching and Recreating Library Items

When you select a library item and click the [Detach from original] button on the Properties panel, the link between the selected library item and its source file is broken. When an item is detached from the original it can be edited in the document, but it's no longer a library item and can't be updated when you modify the original library item.

The [Recreate] button on the Properties panel recreates a library item that you may have accidentally deleted or cannot find. When you click the Recreate button, the original library item is overwritten by the current selection.

Using Templates

A great way to maintain design consistency throughout your entire site, or sections within your site, is to finalize the initial page layout and save the page as a template. When you create a new page based on the template, the page will inherit all of the design elements from the template. Without a template, your best hope in maintaining design consistency is to save each new page with a different name. This works to a certain degree but you must update each page by hand. If you accidentally move a table cell border, for example, the entire structure of the layout will shift. Many new vocabularies have been created by Web designers when this happens.

All of the main content pages in your site probably share certain similar characteristics, such as a page header, navigation bar, content area, and page footer. If these elements are in the same location on each page, visitors to your site can relax knowing that they don't have to relearn your navigation scheme each time they jump to another page.

Also, some pages may require images in one location and tables or lists in another location. Other pages may not use these elements at all. You can include any or all of the content items needed for a given page. Those who use your templates (see the following note) can elect to show just those elements they need to get the job done and hide the rest. Folks who use your template can only add content; they cannot change the layout or toss your design in disarray. A template effectively locks content providers out of the design areas they don't need to be tampering with. Now that's control!

Another great aspect of using Dreamweaver templates is the ability to instantly update the look of your site. When you make changes to a template, all of the pages based on the template are automatically updated (unless you choose to defer the update). You can update the pages later by choosing Modify→Templates→Update Pages.

 NOTE! *Large sites generally require a team of Web page developers. For example, one developer's job may be to keep all of the links functional. Another's job may be to design the site navigation, etc. If you're working solo, you are responsible for all of these tasks, and many more.*

Creating a New Template

You can create a template from a new, blank HTML document or you can save an existing page as a template. We use the latter approach in this lesson. The New Document dialog box provides several options for creating new templates and template-based pages. When you create and save a template, Dreamweaver creates a Template folder in the root folder of your local site to store the template. Template files use the .dwt extension.

 ## Hands-On 11.7   Save a File as a Template

In this exercise, you will save an existing page as a template for the Dolphin Watch site.

1. Open dolphin_watch.htm from the lesson_11 folder.
   This file is linked to dolphin_watch.css.

2. Choose File→Save as Template.
   This opens the Save as Template dialog box.

3. Save the file with the default name **dolphin_watch** in the current local site.
This opens the Update Links alert box. Updating the links will allow Dreamweaver to keep the paths to links and images correct.

4. Choose Yes.
Dreamweaver creates a Templates folder in the root level of your local site and stores the template in it. You may need to click the Refresh button on the Files panel to see the Templates folder.

5. Observe the new filename at the top of the Document window.
The file you are working with now is < <Template> > (dolphin_watch.dwt). The file you used to create the template is closed. No changes were made to that document.

6. Click the Assets tab in the Files panel group.
Because you have a template open, dolphin_watch.dwt may open the Templates category automatically. If not, choose the Templates category. The template you just created appears in the list, and any future templates you create will also appear here.

7. Click the Files tab in the Files panel group.

8. Leave the file open.

⚠️**WARNING!** *Do not move templates out of or put any non-template files in the Templates folder. Also, do not move the Templates folder out of your local root folder. Doing so will cause path errors in the templates.*

Defining Template Regions

Dreamweaver templates consist of regions that are either locked or unlocked. By default, all regions on any page created from a template are locked. To make the template useful, you must define one or more template regions. Dreamweaver defines a variety of template regions. The three regions we explore in this lesson are editable regions, repeating regions, and optional regions.

Editable Regions

An editable region allows content to be edited within a defined area in a template-based page. It is imperative that a template contain a minimum of one editable region; otherwise, pages based on the template will be locked and template users cannot change the content. That would be like giving someone a book in which all the pages are glued together. (Hey! That might be fun to do on April Fool's Day.)

When editing a template or a template based page, template regions are enclosed by a light blue box with a tab at the top that displays the region name. In the following illustration, the region name is "text."

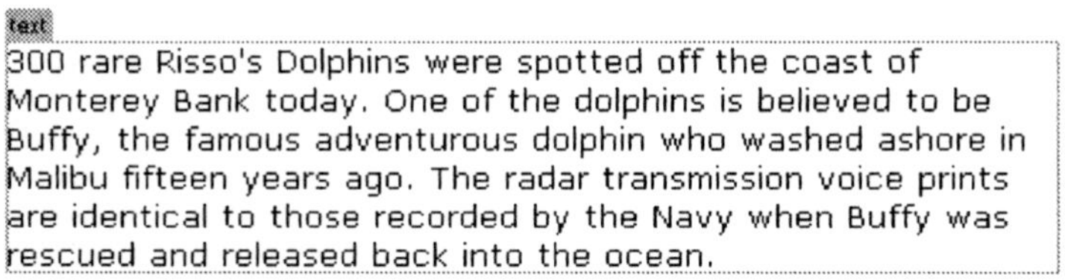

> text
> 300 rare Risso's Dolphins were spotted off the coast of Monterey Bank today. One of the dolphins is believed to be Buffy, the famous adventurous dolphin who washed ashore in Malibu fifteen years ago. The radar transmission voice prints are identical to those recorded by the Navy when Buffy was rescued and released back into the ocean.

Repeating Regions

A repeating region is a section of a template that can be duplicated as often as necessary in a template-based page.

Use these repeating region controls to add, delete, and move an entry up or down.

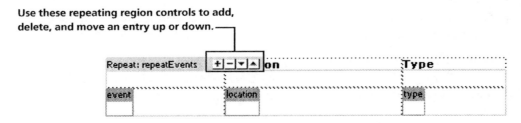

When you add a repeating region entry, a copy of the entire repeating region is added.

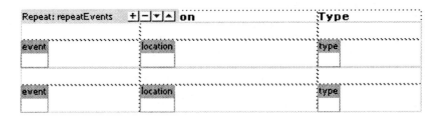

To update the content in the repeating regions, the original template must include an editable region in the repeating region.

Optional Regions

An optional region is an area of a template you can set to show or hide in a template-based page. Advanced optional regions allow you to set conditions for displaying optional content in a document.

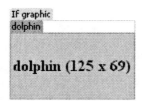

 NOTE! *Optional region names are preceded by the word "If." This is a conditional statement (if...then) that Dreamweaver uses to show or hide the optional region on pages based on the template.*

Inserting an Editable Region

FROM THE KEYBOARD

To insert an editable region:

WIN ONLY
Ctrl + Alt + V

MAC ONLY
Option + ⌘ + V

The first step in modifying a template is to define the areas of the page that should be editable in documents based on the template. This is accomplished by defining one or more editable regions. You can mark an entire table or an individual table cell as editable, but you can't mark multiple table cells as a single editable region. Anything in the template not explicitly defined as editable is locked in pages based on the template.

All of the commands for inserting editable regions can be accessed by choosing Insert→Template Objects. The same commands are available in the Common category of the Insert bar shown in the following illustration.

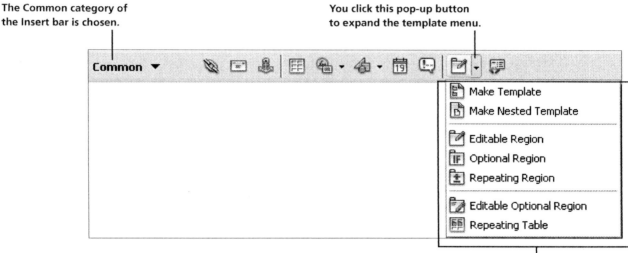

The Common category of the Insert bar is chosen.

You click this pop-up button to expand the template menu.

These options are used to work with template objects.

For the sake of simplicity and consistency, we use commands from the menu bar in this lesson; however, feel free to use the Common category of the Insert bar if you wish.

Hands-On 11.8   Insert an Editable Region

In this exercise, you will define two editable regions.

Before you begin: The dolphin_watch template should still be open.

1. Choose View→Visual Aids and make sure there is a checkmark next to Invisible Elements.

2. Select the Heading Placeholder text.
   The heading will change from page to page so you want to be able to change the heading text on each new page based on the template.

3. Choose Insert→Template Objects→Editable Region.
   This opens the New Editable Region dialog box.

4. Type **heading** in the Name field.
   Each editable region name must be unique and cannot contain special characters. Always choose names that are simple and descriptive.

5. Click OK, and then click outside the heading to deselect the text.
   In the Document window the editable area appears outlined in blue. Notice the blue tab at the top that displays the name of the editable region.

6. Select the paragraph of placeholder text that appears directly below the image placeholder.
   The real text will support the heading so it should be editable on each page.

7. Use the technique outlined in step 3 to define another editable region.

8. Type **text** in the Name field and click OK.
   In the Document window the editable text area appears in a blue outline. The region is identified by a blue tab at the top of the region.

9. Choose File→Save from the menu bar.
   Dreamweaver displays an alert box that tells you users are not able to create new paragraphs.

10. Click OK.

Inserting an Optional Region

When you want your template to include information on some template based pages but not on others, insert an optional region. When creating a new page based on the template, the page author can turn the region on or off. But wait: there's more!

Inserting an optional region doesn't make it editable; it just makes it optional. To make an optional region editable, you have to select the area you want to make editable, and then insert an editable region.

 NOTE! *Dreamweaver provides an Optional Editable Region that is not a replacement for the process we're using here. This type of region contains an optional region with an editable region inside it. Optional Editable Regions have limited capabilities, and it's difficult to insert HTML outside the editable region.*

 Hands-On 11.9   **Insert an Optional Region**

In this exercise, you will insert an optional region for the placeholder graphic.

***Before you begin:** the dolphin_watch template should be open.*

1. Click once on the placeholder graphic to select it.

2. Choose Insert→Template Objects→Optional Region.
   This opens the New Optional Region Dialog box.

3. Ensure that the Basic tab is chosen.

4. Type **graphic** in the Name field and remove the checkmark next to Show by Default.
   Removing the checkmark allows content providers to show the graphic only when needed.

5. Click OK.
   The placeholder is now surrounded by a light blue outline, and the optional region tab reads "if graphic." This is a conditional statement Dreamweaver uses to turn the graphic on or off on any page created from the template.

6. Select the placeholder graphic again.
   Now we need to make the graphic editable.

7. Choose Insert→Template Objects→Editable Region.
   This enables you to replace the image placeholder with a graphic.

8. Type **dolphin** in the Name field and click OK.

9. Save the file but keep it open.

Inserting a Repeating Region

One last aspect we'd like our practice template to have is a repeating region for the small table. Repeating regions enable you to control your page layout by repeating certain items (such as a part number, price, or description) or a row for data (such as a list of items).

You can make a repeating region optional so it appears on some pages but not on others. Also, to make the repeating region useful, you must also make it editable. So, let's see: we have optional, repeating, and editable regions. That's a three-step process!

 ## Hands-On 11.10 Add a Repeating Region

In this exercise, you will add an optional region to a table. Then, you will insert a repeating region and an editable region.

Before you begin: the dolphin_watch template should be open.

1. Click in the small table at the bottom of the page that contains the Event, Location, and Type table headers.

2. Click the <table> tag on the Tag Selector. (It's the last <table> tag on the right.)

3. Choose Insert→Template Objects→Optional Region.

4. Type **events** in the Name field, remove the checkmark next to Show by Default, and then click OK.

5. Drag the insertion point over the two empty rows of the table to select them.
   These will be the repeating rows.

6. Choose Insert→Template Objects→Repeating Region.

7. Type **repeatEvents** in the Name field and click OK.

8. Click in the first empty cell in the last row, and then click the <td> tag on the Tag Selector. (It's the last <td> tag on the right.)

9. Choose Insert→Template Objects—Editable Region.

10. Type **event** in the Name field and click OK.

11. Click in the second cell in the last row, and then click the <td> tag on the Tag Selector.

12. Choose Insert→Template Objects→Editable Region.

13. Type **location** in the Name field and click OK.

14. Click in the last empty cell in the last row, and then click the <td> tag on the Tag Selector.

15. Choose Insert→Template Objects→Editable Region.

16. Type **type** in the Name field and click OK.

The table should now resemble the following illustration:

If events Repeat: repeatEvents Location	Type
event location	type

17. Save and close all files.

 TIP! *If you're having a bad day, you may have trashed your template. When this happens and you've already saved the template, you many want to close the template, delete it from the Assets panel, and start over. Remember, the page you based the template on is still intact.*

Creating Template-Based Pages

Now that we have defined template regions, we can create pages based on a template. Template-based pages are linked to the template; therefore, when you make changes to the template, all of the template-based pages update. You can add a new link or template region after creating multiple pages from the template. The new additions will be added to all pages based on the template when you save the template file.

 WARNING! *Dreamweaver allows you to change an editable region name by clicking the blue tab and typing a new name in the Properties panel. However, be aware that if you've already built pages based on the template, this can create errors. Template-based pages use the name to identify the editable regions and Dreamweaver loses track of where content should go when you rename a region. Fortunately Dreamweaver provides options to remap the region names, but it's best to avoid renaming editable regions unless you absolutely have to.*

QR> **QUICK REFERENCE: WORKING WITH TEMPLATES**

Task	Procedure
Create a new template	■ Start with a blank page or use an existing page. ■ Choose File→Save As Template. ■ Select a site to store the template.
Insert an editable region	■ Select the element that you want to set as an editable region or place the insertion point where you want to insert an editable region. ■ Choose Insert→Template Objects→Editable Region. ■ Enter a unique name for the region.

QR **QUICK REFERENCE: WORKING WITH TEMPLATES (CONTINUED)**

Task	Procedure
Insert an optional region	■ Select the element you want to set as an optional region or place the insertion point in the document where you want to insert the optional region. ■ Select Insert→Template Objects→Optional Region. ■ Specify options for the optional region.
Insert a repeating region	■ Select the text or content you want to set as a repeating region, or place the insertion point in the document where you want to insert the repeating region. ■ Choose Insert→Template Objects→Repeating Region. ■ Enter a unique name for the region.
Create a new page based on a template	■ Choose File→New. ■ In the New Document dialog box, select the Templates tab. ■ In the Templates For list, select the site that contains the template you want to use. The site templates list updates to display templates in the selected site. ■ In the list, select the template you want to use. ■ Click Create to create a new template-based page.
Remove editable, optional, or repeating regions	■ Click the region tab. ■ Choose Modify→Templates→Remove Template Markup.
Detach a page from a template	■ Choose Modify→Templates→Detach from Template.
Update template pages	■ Choose Modify→Templates→Update Pages.

 ## Hands-On 11.11 **Create Template Based Pages**

In this exercise, you will create four template based pages, one for each page referenced in the navigation sidebar (news, sightings, expeditions, and home).

1. Choose File→New from the menu bar.
   This opens the New Document dialog box.

2. (Win) Click the Templates tab. (Mac) Click the Templates button.
   This opens the New from Template dialog box.

3. Follow these steps to create a new template-based page:

Ⓐ Choose your current site from the list of sites you've defined on your file storage location. Your current site name may be different from the one shown.

Ⓑ Select dolphin_watch.

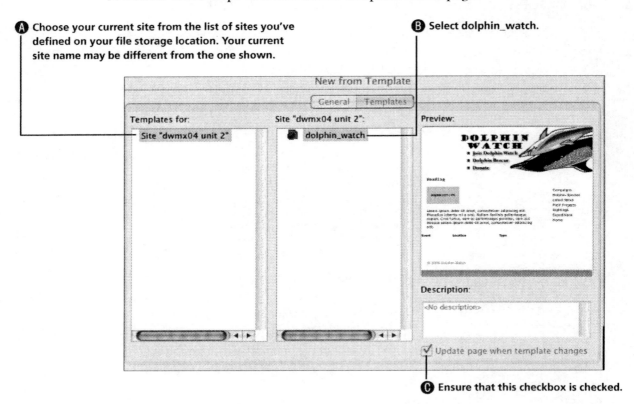

Ⓒ Ensure that this checkbox is checked.

4. Click Create.

The new page looks almost identical to the template, but the optional regions aren't showing. That's because you disabled them. You'll be able to show them on the pages that use them.

5. Use the technique outlined in steps 1–4 to create three more pages.

You should now have a total of four untitled pages. You can use the following shortcut to toggle between open pages in the Document window.

(Mac) Press ⌘+[~] to switch between open pages in the Document window. (Win) Press the page tab to switch between open pages in the Document window.

6. Choose File→Save All.

This opens the Save As dialog box.

7. Ensure that the lesson_11 folder is selected in the current site.

8. Type **expeditions.htm** in the Save As field and click Save.

The file is saved to the current site and the Save As dialog box reappears.

9. Use the technique outlined in step 8 to save the remaining documents with the following names:

- **sightings.htm**
- **news.htm**
- **index.htm**

10. Make index.htm the active page but do not close the other pages.
    The document window appears in a pale yellow outline. The template name, also in pale yellow, appears at the upper-right corner of the document window.

11. Roll the mouse pointer around various regions of the page.
    The "locked" insertion point appears over the regions that you cannot edit.

12. Leave the files open.

You now have a template-based page. What if you want to make changes to this page? Don't worry. Editing template-based pages is a snap.

 Hands-On 11.12 Edit Template-Based Pages

In this exercise, you will edit the editable regions in all of the template based pages.

Before you begin: The index.htm, expeditions.htm, sightings.htm, and news.htm files should be open.

Edit the Homepage

1. Ensure that index.htm is the active page.

2. Select the Heading Placeholder text and type **Introduction** in its place.

3. Delete the placeholder text in the editable region below the heading.

4. Open introduction.txt from the lesson_11/text folder.

5. Copy and paste the text into the editable region marked with the blue text tab.

6. Close the text file.

7. In the Title text field on the Document toolbar, type **Dolphin Watch : How dolphins breathe and communicate**.
   When you're creating template based pages for your site, don't forget to assign each page a unique title.

8. Save and close the file.

Edit the News Page

9. Make news.htm the active page.

10. Select the Heading Placeholder text and type **Latest News** in its place.

11. Delete the placeholder text in the editable region below the heading.

12. Open news.txt from the lesson_11/text folder.

13. Copy and paste the text into the editable region.

14. Use the technique outlined in step 7 to assign a unique title for the page. Use the text of your choosing.

15. Close the text file.

16. Save and close the file.

Edit the Sightings Page

17. Make sightings.htm the active page.

18. Select the Heading Placeholder text and type **Dolphin Sightings** in its place.

19. Delete the placeholder text in the editable region below the heading.

20. Open sightings.txt from the lesson_11/text folder.

21. Copy and paste the text into the editable region.

22. Close the text file.

23. Choose Modify→Template Properties from the menu bar.
This opens the Template Properties dialog box.

24. Follow these steps to show the graphic:

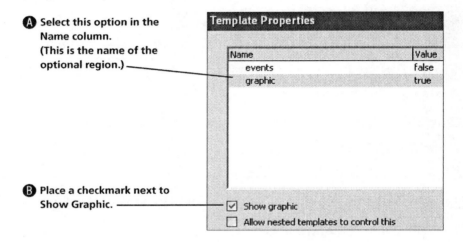

Ⓐ Select this option in the Name column. (This is the name of the optional region.)

Ⓑ Place a checkmark next to Show Graphic.

25. Click OK.
The graphic placeholder is shown on the page.

26. Double-click on the placeholder graphic.
This opens the Select Image Source dialog box.

27. Choose dolph_buffy.gif from the images folder, and then click OK or Choose.
The image replaces the image placeholder.

28. Use the technique outlined in step 7 to assign a unique title for the page. Use the text of your choosing.

29. Save and close the file.

Edit the Expeditions Page

30. Make expeditions.htm the active page.

31. Select the Heading Placeholder text and type **Expeditions** in its place.

32. Delete the placeholder text in the editable region below the heading.

33. Type **Check this page daily for new expeditions**.

34. Choose Modify→Template Properties from the menu bar.

35. In the Name column select events, place a checkmark next to Show Events.

36. Click OK.
The repeating region appears at the bottom of the page.

37. Click in the first empty cell labeled event, type **Dolphin Adventure**, and then press `Tab`.

38. Type **Jamaica** in the location field and press `Tab`.

39. Type **Diving Expedition** in the type field. Do NOT press `Tab`.

40. Click the plus (+) sign to add a new row.

41. Type the data shown in the last row of the following illustration:

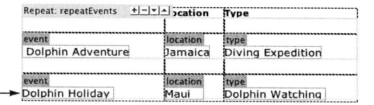

42. Save and close the file.

Modifying a Template

As the template owner, you always have access to the original template, which you can modify to include additional editable regions, add links to template based pages, update copyright information, etc. Even though you can open a template from the Templates folder in your local site, a safer approach is to use the Assets panel. This prevents you from accidentally moving or deleting the template.

If you happen to be working with a template based page and you want to make modifications to the template, choose Modify→Templates→Open Attached Templates.

 Hands-On 11.13 Modify a Template

In this exercise, you will use the small table on the template page to link to the four pages you just created. Then, you will test drive the template-based pages in your browser to make sure all of the links work.

1. Click the Assets tab on the Files panel or choose Window→Assets from the menu bar.

2. Click the Templates button 🖻 on the left side of the Assets panel.

3. Select dolphin_watch.dwt and click the Edit 📝 button at the bottom of the Assets panel.
This opens the template in the Document window.

4. Locate the small table that contains the text News, Sightings, Expeditions, and Home.

5. Select the text News.

6. On the Properties panel, use Browse for File to locate and select news.htm in the list of files in the lesson_11 folder. click OK or Choose.

7. Use the technique outlined in steps 5 and 6 to link the following remaining pages:
   - Sightings—**sightings.htm**
   - Expeditions—**expeditions.htm**
   - Home—**index.htm**

8. Choose File→Save from the menu bar.
   Dreamweaver displays a list of the files that will be updated.

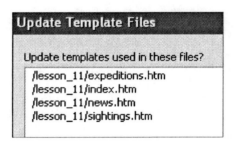

9. Choose Update.
   Dreamweaver opens an Update Pages log that shows the update status.

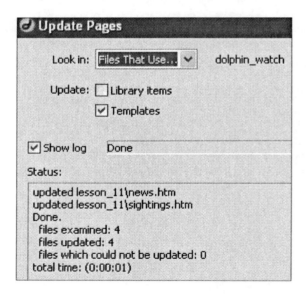

10. Click Close.

11. Close the template file.

12. Open index.htm from the lesson_11 folder.

13. Preview the file in your browser.

14. Click each link in the navigation sidebar.

15. Leave your browser open and return to the Document window.

16. Close all files.

Concepts Review

True/False Questions

1. When you modify a snippet, all pages that contain the snippet update automatically.   TRUE   FALSE

2. The Assets panel is a great place to store frequently used images, colors, URLs, movies, scripts, and links.   TRUE   FALSE

3. Library items can be shared across multiple sites.   TRUE   FALSE

4. Library files are stored in the Library folder and take the .lbi extension.   TRUE   FALSE

5. When you edit a library item, Dreamweaver provides an option to update all pages that use the library item.   TRUE   FALSE

6. When you modify a template linked to numerous pages, you can defer the update.   TRUE   FALSE

7. For ultimate control, it's a great idea to lock all areas of a template.   TRUE   FALSE

8. You can mark an entire table as editable but you can't mark multiple table cells as a single editable region.   TRUE   FALSE

9. Optional regions provide the means for a site contributor to display or hide the optional regions.   TRUE   FALSE

10. If you rename an editable region, all pages based on the template automatically update to reflect the new name.   TRUE   FALSE

Multiple Choice Questions

1. Which of the following elements can be added to the Snippets panel?
   a. An HTML table
   b. CSS code
   c. Text
   d. All of the above

2. Which of the following elements are good candidates for library items?
   a. Frames pages
   b. Headers and footers
   c. External CSS files
   d. None of the above

3. Which of the following regions can be duplicated as often as necessary in a template based page?
   a. Editable
   b. Repeating
   c. Optional
   d. Editable Optional

4. How do you insert editable regions?
   a. Choose Insert→Template Objects→Editable Region.
   b. Use the Common category on the Insert bar.
   c. Select the region and Choose Modify→Template Objects→Editable Region.
   d. Both a and b

 # Skill Builders

Skill Builder 11.1 Create a Snippet

In this exercise, you will create a snippet table.

1. Open breed_directory.htm from the review_11/toy_dogs folder.
   The page contains a small table of links.

2. Select the small table of links.

3. Choose Window→Snippets from the menu bar.

4. Open the My Snippets folder.

5. Click the New Snippet button at the bottom of the Snippets panel.

6. Set the following options in the Snippets dialog box:

Name	**Breed Directory**
Description	**Left Navigation Links**
Snippet Type	Insert Block
Preview Type	Design

7. Click OK.

8. Close breed_directory.htm and leave the Snippets panel open.

9. Open toy_breeds.htm from the review_11/toy_dogs folder.

10. Position the insertion point in the first table cell in the second row.

11. Select the Breed Directory Snippet from the Snippets panel.

12. Click the Insert Snippet button at the bottom of the Snippets panel.

13. Close the Snippets panel.

14. Save the file but leave it open.

Skill Builder 11.2 Create a Library Item

In this exercise, you will practice working with library Items.

1. Select the copyright notice at the bottom of toy_breeds.htm.

2. Choose Modify→Library→Add Object to Library from the menu bar.
   This opens an untitled library item in the Assets panel.

3. Type **jtd copyright** and press ⌈Enter⌋ or ⌈Return⌋.

4. Save the file but leave it open.

Skill Builder 11.3 **Create a Template**

In this exercise, you will create a template from the Just Toy Dogs page.

1. Choose File→Save as Template.

2. Save the template as **toy_breeds** to the current site.

3. Choose Yes to update links.

4. Select the Placeholder Heading text (do not select the right-facing double-angle character entity).

5. Choose Insert→Template Objects→Editable Region.

6. Type **breed** in the Name field and press OK.

7. Select the placeholder graphic.

8. Choose Insert→Template Objects→Optional Region.

9. Type **photo** in the Name field, remove the checkmark next to Show by Default, and then click OK.

10. Select the placeholder graphic, if necessary.

11. Choose Insert→Template Objects→Editable Region.

12. Type **showphoto** in the Name field and click OK.

13. Select all of the placeholder text.

14. Choose Insert→Template Objects→Editable Region.

15. Type **description** in the Name field and click OK.

16. Choose File→Save.

17. Close the alert dialog box that warns you about the paragraph.

18. Close the file.

Skill Builder 11.4   Create a Template-Based Page

In this exercise, you will create a page based on the template.

1. Choose File→New from the menu bar.

2. Choose the Templates tab.

3. Select toy breeds from the Template list and click Create.

4. Save the file as **poms.htm** to the review_11/toy_dogs folder.

5. Change the title of the page to **Just Toy Dogs—Pomeranians**.

6. Type **Pomeranians** to replace the heading placeholder text.

7. Choose Modify→Template Properties from the menu bar.

8. Place a checkmark next to Show Photo and click OK.

9. Double-click the image placeholder.
   This opens the Select Image Source dialog box.

10. Choose yahoo.jpg from the list of images in the Images folder.

11. Select and delete all of the description placeholder text.

12. Open poms.txt from the review_11/text folder.

13. Copy the text and paste it into the description editable area.

14. Close the text file.

15. Save the file, and then preview it in your browser.

16. Leave your browser open and return to the Document window.

17. Close all files.

Assessments

Assessment 11.1 Create a Template

In this exercise, you will save an existing document as a template. You will also define editable, optional, and repeating regions.

1. Open frederic.htm from the review_11/frederick folder.

2. Save the file as a template.

3. Insert the template regions shown in the following illustration:

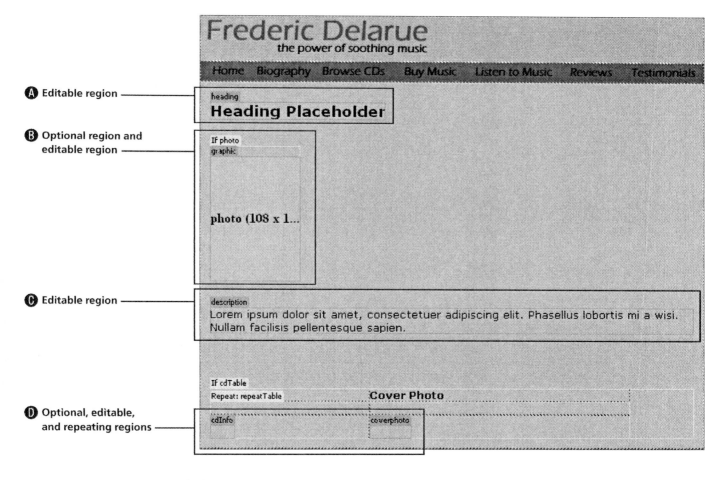

Ⓐ Editable region

Ⓑ Optional region and editable region

Ⓒ Editable region

Ⓓ Optional, editable, and repeating regions

4. Save and close the template file.

Assessment 11.2   Create Template-Based Pages

In this exercise, you will create a template-based page from the frederic template to create a Browse CDs page, and a Biography page. The text for the biographical information is stored in the review_11/text folder. The name of the file is bio.txt.

1. Create a new template-based page named bio.htm. Save it to the review_11/frederic folder.

2. Replace the Heading Placeholder text with Biography.

3. Modify the template properties to show the optional graphic region.

4. Replace the image placeholder with frederic.jpg, which is located in the images folder.

5. Open bio.txt from the review_11/text folder.

6. Copy and paste the text in the description editable region below the graphic, and then close the text file.

   The final version of the file bio.htm is shown in the following illustration:

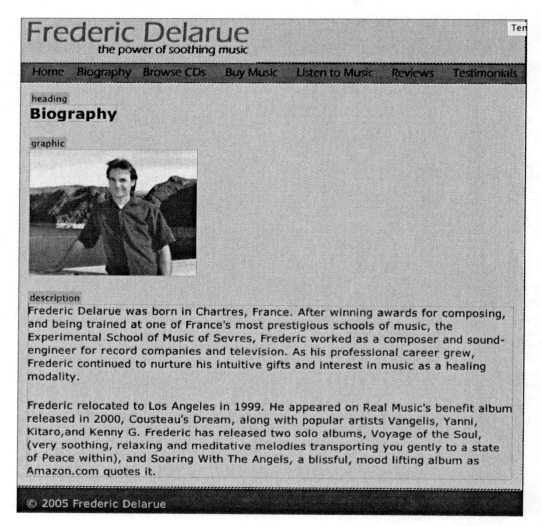

7. Save and close the file.

8. Create another template-based page named browse.htm. Save it to the review_11/frederic folder.

9. Replace the Heading Placeholder text with Browse CDs.

10. Modify the template properties to show the optional graphic region and the optional repeating region.

11. Use the following illustration to complete the repeating region.
   The two graphics are named soaringwiththeangels.jpg and voyageofthesoul.jpg. Both are located in the images folder.

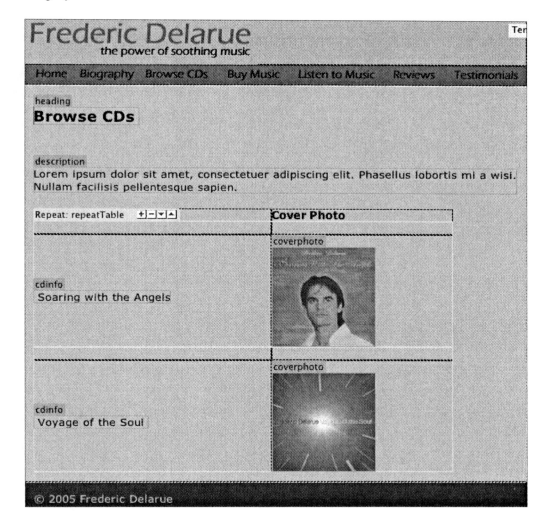

12. Save and close all files.

Critical Thinking

Critical Thinking 11.1   On Your Own

Jeffrey Springer just finished his Dreamweaver course at Lodi Community College. As a reward, he took what he thought would be a brief vacation to Maui. However, two days after arriving he spotted an ad in a local flyer. A neighborhood tourist bureau was in need of someone with Dreamweaver MX 2004 skills and the pay and benefits were awesome. Jeffrey has always dreamed of spending his free days surfing and hiking but he never thought the opportunity would come so quickly.

Jeffrey passed the audition and received his first assignment. He now asks you to design a template he can use to add new content pages to the Hawaii tourist site. Jeffrey has already designed the homepage.

All of the files for this exercise are located in the review_11/hawaii folder.

Test Drive the Homepage

■ Open index.htm in your browser. The homepage is a two-frame frameset that contains a left and right frame. The only functional links are Travel Tips and Home. A click on the Travel Tips link opens travel.htm in the right frame; a click on the Home link opens a page named content.htm in the right frame. The home page is shown in the following illustration:

Create the Template and the Template-Based Pages

- Use the travel.htm file as your starting point for creating a template. Or, you can create a new blank page and save it as a template.

- The template design should contain an editable, an optional, and a repeating region.

- Create the template-based page shown in the following illustration. (The bride.jpg image shown is located in the images folder.)

- Use the Weddings and Honeymoons text on the nav_left.htm file to link to the new wedding page you created from the template.

- When previewed in your browser, the wedding page should open in the right frame when the link to Weddings and Honeymoons is clicked. The final version of the page is shown in the following illustration.

- Leave the file open if you want to continue this in the next Critical Thinking exercise.

A A click on the link to Weddings & Honeymoons...

Wedding Packages

Family Fun
Outdoor Adventure
Weddings & Honeymoons
Business & Education
Culture & History
Travel Tips
home

Whether this is the first or the fifth, this wedding will be one you will never forget. Our wedding packages ensure a high level of quality and service. We will take care of all the details so you can relax and enjoy being in love.

Wedding Package	Price
Plumeria Basic	$250
Plumeria Deluxe	$1450
No Orchids	$25

B ...opens a wedding page that contains editable, optional, and repeating regions.

Critical Thinking 11.2   On the Web

Use your browser and favorite search engine to research the following Hawaiian topics needed to complete the Hawaii pages:

- Family fun

- Outdoor Adventure

- Business and Education

- Culture and History

- Travel Tips

Create new content pages for each topic. Link all of the new pages to the navigation links in the left frame. Close all the files when complete.

Unit 3

Advanced Skills

Dreamweaver MX 2004 includes all of the tools you need to provide interaction between you and your site visitors. In this unit, you will learn how to design forms to gather information from your site visitors, how to use Dreamweaver behaviors to create interactive Web page features such as rollover images and swapping two or more images with a single event, how to combine layers and Cascading Style Sheets (CSS) to create sophisticated page layouts, and how to animate layers with timelines. You will also edit HTML, optimize your pages for better search results, clean up HTML and Word HTML documents, and validate code.

Lesson 12: Working with Forms

Lesson 13: Working with Behaviors

Lesson 14: Working with Layers

Lesson 15: Working with HTML

LESSON 12

Working with Forms

In this lesson, you will learn how to design forms for your Web site. Forms provide two-way communication between your site and its visitors. For example, you can design a form that requests your visitor's name and email address, or provide a form field they can use to give you feedback about your site. Fortunately, Dreamweaver's form objects make the form design process easy. A form object consists of the form and elements within the form that are used to gather information, such as text fields, menus, radio buttons, and checkboxes.

This lesson teaches you the basics of designing a form, adding form objects, and setting their properties. You will also learn how to validate required text input fields to help ensure that your form captures the essential data you are seeking.

Case Study

Zoya Borodkina is a matchmaker. Her yenta power propelled her into the spotlight last year when she launched Party of Two, a free online dating service sponsored by several upscale local restaurants. Potential candidates fill out a form on the Party of Two's Make a Date page. When the form is submitted, Zoya reviews the data and when she finds a match, she sends the lucky couple an email. This process sure beats the old one, which required the use of hundreds of index cards.

The form is well organized and labeled so users know exactly what's required. To ensure that the most important text fields aren't empty, she uses form validation. When the form is successfully submitted, a form results page is returned so users are assured that the data has been received. Oy vey, now it's breath holding time.

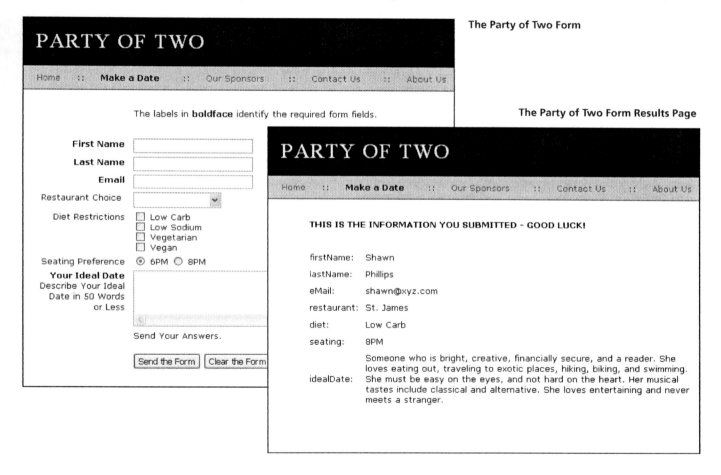

The Party of Two Form

The Party of Two Form Results Page

Understanding How Forms Work

Before you begin building forms (a Web page with a series of data fields to complete), you need a basic understanding of how they work. In a nutshell, when a visitor to your site sees the form, they are directed to fill out the fields. Usually near the bottom of the form is a Send or Submit button. When the visitor clicks the button, the browser looks at the URL specified in the <form> tag, and then sends the data to that address. The address is usually to you or your Internet service provider's server (master computer). The ball is then in the server's court. If you've done your job correctly, the server uses the script (short programming code) specified in the form, processes the form data, and then sends a confirmation that the data has been received. This is called server-side processing because all scripts your forms use must reside in a folder on your server. Here, we explore this process in greater detail.

When you insert a form, Dreamweaver adds the <form> tag in Code view. The opening <form> tag indicates the beginning of the form and its properties; the closing </form> tag marks the form's end.

```
<form name="form1" method="post" action=""> </form>
```

The <form> tag contains three essential properties that you need to modify in order to process the form data: name, method, and action. When you select a form, the default properties appear in the Properties panel.

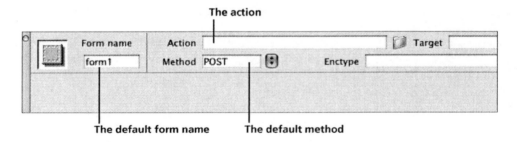

The action

Form name | Action | Target
form1 | Method POST | Enctype

The default form name | **The default method**

Use the Properties panel to set form and form object properties.

The Action Property

The action property specifies the URL of the script you use to process the information submitted in the form. The most widely used form processing script is Common Gateway Interface (CGI). CGI scripts are written in Perl or another programming language such as C, C++, or Python. Forms can also be processed by other server-side technologies such as ASP, ASP.NET, ColdFusion, PHP, or JSP, which function essentially in the same way as CGI scripts. Server-side scripts allow two-way communication. For security reasons, scripts are kept in special directories on your server and you must have permission to use them. Before spending a lot of time designing forms, check with your server administrator and find out what type of scripting technology is supported. Many Web hosting companies provide free form processing scripts already securely set up for use on their servers.

NOTE! *The specifics of setting up scripts are well beyond the scope of this book. Unless you are using forms to process secure data, chances are your Web hosting service or your Web server administrator already has scripts you can use to process your forms.*

The form you design in this lesson is processed by a custom ASP server-side script for demonstration purposes only. The form data isn't stored on a server.

The Method Property

The method property determines which method to use when processing information submitted in the form. The method property has two possible values: Post or Get. Post is the default and most commonly used method to send information to your server. The Get method is an older method that is marked for deletion in future HTML versions due to security risks to a server.

The Name Property

The name property is a unique identifier for forms and form elements. The first form you insert is named form1, until you change it.

Forms and all form objects should have a unique name that describes the information you are gathering. For example, if you're collecting information about museums, you might want to use the name "museums" for your form.

TIP! *Do not use spaces or special characters. Names are case-sensitive when used with scripts such as CGI or JavaScripts.*

When a visitor to your site fills out a form and submits it, the form processing script running on your server matches the name of the form object with the value that the user enters. For example, say the name of a text field is museum_name. The user types **Museum of Modern Man** into the text field, and then submits the form. The form processing script returns the name/value pair, which is simply the name of the form object and the value the user entered. In this case, the script returns: museum_name = "Museum of Modern Man".

Emailing Form Results

If you don't need to store form results on your server, you can have the form results sent to your email. This sounds easy enough, but you need to have a form mail script running on your server in order to retrieve the data and parse it (translate it into something a human can read). Again, contact your Web hosting service for details.

Building a Form

The first step in building a form is to insert a form object on the page and set its properties. A form inserted onto a page appears as a dashed red outline, which is a visual aid that defines its boundaries. A form stretches all the way across the page unless you insert the form inside a table set to a fixed width or percentage value that's less than 100%.

A form object appears as a red dashed rectangular outline.

In this lesson, you will use the Forms category on the Insert bar. If you are menu driven, feel free to choose Insert→Form, and then choose the appropriate form object from the menu bar.

The Forms Category on the Insert Bar

The Forms category on the Insert bar provides a series of buttons you can use to insert forms and other form objects, as well as two buttons you can use to organize more complex forms into sections.

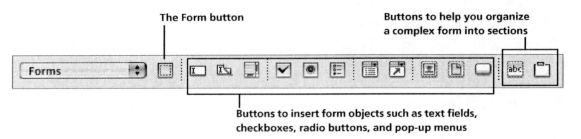

The Form button   Buttons to help you organize a complex form into sections

Buttons to insert form objects such as text fields, checkboxes, radio buttons, and pop-up menus

Every form object must be contained within a form. A form can also contain tables, text, images, and other elements that normally appear on a Web page.

 TIP! *Tables provide structure for form objects and field labels and allow you to line up choices both vertically and horizontally.*

 QR

QUICK REFERENCE: INSERTING A FORM

Insert a form
- Place the insertion point where you want to insert the form.
- Click the Form object in the Forms category of the Insert bar or choose Insert→Form→Form.
- Use the Properties panel to set the Form's properties.

Hands-On 12.1   Insert a Form

In this exercise, you will insert a form object into a table cell, and then drag and drop a pre-designed table inside the red dashed outline that represents the form object.

1. Open party_form.htm from the lesson_12 folder.
   The page contains a banner, a navigation row, an empty row, and another table separated by a paragraph.

2. Place the insertion point in the empty row below the navigation row.

Insert a Form

3. Press the Form ▢ button in the Forms category of the Insert bar or choose Insert→Form→Form from the menu bar.
   The form appears as a red dashed outline and the insertion point is blinking inside the form. If you do not see the form, choose View_Visual Aids, and then click to put a checkmark next to Invisible Elements.

4. Click anywhere in the large table that appears below the form, and then click the <table.bgwhite> tag on the Tag Selector.
   This pre-designed table will save you time and assist you in aligning form objects.

5. Choose Edit→Cut.
   This cuts the table to the Clipboard.

6. Place the insertion point inside the form, and then choose Edit→Paste.
   This pastes the table into the red dashed outline that represents the form object.

7. Click anywhere in the table you just pasted and observe the hierarchy of tags on the Tag Selector.
   The <form> tag precedes the <table.bgwhite> tag. This is your guarantee that the table is housed inside the form object.

8. Click the <form> tag on the Tag Selector.

Set Form Properties

9. Follow these steps to set the form properties:

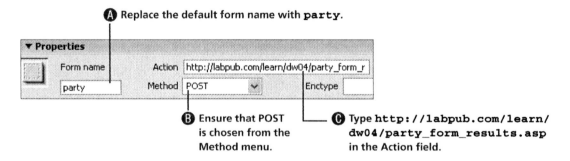

Ⓐ Replace the default form name with **party**.

Ⓑ Ensure that POST is chosen from the Method menu.

Ⓒ Type **http://labpub.com/learn/ dw04/party_form_results.asp** in the Action field.

10. Save the file but keep it open.

Adding Form Elements

Form elements come in a variety of shapes and sizes, and each one has a unique purpose. For example, text fields provide a space to type specific information, a series of checkboxes provide multiple-choice selections, and menus provide a list of items from which to choose. Regardless of which element you add, you must insert it inside the form. The routine you follow for adding form elements requires the same two-step process you used to insert a form and set its properties:

1. Press the form element button in the Forms category of the Insert bar or use the Insert menu to insert the form element into the form.

2. Use the Properties panel to assign a unique name for each new form element, and then set the form element's remaining properties.

It's as simple as that. Each time you select a form element, the Properties panel changes to show the current form element's properties.

Adding Text Fields

Text fields (also called text boxes) enable a site visitor to type text inside a box. Text fields come in two flavors: single line fields for short responses, multi-line fields for longer responses.

Adding Single Line Text Fields

Single line text fields are the perfect choice for gathering information such as a person's name, phone number, or email address, on one line.

Single line text fields are used to capture short words or phrases on a single line.

When you insert a single line text field, Dreamweaver add the <input> tag and its three default properties: name, type, and value.

```
<input name="textfield" type="text" value="">
```

The name property identifies the text field. The type property instructs a browser to display a single line text field. The value property is the value the form processing script sends to the server when the form is submitted.

While the text field is selected, you use the Properties panel to set its properties.

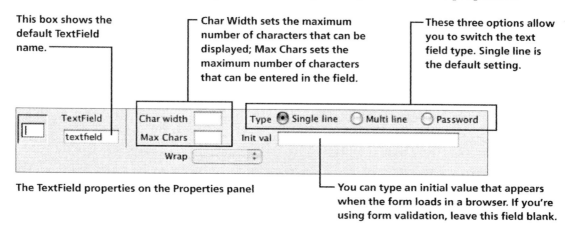

This box shows the default TextField name.

Char Width sets the maximum number of characters that can be displayed; Max Chars sets the maximum number of characters that can be entered in the field.

These three options allow you to switch the text field type. Single line is the default setting.

The TextField properties on the Properties panel

You can type an initial value that appears when the form loads in a browser. If you're using form validation, leave this field blank.

Labeling Form Elements

Your site visitors should never have to analyze a form element in order to understand how to use it. To make your forms user friendly, include a text label that clearly defines the purpose of each form element. For example, if you want someone to type their first name in a text box, precede the text box with a short text label like "First Name".

First Name

A text label identifies the purpose of the form element.

 ## Hands-On 12.2   Insert Single Line Text Fields

In this exercise, you will insert three single line text fields to capture a site visitor's first name, last name, and email address. You will also set properties for the three form elements.

Before you begin: The party_form.htm file should be open from the last exercise.

1. Position the insertion point in the fourth row, third table cell (to the right of First Name).

2. Press the Text Field ▣ button on the Forms tab of the Insert bar or choose Insert→Form→Text Field from the menu bar.

3. Use the technique outlined in step 2 two more times to insert a Text Field for the Last Name and Email rows.
   The text fields should now be positioned as shown in the following illustration:

4. Click anywhere in the first text field.
   This is a fast way to select the text field.

5. Observe the <input> tag on the Tag Selector.
This identifies the currently selected form element.

6. Set the following TextField properties on the Properties panel.

TextField	firstName
Char Width	30
Max Chars	40

7. Select the second text field and set the following properties:

TextField	lastName
Char Width	30
Max Chars	40

8. Select the third text field and set the following properties:

TextField	Email
Char Width	30
Max Chars	40

9. Save the file but keep it open.

Adding Multi-Line Text Fields

Multi-line text fields are ideal for collecting large amounts of information, such as comments and feedback about your site, or anything else that can't be displayed in a single line.

A multi-line text field captures more than one line of text.

When you add a multi-line text field to a form, Dreamweaver adds the <textarea> tag, which the browser uses to display a multi-line text field, and the name property, which identifies the element by name.

```
<textarea name="textarea"></textarea>
```

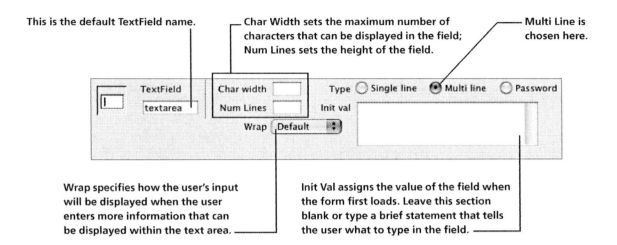

This is the default TextField name.

Char Width sets the maximum number of characters that can be displayed in the field; Num Lines sets the height of the field.

Multi Line is chosen here.

Wrap specifies how the user's input will be displayed when the user enters more information that can be displayed within the text area.

Init Val assigns the value of the field when the form first loads. Leave this section blank or type a brief statement that tells the user what to type in the field.

 Hands-On 12.3 Insert a Multi-Line Text Field

In this exercise, you will insert and set the properties for a multi-line text field.

Before you begin: The party_form.htm file should be open from the last exercise.

1. Place the insertion point in the large empty cell to the right of the text Your Ideal Date.

2. Press the Textarea [icon] button in the Forms category on the Insert bar or choose Insert→Form→Textarea from the menu bar.

3. Observe the <textarea> tag on the Tag Selector.

4. In the TextField field on the Properties panel, type **idealDate**.

5. In the Char Width field, type **50**.

6. In the Num Lines field, type **4**.
   Your form should now resemble the following partial illustration:

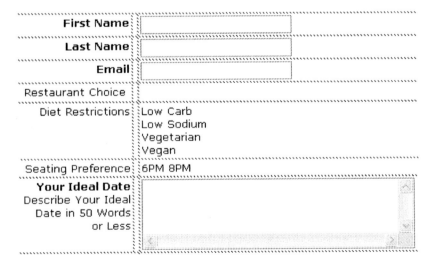

7. Save the file but keep it open.

SETTING TEXT FIELD PROPERTIES

Property	Description
TextField	The default name appears in this field. It is good practice to replace the default name with a name that describes the information you are gathering.
Type	Choosing Single Line results in a single line text field. Choosing Multi Line results in a multiple line scrolling text area. Choosing Password results in a password field that converts readable text to bullets or asterisks to protect it from observation by others. (See note.)
Char Width	This option sets the maximum number of characters that can be displayed in the field.
Max Chars/Num Lines	This option sets the maximum number of characters that can be entered in the field. When you've specified a multi-line text field, the Max Chars box changes becomes the Num Lines box. In this case, you can't limit the amount of text typed; however, you can specify the height of the text field on the screen.
Wrap	This option specifies how input will be displayed when the user enters more information than can be displayed within the defined text area in a multi-line text box.
Init Val	This option assigns an optional value to display in the field when the form first loads in a browser. Leave this field blank if you are using form validation.

 NOTE! *The Password field hides input on the screen but doesn't make the data secure. If you use this field to transmit social security or credit card numbers, you need an encrypted connection between your Web server and the user's computer. Your Web server must be configured to work in SSL (Secure Sockets Layer). Most Web hosting services support this feature, but you should verify this if you're running an e-commerce site.*

Adding Menus and Lists

Menus and lists are great choices for providing your users with preset values from which they can choose.

Menus (also called pull-down or pop-up menus) present users with multiple items, where only one item can be selected.

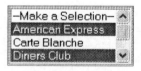

A scrolling list allows users to make multiple selections.

When you insert a menu or a list, Dreamweaver adds the <select> tag and the name attribute, which is the default name of the form element. For the <select> tag to work, you must populate the menu/list with a set of list values. List values are merely menu choices such as, American Express, Carte Blanche, etc.

```
<select name="select"> </select>
```

The properties for list and menu objects change depending on the selection you make. You can easily convert a list to a menu or a menu to a list.

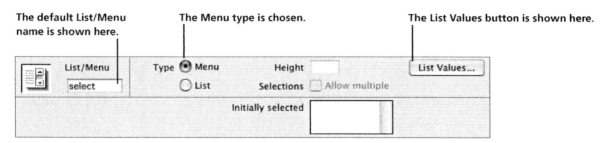

The default List/Menu name is shown here.

The Menu type is chosen.

The List Values button is shown here.

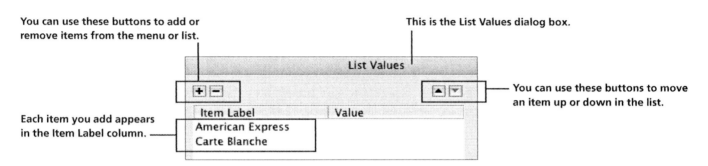

You can use these buttons to add or remove items from the menu or list.

This is the List Values dialog box.

You can use these buttons to move an item up or down in the list.

Each item you add appears in the Item Label column.

The Item Label is required; the Value is optional. If you do not supply a value, the Item Label is used. The following table demonstrates the optional use of the Value property.

Item Label	Value	Value Used by the Form Processing Script
American Express		American Express
American Express	AMEX	AMEX

Hands-On 12.4   Insert a Pop-Up Menu

In this exercise, you will insert and set the properties for a pop-up menu.

Before you begin: The party_form.htm file should be open from the previous exercise.

1. Position the insertion point in the cell directly below the email text field.

2. Press the List/Menu 🔲 button in the Forms category of the Insert bar or choose Insert→Form→List/Menu from the menu bar.

3. Click once on the menu you inserted in step 2 and observe the <select> tag on the Tag Selector.

4. In the List/Menu field on the Properties panel, type **restaurant** to replace the default name.

5. Press the ⬚ List Values... ⬚ button.
   This opens the List Values dialog box.

6. Type **Select a Restaurant** and then press the Add List Value ⊞ button. (You can also press [Tab] twice).
   This enters the text and moves the insertion point to the row below.

7. Use the technique outlined in step 6 to populate the menu with the following choices:
   St. James Vineyard

   The Chop House

   Le Vallauris

   Davey's Hideaway

8. Use the Remove List Value ⊟ button, if necessary, to remove an item from the list.

9. If you like, use the Move Up List Value ▲ button or the Move Down List Value ▼ button to reorder the items in the list.

10. Press OK.

11. In the Initially Selected menu on the Properties panel, select Select a Restaurant.
    This sets Select as Restaurant as the default choice in the list. You should now see this item in the menu.

12. Click the <select#restaurant> tag on the Tag Inspector, and then switch to Code view.

13. Observe the <option> tags that appear below the <select> tag.
    Each <option> tag identifies a list value. The first <option> tag contains the selected property you set in step 11.

14. Switch back to Design view.

15. Save the file, and then preview it in your browser.
    Your form should resemble the following partial illustration:

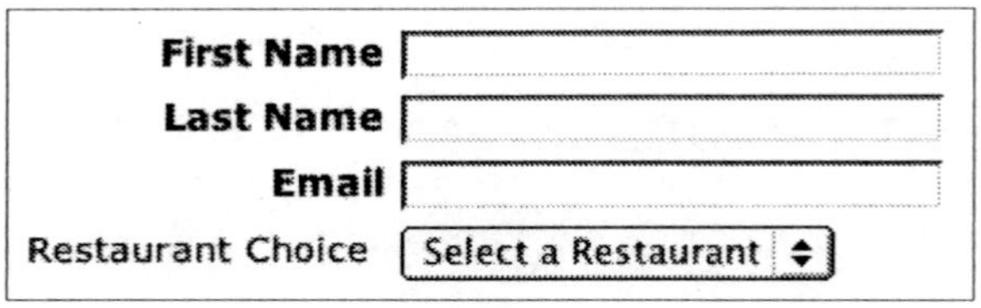

First Name	
Last Name	
Email	
Restaurant Choice	Select a Restaurant ⬍

16. Expand the menu and observe the items in the list.

17. Leave your browser open and return to the Document window.

SETTING LIST/MENU PROPERTIES

Property	Description
List/Menu	This required field assigns a name to the list or menu. The name must be unique.
Type	This option indicates whether the form object is a pop-up menu or a scrolling list. For a list, you can set the height (the number of items displayed at once) and indicate whether multiple items can be selected.
List Values	This option opens the List Values dialog box so you can add items to the list or pop-up menu. Each item in the list has a label (the text that appears in the list). The value property is optional. If you don't type a value, the label is sent to the processing script if the item is selected. Use the plus and minus buttons to add and remove items in the list. Use the up and down arrow buttons to rearrange items in the list.

Adding Checkboxes

Checkboxes provide multiple-choice selections. The user can select one, multiple, or no checkboxes. Each checkbox must be assigned a unique Checked Value. In the following illustration, two checkboxes are checked and two are not.

The user can ignore checkboxes or make multiple selections.

When you add a checkbox to a form, Dreamweaver inserts the <input> tag and the following properties: type, name, and value.

```
<input type="checkbox" name="checkbox" value="checkbox">
```

The type property instructs a browser to display a checkbox. The name property identifies the name of the checkbox. The value property is the text the form processing script sends to the server when the form is submitted.

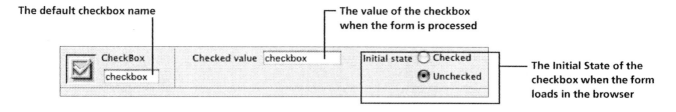

The default checkbox name

The value of the checkbox when the form is processed

The Initial State of the checkbox when the form loads in the browser

Each checkbox in a group shares the same name; however the Checked Value property is different for each checkbox. It specifies the value that is returned when the form is processed. For example, the following illustration shows four checkboxes. The Explorer and Safari boxes are checked.

☑ Explorer ☐ Netscape ☑ Safari ☐ Opera

Say that all of the checkboxes are named browser. The Checked Value for the Explorer checkbox is "Explorer" and the Checked Value for the Safari checkbox is "Safari." When the form is submitted, the form processing script returns:

```
browser="Explorer"
browser="Safari"
```

Hands-On 12.5   Insert Checkboxes

In this exercise, you will insert four checkboxes and set the properties for each. All of the checkboxes share the same name; however the Checked Value property will be unique for each.

Before you begin: The party_form.htm file should be open from the last exercise.

1. Position the insertion point to the left of the text Low Carb.

2. Press the Checkbox ☑ button in the Forms category on the Insert bar or choose Insert→Form→Checkbox from the menu bar.

3. Use the following illustration to insert three more checkboxes:

Diet Restrictions: ☐ Low Carb
                     ☐ Low Sodium
                     ☐ Vegetarian
                     ☐ Vegan

4. Select the first checkbox.

5. Observe the <input> tag on the Tag Selector.

6. In the (Win) CheckBox name or (Mac) CheckBox field on the Properties panel, replace the default text with **diet**.

7. In the Checked Value field, type **Low Carb** to replace the default text.

8. Repeat this process to name all of the checkboxes, and then set the Checked Value property to match the checkbox label as listed.

CheckBox name	diet
Checked Value	Low Sodium
CheckBox name	diet
Checked Value	Vegetarian
CheckBox name	diet
Checked Value	Vegan

9. Save the file but keep it open.

SETTING CHECKBOX PROPERTIES	
Property	**Description**
CheckBox name	Type a unique name for the checkbox. Each checkbox in the group shares the same name.
Checked Value	Type a value for the checkbox. This is the value sent to the form processing script when the form is submitted.
Initial State	Click Checked if you want an option to appear selected when the form first loads in the browser.

Adding Radio Buttons

Radio buttons are typically used in groups. They provide multiple choices but, unlike checkboxes, only one radio button may be selected in a group.

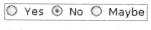

Only one radio button in a group may be selected.

When you add a radio button to a form, Dreamweaver adds the <input> tag and the same three properties that are used for all input elements: name, type, and value.

The name property is the name of the radio button. The type property instructs a browser to display a radio button. The value property is the value the form processing script sends to the server when the form is submitted.

```
<input name="radiobutton" type="radio" value="radiobutton">
```

The default radio button name ⎯ **The default checked value**

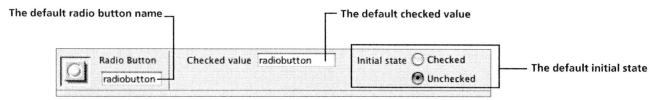

The default initial state

All radio buttons in a group must share the same name and have unique checked values.

!TIP! *Radio buttons are named after mid-century automobile radios. To change the station, you had to press a radio button.*

Hands-On 12.6 Insert Radio Buttons

In this exercise, you will insert and set the properties for two radio buttons.

1. Position the insertion point to the left of the text 6PM.

2. Press the Radio 🔘 button in the Forms category of the Insert bar or choose Insert→Form→Radio Button from the menu bar.

3. In the Radio Button name field on the Properties panel, type **seating**.

4. In the Checked Value field, type **6PM**.

5. On the Properties panel, choose the Checked radio button next to Initial State.

6. Insert another Radio Button to the left of the text 8PM.

7. Type **seating** for the Radio Button name, and then type **8PM** for the Checked Value. *Your form should now resemble the following partial illustration:*

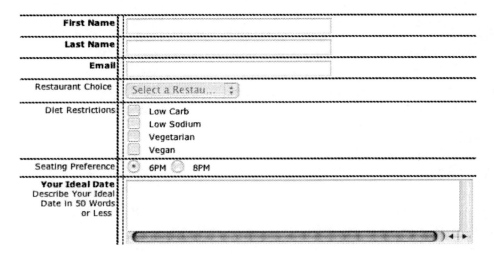

8. Save the file but keep it open.

SETTING RADIO BUTTON PROPERTIES

Property	Description
Radio Button	Type a unique name for the radio button. Each radio button in the same group shares the same name.
Checked Value	Enter the value you want sent to the form processing script when a user selects the radio button.
Initial State	Click Checked if you want an option to appear selected when the form first loads in the browser.

Adding a Submit and a Reset Button

Our form design is almost complete, but it's missing the component that makes the form do something. We need to add a button the user can click to submit the form data. Dreamweaver provides a pre-designed Submit button, which sends the form data to the server, and a Reset button the user can press to clear the form.

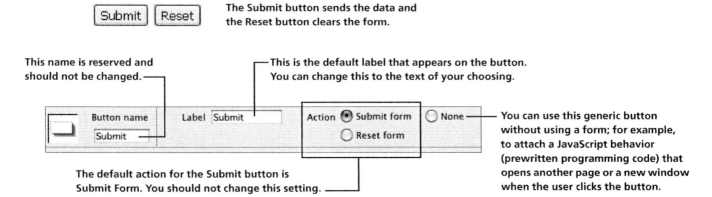

The Submit button sends the data and the Reset button clears the form.

This name is reserved and should not be changed.

This is the default label that appears on the button. You can change this to the text of your choosing.

Button name
Submit

Label Submit

Action ● Submit form ○ Reset form ○ None

You can use this generic button without using a form; for example, to attach a JavaScript behavior (prewritten programming code) that opens another page or a new window when the user clicks the button.

The default action for the Submit button is Submit Form. You should not change this setting.

 Hands-On 12.7 Add a Submit and Reset Button

In this exercise, you will add a Submit button that enables the form data to be processed, and a Reset button to clear the form. You will also set the properties for each button.

1. Position the insertion point below the text Send Your Answers.

2. Press the button ⬚ in the Forms category of the Insert bar or choose Insert→Form→Button from the menu bar.
   Do NOT change the button name.

3. Type **Reserve a Table** to replace the text in the Label field.

4. Click to the right of the Submit button, and then use the technique outlined in step 2 to insert another button.

5. Choose the Reset Form radio button next to Action.
   This switches the button from a Submit button to a Reset button.

6. Type **Clear the Form** to replace the text in the Label field.
Your form should now resemble the following partial illustration:

7. Save the file, and then preview it in your browser.

8. Press the Submit (Reserve a Table) button before filling out the form.
Observe that the form data is processed even though the form fields are blank. This is not a good thing.

9. Partially fill out the form, and then press the Reset (Clear the Form) button.
This resets the form.

10. Leave your browser open and return to the Dreamweaver Document window.

SETTING BUTTON PROPERTIES

Property	Description
Button Name	If you are designing a form, do not change the name Submit. Note that there are two reserved names: Submit sends the form data for processing and Reset clears the form fields or use the default label.
Label	Enter the text you want to appear on the button in the Properties panel's Label field, or use the default label.
Action	Select an action from the Action section. The available actions are: ■ Submit the form for processing when the button is clicked. ■ Reset the form when the button is clicked. ■ Specify an action to be performed when the button is clicked (the None option).

Validating Forms

Imagine how annoying it would be if a customer ordered one of your products but didn't include their shipping address or a new subscriber to your online newsletter didn't include their email address. In situations where it's critical that certain information in the form be included, you might want to consider making some form fields mandatory. If a user submits a form with a blank mandatory field, a message will be displayed that alerts them to fill out the required fields. This form checking procedure is called form validation.

Fortunately, Dreamweaver provides a prewritten JavaScript script (called a behavior) that assists you in the validation process for text fields. You cannot validate menus, radio buttons, or checkboxes. You will learn more about behaviors in Lesson 13, Working with Behaviors.

To open the Behaviors panel, choose Window→Behaviors from the menu bar or press [Shift]+[F4]. To add form validation, you must select the text field you want to validate. The following illustration displays a list of behaviors.

When a form text field is selected, this menu shows a list of behaviors.

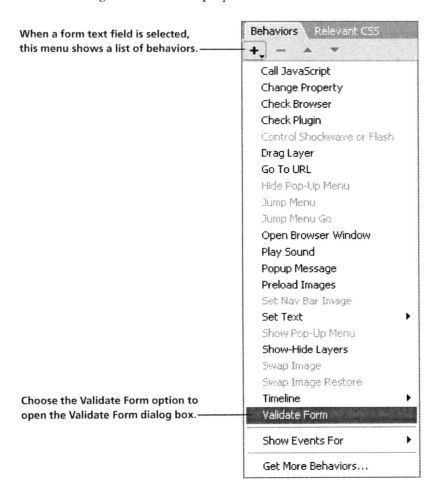

Choose the Validate Form option to open the Validate Form dialog box.

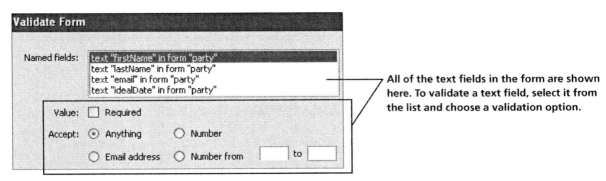

All of the text fields in the form are shown here. To validate a text field, select it from the list and choose a validation option.

Task	Procedure
Validate a form	■ Insert a form that includes at least one text field and one Submit button.
	■ Make sure every text field you want to validate has a unique name.
	■ Select the Submit button.
	■ In the Behaviors panel (Window→Behaviors), click the plus button and select the Validate Form behavior from the list.
	■ Set the validation rules for each text field and click OK.

 Hands-On 12.8 Add Form Validation

In this exercise, you will add form validation to the four text fields.

Before you begin: The party_form.htm file should be open from the last exercise.

1. Click in the form, and then select the <form#party> tag on the Tag Selector.

2. Choose Window→Behaviors from the menu bar.

3. Click the ⊞ button, and then choose Validate Form from the Behaviors list.
   This opens the Validate Form dialog box. The four text fields appear in order in the Named Fields section.

4. In the Named Fields section, ensure that the first line is selected.

5. Place a checkmark next to Value: Required.
   Do NOT close the dialog box until all four fields are validated.

6. Select the second line and place a checkmark next to Value: Required.

7. Select the third line and place a checkmark next to Value: Required. In the Accept section, choose the Email Address radio button.

8. Select the fourth line and place a checkmark next to Value: Required.

9. Press OK.

10. Save the file, and then preview it in your browser.

11. Click the Submit button without filling out the form.
    An alert box should appear that lists the required text fields.

12. Fill out the form and click the Submit button again.
    The form processing script returns the values you entered in the form.

13. Leave your browser open and return to the Dreamweaver Document window.

14. Close the file.

Modifying Form Behaviors

If you need to modify or remove a form behavior, select the <form> tag on the Tag Selector and follow the steps shown in the following illustration:

Use the minus (–) button to remove a behavior.

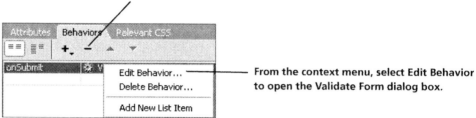

From the context menu, select Edit Behavior to open the Validate Form dialog box.

QUICK REFERENCE: MODIFYING FORM BEHAVIORS

Task	Procedure
Remove a behavior	■ Select the Submit button.
	■ In the Behaviors panel (Window→Behaviors), click the minus button.
Edit a behavior	■ Select the Submit button.
	■ In the Behaviors panel (Window→Behaviors), right-click on Validate Form, and then choose Edit Behavior from the context menu.

Concepts Review

True/False Questions

1. It is not a good idea to change the Submit button's text label.   TRUE   FALSE

2. The Action property specifies the URL of your form processing script.   TRUE   FALSE

3. Server-side scripts allow two-way communication to your server. You must have permission to use them.   TRUE   FALSE

4. Form objects can be rigged to work outside the <form> tag.   TRUE   FALSE

5. The name/value pair is the name of the form object and the value entered.   TRUE   FALSE

6. In a group of radio buttons, a visitor can make multiple choices.   TRUE   FALSE

7. Multi-line text fields are ideal for capturing email addresses.   TRUE   FALSE

8. Every form object should be assigned a unique name.   TRUE   FALSE

9. A form menu presents users with multiple items and only one item can be selected.   TRUE   FALSE

10. You cannot use behaviors to validate any form object other than a text field.   TRUE   FALSE

Multiple Choice Questions

1. Which of the following form properties are mandatory?
   a. Method
   b. Name
   c. Action
   d. All of the above

2. Which of the following statements best describes the method property?
   a. The method used to insert a form object
   b. The method used to process information submitted in a form
   c. The method used to identify the URL of the form processing script
   d. None of the above

3. Which of the following scripts is most widely used to process forms?
   a. Behavior
   b. Java
   c. CGI
   d. Perl

4. Which of the following form objects is the ideal choice for capturing multiple choices?
   a. Scrolling Lists
   b. Radio buttons
   c. Checkboxes
   d. Both a and c

Skill Builders

Skill Builder 12.1   Insert a Form and Set Form Properties

In this exercise, you will insert a form. Then you paste a table that contains form labels into the form.

1. Open questionnaire.htm from the review_12 folder.

2. Place the insertion point at the top of the page, and then press the Form ⬚ button on the Forms category of the Insert bar.

Set Form Properties

3. In the Properties panel, type **inquiry** in the Form Name field.

4. In the Action field, type your email address preceded by mailto: For example, type mailto:bill@labpub.com (use your email address).
   If you have an email account set up on your computer, the email application will open when you submit the form; however, the form data goes nowhere. You must have a form mail processing script in order to actually process the data.

5. Ensure that POST is selected in the Method menu. Leave all other fields blank.

6. Scroll down the page and select the table that contains the form labels.

7. Cut the table to the Clipboard, and then paste it into the form.
   The page should resemble the following illustration:

> # Questionnaire
>
> Thank you for your inquiry about our services. Please fill out the form below and a representative will contact you within the next business day.
>
> | Name * | Tell us about your company. |
> | Company * | |
> | Phone * | |
> | Email * | |

8. Save the file but keep it open.

Skill Builder 12.2   Add a Pop-Up Menu

In this exercise, you will add a pop-up menu to your form.

1. Insert a List/Menu 🖼 in the blank row below the heading text Questionnaire.

2. In the Properties panel, type **request** in the List/Menu Name field.

3. Click the [List Values...] button, and then use the following illustration to populate the menu:

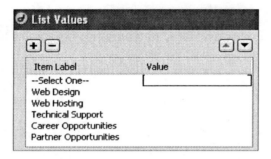

4. Press OK.

5. On the Properties panel, select --Select One-- from the Initially Selected menu.

6. Save the file, and then preview it in your browser.

7. Make selections from the menu to make sure it works properly.

8. Leave your browser open and return to the Document window.

Skill Builder 12.3   Add Four Text Fields

In this exercise, you will add four text fields to your form.

1. Insert a Text Field 🖼 below the label text Name *.

2. In the Properties panel, type **name** in the TextField field, and then type **25** in the Char Width field.

3. Use the technique described in step 1 to add three more text fields below the labels Company *, Phone *, and Email *.

4. Use the technique outlined in step 2 to name each text field and set the Char Width property to 25. Use the names of the labels for the TextField Name field. *Your form should now resemble the following illustration:*

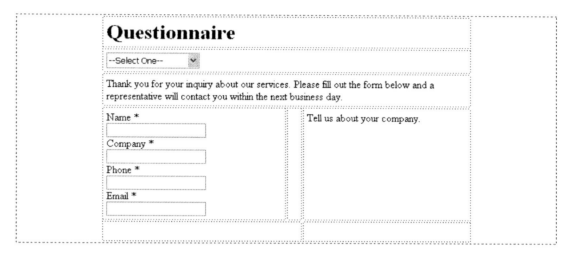

5. Save the file but keep it open.

Skill Builder 12.4 Add a Multi-Line Text Field and a Submit Button

In this exercise, you will add a multi-line text field and a submit button to your form.

1. Place the insertion point below the text Tell Us About Your Company.

2. Press the Textarea ⊞ button in the Forms category of the Insert bar.

3. In the Properties panel, type **comments** in the TextField Name field.

4. Type **25** in the Char Width field.

5. Type **4** in the Num Lines field.

6. From the Wrap menu in the Properties panel, choose Virtual.

7. Place the insertion point in the empty cell below the multi-line text field.

8. Press the Button  button in the Forms category of the Insert bar.

9. In the Properties panel, change the button's label to **Send Your Inquiry**.
   Your form should now resemble the following illustration:

10. Save the file, and then preview it in your browser.

11. Leave your browser open and return to the Document window.

12. Leave the file open.

Skill Builder 12.5   Add Form Validation

In this exercise, you will add form validation to ensure that the required fields aren't blank when your form is submitted.

1. Click in the form and select the <form#inquiry> tag on the Tag Selector.

2. Choose Window→Behaviors from the menu bar.

3. Click the Add Behavior **+** button, and then choose Validate Form from the Behaviors list.
   This opens the Validate Form dialog box.

4. In the Named Fields section, select the first line.

5. Place a checkmark next to Value: Required. Do NOT close the dialog box until all text fields are validated.

6. Use the technique outlined in step 5 to validate the company, phone, and comments text fields.

7. Select the email text field and place a checkmark next to Value: Required. In the Accept section, choose the Email Address radio button.

8. Press OK.

9. Save the file, and then preview it in your browser.

10. Do not fill out the form. Click the Submit button.
    You should see an alert box stating that the required fields cannot be empty.

11. Fill out the form with the information of your choosing and click Submit.
    If you have email set up on your computer, the application should open with an email automatically addressed to you. If you don't have email on your computer, you are likely to get an error message when you submit the form.

12. Leave your browser open and return to the Dreamweaver Document window.

13. Close the file.

 **Assessments**

Assessment 12.1   Create an Order Menu

In this exercise, you will create a new HTML document, insert a table, and insert a form into a table cell. Then you will insert another table inside the form and populate the table with text labels and form objects. You will also validate form text fields.

1. Create a new HTML document named **order_up.htm** in your review_12 folder.

2. Insert a 1 × 1, 600-pixel wide table.

3. Click in the empty table cell and choose Insert→Form→Form from the menu bar.

4. On the Properties panel, click in the Action field and type **mailto:** followed by your email address. (Remember, no space is allowed between mailto: and your email address.)

5. Position the insertion point in the form and insert an 8 × 3, 100% wide table.

6. Add the text and form objects in the illustration (merge the table cells as necessary to accommodate the text):

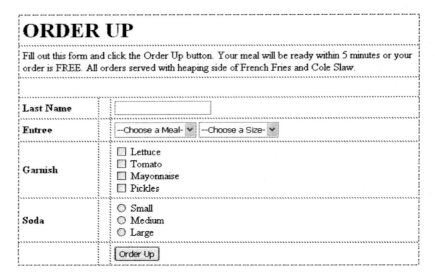

7. Set the properties for each form object.

8. Populate the two pop-up menus as shown in the following illustrations or use the text of your choosing:

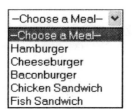 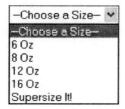

9. Validate the text field object.

10. Save the file, and then preview it in your browser.

11. Fill out the form and submit your order. If you have email set up on your computer, it should open to an automatically addressed email to you.

Assessment 12.2 Apply Styles to Form

In this exercise, you will format the Order Up form you created in the previous exercise.

1. Use the CSS Styles panel to attach the external style sheet order_up.css to order_up.htm. The style sheet is located in the review_12 folder.

2. Follow these steps to apply class styles:

Ⓐ Apply the border style to the outermost table.

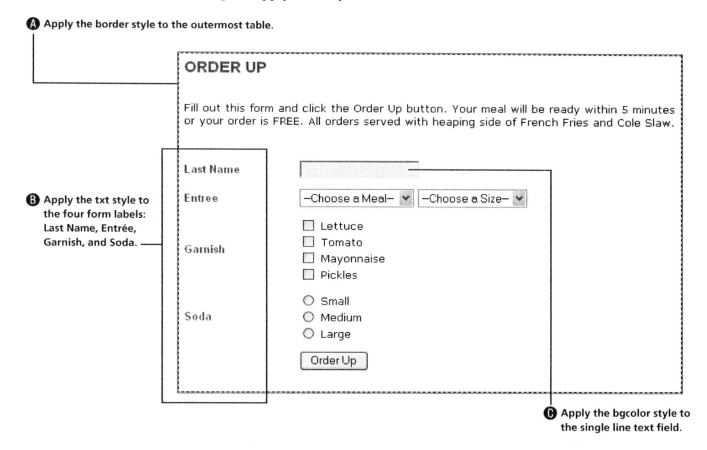

Ⓑ Apply the txt style to the four form labels: Last Name, Entrée, Garnish, and Soda.

Ⓒ Apply the bgcolor style to the single line text field.

3. Feel free to edit the external style sheet to change the page background color, font type, and font size. Make any edits to the three class styles or add additional class styles.

4. Save and close the file.

Critical Thinking

Critical Thinking 12.1   On Your Own

Maria Mendez is a freelance graphic designer and Web site developer. She specializes in helping small businesses and non-profit organizations obtain an Internet presence. Maria asks you to design a form to capture critical client data instead of having to get all the information over the phone. Some potential form fields include the following:

- First Name, Last Name, Email Address

- Pre-existing Site URL or Domain Name

- Approximate number of pages required—Provide a menu of choices

- Have you prepared the site content?—Yes or No

- Please thoroughly describe the type of site you need and its purpose.

- Please describe your target audience.

- Provide options and have the potential client check all that apply; for example: shopping cart, feedback forms, Flash, guest register, chat rooms, message board, database, site search, secure certificate for processing credit cards, other.

- What is the approximate budget allotted for your site development?—Provide a list or menu of choices.

Validate the form fields as necessary to capture critical contact information. Use CSS to format the page. Save the file as **survey.htm** and store it in the review_12 folder.

Critical Thinking 12.2   On Your Own

The form shown in the following illustration represents one of many that should not be unleashed on the public. About the only thing the form has in its favor is the absence of a black background and red text. This is a real form captured from the Web and only the site identity and any proprietary information is missing. The purpose of the form is not quite clear. You will use your critical thinking skills to improve this form.

Name [   ]

Address [   ]

City [   ] State [   ] Zip Code [   ]

Phone [   ] Email [   ]

Did you attend last year? [Click Here ▼]

What is your current status?

☐ Retired ☐ High school ☐ High school graduate ☐ College ☐ Graduate

School and/or organization you are representing: [   ]

Any specific dietary needs? [   ]

If you require lodging please list individuals with whom you would like to room:

[   ]

Do you require parking? [Click Here ▼]   Do you require lodging? [Click Here ▼]

Members in your travel group: [   ]

[Submit]

Open bad_bad_form.htm from the review_12 folder. Determine what's wrong with the form and decide what you can do to make the form useful. Redesign the form and save it in the review_12 folder. Use your creative skills to develop a heading and a statement that will entice users to fill out the form. If time permits, use CSS to format the page and the form.

Critical Thinking 12.3   On the Web

There are many free form processing scripts available on the Web. Some are easier to set up and use than others. Fire up your favorite browser and search engine and type in this string of keywords: **free form processing scripts formmail**. You will find more scripts than you can possibly ever use. All of them will require some tweaking to get them to work with your form. Be sure to contact your Web hosting service to see if they support the technology that your script requires.

LESSON 13

Working with Behaviors

In this lesson, you will learn how to make your Web pages more interactive. Interactive Web pages enhance the user experience by allowing your site visitors to do more than just click links or browse page contents. Interaction is a two-way communication process made possible with Dreamweaver behaviors. A behavior is a combination of an event and an action triggered by the event. One of the most popular events is onMouseover, which occurs when a site visitor rolls his mouse over an image. The action triggered by the event is that the original image is replaced by another image. When the visitor rolls his mouse pointer off the image, the onMouseOut event occurs and the original image is restored or permanently swapped based on the action specified when you created or modified the behavior. This lesson teaches you how to use the Behaviors panel to add actions and events, create rollover images, swap two images with one event, use pop-up messages, open new windows, and attach a behavior to a hotspot on an image map.

Additional learning resources are available at labpub.com/learn/dw04/

Case Study

James Offord is owner of St. James, a popular Palm Springs restaurant that caters to customers seeking a magical dining experience in an exotic setting. James' site is constantly evolving as he provides interactivity to engage site visitors. He uses Dreamweaver behaviors to insert a series of rollover images in the banner navigation bar.

When the mouse rolls over an image...

...the image is swapped with another image.

When the mouse pointer rolls off the image, the original image is restored.

On the Banquet page, James uses the Open Browser Window behavior and the onClick event to open a new window when a visitor clicks a link in an image map.

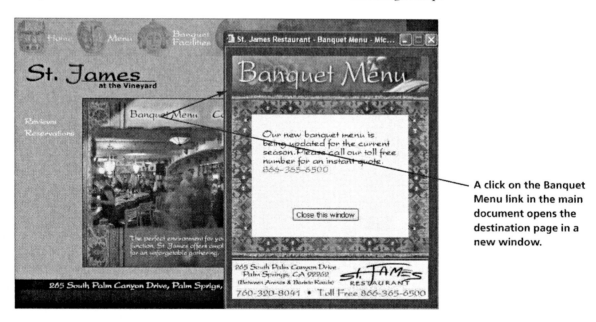

A click on the Banquet Menu link in the main document opens the destination page in a new window.

Understanding Behaviors

Dreamweaver simplifies the process of using JavaScript (see note) functions by providing behaviors, which are prewritten JavaScript code you can incorporate into your Web site to add interactivity.

A behavior is an event with an action triggered by the event. A Web browser sits quietly in the background and waits for an event, such as the page fully loading (onLoad event) or the user clicking on a link (onClick event). When an event occurs, the browser looks to see what action should be taken, as defined by the behavior.

Different events are defined for different page elements; for example, in most browsers onMouseOver and OnClick are events associated with links, whereas onLoad is an event associated with images and the body section of a document.

 NOTE! *JavaScript is a client-side scripting language. This means that the scripts are included on the Web pages and processed by the Web browser. Other scripts, such as the one you used to process form data in the last lesson, are server-side scripts. They are processed by the server and delivered to the user. Dreamweaver behaviors only use client-side scripts.*

Unfortunately, JavaScript works differently in different browsers and in different versions of browsers. Dreamweaver's default setting for browser events is browser versions 4.0 and later, which cover the majority of Web surfers today. If you plan to use interactive elements on your Web site, you should test each behavior in as many browsers as possible. All the behavior examples in this book are based on compatibility with version 4.0 or later of all of the following browsers:

■ Internet Explorer

■ Netscape Navigator

■ Opera

■ Safari

■ Mozilla

Touring the Behaviors Panel

FROM THE KEYBOARD

To open the Behaviors panel:

WIN AND MAC

[Shift]+[F4]

In the Behaviors panel, you add a behavior to a page by specifying an action and the event that triggers the action. Behaviors rely on HTML tags and almost any tag can respond to a user event. To get started with the Behaviors panel, you must select an HTML element and choose a target browser. (You only have to choose a target browser the first time you add a behavior to a page element.) To open the Behaviors panel, choose Window→Behaviors.

In the following illustration, the <body> tag is chosen and the Behaviors panel displays all of the actions that work in version 4.0 or later browsers.

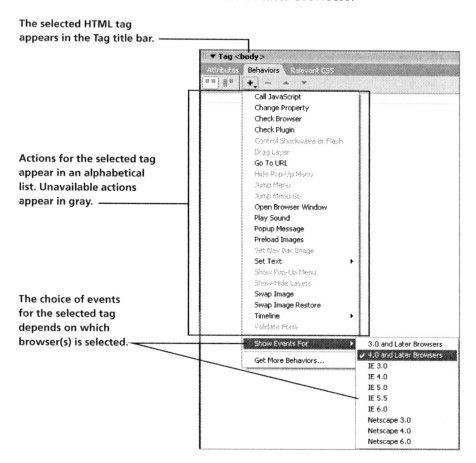

The selected HTML tag appears in the Tag title bar.

Actions for the selected tag appear in an alphabetical list. Unavailable actions appear in gray.

The choice of events for the selected tag depends on which browser(s) is selected.

 NOTE! *If you are designing a site for a company that uses IE 6.0, then that's the obvious setting you should choose. However, in spite of all the events that are available in IE 6.0, many of them don't work in any other browser. If you are designing for the Web, your safest choice is 4.0 and Later Browsers.*

 TIP! *When choosing a browser, use the "set it and forget it" rule. Changing your mind in midstream may make it difficult to edit actions you've already applied using events that no longer apply to the new setting.*

Once you have chosen a target browser, use the Behaviors panel to determine the events available for the selected HTML element. The Behaviors panel toolbar displays two buttons that you can use to work with events: the Show Set Events button and the Show All Events button.

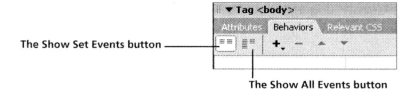

The Show Set Events button

The Show All Events button

The Show Set Events button and the Show All Events button markings are slightly different on the Mac and Win versions of Dreamweaver though they function in the same way. The preceding illustration shows the buttons as they appear in the Win version. The following illustration shows the buttons as they appear on a Mac.

The Show All Events button displays a list of events you can use for the currently selected HTML tag.

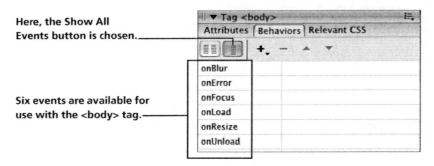

Here, the Show All Events button is chosen.

Six events are available for use with the <body> tag.

The next step is to choose an action to apply to the selected HTML element. For our example, we use the Popup Message action.

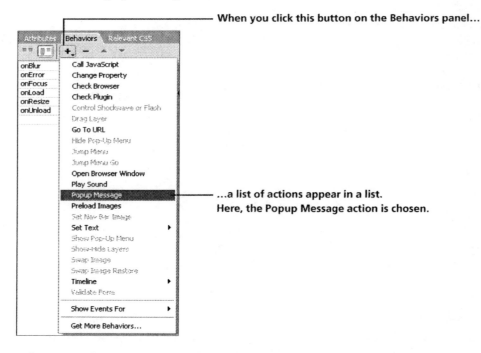

When you click this button on the Behaviors panel...

...a list of actions appear in a list. Here, the Popup Message action is chosen.

When you choose an action from the list of behaviors, Dreamweaver applies the action to the default event, which in our example is onLoad. If this is not the event you want to occur, you can easily choose any of the other events available for the <body> tag.

When an event is set, the Show Set Events button shows the event and the action for the selected HTML element. A translation of this behavior for a browser reads, "When the page fully loads, open a popup message."

The Show Set Events button is selected.

The Events list shows all the events for the selected HTML element.

The Actions list shows the behavior.

As you'll see in the following exercise, it's quite easy to put behaviors to work right away.

Hands-On 13.1   Tour the Behaviors Panel

In this exercise, you will create a new HTML document and observe the events available to the <body> tag.

1. Choose Window→Behaviors to open the Behaviors panel.

2. Create a new HTML document.

3. Save the file as **actions_events.htm** in the lesson_13 folder.

4. Observe the Tag Selector.
   Only the <body> tag is shown because no HTML elements have been added to the page.

5. Click the <body> tag on the Tag Selector.
   This ensures that the correct tag is chosen, just in case you've accidentally added a paragraph break.

6. Click the Add Behavior ⊞ button on the Behaviors panel.

7. From the list of actions, choose Show Events For. Ensure that a checkmark appears next to the option 4.0 and Later Browsers.
   We use this default setting for all behaviors in this book.

8. Click the Show All Events ▦ (Win) or ▦ (Mac) button.
   The six events available to the <body> tag appear in a list.

9. Keep the file open for the next exercise. ∎

Applying Behaviors to an Entire Document

In the previous exercise, you saw the six events available to the <body> tag. Setting an event for the <body> tag affects the entire document. The two most commonly used events for the <body> tag are onLoad and onUnload. The onLoad event is typically used to display a pop-up message, preload a series of images, or set the text of the status bar. The onUnload event is unfortunately used too often by unscrupulous spammers to open an unsolicited new window when you use your browser to try to go someplace else, or to close the browser window.

 Hands-On 13.2   Apply a Behavior to the Entire Document

In this exercise, you will use the onLoad event to display a pop-up message.

Before you begin: the actions_events.htm file should be open.

1. Click the Add Behavior ⊞ button on the Behaviors panel.

2. From the list of actions, choose Popup Message.
   This opens the Popup Message dialog box.

3. Type **SALE! 50% SAVINGS - TODAY ONLY** and press OK.
   The event is shown in the Events list and the action is shown in the Actions list.

onLoad	🔅 Popup Message

4. Save the file, and then preview it in your browser.
When the page loads, the onLoad event occurs and a pop-up message opens in the browser window.

5. Read the message, and then click OK.

6. Leave your browser open, and return to the Dreamweaver Document window.

Editing Actions and Events

After attaching a behavior, you can change the event that triggers the action, add or remove actions, or even attach several actions to a single event. In the following illustration, we've added two more behavior examples that apply to the same event: Call JavaScript and Open Browser Window. When one event triggers several behaviors, you can change the order in which they occur.

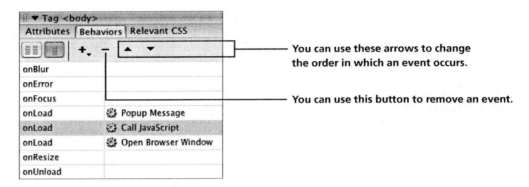

You can use these arrows to change the order in which an event occurs.

You can use this button to remove an event.

The default event to trigger the action appears in the Events column. If this is not the event you want, you can select another event from the Events menu. For example, say you'd like to switch the Open Browser Window from an onLoad event to an onUnload event.

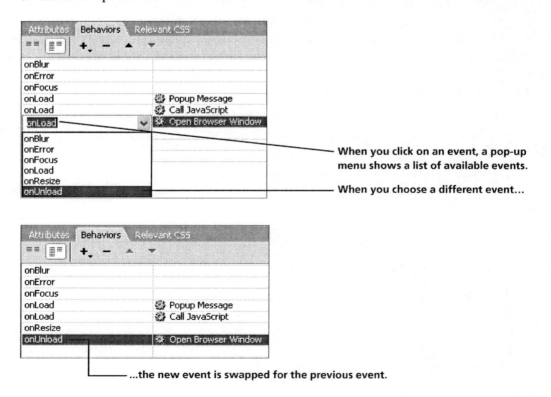

When you click on an event, a pop-up menu shows a list of available events.

When you choose a different event...

...the new event is swapped for the previous event.

A list of all set events appears when you click the Show Set Events button.

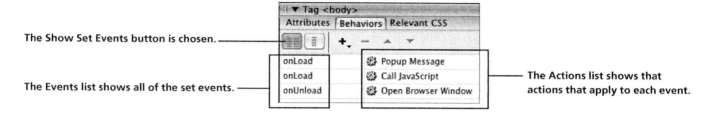

The Show Set Events button is chosen.

The Events list shows all of the set events.

The Actions list shows that actions that apply to each event.

 TIP! *When you need to modify a behavior, double-click the action you want to modify.*

 QR

QUICK REFERENCE: ADDING BEHAVIORS

Task	Procedure
Add a behavior	■ Select an element on the page, such as an image or a link.
	■ Click the Add Behavior ⊞ button on the Behaviors panel.
	■ Choose an action.
	■ Choose an event.

 ## Hands-On 13.3   Add an Event

In this exercise, you will edit one action and add another event to load a new page in the browser when you exit the current window. Then you will remove one of the events.

Before you begin: The actions_events.htm file should be open from the last exercise.

1. Choose Window→Behaviors to open the Behaviors panel.

2. Double-click on Popup Message.
   This opens the Popup Message dialog box.

3. Type **75%** to replace 50%, and then click OK. (Feel free to add additional text of your choosing.)

4. Click the Add Behavior button on the Behaviors panel.

5. From the list of actions, choose Open Browser Window.
   This opens the Open Browser Window dialog box.

6. Click the Browse button and locate and select open_win.htm from the lesson_13 folder, and then click OK (Win) or Choose (Mac).

7. Do not change the default settings in the Open Browser Window dialog box. Click OK.
   The Open Browser Window action is added next to the onLoad event. We want the event to occur with onUnload.

8. Click on onLoad.
   This displays a pop-up menu.

9. From the list of events, choose onUnload.
The new event appears in the Show All Events list.

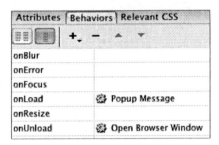

10. Click the Show Set Events button.
The two events appear in the Show Set Events list.

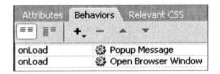

11. Save the file, and then preview it in your browser.

12. Read the revised text in the pop-up message and click OK.

13. Close your browser.
When you close your browser window, the onUnload event occurs and another browser window opens.

14. Close your browser, and then return to the Dreamweaver Document window.

15. Select the Open Browser Window event, and then press the Remove Event button.
This removes the event.

16. Save and close the file.

TIP! *When you're designing pages for your site, hopefully you would never subject unsuspecting visitors to such annoying popup messages and unsolicited new browser windows.*

Applying Behaviors to Text

To apply a behavior to text, you must make the text a link. If you don't want the text to point to a URL, simply create a null link. A null link is one that doesn't actually jump someplace when it's clicked. For the past several lessons, you've been using link placeholders (technically called null links) by typing a number (#) sign in the Link field on the Properties panel to test link states without actually including a URL. This approach is fine for testing link states while you're still developing your Web pages, but to create a null link for a finished page, you should type `javascript:;` (the link must be typed exactly as shown) in the Link field of the Properties panel. This also creates a null link that tells the browser that the link will be handled by the JavaScript of the attached behavior. If you do not have a behavior attached to the link, you can still use the link as a null link to test link states.

Hands-On 13.4   Apply a Behavior to Text

In this exercise, you will create a null text link and use it to swap an image.

1. Open text_link.htm from the lesson_13 folder.

2. Type **Swap Image** at the top of the page.
   To attach a behavior to the text, you must make the text a null link.

3. Select the text, type **javascript:;** in the Link field on the Properties panel, and then press Enter or Return.
   The text doesn't point to a file but it's now armed to receive a behavior.

4. Position the insertion point below the text, and then insert skater_off.gif from the images folder.
   Your page should resemble the following illustration:

5. Select the image and type **skater** in the Name field on the Properties panel.
   The name enables a behavior to uniquely identify the object. If you don't supply a name, Dreamweaver adds the generic name Image1. This naming process is identical to the process you used to name form objects in the last lesson.

   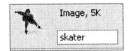

6. While the image is still selected, observe the image tag on the Tag Selector.
   The image tag now reads <img#skater>. The # sign uniquely identifies the image so the script can perform its action on the correct object.

7. Select the text.

8. Click the Show All Events button on the Behaviors panel.
   Observe the events to which the null text link can respond. One of the events is onMouseOver.

9. Click the Add Behavior ⊞ button and, from the list of Actions, choose Swap Image.
   This opens the Swap Image dialog box. In the Images window, notice that the skater image is highlighted.

10. Click the Browse button and select skater_over.gif from the images folder.
This is the image that will replace the skater_off.gif when the page loads in the browser and you roll the mouse pointer over the null text link.

11. Click OK or Choose.
This sets the rollover image source.

12. Ensure that a checkmark appears next to Preload Images and Restore Images onMouseOut, and then click OK.

13. Click the Show Set Events button on the Behaviors panel.
The onMouseOver event swaps the image when the mouse pointer moves over the original image; the onMouseOut event restores the original image when the mouse pointer moves off the secondary image.

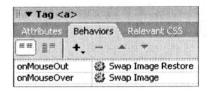

14. Save the file, and then preview it in your browser.

15. Roll the mouse over the text.
The original image is replaced by the rollover image.

16. Roll the mouse off the text.
The original image is restored to its previous state.

17. Leave your browser open and return to the Dreamweaver Document window.

18. Close the file.

Inserting a Rollover Image

In the last exercise, you used a null text link to swap an image with another image using the onMouseOver event. Now that you have "gotten your feet wet" we can explore more advanced behaviors. One of the most common forms of user interaction on a Web page is a rollover image. A rollover image is an image that, when viewed in a browser, changes when the mouse pointer moves over it.

Rollover images require two images: the original (primary) image and the rollover (secondary) image. Both images in a rollover should be the same size; otherwise, Dreamweaver resizes the rollover image to match the proportions of the original image and distortion occurs because the rollover image must share the same space as the original image.

 TIP! *Behaviors are bells and whistles that can add sophistication or "pop" to your site. Overuse can result in drowning out the message you intend to convey.*

You can use either of two methods to insert a rollover image. The method you choose depends on whether the original image is already on the page. If it is, you can use the Common category of the Insert bar or choose Insert→Image Object→Rollover Image from the menu bar. When you use this method, Dreamweaver opens the Rollover Image dialog box that walks you through the entire process of creating a rollover image.

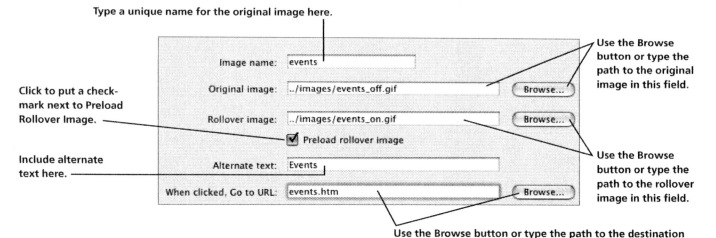

Type a unique name for the original image here.

Use the Browse button or type the path to the original image in this field.

Click to put a check-mark next to Preload Rollover Image.

Use the Browse button or type the path to the rollover image in this field.

Include alternate text here.

Use the Browse button or type the path to the destination file here. If the rollover image is for visual effect only, you can type javascript:; to create a null link.

Preloading Rollover Images

When you check the Preload Rollover Image box, Dreamweaver adds JavaScript to your code that enables a browser to preload the rollover image when the page first loads. This ensures that the rollover effect will occur without hesitation because the rollover image is already stored in the browser's memory. Not choosing this option, depending on the size of the rollover image, can result in a delayed response because the browser has to download the rollover image from the server. If you have many rollover images on the same page, the initial page may take longer to download but it's better to have the wait early to avoid any hesitation when the mouse pointer moves over a rollover image.

NOTE! *When working with rollover images, remember that you are at the very least doubling the number of images. For example, in the following exercise we have a total of 16 rollover images. Double that number and you have 32 images.*

 TIP! *To quickly identify rollover images, you might consider keeping them in a separate folder.*

Hands-On 13.5 Insert a Rollover Image

In this exercise, you will preview a partially completed page of rollover images. Then you will insert two rollover images to complete the side navigation bar.

1. Open st_james.htm from the lesson_13/st_james folder.
   The page contains a small sidebar table of partially completed rollover images. The large gray box is an embedded Flash animation that plays automatically when the page loads in the browser.

2. Preview the file in your browser.

3. Roll the mouse pointer over Reviews and Reservations.
   Each image is replaced by a rollover image. When you roll off each image, the original image is restored. These two links are null links.

4. Roll the mouse pointer over Home in the banner navigation bar.
   This is an example of swapping two images with a single event. You'll see how this is accomplished in the next exercise.

5. Click the Home link.
   This is the homepage. The page reloads and the Flash animation plays again.

6. Leave your browser open and return to the Dreamweaver Document window.

7. Position the insertion point in the first blank table cell (two rows above Reviews).
   This is where you will insert the first rollover image.

8. Choose Insert→Image Objects→Rollover Image.
   This opens the Insert Rollover Image dialog box.

9. In the Image Name text field, select the default generic name and type **events**.
   All rollover images must have a unique name. Use short, descriptive names that can be easily identified. Don't use spaces or special characters and do not begin the name with a number.

10. Click the Browse button next to the Original Image text field and select events_off.gif in the rollover_sj folder. This folder is located in the same location as the images folder and the lesson_13 folder.
    This is the primary image.

11. Click the Browse button next to the Rollover Image text field and select events_on.gif in the rollover_sj folder.
    This image will replace the primary image.

12. Ensure that a checkmark appears next to Preload Rollover image.
    This eliminates any lag that might otherwise occur when the mouse pointer is rolled over the secondary image.

13. Type **Events** in the Alternate text field.

14. Click the Browse button next to the text field When Clicked, Go to URL. Select events.htm from the lesson_13/st_james/ folder.

15. Press OK.

16. Place the insertion point in the empty row below Events.

17. Choose Insert→Image Objects→Rollover Image.

18. Use the following illustration to complete the Insert Rollover Image dialog box:

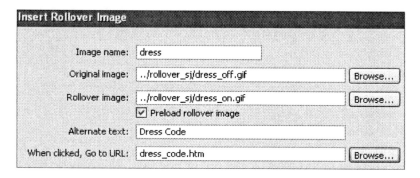

19. Save the file, and then test the rollover images in your browser.

20. Leave your browser open and return to the Dreamweaver Document window. Keep the file open.

Swapping Two Images with One Event

You can create more complex rollovers by swapping two images with a single mouse rollover event. In the following illustration on the left, there are two images. When the mouse pointer is rolled over the Gallery image, both images are replaced with the rollover images shown in the illustration on the right.

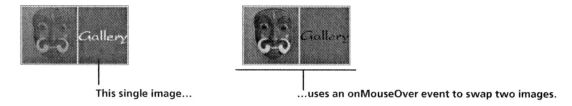

This single image...   ...uses an onMouseOver event to swap two images.

!TIP! *If you make a mistake swapping two images with one event, it's easier to remove the event and start over than trying to troubleshoot the behavior.*

Hands-On 13.6   Swap Two Images with One Event

In this exercise, you will swap two images with one event.

Before you begin: The st_james.htm file should be open.

1. In the banner navigation bar at the top of the page, randomly click on any of the twelve images and view the name that appears in the Properties panel.
   Each image name has been created for you to save time. Remember, these are NOT image filenames; they are unique identifiers the behaviors need to work with the images.

2. Select the Menu text image named menu_off.
   You will use this image to create two rollover images: the menu text image and the menu mask image.

3. Click the Add Behavior button on the Behaviors panel. Then, from the Action list, choose Swap Image.
   This opens the Swap Image dialog box. The selected image is highlighted in the Images window of the dialog box.

4. Click the Browse button and select menu_on.gif from the rollover_sj folder.
   It's a good idea to preview the image.

5. Click OK or Choose. Do NOT close the Swap Image dialog box.
   This attaches the swap image behavior to the selected image and the image name now has an asterisk (*) next to it.

6. From the list of images, select the menu_mask_off.gif image.
   This is the pale mask image located to the left of the text menu image in the banner navigation bar.

7. Click the Browse button, select menu_mask_on.gif from the rollover_sj folder, and then press OK or Choose.
   This attaches the swap image behavior to the selected image and the image name now also has an asterisk (*) next to it.

8. Ensure that a checkmark appears next to Preload Images and Restore Images on onMouseOut and press OK.

9. Save the file, and then test the rollover image in your browser.

10. Leave your browser open and return to the Dreamweaver Document window.

11. If time permits, swap the remaining eight images to complete the top navigation bar.
    The replaced images are easily identifiable in the rollover_sj folder.

12. Close the file.

Opening a New Window

In the beginning of this lesson, you used an onUnload event to open a new window when the current window was closed. Here we explore the proper use of opening a new window. The action to open a new window can be triggered by a variety of events. We'll use an onClick event to open a new window from a clickable area of one large image shown in the following illustration.

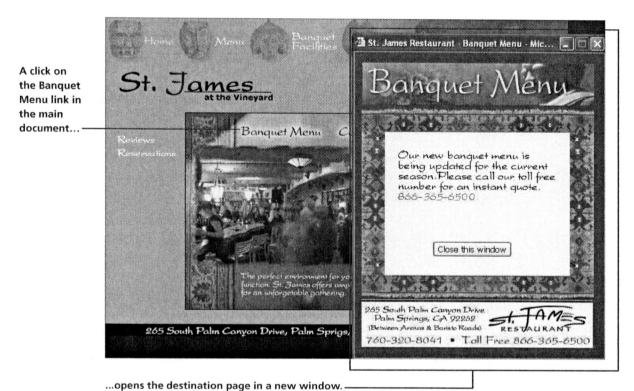

A click on the Banquet Menu link in the main document...

...opens the destination page in a new window.

When you attach the Open Browser Window behavior to an HTML element, Dreamweaver opens the Open Browser Window dialog box. The only required setting is the URL to Display. However, there are a variety of other settings you can use, such as the width and height of the new window and attributes that make the window look like a browser window (the Location toolbar, scrollbars, and a Menu bar).

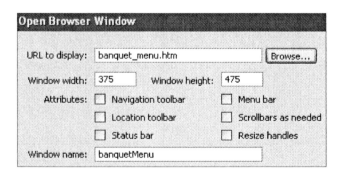

OPEN BROWSER WINDOW DIALOG BOX SETTINGS

Setting	Description
Window Width	Specifies the width of the window in pixels
Window Height	Specifies the height of the window in pixels
Navigation Toolbar	Displays the row of browser buttons (Back, Forward, Home, and Reload)
Location Toolbar	Displays the row of browser options (including the Location text box)
Status Bar	Displays the area at the bottom of the browser window in which messages (such as the load time remaining and the URLs associated with links) appear
Menu Bar	Displays the menu that shows File, Edit, View, History, Help, etc.
Scrollbars as Needed	Specifies that scroll bars should appear if the content extends beyond the visible area
Resize Handles	Specifies that the user should be able to resize the window
Window Name	The name of the new window (name the new window if you want to target it with links or control it with JavaScript)

Adding a Behavior to an Image Map

An image map is a single image that contains one or more clickable areas called hotspots. Image maps have been around since the early days of the Web and the original ones required quite a bit of programming and other wizardry to make them work. Dreamweaver provides all the tools you need to create an image map. Within seconds, you can draw hotspots using the drawing tools on the Properties panel.

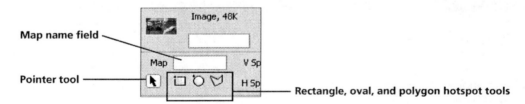

Map name field

Pointer tool

Rectangle, oval, and polygon hotspot tools

When you use a hotspot tool to draw an area on the image, Dreamweaver adds the <map> </map> tags in Code view and assigns the default name Map. Nested inside the <map> tag is the <area> tag that contains three attributes a browser needs to identify the shape, coordinates, and hypertext reference. By default, the hypertext reference is a null link.

```
<map name="Map">
  <area shape="rect" coords="78,15,214,42" href="#">
</map>
```

When you use Behaviors with an image map, the behavior is attached to the <area> tag.

The <map> tag and the <img> tag are tied by the usemap attribute that appears in the <img> tag. The value of the usemap attribute is equal to the name of the image map. A Web browser uses this unique name to find the image map on the page.

```
<img src="../../images/banquet.jpg" width="550" height="305" border="0" alt=""
usemap="#Map">
```

The following illustration shows the image you'll use to create an image map and attach a Behavior to a link that opens the page in a new browser window. Banquet Menu is the portion of the image you'll use to define a hotspot.

Banquet Menu is the area you'll use to draw a rectangular hotspot.

 ## Hands-On 13.7   Add a Behavior to an Image Map

In this exercise, you will create a simple image map and attach a Behavior that opens a page in a new browser window.

1. Open banquet.htm from the lesson_13/st_james folder.

2. Select the large image in the main content area.

3. Click the Rectangle Hotspot Tool ☐ button on the Properties panel.

4. Draw a rectangle around the text Banquet Menu.
   When you release the mouse, the hot spot appears as a translucent blue-green overlay.

5. Observe the <area> tag on the Tag Selector.
   This is the HTML tag that's used to apply the behavior.

6. Click the Add Behavior ➕ button on the Behaviors panel. Then, from the list of actions, choose Open Browser Window.
   This opens the Open Browser Window dialog box.

7. Click the Browse button and select banquet_menu.htm from the lesson_13/st_james folder, and then press OK or Choose.
   This is the page that will open in a new window.

8. Type **375** in the Window Width text field and type **475** in the Window Height text field.
   These dimensions are just a little larger than those required to show the page contents without scrolling in most newer browser windows.

9. Place a checkmark next to Resize Handles.
   This enables site visitors to manually resize the window, if necessary, to view the contents. The Open Browser Window action is added next to the onMouseOver event. We want the event to occur with OnClick.

10. In the Behaviors panel, click on onMouseOver. Then, from the pop-up menu, choose onClick.

11. Save the file, and then open it in your browser.

12. Roll the mouse pointer over the Banquet Menu hot spot.
    Observe the pointing hand symbol that identifies a link.

13. Click the Banquet Menu link.
    This opens the Banquet Menu page in a new window.

14. Close the new window.

15. Leave your browser open and return to the Dreamweaver Document window.

16. Close the file.

Concepts Review

True/False Questions

1. A Behavior is an event with an action triggered by that event.　　　TRUE　　FALSE

2. If you are designing for the Web, your safest choice is to use events for version 4.0 and later browsers.　　　TRUE　　FALSE

3. To set an event for a paragraph, select the <p> tag on the Tag Selector and choose an action from the Behaviors panel.　　　TRUE　　FALSE

4. When an event is set, you use the Show Set Events button to show the event for the selected element.　　　TRUE　　FALSE

5. Setting an event for the <body> tag applies only to the headings on a page.　　　TRUE　　FALSE

6. Client-side scripts must be processed by the Web server, not the Web browser.　　　TRUE　　FALSE

7. Using multiple pop-up messages and opening new windows when a browser is closed is a great way to entertain a site visitor.　　　TRUE　　FALSE

8. To attach a behavior to text, add a null link to the text and attach the behavior to it.　　　TRUE　　FALSE

9. When using rollover images, the replaced image should be slightly larger to make the rollover effect really pop.　　　TRUE　　FALSE

10. Preloading rollover images enables the browser to load all images when the window is first opened so there is no delayed response.　　　TRUE　　FALSE

Multiple Choice Questions

1. Which of the following languages does Dreamweaver use to apply behaviors?
   a. C++
   b. C-
   c. JavaScript
   d. None of the above

2. Which of the following events is used to ensure that an action occurs when the page fully loads?
   a. onFocus
   b. onBlur
   c. onLoad
   d. onGo

3. Which of the following tags is used to apply a behavior to a hotspot in an image map?
   a. <map>
   b. <shape>
   c. <href>
   d. <area>

4. The Behaviors panel is a member of the _____ panel group.
   a. Assets
   b. Tag
   c. Properties
   d. Code

 **Skill Builders**

Skill Builder 13.1   Insert an Image and Apply a Behavior

In this exercise, you will insert an image and apply the Swap Image behavior.

1. Choose Window→Behaviors, to open the Behaviors panel.

2. Create a new HTML document and save it as **rollovers.htm** in the review_13 folder.

3. Insert sparks_off.gif at the top of the page.
   This is the primary image that will be replaced by a rollover image.

4. Select the image and type **sparks** in the Name box on the Properties panel. (Feel free to use another name if you wish.)

5. Click the Show All Events button on the Behaviors panel.
   The <A> next to each user event indicates that the event names are available only for links. Selecting one of these event names automatically adds a null link to the selected image and attaches the behavior to that link instead of to the element itself.

6. Click the Add Behavior **+** button, and then, from the list of actions, choose Swap Image.
   This opens the Swap Image dialog box.

7. Click the Browse button and select sparks_over.gif from the images folder, and then press OK or Choose.

8. Leave the two checkboxes on the Swap Image dialog box at their default checked settings and click OK. Do NOT deselect the image.

9. Observe the Link field on the Properties panel.
   A null link automatically appears in this field. The behavior is attached to the null link, not to the image.

10. Save the file, and then open it in your browser.

11. Test the rollover effect, and then return to the Dreamweaver Document window. Leave the file open.

Skill Builder 13.2   Insert a Rollover Image

In this exercise, you will insert a rollover image and bypass the Behaviors panel to create a rollover image effect.

1. Position the insertion point below the sparks image.

2. Choose Insert→Image Objects→Rollover Image from the menu bar.
   This opens the Insert Rollover Image dialog box.

3. Type **cello** in the Image Name text field and press [Tab].

4. Click the Original Image Browse button, select cello_off.gif from the images folder, and press [Tab].

5. Click the Rollover Image Browse button and select cello_over.gif from the images folder.

6. Ensure that a checkmark appears next to Preload Rollover Image.

7. Type **Playing the Cello** in the Alternate Text field and press Tab.

8. Type **javascript:;** in the When Clicked, Go to URL text field and click OK.

9. Save the file, and then preview it in your browser.

10. Test the new image rollover.

11. Leave your browser open and return to the Dreamweaver Document window.

12. Close the file.

Skill Builder 13.3   Create an Image Map

In this exercise, you will create an image map and apply a behavior to a hot spot. The behavior will swap a transparent spacer with a colorful food image.

1. Open food.htm from the review_13 folder.
   The page contains four images. The large white box with the thin black border contains a transparent spacer image.

2. Click once inside the white box (table cell) to select the transparent spacer.

3. Observe the Width and Height boxes on the Properties panel.
   The image is set to 403 × 316 pixels. A rollover image the same size will replace the spacer image.

4. Select the image that contains the oval hotspot.

5. Use the Oval Hotspot Tool ⬭ button on the Properties panel to draw an oval around the plate of beets, which is the first plate in the lower-left corner of the image.
   Don't overlap the hotspot with the one above it.

6. Use the Pointer Hotspot Tool ⬚ button, if necessary, to move the oval or delete it and start over.

7. Select the hot spot.

8. Click the Add Behavior ⊞ button on the Behaviors panel, and then the list of actions, choose Swap Image.
   This opens the Swap Image dialog box.

9. In the Images window, select image "spacer".
   This is the image that will be replaced with the rollover image.

10. Click the Browse button and select beets.jpg from the images folder.
    This sets the source of the rollover image.

11. Ensure that the two checkboxes are checked, and then press OK.

12. Use the technique outlined in steps 4–9 and draw another oval around the plate of curry, which is located above the middle hotspot. DO leave the hotspot selected.

13. Repeat steps 8–11 but this time select curry.jpg from the images folder.

14. The page should now resemble the following illustration:

15. Save the file, and then preview it in your browser.

16. Roll your mouse pointer over each of the hotspots on the image map.
The invisible spacer image is replaced by the rollover images. When you roll your mouse pointer off the image, the original spacer image is restored.

17. Return to the Dreamweaver Document window.

18. Leave the file open.

Skill Builder 13.4   Use an onClick Event to Swap an Image

In this exercise, you will add an onClick event to swap the invisible spacer image with another image that shows the price of the Mahi entrée, which is the middle hotspot.

1. Select the middle hotspot.
The hotspot already contains an onMouseOver event and a Swap Image action. Now you add another event to switch the invisible spacer when the hotspot is clicked.

2. From the Behaviors panel, choose Swap Image.
This opens the Swap Image dialog box.

3. In the Images window, select the image "spacer".

4. Click the Browse button, select mahi_detail.jpg from the images folder, and then press OK or Choose.

5. Press OK to close the Swap Image dialog box.

6. Observe the events in the Behaviors panel.
   The default event for a Swap Image action is onMouseOver. You need to switch this to an onClick event.

7. Click the Show Set Events button on the Behaviors panel.

8. Select the onMouseOver event you set in this exercise and change it to an onClick event. (It should be the last one in the list.)
   The final events are shown in the following illustration:

9. Save the file and preview it in your browser.
   The rollover images should work as they did previously.

10. Click the middle hotspot.
    The image in the following illustration replaces the spacer image. When you roll the mouse pointer off the image, the original image is restored.

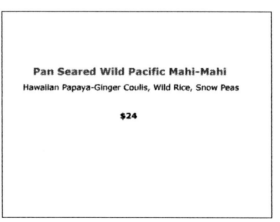

11. Leave your browser open and return to the Dreamweaver Document window.

12. Close the file.

 # Assessments

Assessment 13.1   Insert Behaviors

In this exercise, you will create three rollover effects, add a pop-up message, and open a new window.

1. Open dolphin_news from the review_13 folder.

Swap Three Images

2. Use the Swap Image action and an onMouseOver event to create a rollover effect for each of the images shown in the following illustration. The image names are join, rescue, and donate. The swapped image filenames are join_over.gif, rescue_over.gif, and donate_over.gif. The rollover images are located in the slices folder, which is in the same location as the images folder and the review_13 folder.

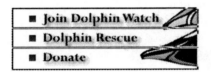

Add a Pop-Up Message

3. Add a Popup Message action and an onClick event to the first image. The popup message should read: **Members receive a 25% discount on all expeditions.**

Open a New Browser Window

4. Add an Open Browser Window action and an onClick event to the second image.

5. Set the new window size to 335 × 340.

6. The file to open in the new window is dolphin_rescue.htm, which is located in the review_13 folder.

7. Save the file but keep it open.

Assessment 13.2 Apply Behaviors to Text

In this exercise, you will apply behaviors to text in the content area of the page.

1. Click in the large table cell shown in the following illustration. Notice that the cell is not empty; it contains an invisible spacer image.

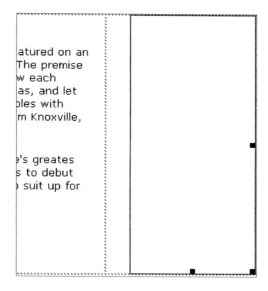

2. Observe the following two illustrations that represent the final version of the exercise.

Ⓐ When the mouse rolls over the Judy Lapinsky link...

Ⓑ ...the spacer image is swapped with the lapinksy.gif image.

A When the mouse rolls over the Dollie Faye Baker link...

News

...tch manager, Judy Lapinsky, is being featured on
... of the new TV hit series Switching Roles. The
... the show is to take two people who do not know
..., and have vastly different careers and phobias,
... switch roles for one week. Judy will switch
... Dollie Faye Baker, a popular country music star
...ville, Tennessee.

...atest fear is singing in public; Dollie Faye's greates
...n water. Stay tuned while Judy prepares to debut
...nd Ole Opry, and Dollie Faye prepares to suit up
...g expedition off the coast of Raratonga.

B ...the spacer image is swapped with the baker.gif image.

3. Select the spacer image and type **spacer** in the Image name box on the Properties panel. (Or, type the name of your choosing.)

4. In the first paragraph, make the text Judy Lapinsky a null link.

5. Add a Swap Image action and an onMouseOver event to the null link.
   The event should swap the spacer image with the lapinsky.gif image.

6. Select the Dollie Faye Baker text and swap the spacer image with the baker.gif image.

7. Save the file.

8. Preview the file in your browser and test the rollover effects.

9. Return to the Dreamweaver Document window and close the file.

Critical Thinking

Critical Thinking 13.1   On Your Own

Frederic Delarue has just released his latest CD, entitled "Dolphins, a Message of Love." Frederic announces the arrival of the new CD by opening a new window, shown in the following illustration, when a visitor opens the Listen to Music page.

The Listen to Music page enables visitors to sample three tracks of the "Dolphins," "Soaring with the Angels," and "Voyage of the Soul" CDs. Frederic needs your help to update the page to make it interactive. The following illustration shows the final version of the page:

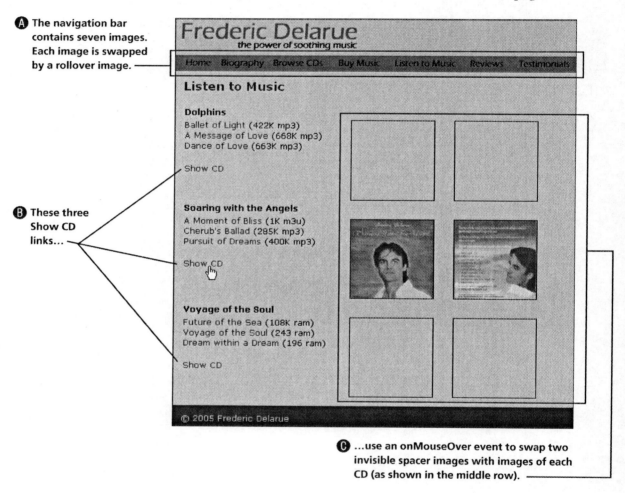

A The navigation bar contains seven images. Each image is swapped by a rollover image.

B These three Show CD links...

C ...use an onMouseOver event to swap two invisible spacer images with images of each CD (as shown in the middle row).

Now you will create the page!

Design the Navigation Bar

Open frederic_music.htm from the review_13 folder. Locate the table row shown in the following illustration. This row will become the navigation bar. Currently, the seven table cells are empty.

The original and rollover image filenames are shown in the following table. The images are located in the rollover_fd folder, which is in the same location as the images folder and the review_13 folder. All of the images should use a null link.

Original Image	Rollover Image
home.gif	home_over.gif
bio.gif	bio_over.gif
browse.gif	browse_over.gif
buy.gif	buy_over.gif
listen.gif	listen_over.gif
reviews.gif	reviews_over.gif
testimonials.gif	testimonials_over.gif

An example of one of the rollover images is shown in the following illustration.

Design the Main Content Area

Insert six spacer images and size them to 124 × 122 pixels. This is the same size of each CD detail image that you'll use to swap the spacer. Be sure to assign each spacer a unique name. For each spacer, use spacer.gif, which is located in the images folder.

The six images are located in the rollover_fd folder and the filenames are shown in the following table.

CD Cover Image	CD Back Image
dolphin_cover.gif	dolphin_back.gif
soaring_cover.gif	soaring_back.gif
voyage_cover.gif	voyage_back.gif

The following illustration shows the rollover images that replace the spacer images in the Soaring with the Angels section of the page.

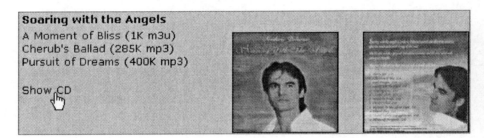

Open a New Window

Your final task is to open a new window when the page first loads in the browser. The filename for the new window is dolphins_window.htm. The file is located in the review_13 folder.

When you finished, save and close the file.

Working with Layers

In this lesson, you will work with layers. Layers are HTML containers that hold text, graphics, tables, forms, media objects, and other layers. Layers are similar to individual table cells but without the table. However, unlike table cells, you can position layers anywhere on the page, stack them on top of each other, show or hide them, and even animate them. Layers are perhaps one of the most popular Dreamweaver features. When combined with CSS, you can create sophisticated page layouts without having to build complex table structures.

This lesson teaches you how to work with layers to create a CSS positioned page layout, apply behaviors to layers, and animate layers with timelines.

Case Study

Byron Whitman designed The Zen Garden to share thought provoking sayings, poems, parables, and stories with friends and fellow students. Byron used layers to precisely position graphic, navigation, and text elements on the page. Each layer is formatted with a series of CSS ID selector styles.

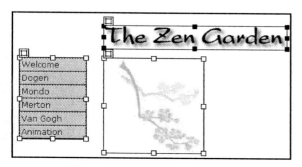

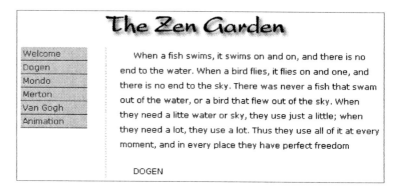

Notice that only three of seven layers appear on the page: the banner graphic, the navigation bar, and the branch graphic. Sitting behind the branch layer are five hidden layers.

The links in the navigation bar named Dogen, Mondo, Merton, and Van Gogh are attached to a Show-Hide behavior. In this illustration, the Dogen link is chosen and the layer named dogen is shown; the other layers are hidden.

To engage site visitors, Byron uses behaviors and a timeline to create interaction and animation. When the page opens, the Buddha image on the right moves slowly behind the text and to the left.

When the Buddha image reaches its destination, a behavior swaps the ghost image with a more colorful version of the same image.

417

Measuring in the Document Window

When you need pixel perfect precision in your page layout, you can add a ruler and a grid to help you size and place layers in the Document window.

Using Rulers

Rulers are especially helpful in resizing and positioning layers. To view rulers, choose View→Rulers→Show. To change the ruler measurements, choose View→Rulers, and then choose Pixels, Inches, or Centimeters.

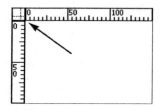

By default, the rulers' zero (or starting) point for measurements starts at the top-left corner.

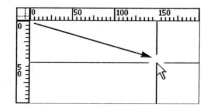

You can change the zero point by clicking and dragging it into the window.

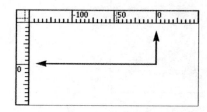

When the zero point is where you want it to be, release the mouse button.

To reset the starting point to the default location, choose View→Rulers→Reset Origin.

Using the Grid

The grid is another handy tool to use when placing layers and other objects by dragging them on the page. To view the grid, choose View→Grid→Show Grid. In the following illustration, a layer is precisely aligned 200 pixels from the left and 50 pixels from the top of the page.

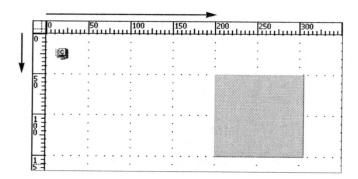

The grid has a "snapping" feature that behaves like a weak magnet. When you use this feature, the border of the layer you're dragging in the Document window snaps to the grid. To turn on snapping, choose View→Grid→Snap to Grid.

To change the default grid setting, choose View→Grid→Grid Settings.

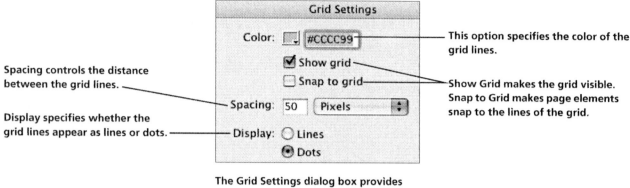

Spacing controls the distance between the grid lines.

Display specifies whether the grid lines appear as lines or dots.

This option specifies the color of the grid lines.

Show Grid makes the grid visible. Snap to Grid makes page elements snap to the lines of the grid.

The Grid Settings dialog box provides options for customizing the grid.

Some people rely heavily on rulers and the grid; others find them distracting. In this lesson we do not require the use of these tools. However, feel free to experiment on your own.

Understanding Layers

The term layer is specific to Dreamweaver. Technically, layers are called CSS positioned elements, but the term layers is a lot more user friendly so that's what we'll call them throughout this lesson. There's really nothing magical about layers; in fact, you can create one with any simple text editor. All you need is a <div> tag and a few CSS positioning properties. Positioning properties are available in the Positioning category of the CSS Style Definition dialog box. These properties determine, for example, the width and height of a layer, its exact location on the page, and how to handle overflow when the layer content is larger than the layer. When you draw or insert a layer, Dreamweaver does all the work for you by placing the CSS positioning properties inside the <div> tag. You'll learn more about the <div> tag and CSS positioning later in this later.

Layers are named as such because they can be positioned in three dimensions. For example, you can set an absolute or relative location for a layer along the pages X and Y axes (left and top). In the following illustration, a layer is positioned exactly 100 pixels from the left and 50 pixels from the top of the page.

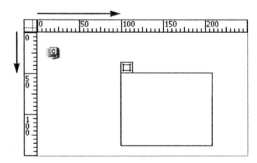

The third dimension, the Z index (stacking order), allows layers to overlap one another. The layer with the highest Z index number gets top billing; the layer with the lowest number is on the bottom. You can change the Z-Index number and move a layer to any position you choose. In the following illustration, the goblins layer has the highest Z-Index number.

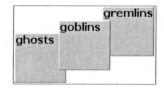

⚠️ **WARNING!** *Like most advanced Web design tools, layers do not work in browsers prior to version 4.0.*

Using the Layers Panel

FROM THE KEYBOARD

To open the Layers panel:

WIN AND MAC

F2

The Layers panel is the control center for managing layers. You use the Layers panel to prevent or enable layer overlaps, change the visibility of layers, nest or stack layers, modify the Z-Index number, and select one or more layers. To open the Layers panel, choose Window→Layers from the menu bar.

The Layers panel is part of the Design panel group. Its neighbor to the left is the CSS Styles panel. The Layers panel is divided into three columns: Visibility, Name, and Z (index).

The Visibility column shows or hides a layer. An open eye indicates a visible layer while a closed eye indicates a hidden layer.

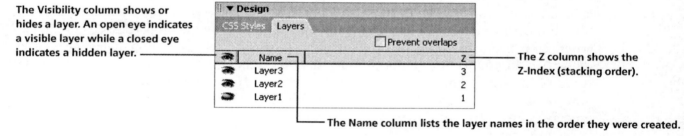

The Z column shows the Z-Index (stacking order).

The Name column lists the layer names in the order they were created.

The Layers panel controls layer visibility, name, and stacking order.

Creating Layers

You can either draw or insert a layer. There is another approach to creating layers but we'll save that for later in this lesson. Layers come in two flavors: inline layers and fully qualified CSS layers.

Inline Layers

An inline layer is one that contains the CSS positioning properties within the <div> tag. This is the type of layer you create automatically when you insert or draw a layer. For example, if you draw a 50 × 50 pixel layer 100 pixels from the top and 100 pixels from the left of the page, Dreamweaver writes the following code:

```
<div id="Layer1" style="position:absolute; left:100; top:100; width:50px; height:50px;
z-index:1">Page content goes here.</div>
```

If you are a hand coder, you can type CSS inside the <div> tag. In the following example, we've added CSS background color and font properties.

```
<div id="Layer1" style="position:absolute; left:100; top:100; width:50px; height:50px;
z-index:1; background-color:#CCCCCC; font-family:Arial, Helvetica, sans-serif;
font-size:12pt">Page content goes here.</div>
```

While this approach is acceptable in some situations, it should not be used to lay out multiple pages in your site because it defeats the goal of separating HTML structure from CSS formatting. Also, if you have inline layers scattered throughout multiple pages in your site and you need to modify them, you'd do well to call on Indiana Jones and his raiders to help you dig through the buried code.

TIP! *Use inline layers for timeline animations or any purpose other than CSS page layout.*

Fully Qualified CSS Layers

A fully qualified CSS layer is a technical term for a layer that does not contain the CSS positioning properties inside the <div> tag. That information is stored in an embedded or linked style sheet.

Using the same previous layer example, let's look at a fully qualified CSS layer:

```
<div id="Layer1">Page content goes here.</div>
```

In the associated style sheet, you will see this:

```
#Layer1 { position:absolute; left:100px; top:100px; width:50px; height:50px; z-index: 1; }
```

If you have multiple pages in your site that use the #Layer1 style (in reality you'd name the layer something more descriptive) and the style resides in an external style sheet, you can modify all of the pages at once by modifying the style's properties in one location.

TIP! *Fully qualified CSS layers are the perfect choice for a CSS page layout.*

For the remainder of this lesson, we will refer to inline and fully qualified layers. It is important to distinguish between the two.

Drawing a Layer

To draw a layer, ensure that you are in Standard mode and use the Draw Layer button on the Layout category of the Insert bar. (You can also draw layers in Expanded Tables mode.)

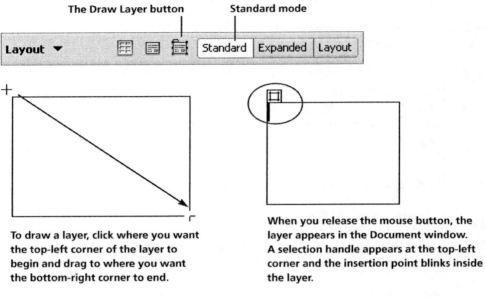

To draw a layer, click where you want the top-left corner of the layer to begin and drag to where you want the bottom-right corner to end.

When you release the mouse button, the layer appears in the Document window. A selection handle appears at the top-left corner and the insertion point blinks inside the layer.

 TIP! *To draw multiple layers, hold down the* Control *key (Win) or* Command *key (Mac).*

FROM THE KEYBOARD

To toggle the display of visual elements:

WIN ONLY
Ctrl + Shift + I

MAC ONLY
⌘ + Shift + I

Along with the layer, a layer marker will appear. It is an invisible element that shows where the layer code appears within the page code. You can move the marker to another location (not recommended), but it doesn't affect the position of the layer; it repositions the layer code in the HTML of the page.

Hands-On 14.1   Draw a Layer

In this exercise, you will make sure that Anchor Points for Layers is chosen in Preferences. Then you will use the Draw Layer button on the Layout category of the Insert Bar to draw a layer.

1. Choose Edit→Preferences (Win) or Dreamweaver→Preferences (Mac).

2. In the Invisible Elements category, ensure that a checkmark appears next to Anchor Points for Layers.

3. Choose Window→Layers from the menu bar.

4. Create a new HTML document and save it as **layer_basics.htm** in the lesson_14 folder.

5. Use the Draw Layer 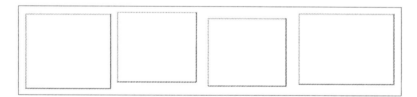 button on the Layout category of the Insert bar to draw a layer approximately one inch square. Do NOT deselect the layer.
If you do not see the layer, choose View→Visual Aids and ensure there is a checkmark next to Layer Borders.

6. Observe the layer marker in the upper-left corner of the page.
This is an invisible element that anchors the layer onto the page and identifies the location of the HTML code for the layer.

7. Observe the Layers panel.
The default layer name is Layer1, and the Z-Index number is 1.

8. Observe the Tag Selector.
<div#Layer1> The layer is identified as #Layer1.

9. Click <div#Layer1> on the Tag Selector.

10. Choose View→Code.
Analyze the CSS properties inside the <div> tag. This is an inline layer.

11. Choose View→Design.

12. Observe the layer properties on the Properties panel.
You can modify all of the CSS positioning properties in the Properties panel.

13. Use the technique outlined in step 5 to draw three more layers. Do NOT overlap the layers.
Your page should now resemble the following illustration:

14. Observe the Layers panel.
The layer names appear in the order they were created. The last layer created has the highest Z-Index number.

15. Save the file but keep it open.

Modifying Layer Properties

When you draw or insert a layer, Dreamweaver uses the default property settings, which in most cases need to be modified. Here we explore how to select, resize, move, delete, rename, align, and set background color and to change the stacking order of layers.

Selecting Layers

As you know, to modify anything on a Web page you must first select it. The same rule applies to layers. Not surprisingly, there are a number of ways to select a layer. The following Quick Reference details the most commonly used methods.

QUICK REFERENCE: SELECTING LAYERS

Task	Procedure
Select layers	■ Click the layer's selection handle, or ■ Click the layer's name in the Layers panel, or ■ Click the layer marker, or ■ Click the layer's border.
Select multiple layers	■ Hold down the [Shift] key while selecting layers in the Document window, or ■ Hold down the [Shift] key while selecting layer names in the Layers panel.

Hands-On 14.2   Select Layers

In this exercise, you will practice selecting layers.

Before you begin: The layer_basics.htm file should be open.

1. Click anywhere in the first layer, and then click the layer's selection handle.
   This selects the layer, and eight sizing handles surround the layer. The layer name appears highlighted in the Layers panel.

2. In the Layers panel, click Layer2.
   This selects the layer in the Document window.

3. Click the third layer marker [⬛].
   This selects the layer in the Document window and highlights the layer name in the Layers panel.

4. Click any layer border.
   This is a shortcut for selecting a layer.

5. While holding down the [Shift] key, click anywhere on each of the four layers.
   Pay close attention to the last layer you clicked. It's the one with the solid black sizing handles. You'll find this feature useful for aligning and resizing multiple layers.

6. Click anywhere off the layers to deselect them.

7. Keep the file open for the next exercise.

Moving Layers

There are a variety of techniques you can use to move a layer. Here, we explore a few of our favorites.

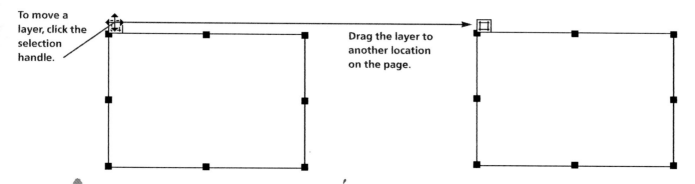

To move a layer, click the selection handle.

Drag the layer to another location on the page.

TIP! *You can also move a layer by clicking anywhere on its border and dragging it (avoid dragging the sizing handles) to another location on the page.*

For less speed, but greater precision, you can move a layer using the keyboard. First select the layer, and then do one of the following:

■ To move a layer one pixel at a time, press the corresponding keyboard arrow key.

■ Press ⌈Shift⌋ while using an arrow key to move a layer 10 pixels at a time.

You can also control the placement of a layer using the Properties panel. Dreamweaver measures a layer's position relative to the left and top edges of the page. The L (Left) box specifies the distance from the left edge of the page to the left edge of the selected layer; T (Top) specifies the distance from the top edge of the page to the top left edge of the selected layer.

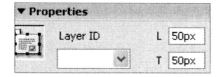

TIP! *You cannot drag a layer completely off the page; however, you can type a negative number in the Properties panel, or use the keyboard to nudge the layer off the page.*

Resizing Layers

You can change the width and height of a layer before or after you add content to the layer. While a layer is selected, drag one of the eight sizing handles that surround the layer to increase or decrease the layer size.

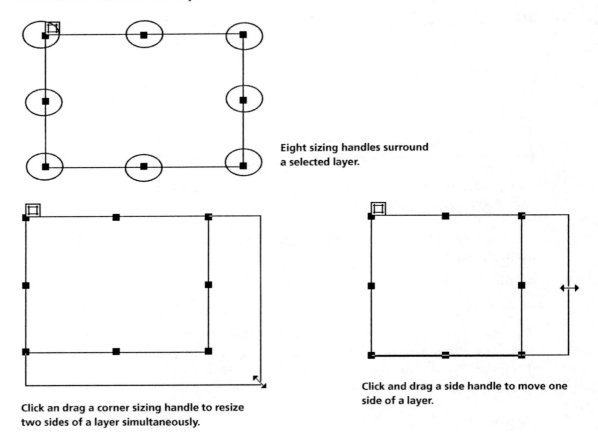

Eight sizing handles surround a selected layer.

Click an drag a corner sizing handle to resize two sides of a layer simultaneously.

Click and drag a side handle to move one side of a layer.

You can also use the keyboard to resize a layer. First, select the layer, and then do one of the following:

- Press the [Control] (Win) or [Command] (Mac) key and press the arrow keys to change the layer's size by one pixel. The up and down arrow keys adjust the layer's height; the left and right arrows affect its width.

- To change the size 10 pixels at a time, press [Shift]+[Control] (Win) or [Shift]+[Command] (Mac) and press the arrow keys.

You can also type the width of the layer in the W (width) text box and the height of the layer in the H (height) text box on the Properties panel.

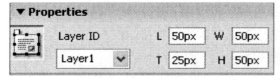

 TIP! *To resize multiple layers at once,* [Shift]+*click two or more layers to select them, and then type a new width and height in the Properties panel.*

Hands-On 14.3   Resize and Move Layers

In this exercise, you will practice resizing and moving layers.

Before you begin: The layer_basics.htm file should be open.

1. Select the fourth layer. Keep the fourth layer selected for the entire exercise.

2. Drag a corner sizing handle until the layer is approximately 50% larger.

3. While holding down the [Control] key (Win) or [Command] key (Mac), press the left arrow key three times.
   This reduces the width of the fourth layer by three pixels.

4. While holding down the [Shift]+[Control] (Win) or [Shift]+[Command] (Mac), press the down arrow key two times.
   This increases the height of the fourth layer by 20 pixels.

5. In the Properties panel, type **100px** in the W box and type **100px** in the H box.
   This shortcut sets the fourth layer to 100 pixels wide and 100 pixels high.

6. Select the fourth layer, and then press [Delete] or [Backspace].
   This deletes the fourth layer, leaving you with three layers.

7. Resize the remaining layers and move them around to form a pattern similar to the following illustration:

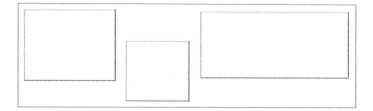

8. Save the file but keep it open.

Aligning Layers

The Align layer commands provide options to align one or more layers with a border of the last layer selected. The Align options are Left, Right, Top, and Bottom.

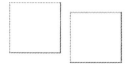

Say you want to align the top of the layers shown here to the top of the first layer.

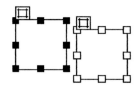

Select the first layer last. The last selected layer is identified by solid black sizing handles.

Choose Modify→Align→Top to align the second layer to the top of the first layer.

The Align layer commands also provide options to resize multiple layers simultaneously. For example, select two or more layers and choose Modify→Align→Make Same Width or Make Same Height. The first selected layers change to the width or height of the last selected layer.

 ## Hands-On 14.4   Align Layers

In this exercise, you will practice aligning multiple layers.

Before you begin: The layer_basics.htm file should be open.

1. While holding down the ⟨Shift⟩ key, select Layer1, Layer2, and Layer3 in the Layers panel.
   Observe Layer3, which is the last layer you selected.

2. Choose Modify→Align→Top.
   Layer1 and Layer2 snap into the same top alignment position as Layer3.

3. Choose Modify→Align→Make Same Height.
   The three layers are now the same height.

4. Choose Modify→Align→Make Same Width.
   The three layers are now the same width.

5. Save the file but keep it open.

Renaming Layers

By default, Dreamweaver names each successive layer Layer1, Layer2, Layer3, etc. It's a good idea to provide unique descriptive names for your layers so you can easily identify them when working in the Layers panel and when defining CSS styles for layers.

 Layer names must start with a letter and can only contain letters and numbers. Do not use spaces or punctuation. No two elements on a Web page should have the same name.

To rename a layer, double-click the layer name in the Layers panel and type the new name. Or, type a new name in the Layer ID box on the Properties panel.

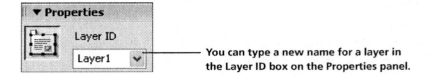

You can type a new name for a layer in the Layer ID box on the Properties panel.

Setting Background Image and Color

You can set a layer's background properties the same way you set table or table cell background properties: select the layer and use the Bg Color box on the Properties panel. To add a background image to the layer, click the Browse for file icon next to the Bg Image field and select an image from your site's image folder.

You can use Browse for File to locate an image in your site's image folder.

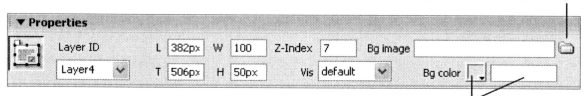

Use the Bg Color box to pick a color or type a color hex code in the hex code color field.

Changing the Stacking Order

When layers overlap, you can swap the stacking order by adjusting the Z-Index of each layer. The Z-Index determines the order in which layers are drawn in a browser. The layer with the highest Z-Index number appears atop layers with lower Z-Index numbers. It is possible for two layers to have the same Z-Index number. When this occurs, the layer that appears in the code first appears on top.

The Z-Index number of Layer2 is higher than Layer1 so Layer1 is behind Layer2.

Layer2 is the image of the prospective groom.

The Z-Index number of Layer1 is now higher than Layer2.

Layer1 now sits on top of Layer2.

To change a layer's stacking order, click once on the Z-Index number in the Layers panel or select the layer and type a new number in the Z-Index field on the Properties panel.

You can use the Properties panel to change the Z-Index number.

Hands-On 14.5   Rename Layers and Change Stacking Order

In this exercise, you will rename layers, set background color, and change the stacking order.

Before you begin: The layer_basics.htm file should be open.

1. Select Layer1.

2. Use the Bg Color box on the Properties panel to color the layer red.

3. Now color Layer2 blue and color Layer3 green.

4. In the Layers panel, double-click on Layer1.

5. Type **red** for the new layer name and press [Enter] or [Return].

6. Now name Layer2 **blue** and name Layer3 **green**.
   The layer names should now match the following illustration:

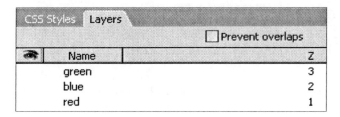

7. Rearrange the layers so they are stacked in the order shown in the following illustration.
   Layer red is on the bottom, blue is in the middle, and green is on top.

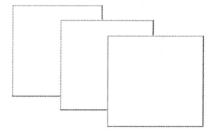

8. In the Layers panel, reverse the Z-Index numbers of the three layers.
   The red layer should now be on top.

9. Save the file but keep it open.

Changing Layer Visibility

Now you see them, now you don't. Changing the visibility of layers can be useful when you're working with page layouts using layers and CSS positioning, or when you're using layers with behaviors or timelines.

The eye icon at the top of the column controls the visibility of all layers.

You can control individual layer visibility by clicking an eye icon next to the layer name. A closed eye icon indicates a hidden layer.

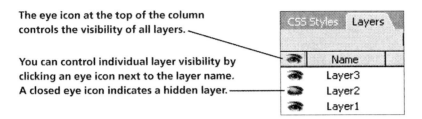

 Hands-On 14.6   Change Layer Visibility

In this exercise, you will show and hide layers.

Before you begin: The layer_basics.htm file should be open.

1. Click the eye icon at the top of the Visibility column in the Layers panel.
   This places an open eye icon to the left of each layer name.

2. Repeat step 1.
   The eye icons next to each layer name are now closed, and all layers are hidden.

3. Click the closed eye icon next to blue.
   The closed eye icon is now an open eye icon and the layer is visible.

4. Repeat step 3 to show each layer.

5. Save and close the file.

Controlling Overflow

When you insert content into a layer, the layer expands to accommodate the content. This default expansion behavior can ruin a carefully crafted CSS page layout design unless you understand how to control the content overflow. You control the overflow by setting one of four properties in the Overflow menu on the Properties panel.

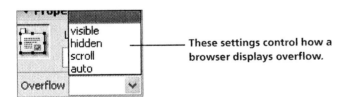

These settings control how a browser displays overflow.

SETTING OVERFLOW PROPERTIES

Property	Definition
Visible	This default setting increases the layer's size so all content is visible. The layer expands down and to the right.
Hidden	This setting maintains the layer's size and clips any content that doesn't fit. No scroll bars are provided.
Scroll	This setting adds scroll bars to the layer regardless of whether the contents exceed the layer's size. This option is not displayed in the Document window; you must preview the file in your browser. This feature works in IE or Netscape 6 or higher.
Auto	Makes scroll bars appear only when the layer's contents exceed its boundaries. You must preview the file in your browser to see this effect.

 Hands-On 14.7   Control Content Overflow

In this exercise, you will use the Overflow menu on the Properties panel to control content overflow. You will also explore a basic CSS page layout and observe an inline layer and a fully qualified layer.

1. Open overflow.htm from the lesson_14 folder.
   The page contains two empty layers, an image, and a text block.

2. Open the Layers panel. Select the banner layer.

3. In the Properties panel, observe the width and height of the layer.
   The layer is 275 × 35 pixels, which is the size of the banner graphic.

4. Drag and drop the banner graphic, The Zen Garden, in the banner layer.

5. In the Layers panel, select the koan layer.

6. In the Properties pane, observe the width and height of the layer.
   The layer is 275 × 100 pixels.

7. Click the CSS Styles tab, which is located to the left of the Layers tab on the Design panel group.

8. Notice the embedded style named #koan.
   This is an advanced ID selector style used to control the positioning and formatting of the koan layer and its contents.

9. Select all of the text on the page and drag and drop it into the empty layer.
   The layer expands to accommodate the content, and the text in the layer is formatted with the #koan style.

10. Select the koan layer.

11. In the Properties panel, choose Auto from the Overflow menu.
    The effects of this setting are not apparent in the Document window. You must open the file in your browser.

12. Save the file, and then preview it in your browser.
    The layer's content exceeds the layer's size, and a vertical scroll bar appears.

13. Leave your browser open and return to the Dreamweaver Document window.

14. Select the koan layer again, and then choose Visible from the Overflow menu.
    This is the default setting.

15. Save the file, and then preview it in your browser.
    The Visible property setting allows the layer to expand to show all of its contents.

16. Leave your browser open and return to the Dreamweaver Document window.

17. Select the banner layer.

18. Switch to Code view.
    Observe that the <div> tag contains CSS positioning properties. This is an inline layer.

19. Look directly above this layer in Code view and locate the koan layer, which is identified by <div id="koan">.
    This is a fully qualified CSS layer. Observe that not formatting properties appear inside the <div> tag.

20. Still in Code view, scroll to the top of the page and locate the #koan style.
    This is an embedded CSS advanced ID selector style that controls the formatting of the layer's contents. Observe that the last property in the style is Overflow, which is the style you applied in step 14.

21. Switch to Design view.

22. Close the file.

Designing a CSS-Positioned Page Layout

As more and more Web browsers support the use of CSS, some designers are abandoning their table-based layout for CSS Page layout. The most important benefit of CSS is that they allow separation of your content from its presentation. Because CSS files are typically stored separate from the Web pages themselves, a consistent look and feel can be applied throughout the site from a common source. For example, changing the color and size of your headers in a single linked CSS file will update the look of all headers throughout the site, instantly and uniformly.

The majority of Web sites still use table-based layouts but this is slowly changing. If you plan to use CSS to design your page layout, test your pages in as many different browsers as possible.

TIP! *Identifying your target audience early on will enable you to make wise design choices.*

To design a CSS page layout, you need to start thinking about dividing your Web page into sections.

Dividing Your Web Page into Sections

The <div></div> tag is a generic tag that has no predefined presentational features. Presentational features are provided by CSS. The tag was introduced in HTML 4.0 as a means to define logical divisions within a Web page. This means that when you use a <div> tag for page layout, you are indicating that the enclosed content is a specific section of the page.

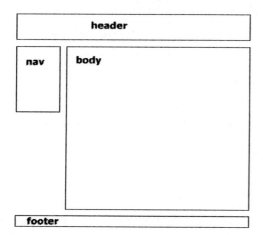

A basic Web page may have these divisions.

```
<div id="header">header</div>
<div id="nav">navigation</div>
<div id="body">body</div>
<div id="footer">footer</div>
```

For the divisions to work with CSS, each division must have a unique ID selector style.

The <div> element, when combined with ID selector styles, allows you to position and format sections of the page. For example, say you want to position the header section 10 pixels from the top and 10 pixels from the left of the page, and you want the header to be 600 × 50 pixels. You would use the New CSS Style dialog box to create an ID selector named #header, and then you would use the Positioning category of the CSS Style Definition dialog box to create the following style:

```
#header { position:absolute; top:10px, left:10px; width:600px; height:50px }
```

To create the layer, select the content for the page header and choose Insert→Layout Objects→Div Tag. Then, from the Insert Div dialog box, choose Header from the ID Menu and Wrap Around Selection from the Insert menu. The result is a fully qualified CSS layer that snaps into the exact position specified by the CSS ID selector style.

Defining CSS Positioning Properties

In Lesson 9, Working with Styles, you learned how to redefine HTML tags, create class selector styles, create contextual selector styles, and anchor pseudo-classes. Here we explore how to create CSS ID selector styles for layers. Since a layer is basically a box, you can use all of the categories in the CSS Style Definition dialog box plus one more that's reserved for layers (Positioning).

Unless you're using a layer for a timeline animation, each layer should have a unique style that defines the positioning and placement of the layer.

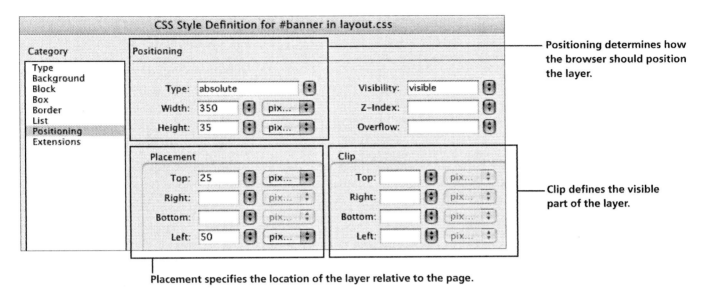

Positioning determines how the browser should position the layer.

Clip defines the visible part of the layer.

Placement specifies the location of the layer relative to the page.

You should leave any fields that are not important to the style empty. As you will see later in this lesson, there are only a few properties you will use time and again, and they're easy to understand.

Planning a CSS Page Layout

The approach we use to plan a CSS positioned page layout is based on the assumption that you're not a professional graphic artist. If you are, please excuse our simplistic approach and know that there are many paths to the mountain top, but once you reach the summit, the view is always the same. (Perhaps I've been hanging out at The Zen Garden too much!)

When you're planning your own CSS page layout, you need a blueprint. The following guidelines are merely suggestions:

1. Assemble images, text, and any other content on the page.

2. Draw and position each layer on the page.

3. Record the position and dimensions of each layer.

4. Record a unique identifier for each layer that represents a section of the page; for example, id="header", id="footer".

5. Delete the layers that represent your page sections.

6. Create ID selector styles for each deleted layer.

7. Select the content for a layer, insert a <div> tag, and wrap the <div> tag around the selection to create a fully qualified CSS layer.

You may be thinking, "Why on earth would I delete the layers after going to all the trouble drawing and positioning them?" That's a logical question and here is the answer: You may recall in the beginning of this lesson, when you insert or draw a layer, Dreamweaver inserts the positioning properties **inside** the <div> tag, which creates an inline layer.

```
<div id="Layer1" style="position:absolute; width:200px; height:115px; z-index:1;
left:100px; top:100px;"></div>
```

You need to keep all formatting properties outside of the <div> tag because when you create styles for the layer content, the inline styles will override internal and external styles. This makes managing multiple pages based on a CSS page layout extremely difficult.

A better approach is to define the styles upfront and apply them to a <div> tag. The result is a fully qualified CSS layer that's very easy to maintain with CSS. This is the approach we use in the following exercises.

 ## Hands-On 14.8   Define ID Selector Styles for Layers

In this exercise, you will create ID selector styles for a banner graphic, a regular graphic, and a text block.

1. Open zen_garden.htm from the lesson_14 folder.
   The page contains a banner graphic, an image of a branch, and a small block of text.

2. Choose Window→CSS Styles, if necessary to open the CSS Styles panel.

3. Click the New CSS Style ⬚ button on the CSS Styles panel.
   This opens the New CSS Style dialog box.

4. Set the options in the New CSS Style dialog box fields according to the following table:

Selector Type	Advanced (IDs, contextual selectors, etc)
Selector	**#banner**
Define In	This Document Only

5. Click OK.
   The CSS Style Definition dialog box opens.

6. Choose the Positioning category and set the following Positioning properties:

Type	Absolute
Width	268 pixels
Height	28 pixels
Z-Index	1
Top	50 pixels
Left	200 pixels

7. Click OK.

8. Observe the #banner style in the CSS Styles panel.

9. Use the technique outlined in steps 3–6 but use **#content** for the style name.

10. Set the following Positioning properties and click OK:

Type	Absolute
Width	390 pixels
Height	200 pixels
Z-Index	2
Top	100 pixels
Left	200 pixels

11. Use the technique outlined in steps 3–6 but use **#pic** for the style name.

12. Set the following Positioning properties and click OK:

Type	Absolute
Width	130 pixels
Height	147 pixels
Z-Index	3
Top	100 pixels
Left	50 pixels

13. Save the file.

How did I know the position and dimensions of each layer? I drew three layers and positioned them where I wanted them. Then, I wrote down the positioning properties, and then deleted each layer.

Applying Layer Styles

Once you've created the ID selector styles, you select the content to appear inside the layer. Then you insert a <div> tag, choose the ID selector name, and wrap the <div> tag around the selection. To insert a <div> tag:

■ Select the content on the page to which you intend to apply the style.

■ Choose Insert→Layout Objects→Div Tag or use the Insert Div Tag ⊞ button in the Layout category of the Insert bar.

When you insert a <div> tag, the Insert Div Tag dialog box opens. From the ID menu, you choose the name of the style; from the Insert menu, you choose Wrap Around Selection.

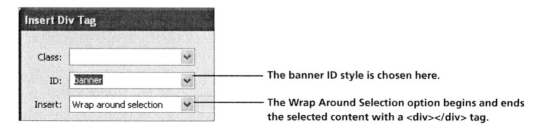

The banner ID style is chosen here.

The Wrap Around Selection option begins and ends the selected content with a <div></div> tag.

When you click OK, the layer appears on the page with the ID style applied to it. This is the code generated as a result of applying the ID style and wrapping the <div> tag around the banner graphic from the previous exercise.

```
<div id="banner"><img src="../images/zen_garden.gif" width="268" height="28"
alt="Zen Garden"></div>
```

This creates a fully qualified CSS layer, which is beautiful because the <div> tag contains HTML content only, not formatting instructions. All of the formatting instructions are embedded in the head of the page.

```
#banner {
position: absolute;
width: 268px;
height: 28px;
Z-Index: 1;
top: 50px;
left: 200px; }
```

Once you've applied an ID style to a layer on the page, the ID name will no longer appear in the ID menu. That's because you can use only one ID selector per page.

 Hands-On 14.9   Apply the ID Selector Styles

In this exercise, you will apply the ID selector styles to create three layers.

Before you begin: The zen_garden.htm file should be open.

1. Select the Zen Garden banner graphic.

2. Use the Insert Div Tag ▦ button on the Layout category of the Insert bar or choose Insert→Layout Objects→Div Tag from the menu bar.
   This opens the Insert Div Tag dialog box.

3. From the ID menu, choose banner and from the Insert menu, choose Wrap Around Selection. Click OK.
   This creates a layer that is precisely positioned on the page. The <div></div> tag is now wrapped around the banner graphic.

4. On the Tag selector, click <div#banner>.

5. Switch to Code view.
   Observe the <div> tag. The only code inside the <div> tag is the ID. This is a fully qualified CSS layer.

6. While in Code view, scroll to the top of the page and locate the internal CSS ID styles you defined in the previous exercise.
   The ID in the <div> tag is the style name. When you modify a style, the contents of the layer update automatically.

7. Switch to Design view.

8. Select all of the text on the page.

9. Repeat step 2.

10. From the ID pop-up menu, choose content and from the Insert menu, choose Wrap Around Selection.
    Observe that the banner style no longer appears in the ID menu. That's because you can only apply an ID selector style once per page.

11. Click OK.

12. Select the remaining graphic.

13. Repeat step 2.

14. From the ID menu, choose pic and from the Insert menu, choose Wrap Around Selection. Click OK.
    This completes the positioning of the three layers. Your page should now resemble the following illustration:

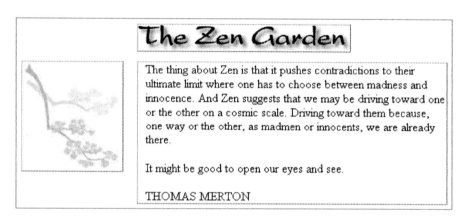

15. Save the file but keep it open.

Modifying ID Selector Styles

The main objective in the last exercise was to create fully qualified CSS layers and position them on the page. It's easier to focus on a few properties at a time rather than defining all of the styles for your layers. We need to dress up the drab content layer by changing the font and font size, adding some padding, and applying a decorative border to the left margin.

 Hands-On 14.10 Modify an ID Selector Style

In this exercise, you will edit the #content style.

Before you begin: The zen_garden.htm file should be open.

1. In the CSS Styles panel, select #content.

2. Click the Edit Style button on the CSS Styles panel.
   This opens the CSS Style Definition dialog box. You might want to move the dialog box away from the content layer so you can see the results of the style each time you click Apply.

3. Choose the Type category, and set the following properties:

Font	Veranda, Arial, Helvetica, Sans-Serif
Size	Small

4. Click Apply. Do NOT close the dialog box.
   This updates the style in the CSS Styles panel. Observe the changes to the content layer formatting in the Document window.

5. Choose the Box category.
   The width and height dimensions are already set. The Width and Height boxes here are the same as the ones you set using the Positioning category.

6. In the Padding column, remove the checkmark next to Same for All.

7. Type **10px** in the Left menu.
   This is a shortcut that enables you to type the unit of measure directly next to the size.

8. Click Apply. Do NOT close the dialog box.
   This adds four pixels of space to the left side of the layer.

9. Choose the Border category.

10. Remove the checkmarks from the Style, Width, and Color columns.

11. From the Style Left menu, choose Dotted.

12. From the Width Left menu, choose Thin.

13. In the Color Left hex color box, type **#FFC4CC** or use the Color box and choose a color.

14. Click Apply, and then click OK.
    You won't see the proper formatting for the layer border until you preview the file in your browser.

15. Save the file, and then preview it in your browser.
    The page should resemble the following illustration:

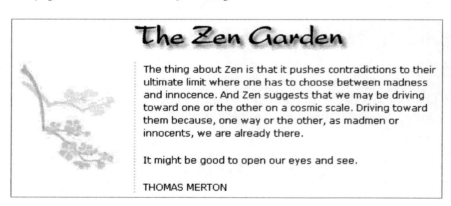

16. Leave your browser open and return to the Dreamweaver Document window.

17. Close the file.

Adding a Show-Hide Layers Behavior

In Lesson 13, Working with Behaviors, you created rollover images and a number of other interactive events using Dreamweaver behaviors. There is also a behavior you can use to show and hide layers. Imagine clicking a link and watching the layer content change without jumping to another page. Now that's saving bandwidth! Let's get this show on the road and see how the behavior works.

 Hands-On 14.11 Tour an Interactive Layers Page

In this exercise, you will open a page that contains a series of links that show and hide a series of layers. The last link doesn't work yet.

1. Open zen_garden_behaviors.htm from the lesson_14 folder.

2. Open the layers panel.

3. Observe the layers in the Layers panel.
   The last four layers are hidden, as indicated by the closed eye ⬤ icon.

4. Click the closed eye ⬤ icon next to dogen.
   The closed eye becomes an open eye, and the layer is now visible even though it's partially hidden by the layer that's stacked on top of it.

5. Click the open eye ⬤ icon next to dogen, and then click the blank space.
   The closed eye icon reappears and the layer is hidden.

Test Drive the Interactive Page

6. Press F12 to preview the file in your primary browser.

7. Click the Dogen link.
   A Behavior hides all of the stacked layers and shows the dogen layer.

8. Click the remaining links.
   The Van Gogh link doesn't do anything. You'll apply a behavior to this link in the next exercise.

9. Click the Welcome link.
   A Behavior hides all of the stacked layers and shows the welcome layer.

10. Leave your browser open and return to the Dreamweaver Document window.

Add a Show-Hide Behavior

11. In the Document window, select the text Van Gogh.

12. Observe the Link field on the Properties panel.
    You may recall that the null link javascript:; is used to apply a behavior to text by making the text a link that doesn't jump anywhere when it's clicked.

13. Choose Window→Behaviors from the menu bar.
    This opens the Behaviors panel.

14. Click the Add Behavior ⊕ button and choose Show-Hide Layers from the list of actions.
This opens the Show-Hide Layers dialog box. Your objective is to hide the welcome, dogen, mondo, and merton layers, and to show the banner, vangogh, and nav layers. You do this by making a selection from the Named Layers list and clicking the Show or Hide button.

15. Click Hide next to all the layers **except** banner, vangogh, and nav.

16. Click OK.
The behavior is applied to the onClick event.

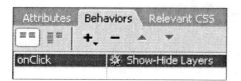

17. Save the file, and then preview it in your browser.

18. Click the Van Gogh link.
A Behavior hides the welcome, dogen, mondo, and merton layers and shows the vangogh, banner, and nav layers.

19. Leave your browser open and return to the Dreamweaver Document window.

20. Close the file.

Animating Layers

Dreamweaver timelines use DHTML (dynamic HTML) to change the properties of layers and images over time. For example, you can change the position, visibility, and stacking order of a layer as it moves on the page. DHTML is not a language; it's a marketing term that refers to HTML content that can change when downloaded in a browser. The dynamic capabilities are made possible by three technologies: HTML, CSS, and JavaScript. You can also place images into timelines and change the image source over time. However, you can't make images move unless they are contained in a layer.

⚠️ **WARNING!** *Timelines do NOT work in IE5.0 Mac but they do work in Safari Mac browser.*

When you create a timeline, Dreamweaver inserts JavaScript into your Web page. The JavaScript defines all the timeline functionality. If you edit the HTML source, be careful not to delete or move the JavaScript code.

⚠️ **WARNING!** *You must be using Dreamweaver version 7.01 or later to work with timelines. Macromedia didn't include the Timelines panel with the first release of Dreamweaver MX 2004. You can download a free upgrade from macromedia.com. When you install the upgrade, you must enter your serial number to complete the installation.*

Using the Timelines Panel

FROM THE KEYBOARD

To open the Timelines panel:

WIN ONLY

`Alt`+`F9`

MAC ONLY

`Option`+`F9`

The Timelines panel is the command center for working with animations within Dreamweaver. You use the Timelines panel to create, modify, and control how animations play in a Web browser. To open the Timelines panel, open an HTML document and choose Window→Timelines.

The Behaviors channel can be used to set behaviors so they execute in a certain frame.

Frames run horizontally from left to right along the top of the timeline. The number of frames affects the pace of the animation. (Only frames 1-50 are shown here.)

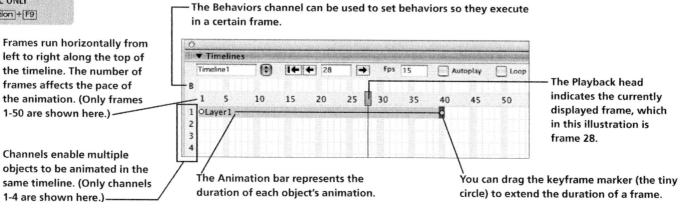

The Playback head indicates the currently displayed frame, which in this illustration is frame 28.

Channels enable multiple objects to be animated in the same timeline. (Only channels 1-4 are shown here.)

The Animation bar represents the duration of each object's animation.

You can drag the keyframe marker (the tiny circle) to extend the duration of a frame.

A timeline is made up of channels (vertical axis) and frames (horizontal axis).

Controlling Playback Options

The playback controls enable you to move through all the frames in the animation both backward and forward.

Rewind moves the playback head to the first frame.

This field shows the number of frames that occur per second in your timeline.

Autoplay (if selected) makes the timeline play automatically when the page is loaded in the browser.

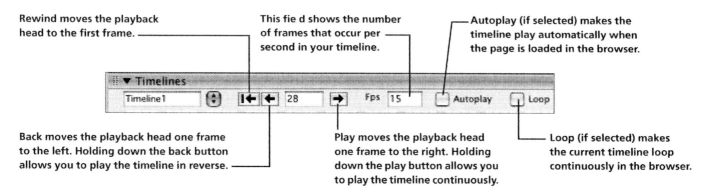

Back moves the playback head one frame to the left. Holding down the back button allows you to play the timeline in reverse.

Play moves the playback head one frame to the right. Holding down the play button allows you to play the timeline continuously.

Loop (if selected) makes the current timeline loop continuously in the browser.

Setting Frames Per Second

You set the frames per second (fps) in the Fps box. This determines the number of frames that occur per second in your timeline. The higher the fps, the faster the animation because more frames are crammed into one second. If you are moving an object around the screen, more frames will make the animation smoother. There is a certain point, however, where the browser can't animate any faster. The default fps setting of 15 is a good place to start. This setting means that 15 frames will take one second to play.

Hands-On 14.12 Create a Timeline Animation

In this exercise, you will insert a layer into the Timelines panel. You will then increase the number of frames and move the layer to its final position in the animation, which is on top of another layer.

1. Open zen_garden_timeline.htm from the lesson_14 folder.
   The page contains three fully qualified CSS layers and one inline layer (the buddha layer). You may recall that an animated layer must be an inline layer.

2. Open the Layers panel.

3. In the Layers panel, ensure that Prevent Layer Overlaps is not checked.
   This enables your animated layer to move over other layers on the screen.

4. In the Layers panel, click each layer name to identify the layer in the Document window.

5. In the Layers panel, select the buddha layer.

6. Choose Modify→Timeline→Add Object to Timeline from the menu bar. (You can also drag layers to the Timeline.)

7. If a message box appears, read the message and close the dialog box.
   The Timelines panel opens and places the object in the first channel in the Timeline. By default, the animation bar extends to frame 15. The name of the layer appears in the Animation bar.

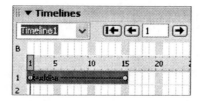

8. Click the keyframe marker at the end of the bar (the tiny circle under frame 15) and drag the marker to frame 60, as shown in the following illustration.
   Increasing the number of frames produces a smoother animation.

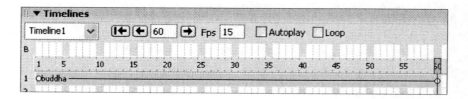

9. In the Document window, click the buddha layer's selection handle.
   This shifts the focus back to the layer.

10. While holding down the ⟨Shift⟩ key, use your keyboard's left arrow key to move the layer to the left 10 pixels at a time. When you approach the home layer, release the ⟨Shift⟩ key and use the left arrow key to nudge the layer until it is centered on top of the home layer. *As you move the layer, a thin line appears to the right of the layer to show the path of the animation in the Document window.*

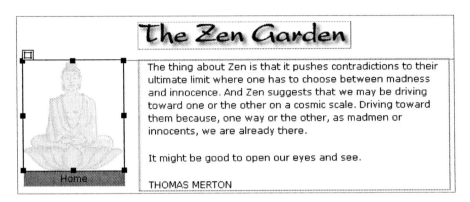

11. Hold down the Play ➡ button to preview the animation.

12. Save the file.

Adding a Behavior to a Timeline

You can add several behaviors to a timeline. To add a behavior, select the frame in the Behaviors channel, and choose Modify→Timeline→Add Behavior to Timeline.

The Behaviors channel ——

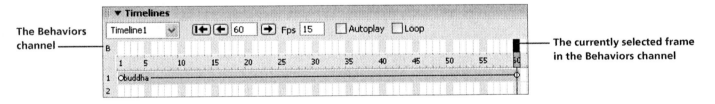

—— The currently selected frame in the Behaviors channel

 Hands-On 14.13 Add a Behavior to a Timeline

In this exercise, you will add a behavior to swap an image when the playback head reaches frame 60 in the timeline.

1. In the Behaviors channel, click the box directly above frame 60.
   The swap image event will occur when the playback head reaches the last frame.

2. Choose Modify→Timeline→Add Behavior to Timeline from the menu bar.

3. Read and then dismiss the information dialog box.
   The Behaviors panel opens.

4. Click the Add Behavior ⊞ button and choose Swap Image from the list of actions.
   The opens the Swap Image dialog box.

5. In the Images window, select image "lotus" in layer "buddha". Click the Browse button and locate and select buddha.gif from the images folder.
   This is the image that will replace the image in the layer when the playback head reaches frame 60.

6. Ensure that a checkmark appears next to Preload images, and then click OK.

7. Place a checkmark next to Autoplay. (Dismiss the information dialog box when it appears.)
   This will play the animation as soon as the browser fully loads the page.

8. Save the file, and then preview it in your browser.
   The ghost image should slowly move to the left. When the playback head reaches the last frame, the behavior should swap the ghost image with a more colorful image of the same size.

9. Leave your browser open, and return to the Dreamweaver Document window.

10. Close the Timelines panel.

11. Close the file.

Concepts Review

True/False Questions

1. Layers are technically referred to as CSS positioned elements. **TRUE   FALSE**

2. Layers can be positioned in three dimensions. **TRUE   FALSE**

3. Layers do not work in browsers prior to version 4.0. **TRUE   FALSE**

4. The <division> tag is used to form a layer. **TRUE   FALSE**

5. An inline layer contains a combination of HTML and CSS properties. **TRUE   FALSE**

6. You must be in Standard mode or Expanded Tables mode to draw a layer. **TRUE   FALSE**

7. When you move a layer marker, the layer is repositioned to the marker location. **TRUE   FALSE**

8. Dreamweaver measures a layer's position relative to the left and top edges of the page. **TRUE   FALSE**

9. When you use the Align layer command, layers are aligned with the border of the first layer selected. **TRUE   FALSE**

10. An ID selector style can be applied to one or more layers on the page. **TRUE   FALSE**

Multiple Choice Questions

1. Which of the following languages is used to create and control a Dreamweaver timeline?
   a. CSS
   b. JavaScript
   c. HTML
   d. All of the above

2. Which of the following represents a fully qualified CSS layer?
   a. <div id="Layer1">content here</div>
   b. <div id="layer1" style="position: absolute; width: 50px; height: 50px; z-index: 1; left: 50px; top: 50px;"></div>
   c. <division id="Layer1">content here</division>
   d. <div class="Layer1">content here</div>

3. Inline layers are the best choice for _____.
   a. CSS page layout
   b. HTML hand coding
   c. Timeline animations
   d. Absolute positioning

4. All elements in a layer are wrapped inside the _____ HTML tag.
   a. <layer>
   b. <div>
   c. <style>
   d. <body>

Skill Builders

Skill Builder 14.1   Create and Modify Layers

In this exercise, you will create and modify three layers.

1. Open balloons.htm from the review_14 folder.
   The page contains three balloon images.

2. Use the Draw Layer ▦ button in the Layout category of the Insert bar to draw three layers of approximately the same width and height of each image.
   Do not overlap the layers.

3. While holding down the [Shift] key, click each layer.
   This allows you to select multiple layers.

4. Type **59** in the W (width) field and **139** in the H (height) field on the Properties panel, and then press [Enter] or [Return].
   This changes the dimensions of each layer to match the dimensions of each image.

5. Drag and drop the red image into the first layer, the blue image into the second layer, and the yellow image into the third layer.

6. While holding down the [Shift] key, click each layer name in the Layers panel.
   This also enables you to select multiple layers.

7. Choose Modify→Align→Top from the menu bar.
   This aligns the top of each layer to the border of the last selection.

8. In the Layers panel, double-click Layer1 and type **red**.

9. Now rename Layer2 **blue** and rename Layer3 **yellow**.

10. Use the technique described in step 6 to select all layers.

11. Choose Modify→Align→Left from the menu bar.

12. Deselect the layers.
    The layers are stacked on top of each other, and the layer with the highest Z-Index number (yellow) is on top.

13. In the Layers panel, modify the Z-Index numbers so blue is the top layer, yellow is the middle layer, and red is the bottom layer.

14. Save and close the file.

Skill Builder 14.2   Define Positioning Styles for a Layer

In this exercise, you will define an advanced ID selector style to position a layer and add padding and a border to a layer.

1. Open balloons_styles.htm from the review_14 folder.
   The page contains one balloon image.

2. Choose Window→CSS Styles from the menu bar.
   This opens the CSS Styles panel.

3. Click the New CSS Style ⊞ button on the CSS Styles panel.
   This opens the New CSS Style dialog box.

4. For the Selector Type, choose Advanced.

5. In the Selector field, type **#red**.
   This defines an advanced ID selector style.

6. For the Define In option, choose This Document Only.
   This option creates an internal style.

7. Click OK.
   This opens the CSS Style Definition dialog box.

8. Choose the Box category.

9. In the Padding section, ensure that a checkmark appears next to Same for All.

10. Type **30px** in the Top box.
    This will add 30 pixels of padding to the top, bottom, left, and right sides of the layer.

11. Choose the Border category.

12. In the Style, Width, and Color sections, ensure that a checkmark appears next to Same for All, and set the following properties:

Style: Top	Ridge
Width: Top	Medium
Color: Top	**#FF0000**

13. Choose the Positioning category, and set the following properties:

Type	Absolute
Width	59 pixels
Height	139 pixels
Z-Index	1
Top	50 pixels
Left	50 pixels

14. Click OK.

15. Leave the file open.

Skill Builder 14.3   Apply a Layer Style

In this exercise, you will apply a layer style to the red balloon image.

1. Select the balloon image.

2. Choose Insert→Layout Objects→Div Tag from the menu bar.
   This opens the Insert Div Tag dialog box.

3. From the ID menu, choose red.

4. In the Insert menu, ensure that Wrap Around Selection is chosen and click OK.
   This creates a layer and the ID style properties are applied to the contents of the layer.

5. Save the file, and then preview it in your browser.
   You must open the file in a browser to preview borders properly.

6. Leave your browser open and return to the Dreamweaver Document window.

7. Close the file.

Skill Builder 14.4   Create a Timeline

In this exercise, you will create a timeline to animate three layers. You will also add a behavior to the time-line that swaps one of the images in a layer to another image.

1. Open balloons_timeline.htm from the review_14 folder.
   The page contains three layers named red, blue, and green. Each layer contains a balloon image. The layers are located halfway down the page. When the animation runs, you want to balloons to float up and to the right.

2. Select the blue layer. Be sure to select the layer, not the image inside the layer. Choose Modify→Timeline→Add Object to Timeline.
   This automatically opens the Timelines panel and adds the selected object to the timeline.

3. Select the yellow layer and drag it to Channel 2, Frame 10 in the timeline.
   This starts the animation for this layer 10 frames later than the first layer.

4. Select the red layer and drag it to Channel 3, Frame 20 in the timeline.

5. Click and drag the first keyframe ⊶ marker to frame 90.

6. Use the technique described in step 5 to drag the other two keyframe markers to frame 90.
   The timeline should now resemble the following illustration:

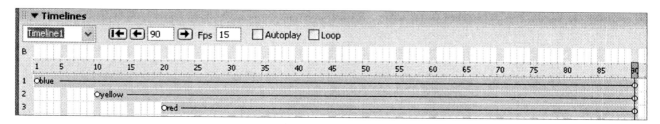

7. Select the first keyframe marker at the end of frame 90.
   This selects the blue layer in the Document window.

8. Drag the blue layer to the top-right area of the page.
   This creates a motion path and you should see the path after you release the mouse button.

9. Use the technique described in steps 7–8 to drag the yellow layer on top of the blue layer.

10. Use the technique described in steps 7–8 to drag the red layer on top of the yellow layer, and then deselect the layer.
    The page should resemble the following illustration. The yellow layer is on top because it has the highest Z-Index number.

11. Hold down the Play ➡ button and test the animation.
    The balloons should float up and to the right.

12. Save the file but keep it open.

Skill Builder 14.5   Add a Behavior to the Timeline

In this exercise, you will add a behavior to the timeline that swaps one of the balloon images with another image. You will also change the visibility property of two images so they disappear just before the Swap Image behavior occurs.

1. Select the keyframe marker in the second channel at Frame 90.

2. From the Vis (Visibility) menu on the Properties panel, choose Hidden.
   This hides the layer when the animation reaches Frame 90.

3. Use the technique described in steps 1–2 to hide the layer in Channel 3.

4. Select the keyframe marker in the first channel at frame 90.

5. Choose Modify→Timeline→Add Behavior to Timeline from the menu bar.
   This opens an information dialog box, and the Behaviors panel.

6. Read the information and close the dialog box.

7. Click the Add Behavior ⊞ button on the Behaviors panel and choose Swap Image from the action list.
   This opens the Swap Image dialog box.

8. In the Images window, select image "blueball" in layer "blue", and then click the Browse button.

9. Select kaboom.gif from the Unit 3 images folder and click OK or Choose.

10. Click OK to close the Swap Image dialog box.
    When the animation reaches Frame 90, the yellow and red layers disappear and the image in the blue frame is swapped with another image.

11. Place a checkmark next to AutoPlay.

12. Save the file, and then preview it in your browser.
    The animation should play as soon as the browser finishes loading the page content.

13. Click the Refresh button on the browser to replay the animation.

14. Leave your browser open and return to the Dreamweaver Document window.

15. Close the file.

■

 **Assessments**

Assessment 14.1 Define Styles for a CSS Page Layout

In this exercise, you will define ID selector styles for a CSS page layout. The final version of Assessments 14.1 through 14.5 is shown in the following illustration. When the final Assessment is completed, the satellite image will move behind the text and float to the top right side of the page.

1. Open lostinspace.htm from the review_14 folder.
   The page contains a banner graphic, a small table of null links, two paragraph blocks, and a satellite image.

Define the #banner Style

2. Create a new Advanced ID selector style named **#banner** and store it in the current document.

3. Set the following Positioning properties in the CSS Style Definition dialog box:

Type	Absolute
Width	250 pixels
Height	31 pixels
Top	37 pixels
Left	250 pixels
Z-Index	4

Define the #nav Style

4. Create another ID selector style named **#nav**.
This style will be used to create a layer to house the small table of links.

5. Set the following positioning properties. The Width and Height properties will be left blank to allow the layer to expand based on the table size.

Type	Absolute
Top	100 pixels
Left	100 pixels
Z-Index	3

Define the #content Style

6. Create another ID selector style named **#content**.

7. Set the following positioning properties:

Type	Absolute
Width	399 pixels
Height	300 pixels
Top	100 pixels
Left	250 pixels
Z-Index	4
Overflow	Auto

8. Save the file but keep it open.

Assessment 14.2   Apply the Advanced ID Selector Styles

In this exercise, you will select elements on the page, insert a series of <div> tags, and wrap the <div> tag around the selection to create the layers.

1. Select the Lost in Space banner graphic.

2. Insert a <div> tag and choose banner from the ID menu. Ensure that Wrap Around Selection is chosen.
This applies the style to the layer and the layer snaps into the position.

3. Select the table and repeat step 2. Apply the nav ID selector style.

4. Select the text and repeat step 2. Apply the content ID selector style.

5. Draw a small layer under the satellite image.

6. Set the following positioning properties in the Properties panel:

Width	100 pixels
Height	115 pixels
Top	241 pixels
Left	100 pixels
Z-Index	1

7. Drag and drop the satellite image into the layer.

8. Select Layer1 and rename it satellite.

9. Save the file but keep it open.

Assessment 14.3   Edit Advanced ID Selector Styles

In this exercise, you will edit the #nav and #content ID selectors.

1. Edit the #nav style to include **#CCCCCC** in the Background category.

2. Edit the #content style to include the following formatting properties in the Type category:

Font	Veranda, Arial, Helvetica, sans-serif
Size	10 points
Line Height	17 pixels

3. Save the file, but keep it open.

Assessment 14.4   Create ID Contextual Selector Styles

In this exercise, you will create ID contextual selector styles for the links that appear in the #nav layer. Don't forget to take advantage of the Apply button each time you add additional properties to the style.

1. Create an ID contextual selector style named **#nav a**.
   This contextual selector style will apply to all links in the #nav layer. Be sure to leave a space between the two selector names.

2. Set the following properties in the Type category:

Font	Veranda, Arial, Helvetica, sans-serif
Size	9 points

3. Set the following properties in the Box category:

Padding	3 pixels

   Place a checkmark next to Same for All.

4. Set the following properties in the Border category (remove all three checkmarks):

Bottom Style	Solid
Bottom Width	1 pixel
Bottom Color	#000000

5. Set the following properties in the Block category:

Display	Block

6. Create another ID contextual selector style named **#nav a:link, a:visited**.
   Here we set the color of the link before and after it's been clicked to the same color (for simplicity).

7. Set the following properties in the Type category:

Color	#333333
Decoration	None

8. Create another ID contextual selector style named **#nav a:hover**.
   This style sets the link state color when the mouse rolls over the link.

9. Set the following properties in the Type category:

Color	#FFFFFF
Decoration	None

10. In the Background Category, set the Background Color to **#000000**.

11. Save the file, and then preview it in your browser.

12. Test the rollover links.

13. Leave your browser open and return to the Dreamweaver Document window.

14. Leave the file open.

Assessment 14.5   Add a Timeline Animation

In this exercise, you will design a timeline animation that moves the satellite layer behind the content layer and up to the top-right corner of the page.

1. Open the Timelines panel.

2. Drag the satellite layer to Channel 1 in the Timelines panel.

3. Drag the keyframe marker to Frame 90.

4. Drag the satellite layer up and to the top-right corner of the page.

5. Change the Visibility setting to make the image disappear when the playback head reaches the last frame.

6. In the table of links, select the text Animation.

7. Add a Play Timeline Behavior and use the default onClick event.

8. Save the file, and then preview it in your browser.

9. Click the Animation link.

10. Refresh your browser window if you want to play the animation again.

11. Leave your browser open and return to the Dreamweaver Document window.

12. Close the file.

Critical Thinking

Critical Thinking 14.1   On Your Own

Bonnie Bixley received her Bachelor of Arts degree last year and married Robert Klein, a classmate she's known since her freshman year. Bonnie and Robert's parents gave them the graduation gift they had been dreaming about: their own wedding resource Web site. Today, Tying the Knot gets several thousand hits a day. Bonnie asks you to design the homepage shown in the following illustration. Each layer contains a unique ID selector style that is linked to an external style sheet.

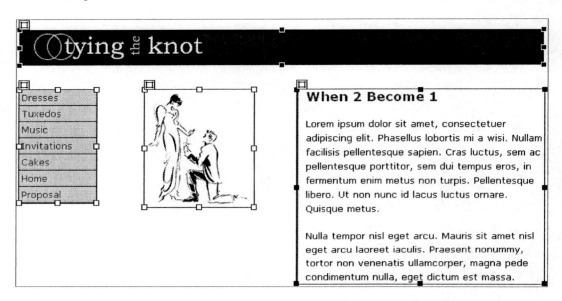

TIP! *(When you receive an HTML document check immediately for dependent files.)*

Use the following guidelines to identify the dependent files:

■ Open index.htm from the review_14 folder.

■ Open the CSS Styles panel.

- The page is linked to an external style sheet named theknot.css and it's in the same location as the current file.

- Carefully observe the following four styles you will apply to the four elements on the page:

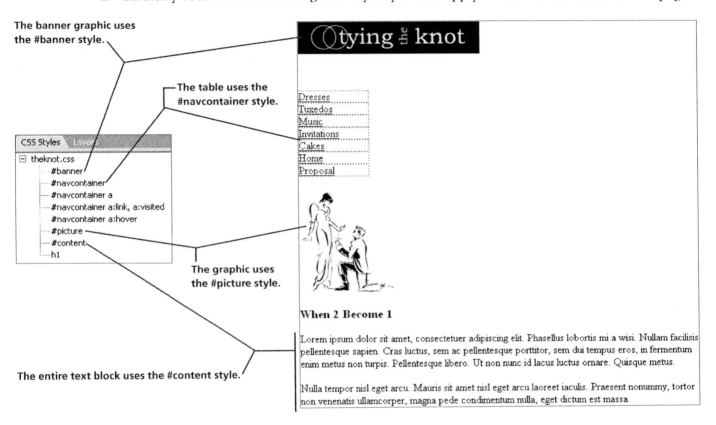

The banner graphic uses the #banner style.

The table uses the #navcontainer style.

The graphic uses the #picture style.

The entire text block uses the #content style.

- Wrap a <div> tag around each element on the page and apply the appropriate ID selector style to convert the selection to a layer.

- When the homepage design is complete, open dresses.htm and tuxedos.htm from the review_14 folder.

- Attach each page to theknot.css.

- When the page elements have been coveted to layers, link the pages together and to Home and Proposal.

- The remaining links on each page (Music, Invitations, and Cakes) are null links.

- Save all files.

Critical Thinking 14.2   On Your Own

Robert Klein has asked you to design a timeline animation that brings a couple together on the Tying the Knot Proposal page. The purpose of the animation is to engage site visitors and demonstrate that yes, some men still get down on their knees when presenting the ring.

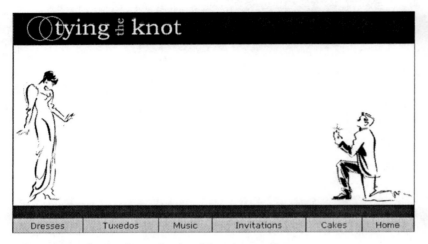

Robert wants the timeline to begin with an image of a woman standing at the left side of the page and a man kneeling at the right side of the page.

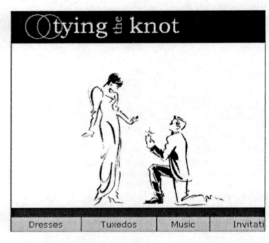

As the animation plays, the two graphics move toward each other and stop when the last frame is reached.

Open proposal.htm from the review_14 folder. The stage is set; however, you need to add two layers and insert the images. Draw a layer on the left side of the page and insert her.gif from the images folder. Resize the layer so it's the same size as the image.

Draw another layer on the right side of the page and insert him.gif from the images folder. Resize the layer so it's the same size as the image.

Select layer1 and rename it **her**; select layer2 and rename it **him**. Create the timeline and check the Autoplay box.

Save the file and preview the file in your browser. Close all files.

Critical Thinking 14.3   On Your Own

This exercise is a brain teaser! It involves working with Z-Index numbers so that two animated layers pass over or under the correct layers. Three generic buttons, which are part of the form object, use behaviors to control the animation in the browser.

Open planets_timeline.htm from the review_14 folder. Observe the five layers shown in the following illustration:

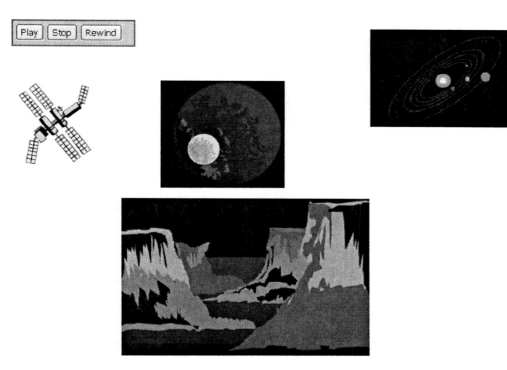

Use the Layers panel to identify each layer by name.

Design a timeline using the following illustrations as a guide. The satellite layer should pass over the planet layer and move horizontally to the right of the page. The galaxy layer should glide diagonally to the left and pass under the planets and crater layers.

Make the satellite and galaxy layers disappear just before the timeline reaches the last frame.

Click each of the three buttons and observe their properties in the Properties panel. Add the Play Timeline Behavior to the Play button, the Stop Timeline Behavior to the Stop button, and the Go to Timeline behavior to the Rewind button.

Remember, it's much easier to work with a white page background. Once the animation working, you should change the page background to black.

Save and close the file when you are finished.

LESSON 15

Working with HTML

In this lesson, you will use several tools that enable you to edit HTML code by hand. Working in Dreamweaver's Design view is like looking under the hood of a luxury car—the masterfully crafted engine makes the car run smoothly. The same thing applies to getting under the hood of Dreamweaver and discovering an array of masterfully crafted tools you can use to optimize your Web pages. When you've learned to use these tools, Jeff Gordon could not get better service at a pit stop for the Indi 500. This lesson teaches you how to edit code in Design and Split view, optimize your pages for better search results, clean up HTML and Word HTML documents, and validate code.

Case Study

Andrew Sheraton just completed his Dreamweaver studies at Joshua Tree Community College and landed a job at Just in Time Design. Andrew's first assignment is to complete the final prep work on the HTML documents before they're published. He begins by using Dreamweaver's Quick Tag Editor to make minor adjustments to the code.

```
Edit tag: <table width="667" border="0"
          align="center" cellpadding="0"
          cellspacing="0" summary="Dolphins are
          among the most intelligent and interesting
          creatures on Earth. This section covers how
          they breathe, and communicate with other
          mammals.">
```

One of the vital lessons Andy learned in school was that just because you build a Web site, there is no voodoo that automatically draws visitors. Knowing this, he scrutinizes each page to ensure that the titles accurately describes the content. He then adds two meta tags to the head of each page to help search engines index the content correctly. He also inserts some invisible HTML comments that provide information for site visitors who actually enjoy studying code.

Andy's final tasks include cleaning up the HTML and Word HTML code and validating each page to ensure they work with HTML 4.01 standards. In the following partial illustration, Andy found 47 warnings on just one page.

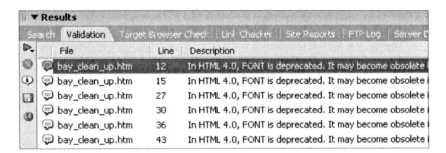

Within 30 seconds he was able to clean up the code to produce a valid HTML document:

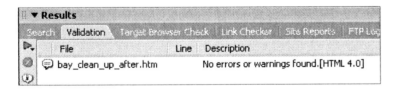

Working with HTML in Design View

Dreamweaver is much more than a visual editor; it provides a variety of tools and resources for hand coding, code editing, cleaning up sloppy code, and validating code. This lesson will give you a basic introduction to Dreamweaver's code editing and troubleshooting features.

Using the Quick Tag Editor

If you are a seasoned coder, you can jump into Code view and write the HTML from scratch. Most of the time, however, Web designers work in Dreamweaver's visual authoring environment and do not write code.

FROM THE KEYBOARD

To open the Quick Tag Editor:

WIN ONLY
[Ctrl]+[T]

MAC ONLY
[⌘]+[T]

You may occasionally find the need to make a quick adjustment to code without switching out of Design view. For example, say you've designed tables for a client and you realize that some require a summary (a table description read aloud by screen reader programs). Once you've inserted a table, the only way to add a summary is to edit the <table> tag in Code view or you can use the Quick Tag Editor without leaving Design view. (The Quick Tag Editor is not available in Code view.)

To open the Quick Tag Editor, use the Quick Tag Editor ✍ button on the Properties panel.

Depending on what you've selected in the Document window or on the Tag Selector, the Quick Tag Editor opens in one of the following modes:

FROM THE KEYBOARD

To cycle through the three quick tag modes:

WIN ONLY
[Ctrl]+[T]

MAC ONLY
[⌘]+[T]

Insert HTML—Use this mode to type a new HTML tag. This mode opens if nothing is currently selected in the Document window.

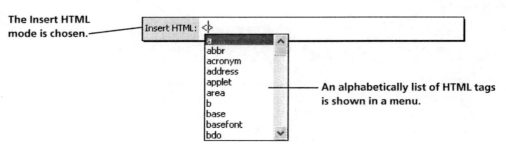

The Insert HTML mode is chosen.

An alphabetically list of HTML tags is shown in a menu.

Edit tag—Use this mode to change the tag of the current selection on the page. In the following illustration, a heading 1 <h1> tag is selected.

Wrap tag—Use this mode to begin and end the current selection with the same tag.

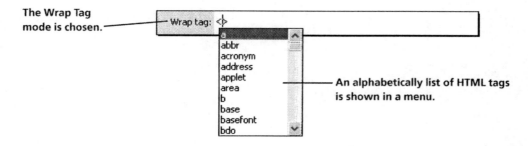

The Wrap Tag mode is chosen.

An alphabetically list of HTML tags is shown in a menu.

TIP! *You can move the Quick Tag Editor to different positions by clicking and dragging the gray area on the left.*

If you make a mistake while editing a tag, press the Esc key to close the Quick Tag Editor.

 ## Hands-On 15.1   Use the Quick Tag Editor

In this exercise, you will use the Quick Tag Editor to add a table summary, insert an HTML tag, and wrap a tag around a text selection.

1. Open dolphin_intro.htm from the lesson_15 folder.

2. Click anywhere in the main content area under the Introduction heading.

Edit an HTML Tag

3. Click the far right <table> tag on the Tag Selector.
   The nested table is now outlined with a thick black border to indicate that it is selected.

4. Click the Quick Tag Editor 🖎 button on the Properties panel.
   This opens the Quick Tag Editor. You can click the gray area and drag the editor to another location.

   ```
   Edit tag: <table width="667" border="0"
             align="center" cellpadding="0"
             cellspacing="0">
   ```

5. Place the insertion point just before the > character at the end of the opening table tag.

6. Press the Spacebar and type **su**.
   A code hints menu opens and the word summary is highlighted in the list of available table properties.

7. Press Enter or Return.
   This adds the summary property to the opening table tag and the insertion point is blinking between two quotation marks.

8. Type **Dolphins are among the most intelligent and interesting creatures on Earth. This section covers how they breathe, and communicate with other mammals.**

9. The opening <table> tag should now match the following illustration:

   ```
   Edit tag: <table width="667" border="0"
             align="center" cellpadding="0"
             cellspacing="0" summary="Dolphins are
             among the most intelligent and interesting
             creatures on Earth.This section covers how
             they breathe, and communicate with other
             mammals.">
   ```

10. Press [Enter] or [Return].
    You will not see visual evidence of the table summary; however, screen readers can now speak the summary text to blind readers.

Insert an HTML Tag

11. Place the insertion point to the right of the word Others, which is the last word in the last paragraph.
    This is where you will insert a horizontal rule.

12. Click the Quick Tag Editor button on the Properties panel.
    This opens the Quick Tag Editor in Insert HTML mode.

13. Type **hr**.

14. Observe that hr is highlighted in the menu.

15. Press [Enter] or [Return].
    This inserts the hr tag in the Editor window and moves the insertion point to the right.

16. Press the spacebar and type **si**.
    The word size is highlighted in the list of available horizontal rule properties.

17. Press [Enter] or [Return].
    This inserts the size attribute and the insertion point is blinking between two quotation marks.

18. Type **1** and press [Enter] or [Return].
    This inserts a one pixel high horizontal rule below the last paragraph.

Wrap a Tag Around a Selection

19. In the copyright notice at the bottom of the page, select the text tm.

20. Click the Quick Tag Editor button on the Properties panel.
    This opens the editor in Wrap Tag mode.

21. Type **sup** and press [Enter] or [Return] twice.
    The inserts the superscript tag and formats the trademark text as superscript.

22. Save the file but keep it open.

Working with HTML in Split View

As you develop your pages, you will undoubtedly need to change the HTML code. Sometimes all it takes is an accidental line break or other unseen characters to make your page layout unsightly. You could spend hours trying to resolve the conflict in the Document window or you could switch to Code view or Split view and perform surgery at the source. Before we don our surgical gear, let's explore the anatomy of an HTML document:

An HTML 4 document is composed of three parts:

1. A line containing HTML version information

2. A declarative header section surrounded by the <head></head> tags

3. A body, which contains the document's actual content (begins with <body></body> or <frameset></frameset>)

The <!DOCTYPE> declaration (DTD) is the first tag that appears in your HTML document. This tag identifies the HTML version and document type. HTML 4.01 specifies three document types: Strict, Transitional, and Frameset. Each time you create a new HTML document, Dreamweaver automatically adds the Transitional document type shown here.

```
<!DOCTYPE HTML PUBLIC "-//W3C//DTD HTML 4.01 Transitional//EN"
"http://www.w3.org/TR/html4/loose.dtd">
```

NOTE! *If you want to use the free World Wide Web Consortium (W3C) CSS and HTML validation tools, the DTD must be the first element in your document. Don't change the case.*

Following the DTD is the opening <html> tag. This tag is the container for the head and body elements. The head section is reserved for HTML elements that are not displayed in a browser but are nonetheless important to the document. The body section is reserved for the visual elements that appear in a Web browser or are spoken to users with vision problems.

The head section is reserved for non-visual elements.

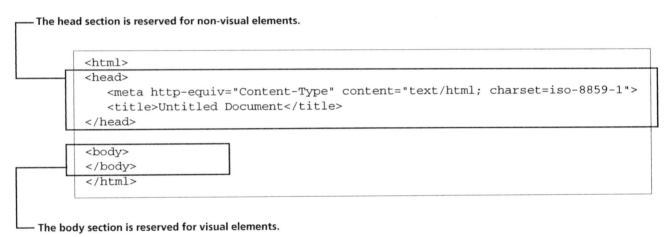

```
<html>
<head>
    <meta http-equiv="Content-Type" content="text/html; charset=iso-8859-1">
    <title>Untitled Document</title>
</head>

<body>
</body>
</html>
```

The body section is reserved for visual elements.

By default, only two tags appear in the head of a new HTML document: a <meta> tag that describes the content type and character set and a <title></title> tag that describes the page contents. Both of these tags are required for valid HTML documents. A valid document is one that conforms to the HTML 4.01 standards set forth by the W3C. You will learn more about meta tags and valid HTML documents later in this lesson.

Using the HTML View Options Menu in Split View

The View Options 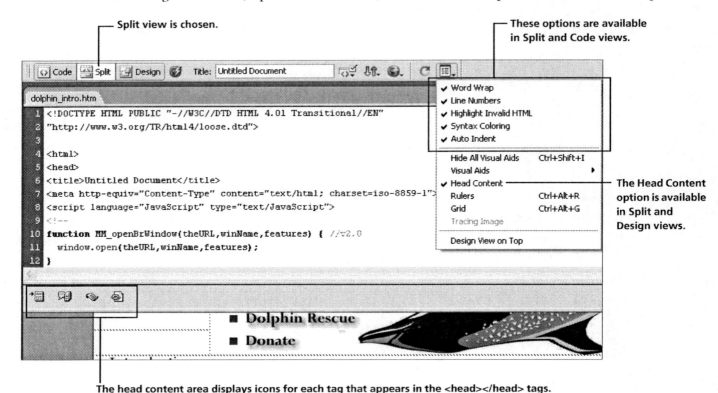 button on the Document toolbar allows you to set options for Code, Split, and Design views. The menu choices depend on which view you're using. In the following illustration, Split view is chosen, and the insertion point is inside the Code pane.

— Split view is chosen.

— These options are available in Split and Code views.

The Head Content option is available in Split and Design views.

The head content area displays icons for each tag that appears in the `<head></head>` tags.

SETTING VIEW OPTIONS MENU IN SPLIT VIEW

Option	Description
Head Content	This option shows the head content area between Code view and Design view.
Word Wrap	This option wraps the code so you can view it without scrolling horizontally. This option doesn't insert line breaks; it just makes the code easier to view.
Line Numbers	This option displays line numbers along the left side of the code. This is a great feature to help you quickly find a line of code.
Highlight Invalid HTML	This option causes Dreamweaver to highlight in yellow HTML that browsers don't support. When you select an invalid tag, the Properties panel displays information on how to correct the error.
Syntax Coloring	This option turns code coloring on and off. To change the coloring scheme, use the Code Coloring category in Dreamweaver Preferences.
Auto Indent	This option makes your code indent automatically when you press Enter or Return while writing code. To change the indent spacing or tags that automatically indent, use the Code Format category in Dreamweaver Preferences.
Design View on Top	This option places Design view on top of Code view.

The following illustration shows a close-up view of the four icons that appear in the Head Content area.

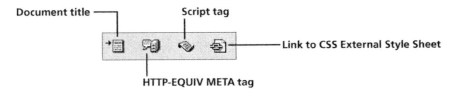

The Head Content area displays icons for all head elements.

 ## Hands-On 15.2   Use Split View to Identify Tags

In this exercise, you will open a page in Split view and identify the tags that appear between the <head> </head> tags.

Before you begin: The dolphin_intro.htm file should be open.

1. Choose View→Code and Design from the menu bar or use the Split button on the Document toolbar.

2. Drag the horizontal bar that separates the two windows approximately two-thirds of the way down to give you more viewing area in the Code window.

3. From the View Options Menu 🔲, on the Document toolbar, choose Head Content.
   This places the head content area between the Document and Code window.

4. Press the Title ⬚ button.
   This highlights the <title></title> tag. Notice that the Properties panel changes to Title properties.

5. Press the Meta 🔲 button.
   This highlights the <meta http-equiv> tag. Notice that the Properties panel changes to Meta properties.

6. Press the Script ⬙ button.
   This highlights the <script> tag. Notice that the Properties panel changes to Script properties.

7. Press the Link ⬙ button.
   This highlights the <link> tag. Notice that the Properties panel changes to Link properties.

8. Stay in Split view and keep the file open.

Optimizing Your Pages for Search Engines

Building your site is a major piece of the Web design pie, but the final slice involves ensuring that your site shows up in a decent ranking in a search engine set of results. Three key elements play a role in helping search engines and directories find you and correctly index the highest level pages in your site. These elements are stored between the <head></head> tags of your HTML documents. In order of importance they are:

- The title tag
- The description meta tag
- The keywords meta tag

Meta tags contain meta data, which is information about a document rather than the document contents. You can assist search engines by adding a meta tag that **describes** the page contents, and another that contains **keywords** a potential visitor might type in a search engine search field. When you add the description and keywords meta tags to your document, you make it much easier for search engine robots to understand how to categorize your site. Your page titles, headings, meta tags, body copy, and other elements all play a role in getting a decent ranking in search results.

The most valuable feature meta tags offer is the ability to control to some degree how your Web pages are described in search results by some search engines. Here, we explore how to optimize the page title and how to add the description and keywords meta tags to the correct location in your HTML document.

Optimizing the Page Title

Without question, the title tag of your page is the single most important factor to consider when optimizing your Web pages for search engines. This is because most search engines place a high level of importance on keywords found in your title tag. The title tag is also what search engines usually use for the title of your listing in the search results.

 TIP! *Each page of your site should have a title tag that contains the most important keywords and keyword phrases that relate to the page content.*

Google will display up to 66 characters of a title tag and crop any additional characters. Yahoo! has a cutoff in presenting titles of 120 characters, which is substantially longer and gives you more room to present longer titles. If your title exceeds 120 characters, the title will be cropped whether the display title ends in a complete word or not. You can create a longer title if you wish, but be aware that anything beyond 120 characters will be cropped in the Yahoo! search results.

Adding and Optimizing the Description

Many search engine robots read the contents of the description meta tag. Some use the information to index your pages in their databases and some also display the information on the search results page (instead of displaying the first few lines of your document text). Some search engines limit the number of characters they index, so it's a good idea to limit your description to approximately 200 characters. Following is an example of a description meta tag.

```
<meta name="description" content="This would be the description of the page
contents. Your most important keyword phrases should appear in this
description.">
```

The following guidelines will help ensure that your site description is accurate:

- Accurately describe the content of your page to entice potential visitors to click on your listing in search results.

- Include three or four of your most important keyword phrases, especially those used in your title tag and page copy.

- Move your most important keywords to the beginning of your description.

The correct placement for both browser and search engine meta tags is between the <head> and </head> tags within the HTML the makes up your page. Their order does not really matter, but most people usually place the description first, followed by the keywords.

Adding and Optimizing the Keywords

Many search engine robots read the contents of the keywords meta tag and use the information to index your pages in their databases. Because some search engines limit the number of keywords or characters they index, or ignore all keywords if you go beyond the limit, it's a good idea to use a few well-chosen keywords. Limit keywords to 250–1024 characters. Enter your keywords, separated by commas, as shown in the following example:

```
<meta name="keywords" content="keywords phrase 1, keywords phrase 2, keywords
phrase 3, etc.">
```

 TIP! *Choose keywords that are relevant to your site. Also, avoid excessive repetition as many search engines will penalize your rankings for attempting to abuse their system.*

It can take up to three months to get indexed by some search engines and even longer to get a reasonable ranking. It is a slow process so take your time and do things right from the beginning.

USING DESCRIPTION AND KEYWORDS META TAGS		
Tag Name	**Example**	**Description**
Description	`<meta name="description" content="...summary of Web page...">`	Used by some search engines to describe your document in search results
Keywords	`<meta name="keywords" content="keyword phrase 1, keyword phrase 2, keyword phrase3">`	Used by some search engines to index your document (in addition to words from the title and document body)

 ## Hands-On 15.3   Add Meta Tags to Your HTML

In this exercise, you will optimize a page title and add the description and keyword meta tags to your HTML.

Before you begin: The dolphin_intro.htm file should be open in Split view.

Optimize the Page Title

1. Press the Title ⁺▣ button in the head content area that separates the Document and Code windows.
   This selects the <title></title> tag and its contents in the Code window. The Properties panel changes to Title properties.

2. In the Properties panel Title field, type **Urgent call to action. Help rescue stranded dolphins on California beaches**. Press ⎡Enter⎤ or ⎡Return⎤.

3. Position the insertion point directly below the <title></title> tags in the Code window.

Insert the Description Meta Tag

4. Choose Insert→HTML→Head Tags→Description. (You can also use the HTML category of the Insert bar to insert meta tags.)
   This opens the Description dialog box.

5. Type **Dolphin Watch performs rescue, rehabilitation, research, education, and release of stranded marine mammals including dolphins and whales on California beaches**. Press OK.

6. Position the insertion point directly below the description meta tag.

Insert the Keywords Meta Tag

7. Choose Insert→HTML→Head Tags→Keywords.
   This opens the Keywords dialog box.

8. Type **Dolphin Watch, marine animals, marine rescue, stranded marine mammals, dolphin rescue, dolphins, California beaches, dolphins and whales, Cetaceans, mammal rehabilitation**. Press OK.

9. Save the file but stay in Split view.

Adding Comments

Comments are programming notes you leave in the code. Comments don't show in the browser window, but anyone can see the comments in the HTML source code. Comments can be used for a variety of purposes, including setting off a section of code for troubleshooting purposes, adding a reminder of when you created or updated the file, or recording who made the last revision. You can also use comments to isolate sections of a document to help you quickly identify nested tables, scripts, or which part of the document constitutes the footer and copyright information. A comments looks like this:

```
<!-- Add a banner graphic here -->
```

Dreamweaver uses its own comments to identify library items and parts of a template. The following comment is a library item example:

```
<!-- #BeginLibraryItem "/Library/sidebar.lbi" -->
```

When cleaning up your HTML code, you must be able to identify the comments you've added from those used by Dreamweaver.

 Hands-On 15.4 Add a Comment

In this exercise, you will add two comments that help identify two sections of a Web page. First, you will ensure that the Invisible Elements category of Dreamweaver preferences is set to show comments.

Before you begin: The dolphin_intro.htm file should be open in Split view.

1. Choose Edit→Preferences (Win) or Dreamweaver→Preferences (Mac).

2. From the Invisible Elements category, ensure that a checkmark appears next to Comments. Press OK.

3. In the Design window, position the insertion point before the word Dolphins (first word in the first paragraph).

4. Choose Insert→Comment.
   This opens the Comment dialog box.

5. Type **This section describes how dolphins breathe**. Press OK.
   In the Design window, the comment invisible marker appears as a yellow symbol with an exclamation point. In the Code window, the comment is highlighted.

6. In the Design window, position the insertion point before the word Dolphins (first word in the second paragraph).

7. Type **This section describes how dolphins communicate and navigate**. Press OK.

8. Click on either of the comment invisible markers.
   The Properties panel displays the comment and allows you to edit the comment text in Design view.

9. Choose View→Design from the menu bar or use the Design button on the Document toolbar.

10. Save and close the file.

Validating Your Code

To further optimize the code in your documents, you can run Validate Markup to examine the code for tag and syntax errors. This allows you to check your documents for compliance with the published standards for the various markup languages Dreamweaver supports. So, for example, you can a check your document's source code to make sure all the tags are valid according to the HTML 4.01 specification from the W3C (World Wide Web Consortium).

FROM THE KEYBOARD

To run Validate Markup:

WIN AND MAC

[Shift]+[F6]

To run Validate Markup, choose File→Check Page→Validate Markup or use the Validation tab on the Results panel.

Validator Preferences let you choose how your code is validated. The recommended settings are shown in the following illustration.

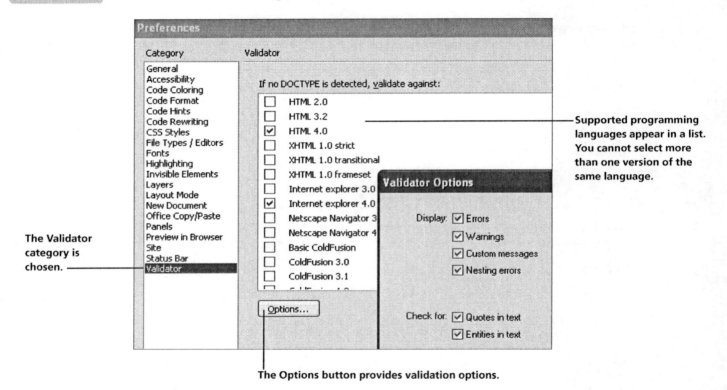

The Validator category is chosen.

Supported programming languages appear in a list. You cannot select more than one version of the same language.

The Options button provides validation options.

Any errors or warnings that Dreamweaver finds are displayed on the Validation tab of the Results panel.

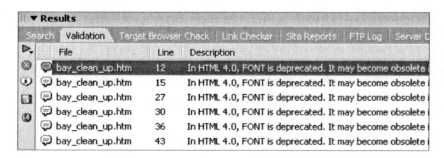

Hands-On 15.5   Validate Your Code

In this exercise, you will validate the code for an HTML 4.01 document.

1. Open bay_clean_up.htm from the lesson_15 folder.
   This document contains typical code violations you're likely to encounter in older Web pages.

2. Choose File→Check Page→Validate Markup from the menu bar.
   This opens the Results panel and a list of potential problems are shown below the Validation tab.

3. Scan the list of warnings that appear in the list.
   Dreamweaver warns you that the <font> tag may no longer be supported in future versions.

4. Close the Results panel group.
   You will fix the warnings in the next exercise.

5. Keep the file open.

 Though Dreamweaver's HTML validator is useful, it cannot find every error. To be certain that your pages are valid, use the free HTML validation service provided by the World Wide Web Consortium at http://validator.W3.org. You can upload a file from your file storage location or type the URL of a page on your server. You'll get a chance to do this in Critical Thinking 15.2.

Cleaning Up HTML

There will undoubtedly be times when you have to work with HTML written by a sloppy hand coder or in a program other than Dreamweaver. You should clean up all code before publishing the page to your server. Fortunately, Dreamweaver has a useful command called Clean Up HTML that automatically removes leftover tags and provides the option to specify exactly which tag(s) to remove. You can run this command in Design, Split, or Code view. To clean up HTML, choose Commands→Clean Up HTML from the menu bar. This opens the Clean UP HTML / XHTML dialog box.

These options allow you to remove tags. ——————

These options allow you to combine nested <font> tags and show a log when completed.——

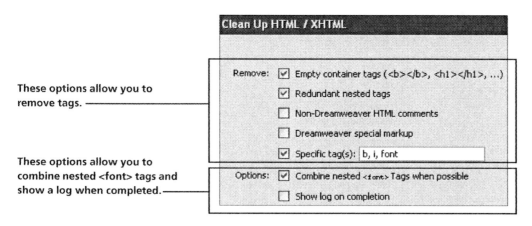

SETTING THE CLEAN UP HTML DIALOG BOX OPTIONS

Option	Description
Remove Empty Container Tags	This option removes any tag pairs that have no content between them. For example, <b></b> and <font color="#FF0000"></font> are empty tags.
Remove Redundant Nested Tags	This option removes all repetitive instances of a tag. For example, in <b>There are not enough<b>cookies</b>in the bag</b>, the <b></b> tags surrounding the word cookies are redundant and would be removed.
Remove Non-Dreamweaver HTML Comments	This option removes all comments not inserted by Dreamweaver. For example, <!-- insert logo here --> would be removed, but <!-- #BeginLibraryItem "/Library/sidebar.lbi" --> wouldn't because it's a Dreamweaver comment that marks the beginning of a library item.
Remove Dreamweaver Special Markup	This option removes comments that Dreamweaver adds to code to allow documents to be automatically updated when templates and library items are updated. If you select this option when cleaning up code in a template-based document, the document is detached from the template. Use this option with caution.
Remove Specific Tag(s)	This option removes tags specified in the adjacent text box. Use this option to remove custom tags inserted by other visual editors and any tags you don't want to appear on your page. Separate multiple tags with commas (for example, font, blink).
Combine Nested <font> Tags When Possible	This option consolidates two or more font tags when they control the same range of text. For example, <font size="4"> <font color="#000000">The Cookie Monster</font></font> would be changed to <font size="4" color="#000000">The Cookie Monster</font>.
Show Log On Completion	This option displays an alert box with details about the changes made to the document as soon as the cleanup is finished.

Cleaning Up the Font Tag

If you began your Dreamweaver studies with this book, chances are you haven't been using the dreaded <font> tag you saw in the last exercise. That's because Dreamweaver MX 2004 uses CSS instead of HTML tags by default to specify the font. The <font> tag was marked for deprecation (extinction) in HTML version 4.0 and will not be supported in future browsers.

So, if you've never used the <font> tag, why should this concern you? Because there are millions of documents that still use the <font> tag and one day you may face the task of cleaning up some of them. It is not uncommon to have hundreds of occurrences of the <font> tag on a single page. When you clean them up, you'll usually cut the file size dramatically, and the pages will load a lot faster.

Hands-On 15.6   Clean Up HTML

In this exercise, you will clean up HTML to remove font tags.

Before you begin: The bay_clean_up.htm file should be open.

1. Observe the download size on the Status bar.
   The download size is 7K.

2. Scroll to the bottom of the page and click in the Fixed-Price Menu table.

3. Click the <table> tag on the Tag Selector.
   This selects the Fixed-Price Menu table.

4. Choose View→Code.

5. Scroll down the page and observe the amount of code it takes to modify the font face and size.

6. Scroll slowly up the page and observe the occurrences of the <font> tag scattered throughout the rest of the page.

7. Choose Commands→Clean Up HTML from the menu bar.
   This opens the Clean Up HTML / XHTML dialog box.

8. Place a checkmark next to Specific Tag(s) and type **font** in the text field.

9. Leave the other checkboxes at their default settings and press OK.
   An alert box opens and informs you that 46 specified tags were removed.

10. Press OK.

11. Observe the download size on the Status bar.
    The download size is reduced by approximately 50%.

12. Scroll through the code one more time and observe how much cleaner it is without 46 font tags!

13. Choose File→Check Page→Validate Markup from the menu bar.
    The page passes the Dreamweaver validation test and no warnings are listed.

14. Save and close the file.

15. Return to Design view.

Cleaning Up Word HTML Documents

Many people save their Word documents as HTML files without realizing how atrocious the resulting code is. The first time I saved a Word document as a Web page and opened the file in Dreamweaver code view, it looked like my cat had fallen asleep on the keyboard. It's a frightening sight and the code cannot pass any Web page validation test, as you will see later.

Dreamweaver's Clean Up Word HTML command can strip most of the proprietary Word XML tags, Word-only mso styles, inline CSS styles, and a lot of other tags that should not be in an HTML document. Unfortunately, the Clean Up Word HTML dialog box doesn't list Word 2003 (Win) or Word X (Mac).

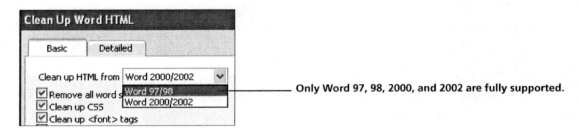

Only Word 97, 98, 2000, and 2002 are fully supported.

When running Clean Up Word HTML on a Word 2003 document, the following warning message appears after Dreamweaver tries to detect which version of Word created the document: "Dreamweaver was unable to determine the version of Word used to generate this document. You may manually select a version from the dropdown menu. However, if the incorrect version is selected, the import filter may not work correctly."

No warning message appears with Word X when running Clean Up Word HTML, but Dreamweaver automatically selects Word 2000/2002. Microsoft Word 2003 for Windows was released on October 21, 2003, which was after Dreamweaver MX 2004 was released (September 10, 2003). Word X for Macintosh was released on November 19, 2001. Dreamweaver currently recognizes Word X documents as Word 2000/2002 documents.

If your version of Word is not supported, see the Word 2003 Workaround section on page 482.

 ## Hands-On 15.7   Clean Up a Word HTML Document

In this exercise, you will clean up a Word 2002 HTML document. This process cleans up the majority of Word proprietary tags. You will use the Clean Up HTML command to finish the job.

1. Open clean_up_word2002.htm from the lesson_15 folder.
The document looks rather harmless; you'd hardly know that code monsters are lurking behind the scene.

2. Observe the file download size.
The text-only file is a whopping 8K in size.

3. Switch to Code view.

4. Start at the top and scroll slowly down the page. Observe all the bloated code.
The red squiggly lines indicate invalid code.

5. Scroll to the top of the page.

6. Choose File→Check Page→Validate Markup from the menu bar.
   All of the red icons to the left of the filename represent errors, not warnings.

Clean Up the Word HTML

7. Choose Commands→Clean Up Word HTML from the menu bar.
   This opens the Clean Up Word HTML dialog box.

8. Remove the checkmark next to Set Background Color.
   This prevents Dreamweaver from inserting the background color attribute inside the <body> tag. Background color is more correctly specified with CSS.

9. Leave all of the other default settings on both the Basic and Detailed tabs as they are and press OK.
   An alert box opens and displays the clean up HTML results.

```
Clean up word HTML results:
4 meta tags removed
15 instances of word XML removed
3 word [if...]'s removed
6 empty paragraphs removed
5 margin defines removed
8 instances of unneeded inline CSS removed
51 word-only "mso" styles removed
1 instances of unused CSS style definitions removed
Source formatting applied
```

10. Press OK.
    The proprietary Word HTML code is removed.

11. Repeat step 6 to run the validation command again.
    Dreamweaver validates the document but you still need to clean up the CSS inline styles.

12. Locate line 14 in the code and observe the CSS inline style inside the <span> tag: <span style='font-family:Georgia'>Self-Empowerment through Learning</span>.

Clean Up the HTML

13. Choose Commands→Clean Up HTML from the menu bar.

14. Place a checkmark next to Specific Tag(s) and type **span** in the text field.

15. Press OK.
    An alert box opens and informs you that 9 specified tags were removed.

16. Press OK.

Delete the Internal CSS Style

17. Choose Window→CSS Styles.
    This opens the CSS Styles panel.

18. Select the <style> tag in the CSS Styles panel and press the Delete CSS Style button on the bottom of the panel.
    The internal style does nothing so it should be deleted. This leaves you with a clean HTML document.

19. Choose File→Check Page→Validate Markup from the menu bar.
The page passes the Dreamweaver validation test and no warnings are listed.

20. Close the Results panel.

21. Return to Design view.

22. Observe the file download size.
The download size is now only 2K.

23. Save and close the file.

Word 2003 Workaround

The Clean Up Word HTML command should work with (Mac) Word X files and (Win) Word 2003 files. When you receive the version warning with Word 2003 files, close the alert box, and click OK to run Clean Up Word HTML and most of the invalid markup will be removed.

Perhaps a better solution than saving a Word document as a Web page is to copy the text in a Word document and paste it into Dreamweaver using one of the following three methods. Each Paste command results in different HTML code, so experiment with each and decide which works best for you:

- Edit→Paste

- Edit→Paste Formatted

- Edit→Paste Text

Remember, when you clean up a Word HTML document, you need to add the <!DOCTYPE> tag if you want to be able to validate your pages against the World Wide Web Consortium's HTML and CSS validation services—as described in the Working with HTML in Split View section.

Concepts Review

True/False Questions

1. To add a summary to an existing table, choose Insert→Table Objects→Summary from the menu bar.   TRUE   FALSE

2. The Quick Tag Editor is available in Design and Code view.   TRUE   FALSE

3. The <!DOCTYPE> declaration identifies the HTML version the document uses.   TRUE   FALSE

4. Meta tags contain meta data, which is information about a document rather than document content.   TRUE   FALSE

5. The head section of an HTML document is reserved for visual elements.   TRUE   FALSE

6. The title element plays the greatest role in helping search engines find your site.   TRUE   FALSE

7. The View Options menu allows you to set options for Code and Design views.   TRUE   FALSE

8. The use of meta tags guarantees that your site will be indexed by search engine robots.   TRUE   FALSE

9. The description meta tag should contain a comprehensive list of keywords potential visitors can use to find your site.   TRUE   FALSE

10. It's a good idea to clean up Word HTML documents to make them compatible with most browsers.   TRUE   FALSE

Multiple Choice Questions

1. Which of the following modes is available in the Quick Tag Editor?
   a. Insert HTML
   b. Edit tag
   c. Wrap tag
   d. All of the above

2. Which of the following tags was declared obsolete in HTML 4.0 and should be avoided?
   a. <div>
   b. <spam>
   c. <font>
   d. <class>

3. _____ are those you can leave for yourself or others working on your site.
   a. Design notes
   b. Invisible notes
   c. Comments
   d. Both a and b

4. A few well chosen keywords should be positioned in front of the following locations in the Description meta tag?
   a. Beginning
   b. Middle
   c. End
   d. It doesn't matter

 **Skill Builders**

Skill Builder 15.1   Use the Quick Tag Editor

In this exercise, you will use the Quick Tag Editor to modify table properties.

1. Open museum.htm from the review_15 folder.
   The table needs a few adjustments. The text in the first cell should be a heading 1, and the cell with the gray background color is too dark.

2. Select the text The Guggenheim Museum.

3. Click the Quick Tag Editor 📝 button on the Properties panel.
   The Quick Tag Editor opens in Wrap Tag mode.

4. Type **h1** and press [Enter] or [Return] twice.
   This formats the text as a heading 1.

5. Click in the table cell with the gray background color.

6. Right-click the <td> tag on the Tag Selector.

7. Choose Edit Tag from the pop-up menu.
   The Quick Tag Editor opens in Edit Tag mode. This is another way to open the Quick Tag Editor.

8. Select the text inside the tag exactly as shown in the following illustration:

   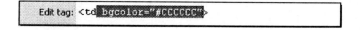

9. Press [Delete] or [Backspace].
   This deletes the background color property from the <td> tag.

10. Press [Enter] or [Return] twice.
    The table cell inherits the page background color.

11. Save the file.

Skill Builder 15.2   Add Meta Tags and a Comment

In this exercise, you will add description and keywords meta tags, and a comment.

1. Choose Insert→HTML→Head Tags→Description from the menu bar.

2. In the Description text box, type **History of Frank Lloyd Wright's design for Solomon R. Guggenheim Museum, New York**. Press OK.

3. Choose Insert—HTML→Head Tags→Keywords from the menu bar.

4. In the Keywords text box, type **Guggenheim museum, Solomon R. Guggenheim museum, History New York museums, New York art, art museums, museums, New York culture, visiting Guggenheim museum**. Press OK.

5. From the View Options Menu 🗐 on the Document toolbar, choose Head Content.
   The head content area appears directly above the Document window when you're working in Design view.

6. Click each of the four icons in the Head Content area and observe the properties on the Properties panel.
   You can use the Properties panel to edit head content without leaving Design view.

7. Save the file and keep it open.

Skill Builder 15.3   Run Validation and Clean Up HTML

In this exercise, you will run validation on a page to get an idea of the potential problems. You will then clean up the HTML and run validation again.

1. Choose File→Check Page→Validate Markup from the menu bar.
   The Results panel lists four warnings and one error on the Validation tab. Leave the Results panel open.

2. Choose Commands→Clean Up HTML from the menu bar.
   This opens the Clean Up HTML / XHTML dialog box.

3. Place a checkmark next to Specific tag(s) and type **font** in the text field.

4. Press OK.
   A clean up summary alert box opens and states that four specified tags were removed.

5. Press OK again.

6. Click the green triangular arrow on the Results panel. From the menu, choose Validate Current Document.
   This refreshes the Results panel, which now shows no errors or warnings.

7. Close the Results panel group.

8. Save and close the file.

 # Assessments

Assessment 15.1 Clean Up Dreamweaver Special Markups

In this exercise, you will clean up Dreamweaver special markup to remove comments in a template-based document. When you run this command, the document is detached from the template.

1. Open dolphin_news.htm from the review_15 folder.

2. Run the Clean Up HTML command to remove Dreamweaver special markup.

3. Replace the links in the right column (News, Expeditions, Sightings, Home) with null links.

4. Validate the markup to ensure there are no errors.

5. Save the file, and then preview it in your browser.

6. Click the Dolphin Rescue graphic link. This opens dolphin_rescue.htm in a new window. Observe the default window location. Without tweaking the JavaScript code, you have no control over the new window location.

7. Close the new window.

8. Leave your browser open and return to the Document window.

9. Keep the file open.

Assessment 15.2 Edit JavaScript Code

In this exercise, you will add horizontal and vertical properties to JavaScript code. This will place the window in an exact location on the visitor's screen.

1. Select the Dolphin Rescue graphic link.

2. Click on the <a> tag on the Tag Selector.

3. In Code or Split view, locate this block of code:

```
<a href="#" onClick="MM_openBrWindow('dolphin_rescue.htm', ','width=335,height=340')">
<img src="../slices/rescue.gif" alt="" name="rescue" width="278" height="30" border="0"
id="rescue"></a>
```

4. After the value of the window height property, type a comma and the following code without spaces: **screenX=100,screenY=150,left=100,top=150**.

5. Compare your revised code to the final version shown here:

```
<a href="#" onClick="MM_openBrWindow('dolphin_rescue.htm','','width=335,height=340,
screenX=100,screenY=150,left=100,top=150')"><img src="../slices/rescue.gif" alt=""
name="rescue" width="278" height="30" border="0" id="rescue"></a>
```

6. Save the file, and then test the new window location in your browser.

7. Close the new browser window.

8. Leave your browser open and return to the Document window.

9. Switch to Design view.

10. Leave the file open.

Assessment 15.3 Use a Code Snippet to Close a Window

In these exercise you will insert a Close Window button. This button is a predefined code snippet.

1. Open dolphin_rescue.htm from the review_15 folder.

2. Open the Snippets panel and locate the Form Elements folder.

3. Insert the Close Window Button snippet in the location shown in the following illustration.

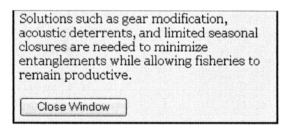

4. Save the file, and then open Dolphin news.htm in your browser.

5. Click the Dolphin Rescue link to open the new window.

6. Click the Close Window button.

7. Return to the Dreamweaver Document window.

8. Save the dolphin_news.htm file but leave it open.

9. Close the dolphin_rescue.htm file.

Assessment 15.4   Optimize the Page for Search Engines

In this exercise, you will optimize the Dolphin News page for search engines.

1. Define a descriptive title for the page.

2. Insert a description meta tag and describe the page contents.

3. Insert a keywords meta tag and add keywords and keyword phrases.

4. Insert comments that describe the two paragraphs of text.

5. Validate the file again to ensure that the code conforms to the HTML 4.01 standard.

6. Save and close the file.

Critical Thinking

Critical Thinking 15.1   On Your Own

The San Diego Restaurant Review chose Tango for their Restaurant of the Year award. Luz Morales, the restaurant critic, sent the review to you in Word 2002 format and needs the page published on their Web site. As a new production team member at Just in Time Design, you know that all pages must be validated before they're published.

To whet your appetite, Tango sent a slab of ribs marinated in their famous Chimichurri sauce and a case of Quilmes beer. Now get to work!

The following guidelines will help get you started:

- Open tango_word2002.htm. The file is riddled with invalid markup.

- Clean up the Word HTML, and then clean up the HTML by removing all occurrences of the span tag.

- Delete the internal CSS style that was created by Word.

- Attach the external style sheet named tango.css. Feel free to modify the styles if you wish.

- Define a page title and add the description and keywords meta tags.

- Insert tango.gif, which is located in the images folder.

- Save the file.

- An example of the final valid document is shown in the following illustration:

TANGO

The dance legend lives on at Tango, the hottest Argentinean restaurant this side of the Pacific. The rustic dining room walls are filled with stunning portraits honoring the legends of tango dancers Casimiro Ain, Juan C. Copes, Virulazo, Petroleo, Bernabe Simarra, and El Cachafaz.

Tango's speciality begins with the aging process of all meats, which arrive fresh from daily. This combined with their best kept secret, the essence of Tango's Chimichurrii sauce, a combination of olive oil, lemon juice, garlic, herbs, spices and fennel, provides a taste sensation not to be forgotten.

Start with the Pollo Rio Negro, marinated for twenty-four hours and served straight from the vast clay ovens that flank the entire length of the kitchen. If you're really hungry, order a party platter of Parrillada Mixta Pampera, a traditional Argentine mixed grill. You have to see it to believe it. Meats are marinated in spicy Chimichurri sauce, adding a wonderful flavor to the tender offerings. Tango also serves excellent seafood for those with a taste for ocean fare.

Carnivores will enjoy the famous Tango steak, a 22 oz sirloin served black on the outside and pink on the inside, Pincho Torro Caliente, 18 oz T-bone steak, veal chop, and much more. While many restaurants are currently serving Churrasco steak, Tango's version is the original and still the very best. Be sure to enjoy one of their exclusive Argentine wines, available only at Tango.

The Argento Chardonnay 2003, produced in the high vineyards of Agrelo is an absolute must while you're waiting at the bar enjoying the exotic dancers that swing and sway to 1930s authentic tango music.

Critical Thinking 15.2   On the Web

You might be able to sleep better at night knowing that your HTML files are indeed valid. Use the following guidelines to validate tango_word2002.htm from the previous exercise:

■ Ensure that the DTD appears in the first line of code and that the meta tag that describes the content type and character set is in place.

■ Point your browser to http://validator.w3.org/.

■ Use the Browse button in the Validate by File Upload section shown in the following illustration to locate tango_word2002.htm in your local file storage location and press Check.

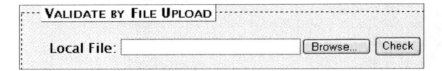

■ If your page is valid, you will see this message: THIS PAGE IS VALID HTML 4.01 TRANSITIONAL!

■ If the page is not valid, you will see this message: THIS PAGE IS NOT VALID HTML 4.01 TRANSITIONAL! Below this disappointing message, you will see comprehensive explanations that describe each error.

Critical Thinking 15.3   On Your Own

There are numerous search engine and directory services on the Web, and you should be listed with as many as possible. You can pay someone to list your site or you can do it yourself. Currently, the two most popular search engines are Yahoo! and Google. These two are your best bets to start. You usually have to do some poking around on a search engine site to figure out how to get your site listed.

Go to http://www.yahoo.com and look for the link to How to Suggest a Site, which at the time of this writing was located at the bottom of the page. Follow the link and learn how to suggest your site.

Go to http://www.google.com and follow the link to About Google. Find and read the links about Webmaster Info and Submitting Your Site.

APPENDIX

Using File Storage Media

This appendix contains instructions for downloading and unzipping the exercise files used with this book, and an overview for using this book with various file storage media.

In This Appendix

The following topics are addressed in this appendix:

Topic	Description	See Page
Downloading the Student Exercise Files	Retrieving the exercise files and copying them to your file storage location	493
Working with File Storage Locations	Using alternative media	494
Using a USB Flash Drive	Storing your work on a USB flash memory drive	494
Using the Hard Drive	Storing your work in the Documents folder on the computer's hard drive	496
Using a Network Drive Folder	Storing your work in a custom folder on a network	496

Downloading the Student Exercise Files

The files needed to complete certain Hands-On, Skill Builder, Assessment, and Critical Thinking exercises are available for download at the Labyrinth Website. Use the following instructions to copy the files to your computer and prepare them for use with this book.

 Hands-On A.1   Download and Unzip Files

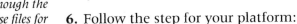

Follow these steps to download a copy of the student files necessary for this book:

1. Launch your Web browser.

2. Enter **labpub.com/students/fdpro05.asp** in the browser's address bar and tap ⏎Enter. *A list of books in the applicable series appears. If you don't see the title for your book in the list, use the links on the left side of the Web page to display the list of books for your series.*

3. Click the link for your book title.
   (Win) A prompt to open or save a file containing the student exercise files appears.
   (Mac) The file should begin downloading to your Desktop automatically.

4. (Win only) Choose the Save File option and start the download process.

5. (Win only) When prompted where to save the file, choose your file storage location and click Save.
   After a pause, the exercise files will begin downloading to your computer. Continue with the next step after the download is complete.

 NOTE!

Although the exercise files for a single lesson can fit on a floppy disk, this storage media is not recommended for use with this book. A USB flash drive is quite affordable, faster, and can store all of the exercise files in a single location.

6. Follow the step for your platform:
   - (Win) Open your file storage location and double-click the newly downloaded zip file.
   - (Mac) Open the file on the Desktop if it was not unstuffed automatically at the end of the download. Choose StuffIt Expander if you are prompted for an application with which to open the StuffIt file.

7. (Win only) Follow the instructions for your file storage location to complete the unzipping process:
   - **USB Flash Drive:** Click the Browse button, navigate to your USB flash drive, click OK, and then click the Unzip button.
   - **My Documents Folder:** Click the Browse button, navigate to the My Documents folder, click OK, and then click the Unzip button.
   - **Network Drive Folder:** Click the Browse button, navigate to your assigned folder on the network drive, click OK, and then click the Unzip button.

8. (Win only) Click the Close button after the files have unzipped.

Working with File Storage Locations

New technologies continue to expand the variety of available computer storage media. The 3½ inch floppy disk has been around since about 1983. That's incredibly ancient in the fast-moving field of computers. It's easy to use other storage media with this book. Potential alternative storage locations include:

- A USB flash drive
- A folder on your local hard drive
- A folder on a network drive

Using a USB Flash Drive

A USB flash drive stores your data on a flash memory chip. You simply plug it into a USB port on any computer and Windows and the Macintosh immediately recognize it as an additional disk drive. USB flash drives typically are able to store 32 megabytes (MB) or more of your data files. Large capacity USB flash drives can store 512 MB or more. The Macintosh displays the flash drive on the Desktop like another disk drive. Windows assigns the flash drive a new drive letter (see next topic).

Most USB flash drives are about the size of your thumb and plug into any available USB port on your computer.

USB Flash Drive Letter (Win)

When you plug in a USB flash drive to a Windows computer, Windows automatically assigns it the next available drive letter. Windows uses drive letters to identify each drive connected to the computer. For example, the primary part of the hard drive is always identified as the C: drive. The CD/DVD drive is typically the D: or E: drive.

⚠️**TIP!** *Your USB flash drive may receive a different drive letter on different computers. This does not affect any files stored on the drive.*

Hands-On A.2   Rename Your USB Flash Drive (Win)

Note to Windows Users: You may find it convenient to rename your USB flash drive to make it easier to recognize when you save or open files.

 TIP! *Some Windows systems may not give you renaming privileges for drives.*

1. Plug the USB flash drive into an available USB port.

2. Open a My Computer window.

3. Right-click your USB flash drive and choose Rename from the context menu.

 NOTE! *In the next step, Windows may display a prompt that you cannot rename this flash drive. You have not done anything wrong! You can use the drive with its current name. You may also want to try renaming it later using a different login.*

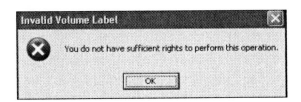

4. Type **FlashDrive** as the new drive name and tap Enter. Click OK if you receive a prompt that you do not have sufficient rights to perform this operation.
   If you were unable to rename the flash drive, don't worry. Renaming the flash drive is a convenience for recognition and has no other effect.

Using the Hard Drive

If you will routinely work with this course on the same compuiter, you can store the exercise files in a folder on the hard drive. Windows users may wish to create a folder in the My Documents folder. Macintosh users should use the Documents folder.

Using a Network Drive Folder

You may use a system connected to a network. There may be a folder on a network server computer in another location that is dedicated to storing your work. Windows users should look for this folder within the My Network Places folder. You may have to navigate deeper into the network drive to locate your personal network drive folder.

Glossary

Absolute links   Links outside your Web site

Absolute path   A path containing an external link to a resource outside the current site; includes the protocol "http" and the URL of the Web page

Browser   A software application used to locate and display Web pages, such as Netscape Navigator, Microsoft Internet Explorer, Opera, Mozilla, and Safari

Cell   In a table, the intersection of a row and a column

Cascading Style Sheets (CSS)   Used to apply styles (font type, font sizes, color, margins); a text-based language that any computer can read

Client   A computer connected to a network that requests actions or files from the network (server) or acts independently (e.g. If you are connected to network and want to print a document, you must request this service from the server)

Contiguous   Adjacent; usually used in reference to table cells

Dependent files   Files (such as images, external style sheets, and other files references in an HTML file) that the browser needs to lead the HTML file

Document-relative path   The URL of resources within your site, where the URL is provided relative to the current page within the site

External styles   Styles stored in a separate style sheet file along with your other Web page documents; used for multiple-pages to ensure formatting consistency

Field   A rectangular box on a forms-based Web page or browser in which data is typed

Form   A Web object consisting of text fields, menus, radio buttons, and checkboxes used to gather information

Frame   A rectangular region of a window that displays a single HTML document; a window or a container for the Web page

Frameset   An HTML document that defines the layout and properties of a set of frames, including the number, size, and placement of frames

Graphics Interchange Format (GIF)   A common format for image files, especially suitable for images containing large areas of the same color; supports 256 colors, supports background transparency and animation

Hexadecimal   A numbering system used by programmers to replace the binary system, which only uses 0 and 1

Homepage   A Web page that serves as an index or table of contents to other documents stored on the site; the default Web page that loads when no other file is specified in the URL

HTML tag   A descriptive marker that provides instructions to your browser

Hypertext Markup Language (HTML)   A text-based language that any computer can read; used to organize pages with devices such as headings, paragraphs, lists, etc.

Internal styles   Styles that appear in the head of your page in Code view; apply to a single document and are not shared with other pages

Internet   A collection of computers all over the world that send, receive and store information; access is gained through an Internet Service Provider (ISP); the Web is just a portion of the Internet

Joint Photographic Experts Group (JPG) Committee that designed the graphics format; JPG images support millions of colors and are best suited for photographs and complex graphics; does not support animation or background transparency

Layer   HTML container that can house text, graphics, tables, forms, media objects, and other layers; a CSS positioned element

Line break   In Web design, an HTML tag that forces text to the next line without adding white space between paragraphs; often used in street addresses

Link   Also called hyperlink; provides navigation through your site

Local site   Web pages and dependent files stored on your local file storage location

Lorem Ipsum   Also called Lipsum; a non-existent language used to simulate the English language; a text placeholder used to lay out pages until final content is available

Paragraph   A line of text ending with an Enter or Return

Pixel   Short for picture element; composed of three sub-dots that form the colors red, blue, and green; pixels are so close together that they appear connected; graphics monitors display pictures by dividing the display screen into thousands (or millions) of pixels

Portable Network Graphics (PNG)   A graphics file format; compresses even smaller than a GIF; supports transparency but not animation; not supported by all browsers

Radio button   Form object used to provide multiple options from which only one selection can be made

Relative link   A link to resources within your site

Resample   To alter an image's resolution; resampling to a higher resolution typically causes little loss of quality while resampling to a lower resolution always causes data loss and usually a drop in quality

Resize   To change an image's height or width

Resolution   The sharpness and clarity of an image; often used to describe graphics monitors, printers, and graphic images; signifies the number of pixels on the entire screen—as the number of pixels increase, so does the screen resolution

Rule   Formatting instruction for styles

Script   A short bit of programming code usually written to automate tasks

Search engine   An automated program designed to find specific information on the Internet as requested by the user

Serifs   Fine lines or curves used to finish off strokes in a letter; help guide readers' eyes through text on printed pages

Server   A master computer connected to many other computers, where the server's job is to provide files or actions as requested by individual computers; usually a high-end, powerful computer with special software

Snippet   A piece of text, HTML, CSS, JavaScript, etc. that is reused on various pages in a site

Style sheet   A group of styles; each style in the style sheet has specific formatting instructions, called rules

Synchronize   To compare data between electronic devices; to determine latest version of a file; to identify new files

Table   A grid of rows and columns that intersect to form cells

Target   Also called the destination; the final location of a hyperlink

Template   An HTML document that contains locked and unlocked regions; content providers cannot edit or modify locked regions on template-based pages

Uniform Resource Locator (URL)   Used to identify a unique resource on the Internet; a Web address

Web-safe colors   The 216 colors that display exactly the same on all computers regardless of operating system

Web site   Refers to a collection of related Web pages and their supporting files and folders

World Wide Web (WWW)   Also called The Web; organized system of Internet servers that support HTML documents; the fun part of the Internet

Index